The Historical Writings

The Historical Writings

FORTRESS COMMENTARY ON THE BIBLE
STUDY EDITION

Gale A. Yee
Hugh R. Page Jr.
Matthew J. M. Coomber
Editors

Fortress Press
Minneapolis

THE HISTORICAL WRITINGS
Fortress Commentary on the Bible Study Edition

Excerpted from the *Fortress Commentary on the Bible: The Old Testament and Apocrypha*
(Minneapolis: Fortress Press, 2014); Gale A. Yee, Hugh R. Page Jr., and Matthew J. M. Coomber, volume editors.

Fortress Press Publication Staff:
Neil Elliott and Scott Tunseth, Project Editors
Marissa Wold, Production Manager
Laurie Ingram, Cover Design.

Copyeditor: Jeffrey A. Reimer

Typesetter: PerfecType, Nashville, TN

Proofreader: David Cottingham

Library of Congress Cataloging-in-Publication data is available

ISBN: 978-1-5064-1581-9

eISBN: 978-1-5064-1582-6

CONTENTS

PUBLISHER'S NOTE

About the Fortress Commentary on the Bible Study Editions

In 2014 Fortress Press released the two-volume *Fortress Commentary on the Bible*. See the Series Introduction (pp. 1–3) for a look inside the creation and design of the Old Testament/Apocrypha and New Testament volumes. While each comprehensive commentary volume can easily be used in classroom settings, we also recognized that dividing the larger commentaries into smaller volumes featuring key sections of Scripture may be especially helpful for use in corresponding biblical studies courses. To help facilitate such classroom use, we have broken the two-volume commentary into eight study editions.

Please note that in this study edition the page numbers match the page numbers of the larger Fortress Commentary on the Bible volume in which it first appeared. We have intentionally retained the same page numbering to facilitate use of the study editions and larger volumes side by side.

The Historical Writings was first published in Fortress Commentary on the Bible: The Old Testament and Apocrypha.

ABBREVIATIONS

General

AT	Alpha Text (of the Greek text of Esther)
BOI	Book of Isaiah
Chr	Chronicler
DH	Deuteronomistic History
DI	Deutero-Isaiah
Dtr	Deuteronomist
Gk.	Greek
H	Holiness Code
Heb.	Hebrew
JPS	Jewish Publication Society
LXX	The Septuagint
LXX B	Vaticanus Text of the Septuagint
MP	Mode of production
MT	Masoretic Text
NIV	New International Version
NRSV	New Revised Standard Version
OAN	Oracles against Nations (in Jeremiah)
P.	papyrus/papyri
P	Priestly source
PE	Pastoral Epistles
RSV	Revised Standard Version
TI	Trito-Isaiah

Books of the Bible (NT, OT, Apocrypha)

Old Testament/Hebrew Bible

Gen.	Genesis
Exod.	Exodus
Lev.	Leviticus
Num.	Numbers
Deut.	Deuteronomy

Josh.	Joshua
Judg.	Judges
Ruth	Ruth
1 Sam.	1 Samuel
2 Sam.	2 Samuel
1 Kgs.	1 Kings
2 Kgs.	2 Kings
1 Chron.	1 Chronicles
2 Chron.	2 Chronicles
Ezra	Ezra
Neh.	Nehemiah
Esther	Esther
Job	Job
Ps. (Pss.)	Psalms
Prov.	Proverbs
Eccles.	Ecclesiastes
Song.	Song of Songs
Isa.	Isaiah
Jer.	Jeremiah
Lam.	Lamentations
Ezek.	Ezekiel
Dan.	Daniel
Hosea	Hosea
Joel	Joel
Amos	Amos
Obad.	Obadiah
Jon.	Jonah
Mic.	Micah
Nah.	Nahum
Hab.	Habakkuk
Zeph.	Zephaniah
Hag.	Haggai
Zech.	Zechariah
Mal.	Malachi

Apocrypha

Tob.	Tobit
Jth.	Judith
Gk. Esther	Greek Additions to Esther
Sir.	Sirach (Ecclesiasticus)

Bar.	Baruch
Let. Jer.	Letter of Jeremiah
Add Dan.	Additions to Daniel
Pr. Azar.	Prayer of Azariah
Sg. Three.	Song of the Three Young Men (or Three Jews)
Sus.	Susanna
Bel	Bel and the Dragon
1 Macc.	1 Maccabees
2 Macc.	2 Maccabees
1 Esd.	1 Esdras
Pr. of Man.	Prayer of Manasseh
2 Esd.	2 Esdras
Wis.	Wisdom of Solomon
3 Macc.	3 Maccabees
4 Macc.	4 Maccabees

New Testament

Matt.	Matthew
Mark	Mark
Luke	Luke
John	John
Acts	Acts of the Apostles
Rom.	Romans
1 Cor.	1 Corinthians
2 Cor.	2 Corinthians
Gal.	Galatians
Eph.	Ephesians
Phil.	Philippians
Col.	Colossians
1 Thess.	1 Thessalonians
2 Thess.	2 Thessalonians
1 Tim.	1 Timothy
2 Tim.	2 Timothy
Titus	Titus
Philem.	Philemon
Heb.	Hebrews
James	James
1 Pet.	1 Peter
2 Pet.	2 Peter
1 John	1 John

2 John	2 John
3 John	3 John
Jude	Jude
Rev.	Revelation (Apocalypse)

Journals, Series, Reference Works

ABD	*Anchor Bible Dictionary*. Edited by David Noel Freedman. 6 vols. New York: Doubleday, 1992.
ACNT	Augsburg Commentaries on the New Testament
AJA	*American Journal of Archaeology*
AJT	*Asia Journal of Theology*
ANET	*Ancient Near Eastern Texts Relating to the Old Testament*. Edited by J. B. Pritchard. 3rd ed. Princeton: Princeton University Press, 1969.
ANF	*The Ante-Nicene Fathers*. Edited by Alexander Roberts and James Donaldson. 1885–1887. 10 vols. Repr., Peabody, MA: Hendrickson, 1994.
ANRW	*Aufstieg und Niedergang der römischen Welt: Geschichte und Kultur Roms im Spiegel der neueren Forschung*. Edited by Hildegard Temporini and Wolfgang Haase. Berlin: de Gruyter, 1972–.
ANTC	Abingdon New Testament Commentaries
AOAT	Alter Orient und Altes Testament
AbOTC	Abingdon Old Testament Commentary
AOTC	Apollos Old Testament Commentary
A(Y)B	Anchor (Yale) Bible
BA	*Biblical Archaeologist*
BAR	*Biblical Archaeology Review*
BDAG	Bauer, W., F. W. Danker, W. F. Arndt, and F. W. Gingrich. *Greek-English Lexicon of the New Testament and Other Early Christian Literature*. 3rd ed. Chicago: University of Chicago Press, 1999.
BEATAJ	Beiträge zur Erforschung des Alten Testaments und des Antiken Judentum
Bib	*Biblica*
BibInt	*Biblical Interpretation*
BJRL	*Bulletin of the John Rylands University Library of Manchester*
BJS	Brown Judaic Studies
BNTC	Black's New Testament Commentaries
BR	*Biblical Research*
BRev	*Bible Review*
BSac	*Bibliotheca sacra*
BTB	*Biblical Theology Bulletin*
BZAW	Beihefte zur Zeitschrift für die alttestamentliche Wissenschaft
CAT	Commentaire de l'Ancien Testament

CBC	Cambridge Bible Commentary
CBQMS	Catholic Biblical Quarterly Monograph Series
CC	Continental Commentaries
CH	*Church History*
CHJ	*Cambridge History of Judaism.* Edited by W. D. Davies and Louis Finkelstein. Cambridge: Cambridge University Press, 1984–.
ConBNT	Coniectanea biblica: New Testament Series
ConBOT	Coniectanea biblica: Old Testament Series
CS	Cistercian Studies
CTAED	*Canaanite Toponyms in Ancient Egyptian Documents.* S. Ahituv. Jerusalem: Magnes, 1984.
CTQ	*Concordia Theological Quarterly*
CurTM	*Currents in Theology and Mission*
ExpTim	*Expository Times*
ETL	*Ephemerides Theologicae Lovanienses*
ExAud	*Ex auditu*
FAT	Forschungen zum Alten Testament
FC	Fathers of the Church
FRLANT	Forschungen zur Religion und Literatur des Alten und Neuen Testaments
HAT	Handbuch zum Alten Testament
HBT	*Horizons in Biblical Theology*
HNTC	Harper's New Testament Commentaries
HR	*History of Religions*
HSM	Harvard Semitic Monographs
HTKAT	Herders Theologischer Kommentar zum Alten Testament
HTR	*Harvard Theological Review*
HTS	Harvard Theological Studies
HUCA	*Hebrew Union College Annual*
HUCM	Monographs of the Hebrew Union College
HUT	Hermeneutische Untersuchungen zur Theologie
IBC	Interpretation: A Bible Commentary for Teaching and Preaching
ICC	International Critical Commentary
Int	*Interpretation*
JAAR	*Journal of the American Academy of Religion*
JAOS	*Journal of the American Oriental Society*
JBL	*Journal of Biblical Literature*
JBQ	*Jewish Bible Quarterly*
JECS	*Journal of Early Christian Studies*
JJS	*Journal of Jewish Studies*
JNES	*Journal of Near Eastern Studies*

JNSL	*Journal of Northwest Semitic Languages*
JQR	*Jewish Quarterly Review*
JRS	*Journal of Roman Studies*
JSem	*Journal of Semitics*
JSJ	*Journal for the Study of Judaism in the Persian, Hellenistic, and Roman Periods*
JSNT	*Journal for the Study of the New Testament*
JSOT	*Journal for the Study of the Old Testament*
JSOTSup	Journal for the Study of the Old Testament Supplement Series
JSQ	*Jewish Studies Quarterly*
JSS	*Journal of Semitic Studies*
JTI	*Journal of Theological Interpretation*
JTS	*Journal of Theological Studies*
JTSA	*Journal of Theology for Southern Africa*
KTU	*Die keilalphabetischen Texte aus Ugarit.* Edited by M. Dietrich, O. Loretz, and J. Sanmartín. AOAT 24/1. Neukirchen-Vluyn: Neukirchener, 1976.
LCC	Loeb Classical Library
LEC	Library of Early Christianity
LHB/OTS	Library of the Hebrew Bible/Old Testament Studies
LW	*Luther's Works.* Edited by Jaroslav Pelikan and Helmut T. Lehmann. 55 vols. St. Louis: Concordia; Philadelphia: Fortress Press, 1958–1986.
NAC	New American Commentary
NCB	New Century Bible
NCBC	New Cambridge Bible Commentary
NedTT	*Nederlands theologisch tijdschrift*
Neot	*Neotestamentica*
NICNT	New International Commentary on the New Testament
NICOT	New International Commentary on the Old Testament
NIGTC	New International Greek Testament Commentary
NovT	*Novum Testamentum*
NPNF[1]	*The Nicene and Post-Nicene Fathers*, Series 1. Edited by Philip Schaff. 14 vols. 1886–1889. Repr., Grand Rapids: Eerdmans, 1956.
NTL	New Testament Library
NTS	*New Testament Studies*
OBT	Overtures to Biblical Theology
OTE	*Old Testament Essays*
OTG	Old Testament Guides
OTL	Old Testament Library
OTM	Old Testament Message
PEQ	*Palestine Exploration Quarterly*
PG	Patrologia graeca [= Patrologiae cursus completus: Series graeca]. Edited by J.-P. Migne. 162 vols. Paris, 1857–1886.

PL	John Milton, *Paradise Lost*
PL	Patrologia latina [= Patrologiae cursus completus: Series latina]. Edited by J.-P. Migne. 217 vols. Paris, 1844–1864.
PRSt	*Perspectives in Religious Studies*
QR	*Quarterly Review*
RevExp	*Review and Expositor*
RevQ	*Revue de Qumran*
SBLABS	Society of Biblical Literature Archaeology and Biblical Studies
SBLAIL	Society of Biblical Literature Ancient Israel and Its Literature
SBLDS	Society of Biblical Literature Dissertation Series
SBLEJL	Society of Biblical Literature Early Judaism and Its Literature
SBLMS	Society of Biblical Literature Monograph Series
SBLRBS	Society of Biblical Literature Resources for Biblical Study
SBLSCS	Society of Biblical Literature Septuagint and Cognate Studies
SBLSP	*Society of Biblical Literature Seminar Papers*
SBLSymS	Society of Biblical Literature Symposium Series
SBLWAW	SBL Writings from the Ancient World
SemeiaSt	Semeia Studies
SJT	*Scottish Journal of Theology*
SNTSMS	Society for New Testament Studies Monograph Series
SO	Symbolae osloenses
SR	*Studies in Religion*
ST	*Studia Theologica*
StABH	Studies in American Biblical Hermeneutics
TD	*Theology Digest*
TAD	*Textbook of Aramaic Documents from Ancient Egypt*. Vol. 1: *Letters*. Bezalel Porten and Ada Yardeni. Winona Lake, IN: Eisenbrauns, 1986.
TDOT	*Theological Dictionary of the Old Testament*. 15 vols. Edited by G. Johannes Botterweck, Helmer Ringgren, and Heinz-Josef Fabry. Translated by David E. Green and Douglas W. Stott. Grand Rapids: Eerdmans, 1974–1995.
TJT	*Toronto Journal of Theology*
TNTC	Tyndale New Testament Commentaries
TOTC	Tyndale Old Testament Commentaries
TS	*Theological Studies*
TZ	*Theologische Zeitschrift*
VE	*Vox evangelica*
VT	*Vetus Testamentum*
VTSup	Supplements to Vetus Testamentum
WBC	Word Biblical Commentary
WSA	Works of St. Augustine: A Translation for the Twenty-First Century
WUANT	Wissenschaftliche Untersuchungen zum Alten und Neuen Testament

WUNT	Wissenschaftliche Untersuchungen zum Neuen Testament
WW	*Word and World*
ZAW	*Zeitschrift für die alttestamentliche Wissenschaft*
ZBK	Zürcher Bibelkommentare
ZNW	*Zeitschrift für die neutestamentliche Wissenschaft und die Kunde der älteren Kirche*

Ancient Authors and Texts

1 Clem.	*1 Clement*
2 Clem.	*2 Clement*
1 En.	*1 Enoch*
2 Bar.	*2 Baruch*
Abot R. Nat.	*Abot de Rabbi Nathan*
Ambrose	
Paen.	*De paenitentia*
Aristotle	
Ath. Pol.	*Athēnaīn politeia*
Nic. Eth.	*Nicomachean Ethics*
Pol.	*Politics*
Rhet.	*Rhetoric*
Augustine	
FC 79	*Tractates on the Gospel of John, 11–27.* Translated by John W. Rettig. Fathers of the Church 79. Washington, DC: Catholic University of America Press, 1988.
Tract. Ev. Jo.	*In Evangelium Johannis tractatus*
Bede, Venerable	
CS 117	*Commentary on the Acts of the Apostles.* Translated by Lawrence T. Martin. Cistercian Studies 117. Kalamazoo, MI: Cistercian Publications, 1989.
Barn.	*Barnabas*
CD	Cairo Genizah copy of the Damascus Document
Cicero	
De or.	*De oratore*
Tusc.	*Tusculanae disputationes*
Clement of Alexandria	
Paed.	*Paedogogus*
Strom.	*Stromata*
Cyril of Jerusalem	
Cat. Lect.	*Catechetical Lectures*
Dio Cassius	
Hist.	*Roman History*

Dio Chrysostom
    Or.   *Orations*
Diog. Diognetus
Dionysius of Halicarnassus
    Thuc.   *De Thucydide*
Epictetus
    Diatr.   *Diatribai (Dissertationes)*
    Ench.   *Enchiridion*
Epiphanius
    Pan.   *Panarion (Adversus Haereses)*
Eusebius of Caesarea
    Hist. eccl.   *Historia ecclesiastica*
Gos. Thom.   *Gospel of Thomas*
Herodotus
    Hist.   *Historiae*
Hermas, *Shepherd*
    Mand.   *Mandates*
    Sim.   *Similitudes*
Homer
    Il.   *Iliad*
    Od.   *Odyssey*
Ignatius of Antioch
    Eph.   *To the Ephesians*
    Smyr.   *To the Smyrnaeans*
Irenaeus
    Adv. haer.   *Adversus haereses*
Jerome
    Vir. ill.   *De viris illustribus*
John Chrysostom
    Hom. 1 Cor. *Homiliae in epistulam i ad Corinthios*
    Hom. Act.   *Homiliae in Acta apostolorum*
    Hom. Heb.   *Homiliae in epistulam ad Hebraeos*
Josephus
    Ant.   *Jewish Antiquities*
    Ag. Ap.   *Against Apion*
    J.W.   *Jewish War*
Jub.   *Jubilees*
Justin Martyr
    Dial.   *Dialogue with Trypho*
    1 Apol.   *First Apology*

L.A.E.	*Life of Adam and Eve*
Liv. Pro.	*Lives of the Prophets*
Lucian	
Alex.	*Alexander (Pseudomantis)*
Phal.	*Phalaris*
Mart. Pol.	*Martyrdom of Polycarp*
Novatian	
Trin.	*De trinitate*
Origen	
C. Cels.	*Contra Celsum*
Comm. Jo.	*Commentarii in evangelium Joannis*
De princ.	*De principiis*
Hom. Exod.	*Homiliae in Exodum*
Hom. Jer.	*Homiliae in Jeremiam*
Hom. Josh.	*Homilies on Joshua*
Pausanias	
Descr.	*Description of Greece*
Philo	
Cher.	*De cherubim*
Decal.	*De decalogo*
Dreams	*On Dreams*
Embassy	*On the Embassy to Gaius (= Legat.)*
Fug.	*De fuga et inventione*
Leg.	*Legum allegoriae*
Legat.	*Legatio ad Gaium*
Migr.	*De migratione Abrahami*
Mos.	*De vita Mosis*
Opif.	*De opificio mundi*
Post.	*De posteritate Caini*
Prob.	*Quod omnis probus liber sit*
QE	*Quaestiones et solutiones in Exodum*
QG	*Quaestiones et solutiones in Genesin*
Spec. Laws	*On the Special Laws*
Plato	
Gorg.	*Gorgias*
Plutarch	
Mor.	*Moralia*
Mulier. virt.	*Mulierum virtutes*
Polycarp	
Phil.	*To the Philippians*

Ps.-Clem. Rec.	*Pseudo-Clementine Recognitions*
Pss. Sol.	*Psalms of Solomon*
Pseudo-Philo	
L.A.B.	*Liber antiquitatum biblicarum*
Seneca	
Ben.	*De beneficiis*
Strabo	
Geog.	*Geographica*
Tatian	
Ad gr.	*Oratio ad Graecos*
Tertullian	
Praescr.	*De praescriptione haereticorum*
Prax.	*Adversus Praxean*
Bapt.	*De baptismo*
De an.	*De anima*
Pud.	*De pudicitia*
Virg.	*De virginibus velandis*
Virgil	
Aen.	*Aeneid*
Xenophon	
Oec.	*Oeconomicus*

Mishnah, Talmud, Targum

b. B. Bat.	*Babylonian Talmudic tractate Baba Batra*
b. Ber.	*Babylonian Talmudic tractate Berakhot*
b Erub.	*Babylonian Talmudic tractate Erubim*
b. Ketub.	*Babylonian Talmudic tractate Ketubbot*
b. Mak.	*Babylonian Talmudic tractate Makkot*
b. Meg.	*Babylonian Talmudic tractate Megillah*
b. Ned.	*Babylonian Talmudic tractate Nedarim*
b. Naz.	*Babylonian Talmudic tractate Nazir*
b. Sanh.	*Babylonian Talmudic tractate Sanhedrin*
b. Shab.	*Babylonian Talmudic tractate Shabbat*
b. Sotah	*Babylonian Talmudic tractate Sotah*
b. Ta'an.	*Babylonian Talmudic tractate Ta'anit*
b. Yev.	*Babylonian Talmudic tractate Yevamot*
b. Yoma	*Babylonian Talmudic tractate Yoma*
Eccl. Rab.	*Ecclesiastes Rabbah*
Exod. Rab.	*Exodus Rabbah*
Gen. Rab.	*Genesis Rabbah*

Lam. Rab.	*Lamentations Rabbah*
Lev. R(ab).	*Leviticus Rabbah*
m. Abot	*Mishnah tractate Abot*
m. Bik.	*Mishnah tractate Bikkurim*
m. Demai	*Mishnah tractate Demai*
m. 'Ed.	*Mishnah tractate 'Eduyyot*
m. Git.	*Mishnah tractate Gittin*
m. Pesaḥ	*Mishnah tractate Pesaḥim*
m. Šeqal.	*Mishnah tractate Šeqalim (Shekalim)*
m. Shab.	*Mishnah tractate Shabbat*
m. Sotah	*Mishnah tractate Sotah*
m. Ta'an.	*Mishnah tractate Ta'anit*
m. Tamid	*Mishnah tractate Tamid*
m. Yad.	*Mishnah tractate Yadayim*
m. Yebam.	*Mishnah tractate Yebamot*
m. Yoma	*Mishnah tractate Yoma*
Num. Rab.	*Numbers Rabbah*
Pesiq. Rab.	*Pesiqta Rabbati*
Pesiq. Rab Kah.	*Pesiqta Rab Kahana*
S. 'Olam Rab.	*Seder 'Olam Rabbah*
Song Rab.	*Song of Songs Rabbah*
t. Hul.	*Tosefta tractate Hullin*
Tg. Onq.	*Targum Onqelos*
Tg. Jer.	*Targum Jeremiah*
y. Hag.	*Jerusalem Talmudic tractate Hagiga*
y. Pesaḥ	*Jerusalem Talmudic tractate Pesaḥim*
y. Sanh.	*Jerusalem Talmudic tractate Sanhedrin*

Dead Sea Scrolls

1QapGen	*Genesis apocryphon* (Excavated frags. from cave)
1QM	*War Scroll*
1QpHab	*Pesher Habakkuk*
1QS	*Rule of the Community*
1QSb	*Rule of the Blessings* (Appendix b to 1QS)
1Q21	*T. Levi*, aramaic
4Q184	Wiles of the Wicked Woman
4Q214	Levi[d] ar (*olim* part of Levi[b])
4Q214b	Levi[f] ar (*olim* part of Levi[b])
4Q226	psJub[b] (4Q *pseudo-Jubilees*)
4Q274	Tohorot A

4Q277	Tohorot B^b (*olim* B^c)
4Q525	*Beatitudes*
4QMMT	*Miqsat Ma'aśê ha-Torah*
4QpNah/4Q169	4Q Pesher Nahum
4Q82	*The Greek Minor Prophets Scroll*

Old Testament Pseudepigrapha

1 En.	1 Enoch
2 En.	2 Enoch
Odes Sol.	Odes of Solomon
Syr. Men.	Sentences of the Syriac Menander
T. Levi	Testament of Levi
T. Mos.	Testament of Moses
T. Sim.	Testament of Simeon

INTRODUCTION

The *Fortress Commentary on the Bible*, presented in two volumes, seeks to invite study and conversation about an ancient text that is both complex and compelling. As biblical scholars, we wish students of the Bible to gain a respect for the antiquity and cultural remoteness of the biblical texts and to grapple for themselves with the variety of their possible meanings; to fathom a long history of interpretation in which the Bible has been wielded for causes both beneficial and harmful; and to develop their own skills and voices as responsible interpreters, aware of their own social locations in relationships of privilege and power. With this in mind, the *Fortress Commentary on the Bible* offers general readers an informed and accessible resource for understanding the biblical writings in their ancient contexts; for recognizing how the texts have come down to us through the mediation of different interpretive traditions; and for engaging current discussion of the Bible's sometimes perplexing, sometimes ambivalent, but always influential legacy in the contemporary world. The commentary is designed not only to inform but also to invite and empower readers as active interpreters of the Bible in their own right.

The editors and contributors to these volumes are scholars and teachers who are committed to helping students engage the Bible in the classroom. Many also work as leaders, both lay and ordained, in religious communities, and wish this commentary to prove useful for informing congregational life in clear, meaningful, and respectful ways. We also understand the work of biblical interpretation as a responsibility far wider than the bounds of any religious community. In this regard, we participate in many and diverse identities and social locations, yet we all are conscious of reading, studying, and hearing the Bible today as citizens of a complex and interconnected world. We recognize in the Bible one of the most important legacies of human culture; its historical and literary interpretation is of profound interest to religious and nonreligious peoples alike.

Often, the academic interpretation of the Bible has moved from close study of the remote ancient world to the rarefied controversy of scholarly debate, with only occasional attention to the ways biblical texts are actually heard and lived out in the world around us. The commentary seeks to provide students with diverse materials on the ways in which these texts have been interpreted through the course of history, as well as helping students understand the texts' relevance for today's globalized world. It recognizes the complexities that are involved with being an engaged reader of the Bible, providing a powerful tool for exploring the Bible's multilayered meanings in both their ancient and modern contexts. The commentary seeks to address contemporary issues that are raised by biblical passages. It aspires to be keenly aware of how the contemporary world and its issues and perspectives influence the interpretation of the Bible. Many of the most important insights of contemporary biblical scholarship not only have come from expertise in the world of antiquity but have also been forged in modern struggles for dignity, for equality, for sheer survival, and out of respect for those who have died without seeing justice done. Gaining familiarity with the original contexts in which the biblical writings were produced is essential, but not sufficient, for encouraging competent and discerning interpretation of the Bible's themes today.

Inside the Commentary

Both volumes of *The Fortress Commentary on the Bible* are organized in a similar way. In the beginning of each volume, **Topical Articles** set the stage on which interpretation takes place, naming the issues and concerns that have shaped historical and theological scholarship down to the present. Articles in the *Fortress Commentary on the Old Testament* attend, for example, to the issues that arise when two different religious communities claim the same body of writings as their Scripture, though interpreting those writings quite differently. Articles in the *Fortress Commentary on the New Testament* address the consequences of Christianity's historic claim to appropriate Jewish Scripture and to supplement it with a second collection of writings, the experience of rootlessness and diaspora, and the legacy of apocalypticism. Articles in both volumes reflect on the historical intertwining of Christianity with imperial and colonial power and with indexes of racial and socioeconomic privilege.

Section Introductions in the Old Testament volume provide background to the writings included in the Torah, Historical Writings, Wisdom, Prophetic Writings, and a general introduction to the Apocrypha. The New Testament volume includes articles introducing the Gospels, Acts, the letters associated with Paul, and Hebrews, the General Epistles and Revelation. These articles will address the literary and historical matters, as well as theological themes, that the books in these collections hold in common.

Commentary Entries present accessible and judicious discussion of each biblical book, beginning with an introduction to current thinking regarding the writing's original context and its significance in different reading communities down to the present day. A three-level commentary then follows for each sense division of the book. In some cases, these follow the chapter divisions of a biblical book, but more often, contributors have discerned other outlines, depending on matters of genre, movement, or argument.

The three levels of commentary are the most distinctive organizational feature of these volumes. The first level, "The Text in Its Ancient Context," addresses relevant lexical, exegetical, and literary aspects of the text, along with cultural and archaeological information that may provide additional insight into the historical context. This level of the commentary describes consensus views where these exist in current scholarship and introduces issues of debate clearly and fairly. Our intent here is to convey some sense of the historical and cultural distance between the text's original context and the contemporary reader.

The second level, "The Text in the Interpretive Tradition," discusses themes including Jewish and Christian tradition as well as other religious, literary, and artistic traditions where the biblical texts have attracted interest. This level is shaped by our conviction that we do not apprehend these texts immediately or innocently; rather, even the plain meaning we may regard as self-evident may have been shaped by centuries of appropriation and argument to which we are heirs.

The third level, "The Text in Contemporary Discussion," follows the history of interpretation into the present, drawing brief attention to a range of issues. Our aim here is not to deliver a single answer—"what the text means"—to the contemporary reader, but to highlight unique challenges and interpretive questions. We pay special attention to occasions of dissonance: aspects of the text or of its interpretation that have become questionable, injurious, or even intolerable to some readers today. Our goal is not to provoke a referendum on the value of the text but to stimulate reflection and discussion and, in this way, to empower the reader to reach his or her own judgments about the text.

The approach of this commentary articulates a particular understanding of the work of responsible biblical interpretation. We seek through this commentary to promote intelligent and mature engagement with the Bible, in religious communities and in academic classrooms alike, among pastors, theologians, and ethicists, but also and especially among nonspecialists. Our work together has given us a new appreciation for the vocation of the biblical scholar, as custodians of a treasure of accumulated wisdom from our predecessors; as stewards at a table to which an ever-expanding circle is invited; as neighbors and fellow citizens called to common cause, regardless of our different professions of faith. If the result of our work here is increased curiosity about the Bible, new questions about its import, and new occasions for mutual understanding among its readers, our work will be a success.

Fortress Commentary on the Old Testament

Gale A. Yee
Episcopal Divinity School

Hugh R. Page Jr.
University of Notre Dame

Matthew J. M. Coomber
St. Ambrose University

Fortress Commentary on the New Testament

Margaret Aymer
Interdenominational Theological Center

Cynthia Briggs Kittredge
Seminary of the Southwest

David A. Sánchez
Loyola Marymount University

READING THE OLD TESTAMENT IN ANCIENT AND CONTEMPORARY CONTEXTS

Matthew J. M. Coomber

As students file into their desks on the first day of my "Introduction to the Old Testament" course, they are greeted with a PowerPoint slide that simply states, in bold red letters, "Caution: Dangerous Texts Ahead!" The students often respond with the mixture of chuckles and uneasy looks that I intend to provoke. To some extent, the slide is offered tongue in cheek, but not entirely. As with any wry statement, the cautionary slide holds an element of truth. The Old Testament contains powerful teachings and radical ideas that have moved the hearts and minds of both adherents and skeptics for millennia.

While the texts of the Old Testament have had a profound effect on societies and cultures for a long span of time, their texts often take a back seat to the Gospels and the Pauline Letters in popular Christian religion. Even though they constitute well over half of the content of Christian Bibles, very few of my students claim to have read much—if any—of the Old Testament or Apocrypha, despite the fact that I teach at a Roman Catholic university in which the vast majority of the students are Christian. In fact, only a handful of my students claim to have been exposed to the stories of the Old Testament outside of either Sunday school or in episodes of the popular cartoon series *Veggie Tales*. Due to this lack of exposure to the Old Testament, I feel compelled to give them fair warning about what they have gotten themselves into by signing up for what may seem like an innocuous required course. I take it as a professional responsibility to alert them to the fact that a keen examination of the ancient Near Eastern library that sits on their desks has the power to change their lives and forever alter the ways in which they experience the world.

Any collection of books containing calls to wage wars of conquest, to resist the temptation to fight while under threat, thoughts on God's role in governance, and meditations on what it means to live *the good life* has the potential to change lives and even inspire revolutions. To assume that the Bible is harmless is both foolish and irresponsible. After all, the Old Testament's contents have been used by some to support slavery and genocide while inspiring others to engage in such dangerous pursuits as enduring imprisonment, torture, and death in attempts to liberate the oppressed. And just as with using any powerful instrument, be it a car or a surgical blade, reading the Old Testament demands care, responsibility, and substantial consideration from those who put it to use.

Books that promote powerful ideas are complex tools that often belong to the readers as much as—if not more than—their authors. The level of consideration required to read, interpret, and actualize such books is magnified when approaching ancient texts such as those found in the Old Testament. These biblical books bridge multiple theological, cultural, and linguistic worlds, which demand multiple levels of understanding and interpretation. Readers must inhabit three worlds (contexts) when reading any of the books of the Old Testament or Apocrypha, from Genesis to 4 Maccabees: (1) the ancient contexts in which they were written, (2) the modern contexts into which the text is being received, and (3) all of those contexts in between wherein interpreters in each generation have shaped the reading of the texts for their own time and place. *The Fortress Commentary on the Bible: The Old Testament and Apocrypha* approaches these ancient texts with due reverence to this complexity. The purpose of this introduction is to explore a few of the many considerations that are required in reading this ancient Near Eastern scriptural library in its ancient and modern contexts.

A Few Considerations on Receiving Ancient Texts with Modern Minds

The word *context*, whether pertaining to events or a book, looks deceptively singular. A student trying to uncover the context of the US civil rights movement will find many contextual viewing points: those of African Americans who rose up against institutionalized oppression, those of segregationists who tried to maintain the status quo, those within the Johnson administration who worked to find a way forward without losing the Democrats' white voters in the South, and the list goes on.

Challenge of Finding an Ancient or Modern Context

The words *ancient context* and *modern context*, when applied to the Old Testament, also need to be considered in the plural. Considering the ancient context, the books of the Old Testament contain the theologies of diverse communities who lived, wrote, argued, and worked to understand their relationship with the divine under a wide variety of circumstances. An attempt to find a single context for the book of Isaiah, for example, is as complex as finding a single sociohistorical setting of the United States, from the colonial period to the present; it cannot be done. The same is true with the modern context. As these religious texts are received in Chicago or Mumbai, on Wall Street or on skid row, they flow into and take on very different meanings and contexts.

Differing Expectations and Intents of Ancient and Modern Histories

Readers in the age of science have certain expectations when reading a history, and these expectations inform how histories—whether written before or after this age—are received. Modern readers want to know, with scientific precision, when, why, and where events happened. Great value is placed on reconstructions of events that are backed up by reliable sources and with as little interpretive bias as possible. A *good* history of the Battle of the Bulge should include not only dates and locations but also eyewitness accounts of allied forces, Wehrmacht and SS divisions, and civilians. Expectations of accuracy and value in objectivity are a service both to the study of the past and to understanding how these events helped to shape the present. However, when dealing with the Old Testament it is easy to project our appreciation for accuracy and disdain for bias onto the ancient texts, which ultimately is not a fair way to approach these ancient texts.

Long before there was even a concept of "Bible," many of the texts of the Old Testament were passed down through oral tradition, only to be written down and finally canonized centuries later; this is evidenced in the repetitive Torah narratives, such as the creation refrain in Gen. 1:1—2:4a and the lyrical hymn of Deborah in Judges 5. To imagine the original texts as printed, bound, copyrighted, and collected works, as we hold them today, is both inaccurate and misleading. Moreover, assuming the intents and expectations of the oral historian to be akin to those of modern historians is misleading, and focusing on accuracy can limit the scope of a passage's message when the intent of the passage rests in the ideas it promotes. Cultures that employ oral tradition do not make dates, places, or accuracy a priority; rather, they are interested in the telling and retelling of a story to develop an understanding or identity that can answer the questions of the times into which they are received. Take the account of King Solomon's wealth in 2 Chron. 9:22-24, for example.

> King Solomon surpassed all the kings of the earth in wealth and wisdom. All the kings of the earth came to pay homage to Solomon and to listen to the wisdom with which God had endowed him. Each brought his tribute—silver and gold objects, robes, weapons, and spices, horses and mules—in the amount due each year (JPS).

Such an account served a purpose to the ancient author and his audience, but the account was certainly not accurate. Putting aside the issue of transoceanic travel for contemporary rulers in the Americas or the South Pacific, Israel held no such wealth in the tenth century BCE, and such superpowers as Egypt and Assyria would never have been compelled to offer tribute. While questions surrounding the reality of Solomon's wealth are not a center of contentious debate in the public sphere, questions pertaining to the creation of the universe are highly controversial; the front lines of this debate can be seen at the doors of the Creation Museum in Petersburg, Kentucky.

Founded by Ken Ham and Answers in Genesis (AiG), a Christian apologetics organization, the Creation Museum is a prime example of how scientific-age expectations are frequently placed on the ancient texts of the Old Testament. With the motto "Prepare to Believe," the museum promotes Gen. 1:1—2:4a as a scientific explanation for the creation of the cosmos, an event that is said to have occurred around 4,000 BCE, as determined through James Ussher's seventeenth-century-CE biblically based calculations. It is important to consider that the questions the Creation Museum seeks to answer do not likely match the agenda of the authors of Gen. 1:1—2:4a, which is connected to the Babylonian myth the *Enuma Elish* and/or the battle between the Canaanite god Baal and Yam, each of which centers on order's conquest of chaos. It also does not take into consideration that those who canonized the Torah followed this story with another creation story (Gen. 2:4b-25), which is juxtaposed with the first, making it unlikely that the ancient intent was to give a *scientific* account of our origins. Furthermore, the authors of the texts believed that the sky was a firmament that held back a great sky-ocean (Gen. 1:6-8), from which precipitation came when its doors were opened, and that the moon was self-illuminating (Gen. 1:14-18). A key danger in treating Old Testament books with modern historical and scientific expectations is not only receiving inaccurate messages about our past but also failing to realize the intent of the authors and the depth of meaning behind the messages they conveyed.

Projecting Modern Contexts onto the Ancient Past

The oft-repeated notion that only the winners write history is not entirely true, for readers rewrite the histories they receive by projecting their own personal and cultural perspectives onto them. The medievalist Norman Cantor stresses how individuals tend to project their own worldviews and experiences onto the past, thereby reinventing the past in their own image (156–58). Whereas Cantor dealt with issues of secular history, biblical history appears to follow suit, as found in such art pieces as Dutch painter Gerard van Honthorst's piece *King David Playing the Harp*. In the painting van Honthorst depicts the king with European-style attire and instrument. In contextually ambiguous passages, such as the land seizures in Mic. 2:1-4, we find scholars filling in the blanks with characters that make more sense in our time than in the ancient past, such as the mafia (Alfaro, 25). It is difficult for a reader not to project his or her own time and culture onto the text, for that is the reader's primary reference point; to escape doing so is likely not possible. But just as complete objectivity is not attainable, an awareness of its hazards can help readers exercise some degree of control regarding how much they project their present onto the past.

Bringing One's Ideology to the Text

Just as readers bring their notions of history to the Old Testament, so also they bring their ideologies. While attempts to view Old Testament texts through the biblical authors' eyes may be made, one's perceptions can never be entirely freed from one's own experiences, which help shape how a particular idea or story is read. This challenge is a double-edged sword. On one side of the sword, the ideology and experiences of the reader may cloud the text's original meaning and intent, causing unintended—and sometimes intentional—misreadings of a passage. When this occurs, the resulting interpretation often tells us more about the social or ideological location of the reader than the biblical characters who are being interpreted. Albert Schweitzer found that nineteenth-century biographies on the life of the "historical Jesus" turned out to be autobiographies of their authors; romantics uncovered an idealist Jesus, political radicals found a revolutionary, and so on (Schweitzer). On the other side of the sword, one finds an advantage shared by oral tradition. Reading a text through one's own experiences can breathe new life into the text and allow it to speak to current circumstances, as found in postcolonial, feminist, and queer interpretations. Since readers cannot fully remove themselves from their own ideological locations, it is important to acknowledge that a reader's ideas and biases are brought to the text and that much is to be learned by considering various interpretations.

Because ideology plays a role in interpretation, it should be noted that history—and biblical histories, in particular—do not exist in the past, but are very much alive and active in the present. YHWH's granting of land to Abraham's dependents, for example, plays a prominent role in the Israel-Palestine conflict. This is addressed by Keith Whitelam and James Crossley, who find the biblical text shaping modern perceptions of land via cartography. A post-1967 war edition of *The Macmillan Bible Atlas* contains a map of Israel with borders that look remarkably similar to the modern-day border with Gaza—despite great uncertainty surrounding ancient Israel's borders—and that is inscribed with Gen. 13:14-15: "The LORD said to Abram . . . 'Lift up your eyes, and look from the place where you are, northward and southward and eastward and westward; for all the land which you see I will give to you and to your descendants forever'" (RSV; see Whitelam 61–62; Crossley 176). Whether one sees this connection in a positive or negative light, clear political implications of the biblical past can be seen.

Differing Views on the Old Testament's History

Another factor to be considered, which is also highly political, is the lack of consensus pertaining to the historicity of biblical narratives and the state of ancient Israel, ranging from the exodus narrative to the Davidic monarchy. The degree to which these events and histories are *real histories* or *cultural memory* has been the subject of much debate and polemic within the academy. Many scholars agree that the story of the Hebrew exodus out of Egypt is cultural memory, with varying degrees of historical truth, ranging from seeing the Hebrews as an invading force to an indigenous movement within Canaan that rose up against exploitative rulers. But one of the most heated debates in the history of ancient Israel has revolved around the dating of the monarchy and the rise of Judah as a powerful state.

The traditional view, often referred to as the *maximalist* perspective, gives greater credence to the Bible's account of the monarchy's history. Scholars of this persuasion accept, to varying degrees, the Old Testament's stories of the rise of Israel beginning with King Saul and continuing on through the destruction of Israel and Judah. So-called *minimalists* give less credence to biblical accounts, relying more on archaeological and extrabiblical sources to develop their views of the monarchy and the presence of a powerful state, for which they find little evidence. While largely unnoticed outside the academy, the debate has caused great animosity within. Maximalist scholars have been accused of burdening archaeology with the task of upholding the biblical narratives (Davies), while minimalists have been accused of attempting to erase ancient Israel from world history (Halpern).

The purpose of addressing the maximalist/minimalist debate in this introduction is to emphasize that biblical scholarship contains diverse voices and points of view on the Bible's history, which will be seen in the commentaries of this volume. It is good that these different perspectives are aired. When approaching an area of history that is of such great importance to so many, yet with so little definitive information available, it is important to articulate and compare different ideas so as to produce and refine the historical possibilities of the Bible's contexts. In this way we see how differing views of biblical interpretation can work as a dance, where partners can complement each other's work, even if tempers can flare sometimes when partners step on one another's toes.

Reading the Old Testament in Its Ancient Context

It is apparent that contemplating the ancient contexts of the Old Testament requires several areas of consideration. While there is no end to the complexities involved with pursuing a greater understating of the world(s) out of which the books of the Old Testament developed, this section is intended to draw the reader's attention to some of the Old Testament's physical environments, political climates, and theological diversity.

Physical Environments of the Old Testament

The geography and ecology of ancient Palestine can easily be overlooked, but their value for understanding the Old Testament should not be underestimated. While the Old Testament represents diverse social settings that span hundreds of years, all of its authors lived in agrarian societies where land, climate, economics, and religion are inseparable. Due to agrarian societies' dire need to ensure successful and regular harvests—whether for survival or with the additional aspiration of building empire—farming practices become incorporated into religious rituals that end up dictating planting, harvesting, and land management. This strong connection between faith and farming led to rituals that served as an interface between spirituality and socioeconomic activities, effectively erasing the lines between religious and economic practice (Coomber 2013). In the end, the ritualization of agrarian economics helps shape perceptions of the deity or deities to which the rituals are connected: the Feast of Unleavened Bread (Exod. 23:14-17), the barley harvest festival incorporated in the Passover feast (Exodus 12; cf. John 19:29, the wheat-harvest Feast of Weeks, also known as Pentecost (Lev. 23:15-21; cf. Acts 2:1), and the fruit-harvest Feast of Booths (Lev. 23:33-36). Thus geography and ecology affected not only the way ancient Hebrews farmed but also how they came to understand God. Moreover, the geographical regions in which many of them farmed influenced these understandings.

Regions of Ancient Israel

Ancient Israel can be divided into a number of geographical areas, each of which presents its own unique environment. Furthest to the west is the *coastal plain*, which held great economic importance in the way of trade. This is especially visible in the development of manufacturing and shipping cities such as Ekron and Ashkelon. Due to the region's trade potential, it was usually controlled by foreign powers and is not frequently mentioned in the Old Testament (e.g., Judges 16; 2 Kings 16; Jer. 25:20; Amos 1:8; Zeph. 2:4).

The lowland *Shephelah* and the *highlands* are just east of the coastal plain, forming an important region of Israel, which is at the center of most of the Old Testament's stories. This fertile land, composed of low hills and valleys, is good for animal husbandry and the cultivation of grains, cereals, nuts, olives, and grapes. These areas were valuable for both subsistence farming and the production of trade goods, in which surrounding empires could engage. The agrarian potential of this area also made Shephelah and the highlands a target for foreign invasion. This region's political influence was heightened by the cities of Jerusalem, Samaria, and Lachish.

The *Jordan Valley*, east of the highlands, contains the lowest natural surface in the world and is part of a fault that extends into Africa. The valley follows the Jordan River from the city of Dan through the city of Hazor and the Sea of Galilee before flowing into the Dead Sea. Aside from the important role that the Jordan Valley plays in Ezekiel's vision of water flowing out of the temple to bring life to the Dead Sea (Ezekiel 47), the region is rarely mentioned.

To the east of the Jordan Valley is the *Transjordan highlands*, which is often referred to as "beyond the Jordan" (e.g., Josh. 12:1). Extending from the Dead Sea's altitude of 650-feet below sea level to the 9,230-foot peak of Mt. Hermon, this region contains a diverse range of topography and climates that allow for the cultivation of diverse agricultural goods, including grains, fruits, timber, and livestock. The agrarian potential of the area attracted a number of peoples, including the Moabites, the Ammonites, and the Edomites.

Whether valued for their sustaining, trade, or defensive capabilities, the topography of ancient Israel and its surrounding lands influenced its inhabitants' ability or inability to find sustenance and pursue their own interests. When empires such as Assyria and Babylon were on the rise, this region attracted their rulers who sought the earning potential of the land, and these events—or the cultural memories they inspired—influenced the Old Testament authors' stories of defeat and are reflected in their perceptions of God's attitudes toward them.

Climatic Challenges

While the land in and around Israel was some of the most sought after in the ancient Near East, its inhabitants endured serious meteorological challenges. The ancient Israelites lived at the crossroads of subtropical and temperate atmospheric patterns—producing rainy winter seasons and dry summers—and the effects of these patterns shaped the ways in which the Hebrews lived: the resulting erratic precipitation patterns result in a 30 percent chance of insufficient rainfall (Karmon, 27). The unpredictability of each growing season's weather pattern meant that the rainfall of a given season could play out in any number of ways, each demanding specific farming strategies for which farmers had little foresight or room for error. Subsequent failed seasons that diminished surpluses could lead to debt and the selling of family members into slavery or even the extinction of a family line.

Everything in society—from the interests of the poorest farmer to the king—depended on successful harvests and access to their crops, and the strong desire for divine assistance is reflected in Old Testament narratives that emphasize fidelity to YHWH. The seriousness placed on securing favorable rainfall and accessing harvests is clear in warnings against following other deities, such as the weather god Baal (e.g., Judg. 2:11; 2 Kings 3:2; Ps. 106:28; Hosea 9:10), God-given visions that foretell rainfall (Genesis 41), and the granting and withholding of rain as reward or punishment (Deut. 11:11-14; cf. 1 Kings 17–18). Additionally, there are strict rules to protect land access (Leviticus 25) and condemnation against abuses (1 Kings 21; Isa. 5:8-10; Mic. 2:1-4).

The physical environments of the Old Testament authors are an important consideration, because they not only affected the way the authors lived but also helped to shape their views of God and the world around them. From the development of the ancient Hebrews' religious rituals to finding either God's favor or wrath in agrarian events (see Zech. 10:1; 1 Kings 17–18), the topography and climatic environments that affected cultivation played key roles in how the biblical authors perceived and interacted with the divine.

Sociopolitical Contexts of the Old Testament

In addition to the challenges presented by Israel's geographic and climatic setting, its strategic location between the empires of Mesopotamia and northern Africa presented a recurring threat. As these empires invaded the lands of ancient Israel for military and economic reasons, the biblical authors and redactors received and transmitted these events into their religious narratives: foreign invasion was often perceived as divine punishment—with the notable exception of the Persians—and the defeat of foreign forces was perceived as a result of divine favor. Before addressing foreign influences on the Old Testament's ancient contexts, a brief overview of Israel's domestic structures should be considered.

Israel's Domestic Sociopolitical Contexts

While ancient Palestine's Mesopotamian neighbors developed cities and urban economies in the Early Bronze Age (3300–2100 BCE), Palestine largely remained a patchwork of scattered settlements that functioned as a peripheral economy, engaging in trade activity as neighboring empires made it lucrative, and receding into highland agriculture when those powers waned (Coomber 2010, 81–92). Adapting to the demands of waxing and waning empires—rather than taking significant steps toward powerful urban economies of its own—resulted in a marked reliance on subsistence strategies on into the seventh century BCE (Coote and Whitelam).

Biblical accounts of Hebrew societal structures present a patronage system that had its roots in small family units called the *bet av* ("father's house"), which together formed a *mishpahah* ("family" or "clan"), which expanded up to the tribe, or *shevet*. When the monarchy was established, the *malkut* ("kingdom") became the top rung. While the *malkut* and *shevet* held the top two tiers, the phrase "all politics is local" applies to ancient Israel: loyalty structures were strongest at the bottom.

Philip Davies and John Rogerson note that the *bet av*, "father's house," likely had a double meaning (32). While it indicated a family unit that included extended lineage and slaves—excluding daughters who left the family at marriage—it likely also denoted the descendants of a common ancestor, who may not have lived under a single roof (e.g., Gen. 24:38). While the *bet avim* grew through the births of sons and the accumulation of wives and slaves, the danger of collapse due to disease, war, and a lack of birth of sons presented a constant threat. Debt was also a threat to a *bet av*, inspiring legal texts that protected its access to arable land (Leviticus 25; Deut. 25:5). It was the patriarch's responsibility to care for the family's economic well-being, as well as to pass on traditions, the history of the nation, and the laws of God (Deut. 6:7; 11:8-9; 32:46-47). The *bet av* also had power over such judicial matters as those of marriage and slave ownership.

Mishpahah denotes a level of organization based on a recognizable kinship (Numbers 1; 26). It had territorial significance, as seen in tribal border lists of Joshua 13–19, and was responsible for dividing the land. While *mishpahah* is difficult to translate, Norman Gottwald offers the useful definition, "protective association of extended families" (Gottwald 1999, 257). If the immediate or extended families of a citizen who had to sell himself to an alien could not redeem him, the *mishpahah* became the last line of protection from perpetual servitude (Lev. 25:48-49).

Shevet refers to the largest group and unit of territorial organization, which was primarily bound together by residence. Military allegiances appear to have belonged to this level, against both foreign and domestic threats—as seen in the Benjamite battles of Judges 12 and 20–21. Gottwald sees the *shevet* as more of a geographic designation pertaining to clusters of villages and/or clans that gathered for protective purposes rather than as representative bodies within a political system (Gottwald 2001, 35).

The *malkut*, or kingdom, is a source of continued contention in the so-called minimalist/maximalist debate mentioned above. The Old Testament account claims that the kingdom of Israel was founded when Saul became king over the Israelite tribes (1 Samuel 9) and continued through the line of David, after Saul fell out of favor with God. Israel's united monarchy is reported to have spanned 1030 to 930 BCE, when King Rehoboam was rejected by the northern Israelites (1 Kgs. 12:1-20; 2 Chron. 10:1-19), leading to the period of the divided monarchy, with Israel in the north and Judah in the south. These two kingdoms existed side by side until Israel was destroyed by Assyria (734–721 BCE). Judah entered into Assyrian vassalage in the 720s and was destroyed by the Babylonians around 586 BCE. Those who give less credence to the biblical account take note that there is little extrabiblical evidence of a monarchy prior to King Omri, aside from the Tel Dan Stele, which refers to "the House of David," which may refer to a king.

While Israel's domestic organizational landscape played a major role in the development of biblical law and narrative, the biblical authors' interactions with surrounding peoples had profound effects on the stories they told. The main imperial influences, from the premonarchical period to the fall of the Hasmonean Dynasty, were Egypt, Philistine, Assyria, Babylon, Persia, the Greeks, and the Romans.

Israel's Foreign Sociopolitical Contexts

The Egyptian Empire played an important role in the development of the Torah, as seen in the stories of Abram and Sarai (Genesis 12), Joseph (Genesis 37–50), and throughout the entire exodus narrative, interwoven into many areas of the Old Testament. The authors of Exodus used the backdrop of Egypt's powerful *New Kingdom* (1549–1069 BCE) to display their faith in YHWH's power, and other books draw on this narrative as a recurring reminder of the Israelites' debt and obligations toward their god (e.g. Deut. 5:15, 24:17-22, 23:7-8; Ps. 106:21; Ezekiel 20; Amos 2:10; Mic. 6:4), and as a vehicle of praise (Psalms 78; 81; 135; 136). The Jewish holiday of Passover, which is referred to throughout the Old Testament, has its roots in this anti-Egyptian epic. A later and weaker Egypt returns to play a role in the story of Judah's lengthy downfall: King Hezekiah (d. 680s) enters into a failed anti-Assyrian alliance with Egypt (Isaiah 30–31; 36:6-9), and King Zedekiah (d. 580s) enters into a failed anti-Babylonian alliance with Pharaoh Hophra (Ezek. 17:15; Jer. 2:36).

While their point of origins are in dispute (Amos 9:7 puts their origin at Caphtor), the Philistines tried to invade Egypt in 1190 BCE, but were repelled by Ramses III, who settled them in the coastal towns of Gaza, Ashkelon, and Ashdod (Deut. 2:23). From there, they continued their incursions along the coastal plain and perhaps even drove out their Egyptian rulers, under the reign of Ramses IV (d. 1149 BCE). They play a key adversarial role in the book of Judges, as found in the stories of Shamgar (Judg. 3:31) and Samson (Judges 13–16). Their military competencies are reflected in the story of their capture of the ark of the covenant in 1 Sam. 4:1—7:2. Fear of the Philistine threat helped influence the people's decision to choose a king to unite the tribes (1 Sam. 8–9). The biblical authors continued to portray the Philistines as a threat to the Israelites, but Philistine influence in the highlands faded as the power of Assyria grew.

Assyria's fearsome power and influence in the region gave them a villain's role in the Old Testament. The biblical authors perceived Assyria's incursions into Israel and Judah as YHWH's punishment for such transgressions as idolatry and social injustice. While archaeological evidence of Philistine-Israelite interaction is scant, there is plenty of archaeological and extrabiblical evidence of Assyria's impact on Israel and Judah.

From the start of its ninth-century conquests, Assyria was feared for its ruthless force. The psychological impact of Assyria's powerful conscripted forces, iron chariots, siege engines, and public mutilations surface in the writings of the Old Testament authors. The Assyrians enforced submission through power and fear, deporting conquered rulers to prevent uprisings (2 Kings 17:6, 24, 28; 18:11). When uprisings occurred, Assyrian troops were deployed from strategically positioned garrisons to flay, impale, and burn the perpetrators, as portrayed in Assyrian palace-reliefs.

In the late eighth century, both Israel and Judah felt the full weight of Assyria's might. The northern kingdom of Israel was destroyed in 721 BCE after joining an alliance of vassals that stopped paying tribute to Assyria. At the end of the century, King Hezekiah entered Judah into a similar alliance with Egypt (Isaiah 30–31), which resulted in the invasion of his kingdom and the siege of Jerusalem. According to 2 Kgs. 18:13-16, the siege was broken when Hezekiah sent a message of repentance to the Assyrian king, Sennacherib, at Lachish, promising to resume his tribute obligations. Other texts in 2 Kings suggest that Sennacherib abandoned the siege to deal with political unrest at home (19:7, 37) or a plague (19:35-36). Despite his efforts to subvert Sennacherib's dominance of Judah, Hezekiah and his successors continued to rule as vassals.

Under the rule of King Nebuchadnezzar, the Babylonian Empire captured Nineveh in 612, destroyed the Egyptians at the battle of Carchemish in 605, and captured Jerusalem in 597, deporting many inhabitants. After a rebellion by King Zedekiah in 586, the Babylonians destroyed Jerusalem and the temple and deported a significant portion of Judah's population (2 Kings 24; 2 Chronicles 36). The prophets Ezekiel, Jeremiah, and Habakkuk saw Nebuchadnezzar's conquest as YHWH's punishment for the sins of the Judean state (Ezekiel 8–11; Jer. 25:1-14; Hab. 1:6-10). The events of the Babylonian conquest are largely supported by archaeology and extrabiblical literature (Grabbe, 210–13).

Biblical claims of the removal of all Judeans but the poorest "people of the land" (2 Kgs. 24:14-16; 25:12; Jer. 52:16, 28-30) are reflected in the archaeological record, which indicates that inhabited sites decreased by two-thirds, from 116 to 41, and surviving sites shrank from 4.4 to 1.4 hectares, suggesting a population collapse of 85 to 90 percent (Liverani, 195). Such a massive exile plays a formidable role in the Old Testament, as described in the stories of significant characters such as Ezekiel and Daniel. Rage associated with this event is found in Psalm 137, which recounts the horrors of the exile and ends with the chilling words "a blessing on him who seizes your [Babylonian] babies and dashes them against the rocks!" (137:9 JPS). The exiled Hebrews who returned to Palestine after the Persians conquered the Babylonians returned to a destroyed Jerusalem that no longer enjoyed the security of a defensive wall. Some of the returnees helped to reshape Judaism with a flourishing priesthood and the composition of scholarly works and biblical texts. While exile is portrayed in negative terms, many Jews remained in the lands to which they had been deported; this had the effect of spreading Judaism outside the confines of Palestine.

After overthrowing his grandfather King Astyages of the Medes in 553 BCE, Cyrus of Persia (d. 530) rapidly expanded his empire, moving westward into Armenia and Asia Minor and east toward India, and defeated Babylon in 539. But unlike previous conquests, the Old Testament treats Persian dominance as a time of hope. As successor to the Babylonian Empire, King Cyrus instituted a policy of allowing victims of Babylonian exile to return to their homelands, where he sponsored their local religions. To the biblical authors, this policy was met with celebration and as a sign of YHWH's love for his people. The authors of 2 Chron. 36:23 and Ezra 1:2 portray King Cyrus as crediting YHWH with his victories and with the mandate to rebuild the temple in Jerusalem; Ezra 1:7 even portrays the Persian king personally returning the vessels that Nebuchadnezzar had seized from the temple four decades before. While the Bible treats Cyrus's policy of return as inspired by YHWH, Davies and Rogerson note that the practice was neither new nor disinterested, as it served to restore the national culture of a large and culturally varied empire (59). It is important to note the great shift in how the biblical authors treated King Cyrus of Persia, as opposed to the kings of the Assyrians and Babylonians, whom they disdained. In Isaiah 40–50, Cyrus is championed as the great savior of the Judean deportees and of the rebuilding of Jerusalem. In fact, while oracles against foreign nations are a key theme in prophetic oracles, none are directed against Persia. Even when their rulers are compliant with the murder of Jews, they are portrayed as either acting against their own desires or out of ignorance (Daniel 6; Esther).

Like the exile, itself, the return from exile plays an important role in the politics and religion of the Old Testament. Accounts of these events are found in the books of Ezra and Nehemiah. While the Bible presents the return as a blessing from God and a time of joy, it does not seem to have been without its hardships. It can be deduced from Ezra and Nehemiah that resettlement involved various tensions; in Ezra 3:3, those who had remained in Judah during the exile, along with other neighboring peoples, take the Canaanites' role in the book of Joshua: "an evil influence which will, unless strenuously rejected, corrupt the 'people of God'" (Davies and Rogerson, 88). It was during the Persian period that the Jerusalem temple was rebuilt and the priesthood gained power and influence.

The long march of succeeding empires continued with the rise of Alexander the Great, who seized control of the Greek city-states in 336 BCE and conquered the Persian Empire before his death in 323. Unlike previous empires that might make their subjects worship a particular deity or relocate to a different region, the Greek ideal of *Hellenism* posed a particular cultural threat. Hellenism promoted a view in which people were not citizens of a particular region, but of the world, enabling the integration of Greek and regional cultures, thus breaking down barriers that separated local peoples from their foreign rulers. Within a hundred years, Koine Greek had become the lingua franca, and Greek philosophy, educational systems, art and attire, politics, and religion permeated the empire. The consequences of Hellenization had profound linguistic, political, and theological effects on the biblical authors who lived and wrote during this period. Jews who lived outside of Israel became more familiar with the Greek language than Hebrew. By the second century CE, Greek had become so widely spoken among the Jewish community in Alexandria, Egypt, that the Hebrew Bible was translated into Koine Greek, which came to be called the Septuagint.

Greek rule eventually led to the severe oppression of the Jewish people at the hands of the usurper king Antiochus IV (d. 164 BCE), who sought to weed out cultural diversity in the Seleucid Empire. King Antiochus, who called himself *Epiphanes* ("god made manifest"), was known for his erratic character, which manifested itself in his brutal hatred of the Jews. Even his allies referred to him by the nickname *Epimanes*—a play on Epiphanes—meaning "the crazy one." He is known for looting the Jerusalem temple to fund his battles against the Ptolemies and for forbidding the Jewish rite of circumcision and sacred dietary laws.

King Antiochus was also known for instigating treachery among the Jewish leadership, giving Jason—of the pro-Greek Onias family—the high priesthood in return for complying with Antiochus's plans to Hellenize Jerusalem by building a gymnasium and enrolling its people as citizens of Antioch (2 Macc. 4:7). Further strife erupted when Menelaus, another aspirant for the high priesthood, offered Antiochus even greater gifts for the office. The rivalry of Jason and Menelaus led to the sacking of Jerusalem, slaughtering of its citizens, and the looting of its temple (2 Macc. 5:11-23; Josephus 12.5.3 §§246–47). The horrors of life under King Antiochus IV are reflected in the horn that emerges from the fourth beast in the apocalyptic vision of Dan. 7:7-8, and is then slain by the "Ancient One" (7:11).

From stripping the temple to pay for his wars to setting up an altar for Zeus in the temple, King Antiochus IV's brutality against the Jews led to a revolt that started in the Judean village of Modein in 167 BCE and spread rapidly throughout the region—as chronicled in 1 and 2 Maccabees and in Josephus's *Antiquities of the Jews* (c. 100 CE). A guerrilla warfare campaign that was led by Judas Maccabeus eventually liberated and purified the temple—an event celebrated today in the Jewish festival of Hanukkah. The Maccabean revolt drove out the Greeks and expanded the borders to include Galilee. While the revolt was successful in ushering in a period of self-rule, the resulting Hasmonean Dynasty fell prey to the lust for power. As civil conflict broke out between two rival claims to the throne, the Roman general Pompey invaded Judea in 63 BCE, seizing control of the region for his empire. In 40 BCE, the Roman Senate appointed an Edomite convert to Judaism, *Herod the Great*, as king of Judea. Despised by his people, the puppet king had to take Jerusalem by force, from where he ruled harshly.

Each of these empires, vying for control over the Southern Levant, brought with them challenges that helped to shape the Hebrew people by influencing the ways they viewed themselves, their God, and their religious practices.

Religious Contexts of the Old Testament

Despite common perceptions of the Bible as a univocal work, the Old Testament represents diverse theologies of communities that spanned centuries and were influenced by the religious systems of their contemporaries. Babylonian and Canaanite musings over the power of order over chaos, as found in the *Enuma Elish* and Baal narratives, are present in Gen. 1:1—2:4a and referenced in Ps. 74:12-17. The authors of the Bible's Wisdom literature exchanged ideas with their foreign neighbors, as found in parallels between the Babylonian story I Will Praise the Lord of Wisdom and the book of Job, and passages from Proverbs that mirror the words of the Egyptian thinkers Ptah-Hotep and Amen-em-opet (e.g., Prov. 22:4; 22:17—24:22). Understanding the diversity of theological perspectives in the Old Testament can aid both exegesis and hermeneutics by giving the reader greater insight into the biblical authors' ideas of God and uncovering layers of meaning that might otherwise go unnoticed.

Monotheism and Henotheism

It should not be assumed that all Old Testament authors were monotheists: many were *henotheists*. Henotheism promotes a multi-god/dess universe in which the adherent gives allegiance to a supreme primary deity. Elements of this outlook appear to be found in God's decision to create humanity "in our image, after our likeness" (Gen. 1:26 RSV), and in YHWH's anxiety over the man that he created becoming "like one of us" in Gen. 3:22. YHWH also expresses his disgust in that the *sons of God* mated with human women, resulting in the birth of the nephilim (Gen. 6:2-4). In the *Song of Moses*, Moses poses the rhetorical question, "who is like you, O Lord, among the gods?" (Exod. 15:11). The writer of Ps. 95:3 proclaims, "YHWH is a great God, the king of all divine beings," while 97:9 asserts that YHWH is "exalted high above all divine beings." These examples pose a number of questions about the biblical authors' views on the divine. Two that will be briefly addressed here concern the identity of God and the role of the other deities being inferred. The supreme deity of the ancient Hebrews is given several names and titles, representing different personality traits and theological views.

Elohim

The name or title *Elohim*, which is usually translated from the Hebrew into English as "God," makes its first appearance in Genesis 1. The name Elohim is used to identify the Hebrews' supreme deity in several Old Testament texts, including those found in the books of Genesis, Exodus, Psalms, and Job. As in the Bible's priestly creation story (Gen. 1:1—2:4a), Elohim is portrayed as an all-powerful, confident, commanding, and somewhat distant deity, whose supremacy and majesty are emphasized.

YHWH

YHWH is an anthropomorphic god who exhibits tendencies toward both kindness and severity and is self-described as a jealous god who, unlike other ancient Near Eastern gods, demands the exclusive allegiance of his followers. The name YHWH, which is often translated into English as "the LORD"—from the Hebrew *adonay*—makes its first appearance in the second creation story (Gen. 2:4b). The name YHWH carries a sense of mystery. Derived from the Hebrew verb *hawah*, meaning "to be," YHWH is difficult to translate, but means something like "he who is" or "he who causes what is." Some believe that YHWH's origins can be traced to the god YHW, who was worshiped in the northwestern region of the Arabian Peninsula known as Midian: this is where Moses first encounters YHWH (Exodus 3).

YHWH has strong associations with Canaanite culture, which highlights discrepancies between biblical directions for the deity's worship and how the deity was worshiped in popular religion. Whereas the biblical authors convey strict messages that YHWH should be worshiped alone, the remains of Israelite homes reveal that other gods and goddesses, such as Asherah—whom the author(s) of Jeremiah refers to as *the queen of heaven*—were worshiped alongside YHWH (Dever, 176–89). Jeremiah 44 appears to give a glimpse into the popular polytheistic or henotheistic religion of sixth-century-BCE Judah. After YHWH threatens the people for worshiping other gods, the women say that they will not listen but will continue the traditions of their ancestors and give offerings to the queen of heaven, who protected them well (Jer. 44:16-17). Further biblical evidence of Asherah's popularity is found in the biblical authors' continual condemnation of her worship, often symbolized through the presence of pillars and poles, as they worked to direct the people toward monotheism (Deut. 7:5; Judg. 3:7-8; 1 Kgs. 14:15, 23; Jer. 17:17-18).

El

The name or title *El* appears around two hundred times in the Old Testament, with frequent use in the ancestor stories of Genesis and surfacing throughout the Old Testament. Its presence poses some interesting questions.

On one level, El is a common Semitic title for "divine being," and can be read as an appellative for "divinity," often compounded with other words such as *el-shadday* ("God Almighty" [Gen. 17:1; Exod. 6:3; Ezek. 10:5]) and *el-elyon* ("God Most High" [Gen. 14:22; Deut. 32:8-9; Ps. 78:35]). In addition to a title referring to God, El is also the name of the chief god of the Canaanite pantheon. Often portrayed as a bearded king on his throne, and referred to as the "Ancient One," El was worshiped in Canaan and Syria both before and after the emergence of Israel. The frequent use of El for God—and the Canaanite god's prominence in Israel—has led many to conclude that El developed into YHWH. Mark Smith asserts, "The original god of Israel was El. . . . Isra*el* is not a Yahwistic name with the divine element of Yahweh, but an El name" (Smith, 32; emphasis on *el* in "Israel" is mine). A cross-pollination of Canaanite and Hebrew religion is found in the use of Canaanite El imagery to describe the "Ancient One" in Dan. 7:9-10 who sits on a throne with white garments and hair as pure as wool. Furthermore, the description of "one like a human being coming with the clouds of heaven," who "came to the Ancient One and was presented before him" (Dan. 7:13), dovetails with images of the Canaanite god Baal coming before El. Whether or not the authors of Daniel 7 envisioned El, the imprint of Canaanite religion appears to have been stamped on ideas of God and passed down through the generations. While not accepted by biblical authors, popular religion in ancient Israel appears to have had a complex network of deities that fulfilled various roles in daily life. (For a helpful overview on differences between "popular" and "official" religion in ancient Israel, see Stavrakopoulou.)

The idea that El was absorbed into YHWH is also supported by the fact that the chief god of the Canaanite pantheon is never condemned in the Old Testament, but his son Baal, consort Asherah, and other gods face vicious condemnation (Num. 25:2; Deut. 4:3; Judg. 6:30; 1 Kgs. 16:31—18:40). Why would the biblical authors attack lesser Canaanite deities but leave the head god unscathed? One possible answer is that El had become synonymous with YHWH; both share a compassionate disposition toward humanity (Exod. 34:6; Ps. 86:15), use dreams to communicate (Gen. 31:24; 37:5; 1 Kgs. 3:5-15), and have healing powers (cf. *KTU* 1:16.v–vi with Gen. 20:17; Num. 12:13; Ps. 107:20 [Smith, 39]).

The Divine Council

As El served as chief of the Canaanite pantheon, YHWH was head of the *divine council*, whose members were often referred to as "the sons of gods." In Gen. 28:12; 33:1-2; Pss. 29:1 and 89:6-9, we find YHWH at the head of subordinate divine beings who are collectively referred to as the "council of Lord" (Jer. 23:18 and the "congregation of El" (Ps. 82:1). In Psalm 82, God attacks the congregants for their oppressive acts against humanity, for which they are doomed to die like mortals (vv. 5-7). In Job 1:6-7, Job's troubles begin when the divine council convenes with YHWH, and God asks "the satan" where he has been. The satan also appears on the divine council in Zechariah, where YHWH delivers judgment between two members of his entourage. The clearest depiction of the divine council's function is in 1 Kgs. 22:19-22, where YHWH seeks guidance and direction from the council, the members of which confer in open discussion before one spirit approaches YHWH with a proposal. Following a common motif in ancient Mediterranean literature, humans are sometimes transported before God and the divine council, as found in a party feasting with Elohim in Exod. 24:9-11 and Isaiah's commission as prophet in Isaiah 6 (Niditch 2010, 14–17).

Concluding Words on the Complexities of the Ancient Context

Reading the Old Testament in its ancient contexts requires a variety of considerations and an understanding that there are divergent views on these contexts. But this complexity should not discourage readers of the Bible from contemplating the origins of the Old Testament books, because a better understanding of their origins results in a broader understanding of their meanings and potential applications to our modern contexts. The authors of this volume's commentaries have worked to give the reader the best possible overview of the sociohistorical contexts that underlie the books of the Old Testament, opening its texts in new ways so that new meanings can be derived. While this section has highlighted some of the many considerations that need to be addressed when reading the "Very Dangerous Texts Ahead," the variety of contexts out of which the Old

Testament's books emerged is paralleled by the diversity of cultures, faiths, and societies into which they have been received.

Reading the Old Testament in Its Contemporary Contexts

Actively engaging the Old Testament in both its ancient and modern contexts enables readers to discover new levels of meaning that would otherwise go unnoticed. Through acknowledging an Old Testament text's historical setting, exploring how it has been interpreted through the millennia, and noticing the questions and challenges that it raises for our contemporary settings, engaged readers are better able to receive multiple levels of meaning that aid the reader in better understanding the biblical authors' intentions and discerning the passage's potential relevance to conversations that are unfolding today.

The Challenge of Bringing Ancient Context in Line with Modern Contexts

To participate in this process, however, is not a simple task. Beyond working to discern the various levels of meaning within the Old Testament, it is of paramount importance for readers to also acknowledge the preconceptions and biases they bring with them as they work to connect the ancient writings to their own world—an issue that is explored at length below.

As humorously demonstrated in A. J. Jacobs's book *The Year of Living Biblically*, it is important to remember that the texts of the Old Testament were not written for twenty-first-century audiences, but for citizens of the ancient world. As he recounts in his book, Jacobs tried to live as literally as possible according to the laws of the Hebrew Bible for one year. His experiment revealed that to live by the rules of the Hebrew Bible is to live as an outlaw in much of the modern world, whether because the Hebrew Bible calls for the execution of people who wear mixed fibers or because it mandates sacrificing animals in urban centers. This clash of ancient and modern cultures occurred in a very serious way in the tragic murder of Murray Seidman. Mr. Seidman's killer referenced Lev. 20:13 as his motivation for stoning the elderly and mentally disabled man (Masterson).

Conversely, some people, like Charlie Fuqua, assert that engaging with the Old Testament's historical contexts is not required. During the 2012 United States election, Fuqua ran for a seat on the Arkansas state legislature and released a book titled *God's Law: The Only Political Solution*. In his book, Fuqua calls for the creation of legal channels that will facilitate the execution of disobedient children, as commanded in Deut. 21:18-21 (2012, 179). While Fuqua's views represent a fringe group of theomonists that include such Christian reconstructionists as Cornelius Van Til and Rousas John Rushdoony, his example illustrates the importance of contemplating the important differences that exist between the biblical authors' societies and those into which their writings are received today. One must ask questions such as, Did the authors of Deut. 21:18-21 actually seek the execution of disobedient children, or did they pose an extreme example to illustrate a point on child rearing? Another important question to consider is, Did Deut. 21:18-21 originate at a time when resources were so scarce and the production of food so difficult that a child who didn't contribute to—but rather threatened——the common good posed a threat to the community's survival? Growing and cultivating food could certainly be a matter of life and death. Fuqua's failure to engage Deut. 21:18-21, choosing instead to blindly subscribe to the text at face value, is a very serious and dangerous matter, especially considering his aspirations for political office. But while vast differences separate the cultures and societies of the Old Testament authors and the world that we inhabit today, a surprising number of connections do exist.

Whether a Judean farmer or an American physician, we all share such aspects of the universal human experience as love, hate, trust, betrayal, fear, and hope—all of which are reflected both in the Old Testament and in our daily lives. Such themes as women working to find justice in societies that offer little, the quest for love along with its dangers and rewards, and people's struggle to understand their relationships with power, whether personal or political, are all found in the stories of the Old Testament and are still highly relevant to us today.

It should be pointed out, however, that earnestly engaging the Old Testament in its ancient and modern contexts is difficult, even hazardous. Several key considerations that help in an engaged reading of the books of the Old Testament are included here, including issues of biblical ownership, methods of interpretation, and approaches to the reception of its texts.

Whose Bible Is It, Anyway?

While the texts of the Old Testament are commonly used with an air of authority and ownership, their ownership is open to question. So, to whom do they belong? Now that their authors are long dead—and their works have passed through generations and around the world—who is the heir of these works? To which community would they turn and say, "The keys are yours"? One problem with answering this question is that the Old Testament's authors and editors did not represent a unified tradition through which a unified voice could be offered. Furthermore, the faiths and cultures of the twenty-first century CE are so far removed from the ancient authors' that they would most likely be utterly unrecognizable to them. On one level, it is a moot question. Those authors are dead, and they do not get a say regarding who uses their works, or how. Be that as it may, it is an important question to consider, for recognizing that the Old Testament has a number of spiritual heirs with divergent views of the divine underscores the vast interpretive possibilities these texts contain. While many faith traditions draw on the books of the Old Testament, the three largest—in order of appearance—are Judaism, Christianity, and Islam.

The Hebrew Bible (the *Tanakh*) of Judaism is composed of twenty-four books, which are divided into the Torah (Law), the Nebiim (Prophets), and the Ketubim (Writings). The Torah gives accounts of the creation, the establishment of the Hebrew people, and their movement out of captivity in Egypt toward the land that was promised to their ancestors. The public reading of the Torah is a religious ritual that culminates with the annual holiday of *Simchat Torah*, which celebrates its completion. Although the Tanakh forms the whole of Jewish biblical literature, it is supplemented by other interpretive collections.

The Christian *Old Testament*, sometimes referred to as the *First Testament*, sets the books of the Tanakh in a different order and serves as the first section of the *Christian Bible*, as a whole. Canonization of the Old Testament varies among different Christian traditions. Roman Catholicism,

Eastern Orthodoxy, and some Protestant groups include the seven additional books in their canon, as well as additions to the books of Esther and Daniel; these additions are called the *deuterocanon* ("second canon") or *Apocrypha* ("hidden"). Many of the books of the Old Testament are popularly seen as a precursor to the coming of Jesus and his perceived fulfillment of the law.

Islam incorporates many of the figures of the Old Testament into its sacred writings, the Holy Qur'an. Giving particular reverence to the Torah and the Psalms, the Qur'an honors Abraham, Isaac, and Moses as prophetic predecessors to the faith's final and greatest prophet, Muhammad (d. 632 CE).

While each of these traditions draws deep meaning and conviction from the Hebrew Scriptures, they also use them in different ways to reflect their own unique spiritual paths and theologies. The question of which group is the rightful heir of the biblical authors is impossible to answer definitively, since each claims to be in fact the rightful heir. The fact that such a diverse pool of people turns to these texts as sacred Scripture amplifies the many possibilities for Old Testament interpretation.

Evolving Views of the Old Testament and Its Interpretation

Whether or not it is done consciously, all readers of the Old Testament are engaged in some level of interpretation; there are no passive readers of the Bible. When people read the books of the Old Testament, they do so actively, bringing their own presuppositions, experiences, and cultural norms to a text. In essence, readers of the Old Testament bridge the ancient to the modern by way of exegesis and hermeneutics.

Exegesis looks at the texts in their ancient contexts, while hermeneutics works to discern how they relate to a modern reader's situation. Biblical scholars and readers have developed a number of methods for bringing the ancient and the modern together, often with specific objectives and theological motives in mind.

Biblical Literalism

Biblical literalism—which asserts that the Bible is the inerrant word of God, unaltered and untainted by human agency during its transmission from God to humanity—is a prevalent form of interpretation in the United States, practiced commonly within fundamentalist and some evangelical communities. The literal meanings of individual biblical texts were long considered alongside allegorical, moral, and mystical interpretations; it was not until the Reformation's second wave, in the seventeenth century, that literalism became a way to approach the Bible as a whole.

Protestant Christians who broke from the authority of Roman Catholicism found a strong sense of liberation in the idea of gaining access to God's direct word through the Scriptures. If an adherent could access God directly through a Bible, what need did they have for such individual or institutional arbitrators as priests, popes, or the Roman Church? Whereas early Reformers like Martin Luther and John Calvin viewed Scripture as being inspired by God with human involvement in its transmission, some of the second wave of Reformers, such as Amandus Polanus (d. 1610) and Abraham Calov (d. 1686), placed even greater emphasis on the Bible's inerrancy. The movement known as Protestant Scholasticism promoted the idea that any human involvement in the creation of the Bible was strictly mechanical; those who wrote the words were merely tools used by God. This was the first time that the idea of the inerrancy of Scripture as a literal interpretive approach was applied to the Bible—as a whole.

Despite the many developments in biblical interpretation that have occurred between the seventeenth and twenty-first centuries CE, many North American Christians still self-identify as biblical literalists. However, almost nobody practices biblical literalism in the strictest sense, for it would be an almost untenable position. The various contributions by the different religious communities that went into the writing of our biblical texts have resulted in contradicting versions of similar content (cf. Exod. 21:2-8 with Deut. 15:12-13). Given these challenges, how could A. J. Jacobs's experiment in living in strict accord with biblical law have any hope of being tenable, or even legal?

Historical Criticism

The influence of the Enlightenment—with its emphases on reason and searching for facts—gave rise to *the historical-critical movement*, which works to reconstruct the ancient contexts of the Bible. Baruch Spinoza (d. 1677) argued that the same scientific principles that were being applied to other areas of knowledge should be applied to the Bible as well. The results, which are still highly influential on how biblical scholarship is conducted today, have challenged such traditionally held Old Testament notions as the Genesis account(s) of the creation, Moses' composition of the Torah, and the historical validity of the Hebrew exodus out of Egypt, to name a few. Scrutinizing a particular text's origins through asking such questions as, Who wrote the text? For what purpose? and, Under what circumstances? Historical critics work to better understand what lies beneath the text.

Historical criticism's influence on biblical scholarship has shaped the way that many theologians read the Bible by adding to our understanding of the ancient contexts behind biblical texts. *Religionsgeschichte* ("history of religions") is a tool of historical criticism that reads biblical texts in their ancient religious contexts. Another historical-critical tool is *form criticism*, which has gleaned new meaning from such passages as the Song of Deborah (Judges 5) by considering their oral prehistory, reconstructing the *Sitz im Leben* ("original setting"), and analyzing their literary genres.

Social-Scientific Criticism

In the late 1970s—with the publication of Norman Gottwald's *The Tribes of Yahweh*—biblical scholars began to look at the books of the Old Testament through the lens of their sociological settings. Since then, numerous scholars have used societal patterns both to fill in many of the hidden contexts that are simply not addressed in the texts themselves and to better understand the societal motivations behind the Old Testament authors' messages.

One advantage to the social-scientific method of interpretation is its ability to inform hermeneutics (again, the application of biblical texts to modern circumstances). Social-scientific models have proven to be of particular use in shedding light on the contexts and motivations behind biblical texts while opening new ways of understanding how those texts might relate to the modern world (Chaney; Coomber 2011). A tempting misuse of social-scientific models of interpretation, however, is to treat the findings gained through social-scientific models as hard evidence that can stand on its own. Social-scientific models that deal with tribalism, urban development, religious-political interactions, or economic cycles can provide insight into how humans—and their systems—are expected to behave; they do not, however, prove how humans and systems did behave. It is for this reason that social-scientific approaches should be used in tandem with all available data, be it archaeological or literary.

Commenting on the great value of using social-scientific models in the interpretation of biblical texts, Philip Esler writes that their use "fires the social-scientific imagination to ask new questions of data, to which only the data can provide the answers" (Esler, 3). In other words, these models are useful for the interpretation of evidence, not as evidence in and of themselves. Social-scientific criticism has proven especially useful in the development of contextual readings of the Old Testament, which address issues ranging from political interpretations of the Bible to interpretations within such minority groups as LGBT (lesbian, gay, bisexual, and transgender) and disabled communities.

Contextual and Reception Readings and Criticisms

Contextual readings of the Old Testament provide excellent examples of how the ancient stories and ideas of the Old Testament can speak to the modern contexts of diverse communities. These forms of criticism, like social-scientific or literary criticism, often take on an interdisciplinary nature. While a plethora of contextual topics have been covered biblically, those that address issues of empire, gender, and race are briefly covered here.

Empire

Just as issues of empire were integral in the formation of the Old Testament, as addressed in the "Reading the Old Testament in Its Ancient Contexts" section above, Old Testament texts continue to influence the ways people approach issues of empire today. On the one hand, the imagery that celebrates conquest in the invasion of Canaan (Joshua) and the glory of Solomon's kingdom (e.g., 1 Kings 4) could be used to support the building of empire. On the other hand, those who challenge the rise or expansion of empires can draw on anti-imperial readings that condemn the conduct of royals and their exploitation of the citizenry (e.g., Micah 3), and legislation against economic injustice in the Torah, Writings, and Prophets.

Pro-imperial readings of the Old Testament can be seen in the building and expansion of US influence, such as the idea of *Manifest Destiny*, which portrays the Christian European settlement of the United States as God's divine will. Manifest destiny involved a reimagining of the Pilgrims—and later European settlers—as the new Hebrews, pushing aside the Native American peoples—who took on the role of Canaanites—in order to create a new Israel. The Rev. Josiah Strong's publication *Our Country* echoes this sentiment in its assertion that God was charging European Christianity "to dispossess the many weaker races, assimilate others, and mold the remainder" (Strong, 178). Reverberations of the Old Testament–rooted Manifest Destiny still surface in aspects of American exceptionalism, which influences the US political spectrum and can be seen in such approaches to foreign policy as "the Bush Doctrine," which works to spread American-style democracy as a path to lasting peace.

Just as the Old Testament has been used for empire building, it has also been used to challenge empire and its institutions. While the exodus narrative helped to shape the idea of Manifest Destiny, it also became a powerful abolitionist force in attacking the institutions of slavery and segregation. During the abolitionist movement, the powerful imagery of the exodus story gave hope and power to free African Americans and slaves alike. The power of the story was harnessed again in the mid-twentieth century, giving strength to those who struggled for racial equality (Coomber 2012, 123–36). Recent biblical scholarship has also turned to the Old Testament to address various issues of modern-day economic exploitation and neoimperialism (e.g., Gottwald 2011; Boer, ed.; West 2010).

A highly influential outcome of the crossing of Bible and empire has been *postcolonial interpretation*. As European empires spread throughout the world, they brought the Bible and Christianity with them. With the twentieth-century waning of European imperialism, colonized and previously colonized peoples have found their own voices in the Bible, resulting in a variety of new interpretations and new approaches to major Old Testament themes. Postcolonial interpretation has enriched the field from Mercedes García Bachmann's use of Isaiah 58 to address issues of "unwanted fasting" (105–12) to raising questions about whether the Christian canon should be reopened to include the folk stories and traditions of colonized Christian communities that feel unrepresented by the current Bible (Pui Lan).

Gender

Studies in gender have also revealed a wide range of interpretive possibilities and have come to the forefront of biblical scholarship during the past four decades. While often treated as the sex of the body, the word *gender* is a complicated term that addresses a variety of factors of embodiment, including mental and behavioral characteristics. *Masculinity* and *femininity*, for example, take on different attributes and expectations depending on the society or culture in which they exist. While gender is an area of study that is continually developing into various branches, both within and outside of biblical studies, one of its most predominant manifestations in biblical studies is found in *feminist criticism*.

Women have been longtime readers and commentators on biblical texts, even though their work has rarely been given the same consideration as their male counterparts, who have long served as the vanguard of the academy. Hildegard of Bingen (d. 1179) authored a commentary on Genesis 1–2 (Young, 262); R. Roberts (d. 1788) composed numerous sermons on a range of texts for a clergyman acquaintance (Knowles, 418–19); and abolitionist Elizabeth Cady Stanton (d. 1902) helped to publish *The Woman's Bible*. These three women serve as but a few examples of women who have made important contributions to biblical studies, though their work is unknown to many.

Feminist criticism continues to be a very effective mode for recovering women's insights, perspectives, knowledge, and the feminine principle in biblical texts, often rescuing those voices and interpretations from centuries of marginalization by patriarchal and even misogynistic interpretation. Elisabeth Schüssler Fiorenza claims that, unlike many other forms of biblical criticism, feminist biblical studies does not owe its existence to the academy but to social movements for change, and also to a desire for the ongoing pursuit of equal participation and equal rights, which have in practice been restricted to a small group of elite men (Schüssler Fiorenza, 8–9). Schüssler Fiorenza argues that since the Bible has most often been used in these struggles for either "legitimating the status quo of the kyriarchal order of domination *or* for challenging dehumanization, feminist biblical interpretation is best articulated as an integral part of wo/men's struggles for authority and self-determination" (9). Like so many forms of contextual and received readings, feminist criticism can serve as a liberating force by revealing perspectives within the Bible's texts that have otherwise gone unnoticed.

An example of recovering the woman's perspective in the Old Testament is found in feminist commentaries on such texts as Isa. 42:14, in which God says,

> For a long time I have held my peace,
>   I have kept still and restrained myself;
> now I will cry out like a woman in labor,
>   I will gasp and pant.

Patricia Tull has highlighted the way in which YHWH adopts the power of a woman in labor to emphasize God's own divine power of creation (Tull, 263). Another example of uncovering women's voices to find justice in patriarchal cultures—which work to subvert women's voices and rights—is found in Sharon Pace Jeansonne's treatment of Tamar as a woman who seizes power to find justice in a society that is set up to stop her from doing so (Jeansonne, 98–106).

Feminist criticism—as with most any other form of biblical criticism—is polyvocal, with a broad spectrum of biblical views, including those who have argued that the Bible might be best left alone (Bal, 14). Male scholars have also engaged with feminist-focused readings of Old Testament texts. Daniel Cohen's midrash on Genesis 3, for example, addresses misogynistic interpretations of the Garden of Eden story (Cohen 141–48).

Similar to some of feminist criticism's attempts to reclaim the women's voice in the Bible and address misogynistic interpretation, *queer criticism* works to uncover LGBT perspectives in the Old Testament and messages that are of importance to LGBT communities. Queer interpretation has addressed a number of such topics, including K. Renato Lings's work on homophobic critiques of the destruction of Sodom in Genesis 19—a text often used to condemn homosexuality—in which he argues that attaching homosexuality to the sin of Sodom was a later interpretive development, unrecognized by biblical authors (Lings, 183–207). Others have shed new light on the ways in which biblical texts are interpreted to affect modern-day political decisions, such as the issue of same-sex marriage (see Stahlberg).

Conclusion

To be an engaged reader of the Old Testament involves simultaneously navigating the worlds of the biblical authors and redactors, as well as all those who have interpreted its texts. It is through approaching a biblical text or idea through these multiple angles that the multilayered meanings of the Old Testament books can be unlocked, not only in regard to the authors' intentions, but also in ways that the biblical writers may have never been able to foresee. These multiple intersections with the biblical text help people to have meaningful conversation and debate on topics ranging from climate change, to same-sex marriage, to the international banking crisis, and more. Naturally, being an engaged reader requires considerable effort, but it is through deliberating on biblical texts in all of their complexity that deeper meaning can be found, and more honest—or at least informed— readings of the Bible's contents can be gleaned.

In this volume, the contributors' commentaries provide a tool through which people can develop their engagement with the books of the Old Testament and Apocrypha. Whether approaching this volume as a researcher, educator, member of the clergy, or student, it is the intent of the *Fortress Commentary on the Old Testament* to inform readers about the Old Testament books' historical contexts, interpretive histories, and the modern contexts with which they engage, while also serving as an opening through which the conversation can be expanded.

Works Cited

Alfaro, Juan I. 1989. *Justice and Loyalty: A Commentary on the Book of Micah*. Grand Rapids: Eerdmans.

Bachmann, Mercedes L. García. 2009. "True Fasting and Unwilling Hunger (Isaiah 58)." In *The Bible and the Hermeneutics of Liberation*, edited by A. F. Botta and P. R. Andiñach, 113–31. Atlanta: SBL.

Bal, Mieke. 1989. *Anti-Covenant: Counter-Reading Women's Lives in the Hebrew Bible*. Sheffield: Almond.

Boer, Roland, ed. 2013. *Postcolonialism and the Hebrew Bible: The Next Step*. SemeiaSt 70. Atlanta: SBL.

Cantor, Norman F. 1992. *Inventing the Middle Ages: The Lives, Works, and Ideas of the Great Medievalists of the Twentieth Century*. Cambridge: Lutterworth.

Chaney, Marvin L. 1999. "Whose Sour Grapes? The Addressees of Isaiah 5:1–7 in the Light of Political Economy." In *The Social World of the Hebrew Bible: Twenty-Five Years of the Social Sciences in the Academy*, edited by Ronald A. Simkins and Stephen L. Cook. *Semeia* 87:105–22.

Cohen, Daniel. 2007. "Taste and See: A Midrash on Genesis 3:6 and 3:12." In *Patriarchs, Prophets and Other Villains*, edited by Lisa Isherwood, 141–48. London: Equinox Publishing.

Coomber, Matthew J. M. 2010. *Re-Reading the Prophets through Corporate Globalization: A Cultural-Evolutionary Approach to Understanding Economic Injustice in the Hebrew Bible*. Piscataway, NJ: Gorgias.

———. 2011. "Caught in the Crossfire? Economic Injustice and Prophetic Motivation in Eighth-Century Judah." *BibInt* 19, nos. 4–5:396–432.

———. 2012. "Before Crossing the Jordan: The Telling and Retelling of the Exodus Narrative in African American History." In *Exodus and Deuteronomy: Texts @ Contexts*, edited by Athalya Brenner and Gale A. Yee, 123–36. Minneapolis: Fortress Press.

———. 2013. "Debt as Weapon: Manufacturing Poverty from Judah to Today." *Diaconia: Journal for the Study of Christian Social Practice* 4, no. 2:141–55.

Coote, Robert B., and Keith W. Whitelam. 1987. *The Emergence of Early Israel in Historical Perspective*. Sheffield: Almond.

Crossley, James G. 2008. *Jesus in an Age of Terror: Scholarly Projects for a New American Century*. London: Equinox.

Davies, Philip. 2000. "What Separates a Minimalist from a Maximalist? Not Much." *BAR* 26, no. 2:24–27, 72–73.

Davies, Philip, and John Rogerson. 2005. *The Old Testament World*. 2nd ed. Louisville: Westminster John Knox.

Dever, William G. 2008. *Did God Have a Wife? Archaeology and Folk Religion in Ancient Israel*. Grand Rapids: Eerdmans.

Esler, Philip F. 2005. "Social-Scientific Models in Biblical Interpretation." In *Ancient Israel: The Old Testament in Its Social Context*, edited by Philip Esler, 3–14. London: SCM.

Fuqua, Charles R. 2012. *God's Law: The Only Political Solution*. Salt Lake City: American Book Publishing.

Gottwald, Norman. 1999. *The Tribes of Yahweh: A Sociology of the Religion of Liberated Israel, 1250–1050* BCE. Sheffield: Sheffield Academic Press.

———. 2001. *The Politics of Ancient Israel*. Louisville: Westminster John Knox.

Grabbe, Lester L. 2007. *Ancient Israel: What Do We Know and How Do We Know It?* London: T&T Clark.

Halpern, Baruch. 1995. "Erasing History: The Minimalist Assault on Ancient Israel." *BRev* 11: 26–35, 47.

Jacobs, A. J. 2007. *The Year of Living Biblically: One Man's Humble Quest to Follow the Bible as Literally as Possible*. New York: Simon & Schuster.

Jeansonne, Sharon Pace. 1990. *The Women of Genesis: From Sarah to Potiphar's Wife*. Minneapolis: Fortress Press.

Josephus, Flavius. 1854. *The Works of Flavius Josephus: Comprising the Antiquities of the Jews, a History of the Jewish Wars, and Life of Flavius Josephus, Written by Himself*. Translated by William Whiston. Philadelphia: Jas. B. Smith.

Karmon, Yehuda. 1971. *Israel: A Regional Geography*. London: Wiley-Interscience.

Knapp, A. Bernard. 1988. "Copper Production and Eastern Mediterranean Trade: The Rise of Complex Society in Cyprus." In *State and Society: The Emergence and Development of Social Hierarchy and Political Centralization*, edited by J. Gledhill, B. Bender, and M. T. Larsen, 149–72. London: Unwin Hyman.

Knowles, Michael P. 2012. "Roberts, R. (ca. 1728–88)." In *Handbook of Women Biblical Interpreters*, edited by M. A. Taylor and A. Choi, 418–20. Grand Rapids: Baker Academic.

Kwok Pui-lan. 2003. "Discovering the Bible in the Non-Biblical World." In *Searching the Scriptures: A Feminist Introduction*, edited by Elisabeth Schüssler Fiorenza, 276–88. New York: Crossroad.

Lings, K. Renato. 2007. "Culture Clash in Sodom: Patriarchal Tales of Heroes, Villains, and Manipulation." In *Patriarchs, Prophets and Other Villains*, edited by Lisa Isherwood, 183–207. London: Equinox.

Liverani, Mario. 2007. *Israel's History and the History of Israel*. Translated by Chiara Peri and Philip Davies. London: Equinox.

Masterson, Teresa. 2011. "Man, 70, Stoned to Death for Being Gay." *NBC10 Philadelphia*. Accessed October 14, 2013. http://www.nbcphiladelphia.com/news/local/Man-70-Stoned-to-Death-for-Homosexuality-Police-118243719.html.

Niditch, Susan. 2010. "Experiencing the Divine: Heavenly Visits, Earthly Encounters and the Land of the Dead." In *Religious Diversity in Ancient Israel and Judah*, edited by Francesca Stavrakopoulou and John Barton, 11–22. London: T&T Clark.

Schüssler Fiorenza, Elisabeth. 2013. *Changing Horizons: Explorations in Feminist Interpretation*. Minneapolis: Fortress Press.

Schweitzer, Albert. 1968. *The Quest of the Historical Jesus: A Critical Study of Its Progress from Reimarus to Wrede*. New York: Macmillan.

Smith, Mark S. 2002. *The Early History of God: Yahweh and the Other Deities in Ancient Israel*. Grand Rapids: Eerdmans.

Stahlberg, Lesleigh Cushing. 2008. "Modern Day Moabites: The Bible and the Debate About Same-Sex Marriage." *BibInt* 16:422–75.

Stavrakopoulou, Francesca. 2010. "'Popular' Religion and 'Official' Religion: Practice, Perception, Portrayal." In *Religious Diversity in Ancient Israel and Judah*, edited by Francesca Stavrakopoulou and John Barton, 37–58. New York: T&T Clark.

Strong, Josiah. 1885. *Our Country: Its Possible Future and Its Present Crisis*. New York: The American Home Missionary Society.

Tull, Patricia K. 2012. "Isaiah." In *Women's Bible Commentary: Twentieth-Anniversary Edition*, edited by C. A. Newsom, S. H. Ringe, and J. E. Lapsley, 255–66. Louisville: Westminster John Knox.

West, Gerald. 2010. "The Legacy of Liberation Theologies in South Africa, with an Emphasis on Biblical Hermeneutics." *Studia Historiae Ecclesiasticae* 36, Supplement: 157–83.

Whitelam, Keith W. 2007. "Lines of Power: Mapping Ancient Israel." In *To Break Every Yoke: Essays in Honour of Marvin L. Chaney*, edited by R. B. Coote and N. K. Gottwald, 40–79. Sheffield: Sheffield Phoenix Press.

Young, Abigail. 2012. "Hildegard of Bingen (1098–1179)." In *Handbook of Women Biblical Interpreters*, edited by M. A. Taylor and A. Choi, 259–64. Grand Rapids: Baker Academic.

THE PEOPLE OF GOD AND THE PEOPLES OF THE EARTH

Hugh R. Page Jr.

The Bible Is Just the Beginning

The Bible is preeminently a book about people. That may strike some as a rather odd assertion given the stature enjoyed by the Bible as sacred text containing, in many faith traditions, everything one needs to know about God and salvation. Nonetheless, some of the more important foci of the Old and New Testaments have to do with the saga of the human family and the women and men that are dramatis personae in this unfolding drama. In the twenty-first century CE, our appreciation of how Scripture narrates that story is much more nuanced than it was perhaps a generation or two ago. We are much more aware of the processes by which traditions are shaped and preserved. We have a deeper understanding of the myriad stages through which the inspired words of prophets, poets, and sages proceed before being canonized: as well as of the place the Bible occupies in the global ecology of sacred texts. Moreover, we recognize that many of the world's sacred texts have important things to say about the human condition. Thus perspectives on what it means to be "people of God," women and men in a special relationship with a transcendent being, or members of a large and diverse human family sharing a common terrestrial abode vary widely. Moreover, in today's world, scholarship in fields such as genetics and anthropology is changing the way we think about human origins and notions of personhood.

It is because of new ideas about humanity and its origins that responsible readers of the Bible must, therefore, examine biblical conceptions of personhood, while keeping in mind the ways in which both the human family in general and those individuals called into special relationship with the God of Israel are construed. In so doing, they must also look at how such ideas have shaped, and continue to influence, notions about the world and its inhabitants today; are related to comparable ideas about personhood in other faith traditions; relate to what scientific evidence reveals about the human family; have been complicit in the exploitation of colonized peoples; and stand in relationship to those ideas about the human family articulated in documents such as the United Nations Declaration of Human Rights and the Declaration on the Rights of Indigenous Peoples. Such a task is necessary if we are to enhance the extent to which the Bible can be deployed as a resource in building a more just and equitable global community. Failure to do so may limit the extent to which members of faith communities for which the Bible is authoritative are able to join in meaningful dialogue about the future of our global community and the institutions that support it. It may also inadvertently lend credence to the idea that religious texts and traditions have no place in conversations about those ideals on which a cosmopolitan global community should be based in the future.

The Earth and Its Peoples—A View from the Ethnographic Record

Science has revealed that modern human beings are the result of a remarkable evolutionary process. We share common African ancestry, and our diversity at this point in time bears witness to an array of migratory, climatic, and genetic adaptations that span hundreds of thousands of years. Our cultural landscape is vast and remarkable in its variation. For example, the comprehensive cultural database maintained by Human Relations Area Files at Yale University (see http://www.yale.edu/hraf/collections.htm) contains information on several hundred cultures.

The *Ethnographic Atlas*, a massive project undertaken by George Peter Murdock (1969) and ultimately brought to full fruition in the 1970s, contains information on more than one thousand distinct groups. As an ethnologist, Murdock was particularly interested in both the comparative study of cultures and the identification of behavioral traits that manifest locally, regionally, and internationally (see especially Murdock 1981, 3). His work calls attention to the breadth of lifeways characteristic of peoples around the world. Scholarship continuing in the vein of Murdock's has led to the identification of some 3,500 cultures on which published data are readily available (see, e.g., Price, 10). Such studies have also resulted in the development of templates for comparing social organization, religious beliefs, and other information about the world's disparate peoples (see Ember and Ember; and Murdock et al.). Needless to say, the vision of the human family derived from this research is remarkable. Social scientists see this diverse collage of languages, customs, and religious traditions as the end result of developmental forces that have been operational for *aeons*. It is also for them a mystery to be probed using the critical tools at their disposal. Ethnographic investigations and theory testing have laid bare and will continue to reveal its undiscovered truths. However, humankind has not revealed, and is not likely to yield, the sum total of its secrets to even the most dogged of investigators. Like the stories of primordial reality we encounter in the biblical book of Genesis, such research offers a place from which to begin pondering what it means to be human.

Human life is, of course, dynamic. New social and religious groups are born constantly. The first two decades of the current millennium have even witnessed the dissolution of geopolitical boundaries, the creation of new nation states, and the birth of new religious movements. Thus notions of culture and personhood in our era are anything but static. Our human family continues to grow and with each passing day becomes more diverse and increasingly complex. Research in the social sciences has increased our understanding of how culture and identity evolve. We know more today than ever before about the ways language, physical environment, and other factors contribute to ideas about what it means to be a fully actualized self and to be in relationship with those other selves that are one's family members, friends, and neighbors. It has also shed light on the role that the collection and preservation of religious lore play in this process. Sacred traditions and texts serve as the repositories for stories about how people and the groups in which they are embedded came to be. They also function as points of reference for the nurture of persons and the communities in which they live.

The challenge we face in an era when such traditions are often read narrowly or uncritically—without an eye toward their implicit limitations—is to create charitable and inclusive approaches that allow us to engage and appropriate them. Such strategies necessitate that we become well versed in the ways that stories, both ancient and modern, shape our identities, beliefs, and relationships with one another. Whether one has in mind venerable tales such as the Babylonian *Enuma Elish* and the so-called Priestly account of creation (Gen. 1:1—2:4a), or modern cinematic myths like the *Matrix* or *Prometheus* sagas, narratives of one kind or another provide a context for understanding who we are and how we choose to live. Returning to the Bible itself, it is arguable that one of its central aims is to inform us of what it means to be finite beings that are threads in a sacred cosmic fabric woven, as it were, by a divine and ineffable artisan.

Ancient Near Eastern Lore and Conceptions of Personhood

In the late nineteenth and early twentieth centuries, scholars such as James Frazer and Stith Thompson began looking seriously at cultural practices and folklore from various parts of the world. The results were remarkable, though not without some degree of controversy. Frazer's efforts included his Victorian-era classic *The Golden Bough* (Frazer 1981) and an equally important, if less celebrated, three-volume work titled *Folk-Lore in the Old Testament* (Frazer 1918a; 1918b; 1918c); and Thompson's work on folklore motifs was pioneering insofar as it laid important groundwork for the comparison of tales from around the world. Although questions remain about the aims and theoretical presuppositions of these early works, their efforts, and those of the scholars following in their immediate footsteps, set the stage for much of the social-scientific research we have seen in the twentieth and twenty-first centuries, even in the field of biblical studies.

Among biblical scholars, the pioneers of form criticism and the so-called myth and ritual school found in this body of information—and other information gathered from ancient Near Eastern sources—a treasure trove useful for contextualizing and interpreting key portions of the Old Testament. Among form critics, Hermann Gunkel must be noted. His collection of essays in *What Remains of the Old Testament* and topical studies of literary *Gattungen* ("forms") as such pertain to the Bible in *The Legends of Genesis* and *The Folktale in the Old Testament* repay—even today—careful reading

(1928; 1964; 1987). Among myth and ritual adherents, Sigmund Mowinckel's work deserves pride of place, especially his *Psalmenstudien* (1966). These pioneers' use of ethnological resources in the study of Scripture were paralleled by those of Johannes Pedersen in his two-volume study of ancient Israelite culture (1926–1940) and extended in subsequent generations by Theodor Gaster's efforts to reclaim and expand the work of Frazer (1950; 1959; 1969); Mary Douglas's exploration of the body as social map (1966); Bruce Malina's use of a circum-Mediterranean paradigm to understand the roles of women and men in the Bible (1989); and others whose work has explored the intersections of Jewish, Christian, Mediterranean, and other cultural traditions both ancient and modern.

Several lessons can be gleaned from this body of research. The first is that people are in some ways "hardwired" to create and tell stories. These stories help in making sense of life crises such as birth, maturation, and death. They are also pivotal in defining the self and the social networks into which individual selves are embedded. A second lesson is that one particular genre, creation stories—whether they focus on the birth of deities (theogonies), the universe (cosmogonies), humanity, tribal confederations, monarchies, or all of the aforementioned—have a direct impact on the ways people understand their place in the world. Creation stories define social and ethnic boundaries, reify social and political hierarchies, and ascribe status based on age, gender, and other ontological and ascribed markers. These two factors should inform the ways information about individuals and groups embedded in poetry, rituals, royal inscriptions, and other texts is understood. A few examples from the ancient Near East are particularly illustrative.

The Mesopotamian flood tradition encountered in the Atrahasis myth has, among its more important purposes, articulation of a basic theological anthropology—one that is based on an understanding of the mutable and immutable dimensions of an, at times, capricious cosmos. Human beings are oddly situated in this power-filled and unstable environment. They are remarkable for three reasons. The first is because they are made of the flesh and blood of a divine insurgent and sacrificed because he led a rebellion against the harsh labor imposed on a subset of deities in the pantheon.

> When the gods themselves were men,
> They did the work. They endured the toil.
> The labor was onerous.
> Massive was the effort. The distress was exceedingly great. (Lambert and Millard, 42
>   [tablet 1.1.1–4], translation my own)

> Let them sacrifice the divine leader.
> Let the gods purify themselves by immersion.
> With his essence—flesh and blood—let Nintu mix the clay,
> So that divinity and humanity may be thoroughly
> Blended in the amalgam.
> For all time let us hear the drumbeat.
> In the flesh of the god let the ghost remain.
> Let her [Nintu] inform him [the slain god] of his token.
> So that there will be no forgetting,
> The spirit will remain. (Lambert and Millard, 58 [tablet 1.4.208–17], translation my own)

The human heartbeat is the "drum" reminding women and men for all time of the immortal lineage that is uniquely their own. The second reason that people are special is due to their being extended kin, as it were, of Atrahasis, the "exceedingly wise one," who managed to survive the great deluge by which all of humanity was destroyed. To them belongs the empowering, yet dangerous, model of this *liminal* ancestor. As William Moran noted more than four decades ago: "The Atrahasis Epic is an assertion of man's importance in the final order of things. It is also a strong criticism of the gods" (Moran, 59).

Humans are also special (see Moran, 60–61) for a third reason: because they are living proof of the imprudence of the gods and goddesses they serve. Created to assume the day-to-day labor deemed too difficult for immortals to bear, the din of their daily existence proved far too disruptive of their divine patrons' and matrons' sleep. Their death was decreed because they were, in a word, "noisy" (Lambert and Millard, 66 [tablet 1.7.354–59]). It is only through the quick-witted intervention of Enki, his personal god, that Atrahasis and his family are able to escape the inundation. Atrahasis is a powerful symbol of what can happen when human perseverance and divine subterfuge are allied.

The Atrahasis myth suggests that people are made of supernatural "stuff" and are heirs to a distinctive lineage. It also emphasizes that in a world filled with danger, the gods who are in control of the fates of women and men do not always have the best interest of the human family in mind. Although all mortals are in a sense beings belonging to and dependent on the gods, the implication of the sobering reality revealed in this myth is that in order to survive, women and men would do well to leverage their inner resources while at the same time relying, should all else fail, on timely divine intervention by those deities with whom they have a special relationship. Such assertions are, of course, in conversation with anthropologies articulated in other lore across a wide spectrum of genres. For example, Gilgamesh—particularly the Old Babylonian version of this Akkadian classic—focuses attention on the unique challenges confronted by one species of individual: monarchs. Of particular interest in this epic are their socialization, capacity to form friendships, quest for lasting renown, and insecurities about death. royal inscriptions, of which exemplars are too numerous to mention, continue in this vein and further define the traits of kings and those subject to their authority. Suzerainty treaties can be said to function in a comparable manner by defining the relationships of sociopolitical aggregates to one another. Sets of laws, like those found in the Code of Hammurabi, reify social status through taxonomies that identify insiders (e.g., king, free men, and those acquitted of offenses) and outsiders (e.g., criminals, widows, and orphans).

Another story, that of the travails of the god Ba'lu from the ancient city of Ugarit, offers a slightly different perspective on human life—this time from West Semitic lore. Unlike the story of Atrahasis, the Ba'lu myth is concerned primarily with how the enigmatic god of the fructifying rains—mainstays of human life—secures his place as head of the pantheon. Although the primary concern of this tale is Ba'lu's contest with rivals for ascendancy to the throne, it lifts the veil concealing the ongoing cosmic struggle between two such forces that inscribe the parameters for human existence: that is, life/fertility, represented by Ba'lu as numen of the storm, and Môtu, the embodiment of death and dissolution. At one point in this saga, he voluntarily submits himself to the authority and power of Môtu. His death, emblematic of nature's cyclic periods of aridity, leads his father 'Ilu, head of the pantheon, and his sister 'Anatu, to bewail its impact on the world. Both give voice to a lament intended, no doubt, to sum up the anguish of all affected by the storm god's departure.

> Ba'lu has died. What is to become of humanity?
> Dagan's child is no more. What will happen to earth's teeming masses? (CAT 1.5.6.23–24; 1.6.1.6–7)

The world and its inhabitants are part of the background landscape against which this divine drama unfolds. Nonetheless, as the narrative progresses, one realizes that each episode has a profound, if at times only partially articulated, impact on the peoples of the earth. Ba'lu returns to life, largely through the intervention of his sister 'Anatu. Eventually, he and Môtu have a fateful encounter that reveals, in no uncertain terms, that they are—and shall remain—in an interminable struggle.

> They fight each other like heroes
> Môtu is strong, as is Ba'lu
> Like raging bulls, they go head to head
> Môtu is strong, as is Ba'lu
> They bite one another like serpents
> Môtu is strong, as is Ba'lu
> Like animals, they beat each other to a pulp
> Môtu falls, Ba'lu collapses. (CAT 1.6.6.16–22)

The two battle to a virtual draw: an indication that the struggle between life and death is ongoing. The hope for "earth's teeming masses" is that the forces of life are able—at the very least—to withstand Death's furious and unrelenting onslaught. To be engaged nobly in the struggle is, therefore, to participate heroically in an age-old struggle that unites every member of the human family as kin. The warp and weft of day-to-day existence finds its ultimate significance in this ongoing cosmic battle. We see a stunning reflex of this mythology in the biblical Song of Songs, where the protagonists are anthropomorphized hypostases of Love (*'ahăbâ*) and Death (*māwet*).

> Seal me to your heart.
> Brand me on your arm.
> Love is equal to Death in its strength.
> Passion rivals Sheol in its ferocity.
> Its flames are a blazing fire.
> It is an eternal inferno. (Song of Songs 8:6, author's own translation)

Additional textual examples from Egypt and Anatolia could be cited, but the above suffice to show how implicit and explicit messaging about people—their nature, connection to one another, and relationship to the divine forces responsible for their creation and support—is conveyed in expressive culture.

The Hebrew Bible, Personhood, and Identity

Biblical references to the earth and its peoples are very much in conversation with these ancient Near Eastern traditions. The opening chapter of the Hebrew Bible contains a remarkable assertion in what scholars have traditionally designated the Priestly account of creation (Gen. 1:1—2:4a): that the world and everything in it is "good." It uses the Hebrew word *ṭôb* to describe its fundamental essence, a word whose semantic range connotes something sweet and pleasurable. Human beings are an important part of the created order. Made on the sixth day, they are distinguished only by gender: male and female. Neither ethnic nor regional markers are noted. All are made according to the divine "form" (*ṣelem*) and "pattern" (*dĕmût*)—that is, God's "image and likeness" according to the NRSV. Theirs are the tasks of reproducing and exercising control of the earth (1:26–28). The word used to describe what will be involved to reach this desired outcome (*kābaš*) connotes a process requiring forceful effort (Oswalt, 430). Also implied here is the idea that this is a laborious enterprise that is both collective and collaborative.

Following this masterful cosmogonic hymn, readers encounter in the remainder of Genesis a "mixed bag" of traditions about the earth's populace representing several sources: fragments of archaic poetry (2:23; 3:14-19; 4:23-24; 49); a descanting creation narrative (2:4b-24); etiological tales (11:1-9); ethnohistorical musings about the origins of particular peoples (4:17-22); an epic about the peregrinations of Israel's ancestors (11:31—36:43); and an extensive novella dealing with a key figure in the national saga: Joseph (37–50). While these materials can be read—as scholarly literature attests—from a variety of perspectives, one thing is very clear: together they tell the story of the God of Israel's relationship with the world and its peoples, some of whom—namely, Abraham, Sarah, and their descendants—are called to take on special responsibilities for the entirety of the human family (12:1-3). In fact, it could be argued that a significant portion of the Genesis tradition (1:1—11:32) has been intended as a creative "riff" on, or response to, Sumero-Akkadian lore (like that found in Atrahasis) about the origins of humanity.

One of the unifying threads holding together the narrative tapestry of Genesis and the remaining books of the Torah/Pentateuch is the story of how the world is affected by the shifting, strained, at times tumultuous, dynamic, and constantly evolving relationships among those who are the offspring of the primordial family. While highlighting theological themes such as *calling* (Exod. 3:1-15); *covenant* (Exod. 6:1-8; 20:1-17); *sin and redemption* (Exod. 32:1-35); *divine immanence and transcendence* (Exod. 25:1—31:18); *holiness* (Lev. 10:3; 20:26); *significant individuals* (Exod. 2:10; 15:20; 2:21; 3:1); *groups* (Exod. 3:8; 6:19); and *events* (Exodus 15; Num. 3:14-16; 9:15-16); these books also articulate a gestalt ("general sketch") for comprehending what it means to be part of a human family. This can entail struggling both to recognize its connectedness and to honor its diversity. It can also involve wrestling with the challenge of managing intergroup crises that influence the welfare of peoples living in proximity; competing for limited resources; and dealing with those changing geopolitical realities that generate population shifts, form new social movements, and give rise to diasporas. It is for this reason that one of the foci of these books, and the sources used therein, is the establishment of social, religious, and other boundaries that determine personhood, group affiliation, and status. For example, the Priestly creation story (Gen. 1—2:4a) can be said to inscribe broad and inclusive parameters for personhood. Since all human beings bear the imprint of the creator's "form" and "pattern," they can be said to belong to a single unified group, for which gender is the only subclassification (1:26-27). The implication of this is that everyone created *by* God belongs *to* God and is therefore part of the "people of God."

Genealogical tables, such as that found in Genesis 10, offer a more nuanced view of group identity based on location, language, and kin group (e.g., 10:5). The story of the Tower of Babel goes a step further in its linkage of linguistic heterogeneity to human hubris and a divine response to quell it (Gen. 11:5-7). Although it can be read simply as an entertaining etiology accounting for the diversity and spread of languages, it does contain a polemical strain resistant to linguistic solidarity, centralized government, and the conscription of resources needed to build monumental structures and to maintain the places—that is, cities—where they are most likely to be found in antiquity. Thus the story seems to be suggesting, on one level, that diversity and difference are preferable to a homogeneity whose consequences, intended or unintended, are to transgress the boundary separating mortals from God.

The block of material inclusive of the ancestral epic and the story of Joseph's rise to Egyptian prominence offers an even more complex picture of the "people of God." On the one hand, the "yes" given by Abram/Abraham to the call of YHWH (Gen. 12:1-3), and the covenant made with him (Gen. 15:18; 17:1-27) by YHWH, serve to distinguish him and his descendants among the "people of God"—that is, as a conduit of blessing to the entirety of the human family (Gen. 12:3). On the other hand, an inversion of status—from "temporary sojourner" to "inheritor" of Canaan (17:6-8)—is also promised, one that sets the stage for what is later described in Joshua and Judges. The story of Joseph's tensions with his brothers, as well as that of the peculiar circumstances leading Jacob and his kin to go to Egypt, set the stage for further musing on several issues. The first is how the kin group through whom all of the "people of God" are to be blessed understands its internal subdivisions (Genesis 49; Deuteronomy 32—33). The second has to do with how the kin group's liberation, covenant at Sinai, sojourn in the wilderness, and occupation of Canaan (Exod. 4:1—20:21; 32:1—35:29; Num. 1:1—36:13; Joshua; and Judges) are construed, particularly in terms of how these sources present Israel's relationship to its neighbors, both as stewards of a unique revelatory experience and part of a larger family of divine offspring. The third concerns the final book of the Pentateuch—Deuteronomy—that serves as the transitional bridge to the Former Prophets. From a literary standpoint, it is a rearticulation and expansion of core precepts first articulated in Exod. 20:1-17. It inscribes very narrow parameters for Israel's self-understanding and relationship to its neighbors. "When you come into the land that the LORD your God is giving you, you must not learn to imitate the abhorrent practices of those nations" (Deut. 18:9).

The book of Deuteronomy has very strict stipulations for the centralization of worship (12:1-28), prophetic practice (18:15-22), the conduct of war (20:1-20), and the care of those without material support (24:14-15, 17-18). All of these grow out of a particular self-understanding, stated most succinctly in what Gerhard von Rad long ago identified as a short creedal statement.

A wandering Aramean was my ancestor; he went down into Egypt and lived there as an alien, few in number, and there he became a great nation, mighty and populous. When the Egyptians treated us harshly and afflicted us, by imposing hard labor on us, we cried to the LORD, the God of our ancestors; the LORD heard our voice and saw our affliction, our toil, and our oppression. The LORD brought us out of Egypt with a mighty hand and an outstretched arm, with a terrifying display of power, and with signs and wonders; and he brought us into this place and gave us this land, a land flowing with milk and honey. (Deut. 26:5-9)

Israel's identity as an "alien" subject to "hard labor" and "oppression," now liberated by YHWH, is the backdrop against which Deuteronomy's exclusive covenantal obligations are formulated. The jealousy of YHWH (Deut. 4:24) establishes impermeable cultural and ethical borders separating Israel from its neighbors. Deuteronomy and the historical narrative of the occupation of Canaan and the flowering of the monarchy are written in accordance with its principles. This so-called Deuteronomistic History (abbreviated Dtr by some scholars) consists of Joshua, Judges, the books of Samuel, and 1 and 2 Kings. It offers a far more complex, yet ultimately less inclusive, vision of the "people of God."

For example, we encounter the technical designation *'am yhwh* ("YHWH's people") in the Pentateuch's oldest strata (e.g., Judg. 5:11, 13—an ancient Hebrew poem; and Num. 11:29; 16:41). Here it refers to either the members of Israel's tribal confederation (Judges) or the Israelite community on the march through the wilderness following its flight from Egypt (Numbers). It is present much more frequently in Dtr, where it denotes those faithful bound by the Deuteronomic covenant (Deut. 27:9—*lĕ'am layhwh*); Israel before the establishment of the monarchy (1 Sam. 2:24); the fallen military contingent that supported Jonathan and Saul (2 Sam. 1:12); and as an *ethnonym* for those under the reign of David (2 Sam. 6:21), Jehu (2 Kgs. 9:6), and Jehoida (2 Kgs. 11:17). We also find the terms *'am hā'ĕlōhîm* or *'am 'ĕlōhîm* ("people of God") used in reference to the Israelite tribal contingent armed for battle (Judg. 20:2) and to those under David's sovereign rule (2 Sam. 14:13). Beyond these references, we encounter the term "YHWH's people" in 2 Chron. 23:16 (paralleling 2 Kgs. 11:17). Another enigmatic reference—to "the God of Abraham's people"—is found in Ps. 47:9, a poem asserting the universal kingship of *'ĕlōhîm* ("God").

Although references to "Yahweh's people" and "people of God" do not appear in the Latter Prophets (Isaiah, Jeremiah, Ezekiel, and the Book of the Twelve) or the Writings (outside of the Chronicler), we can certainly detect a keen interest in the world's peoples in many of these books. In some instances, the focus is decidedly polemical. The pointed critique of Israel's neighbors in prophetic oracles is an excellent example (e.g., Isaiah 14–19; Ezekiel 26–30). The bimodal subdivision of humanity in Proverbs (between those who heed Wisdom's voice and others who do not in Proverbs 8–9). A third case in point is the distinction made between "those who lead many to righteousness" in Dan. 12:3) and their opponents. In others, there is an affirmation of the God of Israel's keen interest in building an inclusive eschatological community (e.g., Isa. 66:18-21) and questioning a culture of entitlement and condemnatory rhetoric among Israelite prophets (Jon. 4:9-11). In Jewish apocryphal literature, we also see an interest expressed in the relationship among peoples. In the Greek Addition F to Esther, an editor has called attention to the different "lots" God has assigned to "the people of God" and to "all the nations" (10:10). The author of the Wisdom of Solomon takes a slightly different tack. While adopting a rhetoric that accentuates the difference between the "righteous" and the "ungodly" (Wisdom), it also calls attention to the common ancestry of humanity:

> there is for all one entrance into life, and one way out. (Wis. 18:9)

What we have, therefore, in the Hebrew Bible are multiple visions of what it means to be "people of God" and "peoples of the earth." Some are narrow. Others are selectively inclusive. All must be read with an eye toward genre, the setting in which the text was produced, and the social, political, and religious circumstances it seeks to address.

It goes almost without saying that biblical writers and their initial audiences were concerned with theological issues such as Israel's election and the implications such issues have on the community's holiness and distinctiveness when compared to its neighbors. In light of this special calling, as it were, boundaries—their creation, maintenance, and occasional erasure—take on particular significance. Maintenance is a sign of covenantal fidelity (Deut. 7:1-6) and purity (Lev. 10:1-3). Periodic transgression is, at least in some instances, a necessary survival strategy. Judges is an excellent case in point (see Page). We see evidence in this book of the crossing of bodily, cultural, and other borders as part of what characterizes Israelite life during that bittersweet epoch when "there was no king in Israel" and "people did what was right in their own eyes" (Judg. 21:25). Israel's identity as a people with a unique identity, mission, and teleological objective is, thus, variously articulated in the Hebrew Bible. These overlapping, competing, and complementary ideas of what it means to be a "people of God" among "the earth's peoples" require attentiveness to the religious objectives, political aims, and eschatological foci of the books in which they are found. Therefore, any attempt to fully reconcile all aspects of these disparate conceptions is likely to meet with frustration. Instead, it is perhaps better to recognize that the Hebrew Bible does not speak with a single voice on the issue of what it means to be part of the human family.

Looking beyond the Bible

One could argue that this absence of uniformity in the Hebrew Bible is an invitation not simply to read, but also to query and "talk back to" its books. Among the questions we should ask is what sources—in addition to Scripture—we ought to consult in making sense of who we are, what our relationship should be to one another, and what our place is in the universe. This process is far more involved than turning to Genesis or some other biblical book for a "proof text" (the practice of using a specific text as the final authoritative word on a given issue). Instead, it requires taking into consideration modern geopolitical realities such as globalization and what the pure, applied, and social sciences are telling us about our biological origins, diversity, and connectedness.

It also makes it incumbent on Bible readers to be aware of how documents such as the United Nations Declaration on Human Rights (1948) and the United Nations Declaration on the Rights of Indigenous Peoples (2007) influence how we think about our rights and responsibilities as people of faith and citizens of the world. For example, article 1 of the former states that "all human beings are born free and equal in dignity and rights. They are endowed with reason and conscience and should act towards one another in a spirit of brotherhood" (United Nations General Assembly 2000, 326). An affirmation of this kind shapes the way one thinks about religious texts and traditions that qualify human freedom, equality, dignity, or rights endowed at birth. Furthermore, according to article 18 of the Declaration, "Everyone has the right to freedom of thought, conscience, and religion; this right includes freedom to change his religion or belief, and freedom either alone or in community with others and in public or private, to manifest his religion or belief in teaching, practice, worship, and observance" (United Nations General Assembly 2000, 327). Such texts can't help but influence our reading and deployment of those parts of the Bible that affirm behaviors that affirm or disagree with these statements and the ideals they represent. In the case of those that run counter, a hermeneutic inclusive of exegesis and critical engagement is warranted. Article 7 section 2 of the United Nations Declaration on the Rights of Indigenous Peoples states that "indigenous peoples have the collective right to live in freedom, peace and security as distinct peoples and shall not be subjected to any act of genocide or any other act of violence, including forcibly removing children of the group to another group" (United Nations General Assembly 2007, 5). Moreover, article 8 section 1 affirms that "indigenous peoples and individuals have the right not to be subjected to forced assimilation or destruction of their culture" (United Nations General Assembly 2007, 5). The reading or deployment of biblical passages that appear to celebrate or support behaviors of this kind can be neither ignored nor interpreted in a way that treats lightly the ways they have been used to justify policies that abrogate the rights of indigenous peoples around the world.

Thus, in our current era, perhaps the Bible should be seen less as the single authoritative source from which the final word on what it means to be "people of God" and "people of the earth" is to be found, and more as one of several interlocutors—including lived experience—informing our consideration of what is an unfolding *mystery* about the larger human experience that we are invited to prayerfully ponder.

Works Cited

Douglas, Mary. 1966. *Purity and Danger*. London: ARK.

Eilberg-Schwartz, Howard. 1990. *The Savage in Judaism: Anthropology of Israelite Religion and Ancient Judaism*. Bloomington: Indiana University Press.

Ember, Melvin, and Carol R. Ember, eds. 1999. *Cultures of the World: Selections from the Ten-Volume Encyclopedia of World Cultures*. New York: Macmillan Library Reference USA.

Frazer, James. 1981. *The Golden Bough*. 1890. Reprint, New York: Grammercy.

———. 1918a. *Folk-Lore in the Old Testament*. Vol. 1. London: Macmillan.

———. 1918b. *Folk-Lore in the Old Testament*. Vol. 2. London: Macmillan.

———. 1918c. *Folk-Lore in the Old Testament*. Vol. 3. London: Macmillan.

Gaster, Theodor H. 1950. *Thespis: Ritual, Myth, and Drama in the Ancient Near East*. New York: Harper & Row.

———, ed. 1959. *The New Golden Bough*. New York: Criterion.

————. 1969. *Myth, Legend and Custom in the Old Testament*. New York: Harper & Row.

Gunkel, Hermann. 1928. *What Remains of the Old Testament and Other Essays*. Translated by A. K. Dallas. New York: Macmillan.

————. 1964. *The Legends of Genesis: The Biblical Saga and History*. Translated by W. H. Carruth. Reprint of the introduction to the author's 1901 *Commentary on Genesis*. New York: Schocken.

————. 1987. *The Folktale in the Old Testament*. Translated by M. D. Rutter. Translation of the 1917 ed. Sheffield: Almond.

Lambert, W. G., and A. R. Millard, eds. 1999. *Atra-Hasis: The Babylonian Story of the Flood*. 1969. Reprint, Winona Lake, IN: Eisenbrauns.

Malina, Bruce. 1989. "Dealing with Biblical (Mediterranean) Characters: A Guide for U.S. Consumers." *BTB* 19:127–41.

Moran, William L. 1971. "Atrahasis: The Babylonian Story of the Flood." *Bib* 52:51–61.

Mowinckel, Sigmund. 1966. *Psalmenstudien: 1921–1924*. Amsterdam: Grüner.

Murdock, George Peter. 1969. *Ethnographic Atlas*. 3rd ed. Pittsburgh: University of Pittsburgh Press.

————. 1981. *Atlas of World Cultures*. Pittsburgh: University of Pittsburgh Press.

Murdock, George Peter, C. S. Ford, A. E. Hudson, R. Kennedy, L. W. Simmons, and J. W. M. Whiting. 1987. *Outline of Cultural Materials*. 5th ed. New Haven: Human Relations Area Files.

Oswalt, J. N. 1980. "Kabash." In *Theological Wordbook of the Old Testament*, edited by R. Laird Harris, Gleason L. Archer, and Bruce K. Waltke, 1:430. Chicago: Moody Press.

Page, Hugh R., Jr. 1999. "The Marking of Social, Political, Religious, and Other Boundaries in Biblical Literature—A Case Study Using the Book of Judges." *Research in the Social Scientific Study of Religion* 10:37–55.

Pedersen, Johannes. 1926–1940. *Israel: Its Life and Culture*. 4 vols. London: Oxford University Press.

Price, David H. 2004. *Atlas of World Cultures: A Geographical Guide to Ethnographic Literature*. 1989. Reprint, Caldwell, NJ: Blackburn.

Rad, Gerhard von. 1966. *The Problem of the Hexateuch and Other Essays*. London: SCM.

Thompson, Stith. 2001. *Motif-index of Folk-Literature: A Classification of Narrative Elements in Folk-tales, Ballads, Myths, Fables, Mediaeval Romances, Exempla, Fabliaux, Jest-Books*. Rev. ed. 6 vols. Bloomington: University of Indiana Press.

United Nations General Assembly. 2000. "Universal Declaration of Human Rights (1948)." In *Sourcebook of the World's Religions: An Interfaith Guide to Religion and Spirituality*, edited by J. Beversluis, 325–28. Novato, CA: New World Library.

————. 2007. *United Nations Declaration on the Rights of Indigenous Peoples*. http://www.un.org/esa/socdev/unpfii/documents/DRIPS_en.pdf.

Reading the Christian Old Testament in the Contemporary World

Daniel L. Smith-Christopher

In nineteenth-century Charleston, South Carolina, the Old Testament seemed to assure Episcopal clergyman Frederick Dalcho that slavery was consistent with Christian faith. The same Old Testament, however, particularly Josh. 6:21, just as powerfully inspired fellow Charleston resident and former slave Denmark Vesey to plan a slave revolt. Those involved in the slave revolt felt assured that God would help them "utterly destroy all in the city, both men and women, young and old, with the edge of the sword" (Edgerton 1999, 101–25). In 2010, Steven Hayward, at that time F. K. Weyerhaeuser Fellow at the American Enterprise Institute, published an essay in which he read the story of Joseph in Egypt as a dire warning against government intervention, and suggested that his reading of these texts from Genesis served as a defense of a free-market, private-property economic system. Also in 2010, John Rogerson, professor of Scripture at Sheffield University, began his book on Old Testament theology, written because he, too, believed that the "Old Testament has something to say to today's world(s)," by stating that he wrote as "an Anglican priest . . . a humanist and a socialist" (Rogerson, 11). Dr. James Edwards, of the Center for Immigration Studies, reads some of the Mosaic laws of the Old Testament as defending firm national borders, low tolerance for immigration rights, and concerns for cultural corruption by outsiders (Edwards 2009 n.p., online), while Dr. Lai Ling Elizabeth Ngan of Baylor University, an Asian American scholar, finds that the Old Testament story about God's listening to the prayers of the "foreign woman," namely Hagar, "redefines boundaries that others have inscribed for her"; the story suggests that modern Christians should uphold the dignity of all peoples and resist denigrating people because of physical or racial differences (Ngan 2006, 83).

These are six Christians, all reading their Old Testament in the contemporary world. The fact that not all of these voices are biblical scholars, however, only serves to highlight the fact that reading the Christian Old Testament in the contemporary world is a complex mixture of the scholarly as well as the popular, stereotyped traditional views as well as innovative new insights, and that reading the Old Testament often strikingly divides readers into quite seriously opposing social and political views. Does this mean that reading the Christian Bible (Old or New Testament) in the modern world is a parade example of Cole Porter's 1934 song "Anything Goes"? Is it a matter of some disappointment that we can still agree with Leo Perdue's 1994 observation that "no commanding contemporary theology has yet appeared to form a consensus" (Perdue 1994, 8)?

I would argue that there is no cause for despair. Quite to the contrary! One of the most fascinating aspects of reading the Christian Old Testament in the contemporary world is not simply that there is unprecedented enthusiasm and diversity among scholars and viewpoints in the field but also that *this diversity itself is part of an ongoing debate and discussion*. At the outset, however, we should clarify that we are interested in thinking about serious readings of the Christian Old Testament, and not merely social or political propaganda that lightly seasons its rhetoric with a few Bible verses.

Marketplaces vs. Museums

Biblical scholarship is separated from religious propaganda not only by the fact that biblical scholarship presumes a basic orientation in the relevant historical contexts of the ancient world, familiarity with a diversity of texts both ancient and modern, and the ability to recognize a good argument supported by credible evidence or reasonable suggestions. These are all essential, of course. What really separates biblical scholarship from propaganda is the fact that biblical scholarship in the contemporary world is part of an ongoing discussion—a discussion that knows *and listens* to the challenges of others and seeks to contribute one's own insights *as part of the discussion*. As in all fields of discovery and intellectual endeavor, the success of biblical scholarship is not to be measured by the achievement of some dominant unanimity, but rather is judged by the quality and results of the participation in the scholarly tasks at hand and the *shared perception* that progress is taking place. We are seeing and understanding biblical texts in ever more profound and provocative ways. However, one of the most striking aspects of the rise of simplistic or propagandist use of the Bible is precisely its refusal to engage in dialogue, self-correction, or even acknowledgment of rival views, beyond the occasional ad hominem dismissal of arguments based solely on their association with groups identified by politicized generalizations—for example, "those liberals."

What we are suggesting is that there is an essential *dialogue* in modern, serious reading of the Bible. So, if this essay on reading the Christian Old Testament is not to be a rehearsal of some of the grand theories generally agreed on, now and forever (like a quiet museum tour of accomplishments), it is time for a new guiding image. I am intrigued by suggestions of the Cuban American New Testament scholar Fernando Segovia, who celebrates diversity in dialogue over the Scriptures. Segovia has famously suggested the "marketplace of ideas," rather like Wole Soyinka's discussion of the Silk Road market town Samarkand, as an image of modern sharing and exchanging of multicultural ideas and friendships (see Segovia and Tolbert; Segovia; Soyinka). An introduction to reading the Christian Old Testament in the contemporary world does not need to provide a historical survey of the "great ideas" that led to the present. Good surveys already exist, if European-dominated ideas are one's particular interest (e.g., Ollenburger; Rogerson 1984; Hayes and Prussner). Marketplaces can be elusive, however. They exist within the totality of the lives of people from everywhere, people who set up stalls and shop. Like the night markets of Auckland, New Zealand, or Darwin, Australia, they appear at designated places, at the designated hours, but otherwise there is only quiet. In short, the image of the marketplace suggests that we need a guidebook.

Laura Pulido, Laura Barraclough, and Wendy Cheng have recently published a marvelous, politically informed tour guide titled *A People's Guide to Los Angeles* (2012). The introduction itself is worth the price of admission. In these preliminary observations, the authors reflect on guidebooks and Los Angeles itself.

> *A People's Guide to Los Angeles* is a deliberate political disruption of the way Los Angeles is commonly known and experienced. . . . Guidebooks select sites, put them on a map, and interpret them in terms of their historical and contemporary significance. All such representations are political, because they highlight some perspectives while overlooking others. Struggles over who and what counts as "historic" and worthy of a visit involve decisions about who belongs and who doesn't, who is worth remembering and who can be forgotten, who we have been and who we are becoming.

They continue,

> Mainstream guidebooks typically describe and interpret their sites through the story of one person—almost always a man, and usually the capitalist who invested in a place, or its architect or designer. In doing so, they reinforce an individualized and masculinist way of thinking about history. Meanwhile, the collectives of people who actually created, built, or used the space remain nameless.

It would be difficult to think of a better series of thoughts to begin an essay on reading the Christian Old Testament in the contemporary world, because biblical analysis is rarely, if ever, written without some contemporary concerns in mind. Modern biblical theologies, for example, now usually identify the perspective of the author in the contemporary world (e.g., Brueggemann 1997; Rogerson 2010). Thus I am quite certain that part of the reason I agree with this need for a new image is that I write as a Christian who was born into, and very self-consciously remain informed by, the Quaker tradition. I also learned a great deal of biblical history, language, and theology from my fellow Christian sectarians the Mennonites, and I was first inspired to think seriously about biblical theology in high school by reading Vernard Eller, a theologian from yet another of my sister sectarian movements, the Church of the Brethren (informally known as the Dunkers). This means that I write as a Christian raised on "counterhistories" of the Christian movement—George Fox on Pendle Hill, Margaret Fell at Swarthmore, Conrad Grebel in Zurich, and Alexander Mack in Philadelphia—in addition to the canonical events of Christian history, such as the councils, the division between Rome and the Eastern Orthodox, Calvin, Luther, Wesley, and so on. I am thus well aware that texts, like towns, are susceptible to decisions about which locations are worthy of a visit, and which locations ought to be "memorialized" as deeply important. We could visit the old, established halls memorializing conquest or power—or we can find the marketplaces where we can encounter new ideas, argue with the "stall keepers" (the authors), make offers and listen to the counteroffers. In short, Christian biblical scholarship is tolerant of a variety of particular views of biblical texts, grammar, history, or theological interpretation. It is quite properly intolerant of the refusal to participate in dialogue with others. One of the hallmarks of propagandist abuses of the Bible in the modern world is the virtual absence of dialogue with other serious students of the Bible—a refusal to appear in the marketplace where ideas are examined and challenged.

It might seem that all this "marketplace" talk runs the risk of privileging process rather than results, and thus avoiding the hard work of evaluating whether ideas are good or bad, and then promoting the good. It is a uniquely contemporary heresy, however, to privilege solitary ideas or accomplishments while overlooking the long processes that often lead to any achievements worthy of celebration. Furthermore, to celebrate dialogue in the development of Christian thought about the Bible has sometimes been thought to be a uniquely modern phenomenon. That is already a mistake. What constitutes the "Old Testament," and even whether to have one, have both been matters of serious debate in Christian history.

The Christian Old Testament as a Product of Dialogue

Let us begin with a deceptively simple question: What constitutes the Old Testament? Christians do not even agree on this! Before the early Christian movement that historians now routinely refer to as "orthodox" arose victorious, the determination of what would be the authorized and foundational writings for Christian faith was a lively debate. The so-called *Festal Letter* 39 of Athanasius, which includes the earliest authoritative "list" of a canon of the Christian Bible, is dated to (a surprisingly late) 367 CE. Before then, debates about texts clearly ranged widely, and this does not even address the interesting continued use of noncanonical lore in popular, pre-Reformation medieval theater in the streets and churches of Europe (see Muir).

Furthermore, Athanasius's fourth-century declaration did not really settle the matter. Protestant, Catholic, and Orthodox Christians have each determined to authorize slightly different Old Testaments. Catholics, staying with the collection of Jewish writings that appeared in some of the old Greek translations known as the Septuagint (LXX), have included a series of books in the Old Testament that Protestants do not recognize, which Catholics call "deuterocanonical," and the Orthodox have chosen to include even a few more of these later Jewish (but still pre-Christian) writings. Protestants usually refer to these works as "the Apocrypha." Having said this, however, the difference between Christian canons has fewer implications for biblical scholarship than one might suspect at first. This is primarily because academic biblical studies, including biblical theological work, now tends to overlook specific church doctrines regarding the categories of "canonical," "deuterocanonical," and "noncanonical" writings. In the biblical studies marketplace, no text, artifact, ancient translation, or geographical context is "off limits" to research, comment, and consideration.

Canonical works obviously get the most attention—but it is hardly exclusive—and commentaries and critical analysis of *noncanonical* writing often make significant contributions to the further understanding of the canonical work as well. But we aren't finished with dialogue in relation to the existence of the Old Testament.

In fact, Christianity was marked by diversity in dialogue from the very beginning, as any sober reading of the arguments discussed in the book of Acts clearly reveals. One reason that dialogue is such an important context for thinking about the Old Testament is the fact that *the very existence of a "Christian Old Testament" was not a matter of widespread agreement in the earliest history of Christianity.* The early Christian convert Marcion (c. 85–160) famously proposed that true Christianity ought to discard any connection whatsoever to Judaism and the Jewish tradition; he embraced only a limited number of writings to represent this clean break between Jesus and the Jewish tradition (he proposed only a version of Luke, and ten Pauline epistles). However, the reaction was furious and widespread. W. H. C. Frend argues that Marcion holds the distinction of being "one of the very few opponents of orthodoxy whom Greek and Latin theologians united in damning. For nearly a century after his death . . . he was the arch-heretic" (212). Clearly, not every idea in the marketplace survives. We can stop cynically humming Porter's "Anything Goes" now.

The first Christian centuries, therefore, bequeath a task to all subsequent generations of readers of the "Christian Old Testament," namely, to take these writings into serious consideration when determining the nature of Christian faith. Furthermore, the vast majority of modern Christian communities (Protestant, Catholic, and Orthodox) have agreed with the church fathers and mothers of the first centuries that Christianity does indeed have a "canon," and that the Hebrew writings are part of it. Is this a settled issue, then? Hardly. Before we can speak of ways the Christian Old Testament is being read in the contemporary world, it is important to acknowledge, however briefly, that there are still ways it is *not* being read, and that it is even effectively ignored, in Christian faith and practice. Marcion still haunts us.

Tourism vs. Engagement: Ignoring the Marketplace?

As Aidan Nichols has recently acknowledged for the Catholic Church (2007), and as many others have suggested for other churches (Jenkins 2006, 42–47), a serious tendency remains among many Christian traditions in the modern world to overlook the larger part of their Bible before the Gospel of Matthew begins. Effectively ignoring the witness of the Old Testament for modern Christian faith and practice has sometimes been referred to as "Neo-Marcionism" (Nichols, 81). Even though few modern Christians would explicitly admit to it, the lack of effective education or preaching in Old Testament/Hebrew Bible studies is an alarming prospect for Christian faith and practice. A Christian theology cannot be true to the historic legacy of the faith tradition if it perpetuates such a neo-Marcionite subordination of these texts. This can happen in a number of ways, but it is more typical of popular and/or propagandist readings of the Bible than in biblical scholarship. In fact, some ways of "reading the Christian Old Testament" are simply ways to avoid it!

For example, there is a huge market for "Bible prophecy" books in the United States. One of the most significant criticisms of this popular literature is not only its total neglect of serious biblical scholarship on the prophetic books of the Old Testament but also its exclusive interest in how the books of the Bible may be "decoded" so that they can be understood to refer to contemporary events—as if the eighth-century-BCE book of Amos were actually speaking about twentieth-century Russia, or second-century-BCE portions of the book of Daniel were actually speaking about the twentieth-century ayatollahs of Iran. This "decoding" process usually neglects the historical content of the Old Testament book at hand in favor of what it is "understood" to be saying about modern times. In short, the actual content is merely a code. Its decoded meaning has nothing to do with what is actually written, when it was written, or who may have written it. One effective way of entirely ignoring a biblical book, then, is to completely reconstruct it without regard to its actual content as a historical work. This may not be Marcion's original idea, but he would clearly approve. This radical transformation of the work has little to do with actual study of it, nor is this part of the serious dialogue taking place about how the books of the Old Testament ought to inform contemporary Christian faith and practice.

This case of wildly popular literature on Bible prophecy in the modern world is particularly ironic. While some Christians frequently fault biblical scholars for not accepting the "plain sense" of the biblical text, it is astounding how carefully the various approaches to Bible prophecy omit any engagement with the most straightforward, or "plain," messages of the prophets of ancient Israel, namely, God's concern for the poor and the judgment threatened against the rich and powerful, those who, in the unforgettable images of Amos and Isaiah,

> trample the head of the poor into the dust of the earth,
>   and push the afflicted out of the way (Amos 2:7)

or who

> join house to house,
>   who add field to field,
> until there is room for no one but you,
>   and you are left to live alone
>   in the midst of the land! (Isa. 5:8)

No decoding seems necessary here. Radically altering the Old Testament texts beyond any credible historical or theological contexts in the process is clearly to do violence to those texts.

Another even more problematic way to virtually ignore the Old Testament in the Christian tradition is the Christian idea that the Old Testament is "old" and therefore largely replaced by the New Testament. Jesus is thus understood to have so reformed Jewish thought, very much as in Marcion's original proposal, that very little of the Old Testament is left of any real importance for Christian theology (save, perhaps, for the Ten Commandments). The dangers of such a "de-Semiticized" Jesus are legion, beginning with the problem of failing to understand Jesus' own faith tradition. For example, the event universally known as the "cleansing of the temple" is incomprehensible apart from recognizing that Jesus cites two Hebrew prophets in the act (Jer. 7:11 and Isa. 56:7). The reactions to Jesus' famous "reading" in his home synagogue in Luke 4 are equally incomprehensible apart from carefully noting the Old Testament references therein. Such examples can be multiplied throughout the New Testament.

Finally, the Hebrew tradition in both its historic and contemporary expressions is revered by a living people. Contemporary Christian scholarship is increasingly open to dialogue with Jewish biblical scholarship. Even though all Christians share most of the books of the Jewish canon with Judaism, there has been historically a significant difference in Jewish study of the Bible as opposed to Christian study (see summaries in Sommer 2012). One of the important characteristics of modern Christian readings of the Old Testament is that Jewish, Roman Catholic, Orthodox, and Protestant Scripture scholars are all in dialogue and discussion with each other in biblical studies on levels unprecedented before the twentieth century, and these dialogues continue in a variety of academic contexts in the twenty-first century.

Exorcising the ghost of Marcion from contemporary Christian scholarship of the Old Testament properly insists that taking the Old Testament seriously for Christian faith and practice involves a consideration of what Old Testament writings can say to the Christian tradition, not vice versa; Christian tradition should not use the Old Testament to buttress predetermined doctrinal ideas derived from the New Testament. Dictating terms to the Old Testament will never allow it to speak to Christian faith and practice in new and challenging ways. That isn't the way a marketplace works, after all, and trying to fix prices and control commodities only leads to other marketplaces.

The Role of Historical Events in the Old Testament for Christian Faith and Practice

We have already determined that the adjective *Christian* in our title means that we are interested in how the Old Testament speaks to Christian faith and practice, and therefore we are interested in discussing the role of "biblical theology." Here we encounter one of the loudest sectors of our marketplace. There are contemporary scholars (see Barr) who maintain an older tradition that suggests Old Testament scholarship should never be primarily "religious" or "theological," but rather historical, examining texts and other ancient evidence and then handing the results over to the theologians. Thus some scholars believe that biblical theology seeks to identify an exclusively *historical* expression of *past* belief (e.g., What did the ancient Israelites believe?). Indeed, the famous inaugural lecture of Johann Gabler in 1787, considered by some to be the "founding document" of this understanding of biblical theology (Gabler, 497), argued quite forcefully for maintaining a clear separation between biblical theology, defined as an exclusively historical enterprise, on the one hand, and systematic ("dogmatic") theology on the other.

It should be acknowledged that many modern biblical scholars would insist on this same separation between the historical and the theological approaches to Old Testament study and firmly place themselves in the "historical questions only" camp. Some scholars, again citing the late James Barr, have no objection to doing Christian theology based on biblical ideas, but believe that the formulation of these religious ideas ought to be a separate task from the exclusively historical task of Old Testament study. There are others who have doubts about religious belief in general or about the viability or validity of the specific religious traditions that make religious use of these writings. Some biblical scholars self-identify as atheists, for example, and there are even contemporary biblical scholars who openly condemn the very notion of a viable contemporary belief informed by the Bible (e.g., Avalos).

Both versions of the "historical analysis only" argument would maintain that it is not only possible but also necessary for a scholar of biblical texts to refrain from allowing contemporary interests or commitments (religious or otherwise) to "bias" or "interfere" with the task of historical analysis. This proposed form of historical analysis is represented as an activity that seeks to emulate scientific methodology as much as possible. The goal of this approach is thus described as "objective knowledge," or at least a close approximation of objective knowledge, even if these scholars were to acknowledge that certain influences or limitations of a time period certainly apply, such as the state of historical, archaeological, and textual studies at the time. In either case, the result is similar: a form of biblical studies that would be understood entirely as an aspect of historical investigation, no different in kind from determining what Shakespeare or Isaac Newton may have "believed," on religious (or any other) questions. Thus, while some may think or hope that their work could contribute to Christian faith and practice, they would carefully leave that task to others.

Interest-Free Biblical Analysis?

Recent debates, however, forcefully challenge many of the methodological assumptions that a bias-free analysis of historical texts is even a possible, much less laudable, goal. The term *postmodernism* is normally assigned to such challenges. Especially since the work of Thomas Kuhn (who gave us the concept of a "paradigm shift," 1996) and Paul Feyerabend (who calls for an "anarchist theory of knowledge," 2010), even the notion of an "objective" *scientific* analysis (science being the purported, even if largely self-appointed, model of objective analysis for all fields of inquiry) has been largely abandoned as both claim and goal. Motivations or interests do not necessarily poison results, but in the postmodern age, we are always vigilant about their influence, and thus the tendency in postmodernism is to declare such "interests" in the work itself. Does this preclude the possibility of doing biblical theology for modern Christian faith and practice? I contend that the postmodern criticism of a "bias-free" analysis of the Bible not only allows an enterprise of biblical theology but also positively encourages it.

The endless debates about the precise meaning of postmodernism need not distract us from a useful insight associated with this term: *all knowledge is contingent.* What we "know" usually depends on what we seek to know, and thus the questions we think to ask. Furthermore, what we investigate is influenced by own concerns, and we also sort out and determine which of our results are the most important. This is all part of the dialogue of diversity and, in twenty-first-century study of the Christian Old Testament, is now a widely acknowledged working assumption. Few would deny the importance of not only the identification of one's own working interests and assumptions in thinking about how the Christian Old Testament can speak to the modern age but also the retrospective work of placing older Old Testament theological writings in important social and historical contexts in ways that deepen our appreciation of their achievements and limitations (Rogerson 1984).

Is There a "Collapse of History" in Christian Old Testament Study?

There is an interesting debate going on in another sector of the marketplace. In his recent important monographs on the problems of Old Testament biblical theology, Leo Perdue refers to a "collapse of history" in recent biblical studies. One of the ways he formulates this point is to ask: Can these predominantly religious texts really help us reconstruct historical events in ancient Israel? If not, how can it be said that Israel's experience is important for contemporary readers who are seeking to read these texts as a guide to events that inform contemporary faith and practice? Perdue alludes to an important ongoing debate that began in the late twentieth century, a debate about our ability to know much actual history from what is available to us both in the Old Testament texts and in the relevant archaeological work (both ancient texts and artifacts) that supplements the study of biblical texts.

Especially after the publication of Thomas L. Thompson's widely cited monograph *The Historicity of the Patriarchal Narratives* (1974), fiery debates ensued between scholars who were divided (often unfairly) into "camps" called "minimalists" and "maximalists." These terms referred to those who despaired of the ability to be confident about historical events at all (thus "minimalists") and those who thought there was actually a great deal more evidence for biblical history than was often acknowledged (so Dever 2001; 2003). An interesting summary view of some of the historical debates is provided by Grabbe.

However, as some contemporary scholars have pointed out (see Brueggemann), these debates about historical events and biblical narratives mask the importance of answering a previous question, namely, whether *establishing that an event happened—or precisely how it happened—automatically dictates a corresponding religious significance to that event.* Clearly, it does not. Even if I can be convinced, for example, that the measurements of the temple provided in Ezekiel 40–48 are precise, accurate dimensions of the Jerusalem temple during the first millennium BCE, this does not strike me as having monumental importance for Christian faith and practice. It may have quite fascinating historical interest, but *theological* significance? This can also apply to less obscure issues. For example, determining that the texts in the opening chapters of the book of Exodus give us a more or less "historically reliable" report of the actual events of Israelites departing from Egypt does not thereby answer the question: Of what significance is the departure from Egypt *for contemporary Christian faith and practice*? Simply agreeing on the *historical* reliability of a biblical passage leaves considerable ground to cover on questions of *significance*. Simply agreeing on the historical details of the exodus, for example, does not thereby make one a liberation theologian. In fact, precious little of the powerful writings of liberation theology, beginning with the 1968 gathering of bishops in Medellín, Colombia (CELAM), actually debated the historical details of the book of Exodus. It is not that the historical story is insignificant; but rather its historical significance, if any, needs to be *part* of the theological argument, and not the entire task.

What happens when different perspectives can no longer be united on a particular reading of biblical events, especially on the accompanying significance of those events? Dominant and influential Old Testament theologies of the past depended on accepting an assigned weight to particular passages or biblical events that were considered central or guiding concepts, and thus critically important for modern theology. For example, Walter Eichrodt proposed that the idea of God's establishing agreements or "covenants" with God's people represents the central notion of the entire Hebrew Bible (Eichrodt 1961; 1967; the original German volumes were published in 1933 and 1935). Gerhard von Rad's equally influential Old Testament theology (Rad 1962; 1965; German 1957 and 1960) argued for the central importance of certain narratives of faith that Israelites allegedly repeated (he used the term "creeds") as indications of their faith, and thus suggested that Israelites were people who identified with such narratives. There is little doubt that such theological arguments, based on readings of the Old Testament, exerted a powerful influence on Christian theological education throughout the Western world in the twentieth century.

However, what if differing perspectives on the part of modern readers of the Bible—especially influenced by differing life situations (ethnicity, gender, etc.)—suggest to some modern readers that different biblical "events" in the Old Testament (whether unquestionably historical or not) are more important than others? Examples are not difficult to cite. On the one hand, after 1968, Latin American biblical scholars (especially Roman Catholic scholars) determined that the Moses and Exodus stories had a powerful message for them in their modern-day circumstances of economic poverty. On the other hand, Native American (Osage) professor of American studies Robert Allan Warrior famously challenged biblical theologians who celebrated the exodus and the entry to a "promised land" by noting that Native Americans frankly had more in common with the beleaguered Canaanites, reminding us that indigenous peoples continue to have an ambiguous relationship with the legacy of the book of Joshua (see Warrior). Nineteenth-century African American slaves also determined that the Jonah and Daniel stories had powerful messages for them in their circumstances of oppression and suppression (Levine; Cone 1992). Finally, recent suggestions view the conquest of Jerusalem in 587 and the subsequent exile of thousands of Judeans (Albertz; Ahn) as a biblical event with serious theological implications (Brueggemann; Smith-Christopher 2002). Nineteenth-century Maori Christians in New Zealand determined that the prophets were powerful examples of a new form of pantribal leadership that had new potential to unite previously fragmented tribal peoples in opposition to growing European settlement, and some even looked to the Davidic monarchy as a model for a new and culturally unprecedented Maori king, and thus an answer to the power and authority of the British Crown (Elsmore 1985; 1989). Is all this also a "collapse of history"? Or is it really the collapse of *dominant readings* of history in the face of alternative decisions about central ideas, events, and themes?

There is little doubt that some Christian biblical scholars and theologians lament the absence of the dominant Old Testament readings. Such a view arguably represents a kind of wistfulness for the "good old days" when a dominant perspective seemed to influence writing and doing (and teaching!) Old Testament theology in Christian institutions of higher learning. Not only does this "hoped-for dominant" perspective do violence to those who were never part of the "dominant perspective" (because they were either gender or cultural minorities, e.g., women, African American,

Asian American, Latino/Latina, or theological minorities such as Anabaptists, Quakers, or Pentecostals), but it is also arguably built on a largely discredited model of intellectual progress that mimics seventeenth- to twentieth-century Western imperial politics and social values—namely, the (intellectual) goal of domination and the vanquishing of opposition.

Surely an alternative to dominance or conquest is concord, dialogue, and cooperation in common causes. If we are to read the Christian Old Testament, and consider it theologically significant, then that theological significance will have to extend to the entire world. The *emerging* Christian world is now based in the Southern Hemisphere (Jenkins 2002). Reading the Christian Old Testament is thus by necessity a global enterprise. The modern marketplace is diverse indeed, and there are a number of ways to recognize this diversity.

Contemporary Worlds in Dialogue

We have seen that Segovia's "marketplace of ideas" does not so much despair of speaking of the past at all, much less signal a "collapse of history." The issue is not whether history can be written any longer. Rather, the issue is how different histories, and different texts, can be understood to matter in differing contexts. Marketplaces can resist organization. Nevertheless, there are perhaps two general ways of sorting the diversity in view. One way is to focus on the identities of the participants themselves, especially in those cases when they consciously and explicitly draw on these identities in their reading of the Bible. The other is to focus on challenges to the human enterprise in local or global contexts. Many of these challenges will require that we marshal our collective wisdom in order to survive as a species, and there are hardly more urgent reasons for biblical scholars to make their contribution to the ideological, spiritual, and political will of people to act in positive ways.

Text and Experience: The Feminist Pioneering of New Questions

New Testament scholar Elisabeth Schüssler Fiorenza points out that it was early feminist critical studies that largely opened up critical readings of both the New and Old Testaments from a perspective informed by particular "interests" (see Schüssler Fiorenza). One of first of these interests was reviewing the long-presumed subordination of women in the narratives of the Bible. It is interesting to see how this work progressed in a variety of different directions, all inspired by gender-related questions. For some feminist readers of the Bible, restating the often unacknowledged positive and powerful roles of women in the Bible is an important corrective to assumptions about the exclusive biblical focus on men (Gafney; Meyers 1988/2013). Phyllis Trible, on the other hand, pioneered the role of an unvarnished focus on destructive texts featuring violence against women, calling them "texts of terror" and thus highlighting dangerous tendencies within historical biblical cultures themselves (see Trible). Renita Weems, similarly, opened a line of investigation on the prophetic use of violent language associated with feminized subjects and objects that also betrayed violent attitudes (e.g., "Lady Jerusalem," Weems 1995). Kathleen O'Connor, Elizabeth Boase, and Carleen Mandolfo have taken this conversation further, suggesting that there is evidence of an ongoing dialogue with "Lady Jerusalem" that began with the violent imagery noted by

Weems in Hosea and Ezekiel, but then continued to Lamentations and Deutero-Isaiah, suggesting that there is acknowledgment of and even repentance for this violence (see O'Connor; Boase; Mandolfo). There are many other directions that studies can go, many of which explicitly identify as feminist, or gender-interested, analysis (see, e.g., Yee 2003).

The feminist approach, far from being a limiting perspective, has moved methodologically from an interest in one formulation of a "minority" perspective—namely, the role of women—to a comparative interest in how this critical approach relates to other issues of "gendering" and "embodiment" in the Bible (homosexuality, prostitution, especially the vexed question of temple prostitution, foreign wives of mixed marriages, gender in relation to slavery, etc.). This approach can also move beyond questions of gender. These early feminist perspectives quite logically moved toward an interest in those who are considered "marginalized" in Hebrew texts—for example, Edomites, Egyptians, Moabites, those lumped together as "aliens" in the Mosaic laws, foreign workers—for other reasons. Interesting work indeed. But what does it have to do with Christian faith and practice?

While not all feminist analysis of the Bible is done with the hope that it will contribute to a more equitable and egalitarian Christian movement in the contemporary world, a considerable amount is.

Cultural Identities and Social Situations in the Marketplace

Feminism is not the only "contemporary interest" that has driven new questions in Christian biblical analysis. Especially those who hope biblical analysis will affect Christian faith and practice have made significant contributions. Already in narratives of freed slaves in North America, African American readers of the Bible were reflecting on their own insights, especially as a countertheology to the European preachers who constantly preached obedience and subservience (see Raboteau; Hopkins and Cummings). In fact, it is possible to trace a twentieth-century flowering of these early readings, some of which began by reexamining the role of explicitly identified Africans in biblical history (see Felder) in a manner similar to those who reexamined the Old Testament stories explicitly about women. One clear goal was to highlight African presence in the Bible that had been neglected in the face of racial prejudice in the modern world against those of African descent. However, in the wake of important calls for a more assertive black theology in the twentieth century (Cone 1970), this project then expanded in different directions in ways very similar to the expansion of gender-related questions (and often intersecting with gender questions, e.g., in "womanist" analysis; see Weems 1991). In the African American context, the appearance of the groundbreaking work *Stony the Road We Trod* (Felder) was a major contribution to the maturing of contemporary, consciously African American biblical scholarship. Included in this collection were essays that dealt not only with historical-critical analysis of the Bible from an African American perspective, but with the use of the Bible in the history of African American interpretation. Further work on African American history of interpretation (Callahan; Wimbush) continues to make important contributions to unique insights into both the later use of Scripture, but also arguments contributing to historical understanding of the texts themselves. Not only is the role of the Bible in African American history itself the subject of important analysis, but African American biblical analysis is also interested in examining texts that have been used historically to suppress both those of explicitly African descent (for example, to defend slavery) and many non-European peoples. A convergence in methods, and sometimes goals, began to emerge that sought to forge alliances across explicitly named cultural or ethnic categories.

So, even though it has followed a different trajectory than African American scholarship, Latino/Latina literature now also holds an important place in the context of the United States. For example, Justo González, Jean-Paul Ruiz, and Miguel De La Torre (2002; 2007) have published monographs and commentaries on Old Testament themes. Interestingly, however, De La Torre has taken a somewhat pessimistic attitude as to whether cross-cultural analysis of the text will influence the general discipline. De La Torre is clear—Euro-Americans are largely not to be trusted for biblical analysis, because "Euroamerican Christians, either from the fundamentalist right or the far liberal left, probably have more in common with each other and understand each other better than they do Christians on the other side of the racial and ethnic divide" (De La Torre 2007, 125). Nevertheless, serious contributions continue to challenge biblical scholars to take seriously the contributions of those who write Old Testament analysis from an openly acknowledged perspective. Gregory Lee Cuéllar, for example, compares passages of Isaiah to the Mexican and Mexican American folk music style known as the *Corrido*, not only to suggest ways that the biblical texts can be understood in contemporary Mexican American communities, but also to propose potential new readings for the book of Isaiah itself (Cuéllar 2008).

While there have been a number of important works from Asian American biblical scholars in the late twentieth century that consciously draw on Asian themes and identity, a significant milestone was the publication in 2006 of the collected volume *Ways of Being, Ways of Reading*. This volume was comparable in many ways to the impact of the 1991 work *Stony the Road We Trod* in the African American scholarly context. It includes retrospective and survey essays, even very personal reflections on academic work (e.g., Yee 2006), as well as examples of contemporary work of some of the most prominent American scholars using cross-cultural approaches.

Finally, in terms of the American context, it is notable that Randall Bailey, Tat-siong Benny Liew, and Fernando Segovia have initiated a dialogue between Latino/a American, Asian American, and African American scholarship, hoping to find common ground in "minority" analysis of the Bible (Bailey, Liew, and Segovia), suggesting the possibilities of a convergence and maturing of methods of analysis, even as they reject any sort of false consensus on similarity of cultural contexts.

Although it is fair to say that readings explicitly related to specific cultural and ethnic identities and traditions continue in the century, attention has tended to turn toward social, political, and economic locations as another significant source of issues that influence the reading of Scripture. In the last quarter of the twentieth century, a number of Old Testament scholars consciously incorporated sociological and anthropological analysis in their ancient historiography of the Bible (Gottwald; Overholt 1992, 2003), and this dialogue with social sciences certainly continues (Chalcraft). Exegetical issues of the most recent writing in Old Testament studies soon converged on a series of questions closely associated with the influence of Edward Said's classic work *Orientalism*, which further built on the early social theories and the observations of the postcolonial theorists Frantz Fanon and Albert Memmi. Once this dialogue with Said's influence was articulated powerfully in the many works of R. S. Sugirtharajah, the rise of postcolonial approaches to Scripture became a significant movement in the early twenty-first century. Sugirtharajah's now classic compendium *Voices from the Margin* signaled a new energy in "interested perspectives" in the reading of the Bible.

The Rise of Postcolonial Biblical Analysis

We have already noted that Christianity—and its Bible—is seeing profound growth in the Southern Hemisphere in the twenty-first century. Twentieth-century Christians in developing societies, especially India, South America, and Africa, began to assert their own perspectives in the analysis of the Bible. After Said's influential work, they began to identify ways in which previous European scholarship contained certain social and cultural assumptions about Western superiority. They then began readings of the Bible within their past experiences of European colonial presence. In the process of reasserting a cultural and/or national identity, however, they soon realized that a reconstruction of cultural identity in the new world could never go back to a purified "precolonial" state, but must always be in dialogue with the social, political, and philosophical realities of having been deeply affected by Western thought and practice. Although in the context of religion and the Bible, one might better speak of "post-Western-missionaryism," the discussions in biblical studies borrowed a term from social and cultural theory to identify their new reviews of the Bible in their own contexts: *postcolonialism*. Postcolonial biblical exegesis provided special tools for Christians in formerly colonized states (or among indigenous peoples in Western European settled lands, North and South America, Australia, and New Zealand). The questions whether, and to what extent, largely imported biblical scholarship was (and is) tainted by imperial goals of control and economic expansion raised serious concerns about those readings of Scripture that seemed deeply involved in that imperial process (De le Torre 2002). A prime example of attempting to counter Western domination was the Latin American assertion that the exodus is the prime event of the Old Testament—and thus liberation is the prime theological theme. However, it is important to note that these questions were being raised largely by Christian Bible scholars. Not all criticism of colonial and missionary policies rejected Christianity and the Bible as an unwanted imposition (see Roberts); sometimes it rather engaged in the more creative task of rereading the texts.

If "postcolonial" contexts include minorities living in multicultural nations, then Fernando Segovia's "Diasporic" approach to reading Scripture becomes especially suggestive. In the American context, this obviously can include African American, Asian American, and Mexican American readings of particular texts that resonate with themes, motifs, or elements of minority existence such that they lead to expositions of Old Testament texts that are suggestive for all readers of the Bible—and not only to fellow members of particular ethnic or cultural groups.

Ethnic and culturally informed readings challenge the notion that European scholarship has a privileged position in biblical scholarship generally, and in the construction of Christian theologies built from Old Testament texts particularly. What we have learned about diversity in dialogue is that the Christian reading of the Old Testament in the contemporary world will be richer, more learned, and more convincing in both textual and historical analysis only if our marketplace grows in its resemblance to the actual diversity of our worlds. What new insights into particular Old

Testament texts await the future BA, MA, or PhD theses and papers written by young Tibetan, Chinese, Navajo, Roma, or Aboriginal Australian students and scholars? What will they see that the rest of us have too quickly dismissed or completely overlooked? In the twenty-first century, we are likely to benefit from an increase of book titles like that of Senegalese American biblical scholar Aliou Niang: *Faith and Freedom in Galatia and Senegal: The Apostle Paul, Colonies, and Sending Gods*.

Let us reaffirm that diversity ought always to lead to dialogue. Agreements, shared insights, and common convictions that we are all learning from the dialogue ought to deliver even the most cynical from the simplistic hope that we Bible scholars would just please get to "the bottom line." Marketplaces don't have a bottom line! Dialogue and haggling over texts is simply the reality. The invitation, therefore, is to listen and learn. Incidentally, lest Christians think that all this is somehow radically new, those familiar with classic rabbinic dialogue and argumentation over religious texts are aware that dialogue with God and with each other is at the heart of theology.

Issues Driving Contemporary Biblical Analysis

Questions from identities and cultural experiences are not, however, the only major and significant sources of urgency in reading and rereading the Christian Old Testament. A number of contemporary global crises have inspired a renewed examination of the ways in which the Bible can be reread. The modern interest in trauma as the psychosocial reality of a world in crisis has recently gained ground in biblical analysis (see O'Connor; Janzen; Kelle). The millions of humans who flee wars and crises as international refugees have also influenced biblical analysis on ancient exile and deportation (see Ahn). The potential list of pressing issues is depressingly long, of course, but it is possible to examine a few examples to illustrate how this section of the marketplace can be organized. In fact, we can move from an example that is already very old but critically ongoing, war and peace in the Old Testament; to an issue that arguably has its roots in the twentieth century, environmentalism; and finally note the signs of a rising issue so new that it has barely begun to generate serious thought among biblical scholars: evolutionary philosophy, transhumanism, and the nature of the person.

War, Peace, and Violence and the Old Testament

Since the fourth century CE, the Christian church has been faced with direct responsibility for violence. The monarchical descendants of the Roman emperor Constantine made Christianity the official religion of the empire, leading into the Byzantine Empire. Biblical study was now intimately connected to the foreign policy of a powerful military machine, and would continue to have foreign policy implications from that time to the present. The continued relevance of the Bible to issues of war and peace is not difficult to discern in the writings of the Christian warriors and their chaplains on the one hand, and the Christian peacemakers and their communities on the other, throughout Western history especially. A clear majority in this debate has supported more violent interpretations, however regretfully they are sometimes offered.

The Jesus who said, "Love your enemies and pray for those who persecute you" (Matt. 5:44), and the Paul who exhorted, "live peaceably with all" (Rom. 12:18), were effectively trumped in Christian faith and practice very early on by an uncritical admiration for the genocidal Joshua and the conquering David (see Davies). There have been a variety of ways in which Christians have responded to the use of the Old Testament as a moral trump over the pacifist Jesus. Once again, the similarities to the methods of feminist biblical analysis are instructive.

For example, especially since the churches in twentieth-century Europe began to mobilize an opposition to the Cold War threats in their own backyards, innumerable monographs have attempted to reexamine the actual practices of Old Testament violence and warfare, either with explicit admiration (so, famously, Yadin), or appropriate levels of horror (Craigie; Niditch; Collins). In modern Old Testament study, then, one is hopefully exposed to the potential dangers of a casual and unguarded use of biblical texts that are so clearly contrary to contemporary moral judgments and international standards of justice.

Finally, similar to those who sought to lift up exemplary moments previously overlooked, there are those who seek to highlight strongly peaceful passages in the Bible that may even have been in critical dialogue with more violent episodes in the canon and thus reveal an internal dialogue or debate that reveals stronger peace voices among the canonical choir (Enz; Smith-Christopher 2007). This approach articulates how a certain form of Hebrew nonviolence would have been a logical expression of theological tendencies that had their roots in the Servant Songs of Second Isaiah and the universalism of the book of Jonah, where we find openness to the repentance of national enemies like the Assyrians, who are portrayed as repenting "... of the violence of their hands." Further developments can affirm the wisdom ethic of peacefulness—an ethic that frequently contrasts self-control over against brute force and earnestly recommends a sober, wise consideration of counsel and diplomacy (Prov. 16:7, 32; 17:27; 24:5-6). In fact, the Wisdom tradition may itself represent precisely a staging place for international discussion, given that wisdom values are as universal in the ancient Near East as any literary themes can be. Ancient Egyptian wisdom, Mesopotamian wisdom, and Greek wisdom all compare quite favorably to ancient Israelite forms.

Texts that reflect an Israelite "exilic" lifestyle, lived in "active nonconformity to the world" (as the famous 1955 Mennonite Church statement puts it), would also build on biblical protests against narrow ethnocentrism (e.g., the book of Ruth, Jacob's apology to Esau, Isaiah 56 and 66, and the striking affirmation in Zechariah 9 of a mixed-race people of God). In fact, there is evidence of a rising protest against violence and narrow self-centeredness (e.g., Ezekiel 40–48) that can be seen to affirm the Deuteronomic critique of the monarchy, and especially the condemnation of the monarchy in the penitential prayers of Ezra 9, Nehemiah 9, and Daniel 9. Thus the fact that there are passages where God is alleged to have called for the massacre of foreign cities does not necessarily cancel out or trump the fact that there are more hopeful passages on this subject as well, texts that openly question whether the stance of the Hebrews toward foreign peoples should be hostile and that envision a different and more peaceful reality (Isaiah 2; 19; Micah 4).

Regrettably, offering a more peaceful reading of the Old Testament will not likely bring about world peace. But if the late Colonel Harry Summers of the Army War College is correct that "it is the passions of the people that are the engines of war" (Summers, 75–76), then perhaps careful biblical analysis will remove at least one major ideological prop and provocation that has certainly been used in the past to excuse quite reprehensible behavior among those who honor the Scriptures (see Trimm).

Environmentalism

Biblical analysis that is driven by ecological concerns can be clearly dated to responses to the famous 1967 article in *Science* by Lynn White, accusing Christianity for providing the "roots" of the ecological crisis in God's injunction to the first couple in Gen. 1:28 to "subdue" and "have dominion" over nature. The late twentieth century then saw an increase of literature that highlighted ways that the Hebrew Bible/Old Testament affirmed a spirituality of care and responsibility for the earth as God's creation. Much of this work owes a great deal to the early writings of Australian biblical scholar Norman Habel (see also Hallman; so now Craven and Kaska; Deane-Drummond). The often-cited "this-worldly" emphasis of much Old Testament ethical discussion, and even the imagery of deep fascination with and appreciation of the created world (Job 38–41; Psalm 147–48), however, continues to inspire further development in pioneering biblical theologies. Genesis portrays God involving Adam in the naming of other creatures (Gen. 2:19) and further records God's intention to "re-create" the world in the Hebrew version of the flood narrative, the basic outlines of which were clearly known to the Jewish people by the time of the Babylonian captivity, and most likely borrowed from Mesopotamian traditions.

A related development is in the direction of animal rights. Concern for animal welfare is not absent from Hebrew law or narrative (Deut. 25:4; Numbers 22). The flood story, of course, involves the considerable responsibility of Noah to preserve animals. The Old Testament strikingly expresses certain visions of peace by referring to changes in the animal kingdom (Isa. 11:6: the wolf living with the lamb) and even hinting that in their first created state, humans were vegetarian (before Gen. 9:4, where eating meat is first explicitly mentioned). Psalm 148 portrays the created animals of the world praising God, and Job famously portrays God's careful attention and knowledge of the details of the animal kingdom (Job 39; on animal rights work, see Linzey 1995; 2009; Miller).

Work in environmentalism more generally, and animal rights specifically, have been parts of a move to appreciate biblical themes that buttress a more responsible care for the earth (Toly and Block). There are, however, some serious economic and even political issues at stake here. On the issue of environmentalism particularly, there has been a serious backlash from those with business interests who see strong environmentalist movements as potential threats to their expansion of industry. Not unexpectedly, then, this reaction has motivated more conservative Christian scholars to reassert a strongly pragmatic and typically short-term ethic of consumption unmitigated by strong concerns for conserving resources in the long term. Christians in this tradition, rarely biblical scholars themselves, are clearly not impressed with nuanced arguments about responsibility for species and their survival. Nor are they likely to be impressed by arguments based largely on Old Testament passages, especially if that concern is perceived as requiring economic sacrifices. An interesting example of this reaction is the work of Steven Hayward, from the conservative think tank the American Enterprise Institute. In a published essay titled "Mere Environmentalism" (the title itself is an homage to evangelical hero C. S. Lewis) and subtitled "A Biblical Perspective on Humans and the Natural World," Hayward suggests that the Genesis narratives promote the hierarchy of creation with humanity at the top. He therefore construes a biblical mandate, not for preservation of the environment, but for a "stewardship" that promotes responsible use of resources and a free-market-driven effort to conquer the "untamed wilderness," and furthermore as free of government intervention as possible. Indeed, Hayward further argues that the story of Joseph in Pharaoh's household is a warning against centralized state control, because Joseph's centralization of resources for the Pharaoh leads directly to the enslavement of the Hebrews. Environmental degradation, therefore, may be a matter calling for repentance, but definitely not for government regulation (33). Finally, Noah offers sacrifice of animals after the flood, Hayward notes, so this story provides no basis for simple preservation, and certainly suggests that animals were to be used for human benefit.

The twenty-first century is likely to see more, rather than less, of this polemical exchange in biblical scholarship. Although more propagandistic approaches have tended to avoid participation in scholarly organizations like the Society of Biblical Literature, we are likely to see more direct engagement over the use, and abuse, of Scripture on various issues of social, and especially economic, importance.

The Nature of the Person: The Rise of Evolutionary Social Science and Philosophy

Finally, it is important in the context of this essay to speculate about issues that may well emerge more fully as the twenty-first century develops. In the wake of Daniel Dennett's polemical 1996 assertion of atheist scientism, titled "Darwin's Dangerous Idea," there is a rise of perspectives represented by the following: "If you believe in a traditional concept of the soul, you should know that there is little doubt that a fuller appreciation of the implications of evolutionary theory . . . is going to destroy that concept"; and, "we must openly acknowledge . . . the collapse of a worldview that has sustained human energies for centuries" (Stanovich, 3). Will biblical studies also be challenged by evolutionary thought? If so, in what way?

In Christian theology and biblical studies, the classic beginning point for discussion of the nature of the human person is the concept of the *imago Dei*, the creation of humanity in the image and likeness of God (Gen. 1:26-27). J. Richard Middleton, for example, seeks to rethink the *imago Dei* debates in a modern context, noting that older Christian theological uses of Genesis 1 were rather strained, and usually presumed that the significance of "the image" and "likeness" of God was precisely human *reason*. Recent discussion has emphasized the royal context of these terms, suggesting that humans are portrayed as royally deputized representations of divine authority and responsibility in the world. Middleton even suggests that the *imago Dei* is, in fact, a politically sophisticated as well as theologically loaded term in Genesis, because here we find the textual staging ground for a narrative culture war against Mesopotamian hegemonic narratives of conquest and subservience. These Mesopotamian narratives were weapons in a philosophical/ideological war that accompanied the invading and conquering armies that conquered both the northern kingdom (722 BCE) and Jerusalem and Judah (597/587).

While it is quite possible to celebrate the theological importance of all humanity from an explicitly evolutionary view of the emergence of *homo sapiens*, it is also clear that some interpretations of human evolution threaten to radically debase and reduce humanity to a mere "sack of genes," with little inherent worth, whose values, art, and faith are mere "spandrels" (that is, accidental and irrelevant by-products) that accompany the real work of genetic reproduction. The value of life is thus no longer inherent in creation, but purely instrumental, as some humans serve as sexual slaves, soldiers, and workers for the shrinking and increasingly ruthless elite. The masses are already once again being pacified by the modern equivalent of bread and circus: ever smaller and more inexpensive sources of digital pornography, graphic violence, and (contra Kant's imperative) the view of fellow humans as means rather than ends.

In this context, religious faith (including, of course, the Bible) is strongly dismissed as "nothing but" the result of evolutionary mechanisms for survival. We perceive deities only because of our ancient and genetically honed "agency detection devices" (instincts that perceive potential threats in the environment). Others suggest that religion was merely a part of a sophisticated social "mate selection" mechanism whereby mates with trustworthy values could be quickly identified. In short, religion is a neural response pattern.

The interesting question is no longer, "Can a biblical scholar believe in evolution and teach Genesis"? Of course they can, and do. What is new is the rising insistence of a form of evolutionary social thought that would dismiss all religious speculation as irrelevant. Such a radically reductionist anthropology seeks to replace the "Eden myth" with an equally implausible and comprehensive "African Savannah myth" that subsumes all humanity into categories of neural survival mechanisms driven by reproductive genes. Does the Old Testament have anything to say in this decidedly modern discussion?

The resources of Wisdom literature and its emphasis on sober assessments of God's moral patterns in the created world provide a foundation beyond Genesis for seeking dialogue with naturalists and biologists. But the issues will continue to press, and will no longer be simply the leisure-time, science-fiction reading of those whose day jobs are in biblical studies. Seeking biblical guidance on the nature of the human person will become increasingly pressing in this century in the light of (1) increased emphasis in the human sciences on "transhumanism," according to which humans can be enhanced by further evolutionary merging with technology; (2) manipulation of genetic information to favor certain human traits (already taking place passively by rejecting human eggs in artificial insemination processes that bear indications of undesired genetic traits); (3) progress in artificial intelligence such that ethical questions are becoming increasingly prominent (when does turning off a machine consist of killing a living being? etc.); (4) further work in cloning; and (5) the location and identification of personhood as directly (and some would say: *only*) a function of neural brain activity, thus raising the possibility of "downloading" human persons into hardware.

Are these exclusively theological issues? Do they have any implications for biblical analysis? Will a biblical analysis arise, for example, driven in part by the prescience of the science fiction writer Philip K. Dick, who anticipated many ethical issues dealing with modern technology? It is possible that biblical scholars will simply suggest that radically new technologies are not the business of textual analysis. However, when those technologies raise serious questions about the nature and value of the human person, it is hard to resist the notion that biblical analysis has something to say to this issue.

Return to the Beginning: Does the Marketplace Matter?
Are There Any Real People There?

Finally, we can pick up on a discussion that was left aside at the very beginning of this essay. What about the clashes among various readings of the Old Testament? Is biblical studies hopelessly mired in disagreements such that, in the end, an individual must simply hum along with Porter's "Anything Goes"?

Appearances, especially in the contemporary world, can be deceiving. The reality of extensive and exciting discussion and debate in biblical studies does not mean that the field is wandering aimlessly. Furthermore, the impressive level of publication and discussion does not mean that there is no consensus of methods or results among biblical scholars. Biblical scholars, like professionals in other fields such as medicine, engineering, or astronomy, certainly stay in touch with each other's work, and through international organizations (the largest being the Society of Biblical Literature) continue to pursue common interests, projects, and even enjoy continued debates and disagreements. It is hardly the case, as philosopher Alvin Plantinga somewhat sourly suggests, that biblical scholars can never agree on anything, explaining (for Plantinga, presumably) why Christians usually do not take their work seriously.

Plantinga may be surprised, however. The influence of biblical scholarship on wider Christian practices might be slow in manifesting itself, but it is absolutely clear. Plantinga should be impressed with the articulate, profound, and serious assessment of the importance of biblical analysis in the 1994 document of the Pontifical Biblical Commission titled "The Interpretation of the Bible in the Church." Calling the historical-critical method of biblical analysis "indispensable for the scientific study of the meaning of ancient texts," the document critically assesses, both positively and negatively, many current approaches to biblical analysis common in universities and biblical scholarship, and recommends much of modern biblical scholarship to the Catholic world more widely. Furthermore, the document famously refers to fundamentalist readings of Scripture as "intellectual suicide." Unimpressed with official declarations by hierarchies? One need only examine the textbooks for Catholic *high school* students, including those explicitly recommended by the bishops, to see the profound impact of biblical scholarship on questions of multiple authorship, historicity, the dangers of literalism, and so on.

Only the most conservative Christians today believe that the only way to treasure the significance of the narratives of Genesis is to take them literally, or believe that Moses wrote every word of the Pentateuch. Only the most fundamentalist Christians today would think that the book of Jonah is about surviving in the gullet of a marine animal, or that nearly one-fifth of the entire population of ancient Egypt left with Moses in the thirteenth century BCE. Furthermore, what many Christians in the church pews and Sunday schools *do* know is that a profound Christian faith can be enriched by learning that an unnamed second prophet we call "Second Isaiah" likely reapplied some of the thought of the eighth-century Isaiah of Jerusalem, but also proclaimed radically new thoughts in the late sixth-century BCE when the Persian emperor Cyrus lived. Furthermore, Christians today know much more about the horrific tragedy of the destruction of Jerusalem in 587, and how Lamentations is a powerful poetic response to that tragedy, and how Psalms contains religious poetry from long after the time of David. None of these ideas are shocking to Christians in the churches any more, and none of them are destructive of anything but the most simplistic of readings of the Old Testament.

Finally, what Christians in the churches surely know is that the Bible invites—indeed nearly demands—the careful attention of many different cultures, genders, ages, and contexts who are brought into dialogue as they listen, read, discuss, and debate the meanings and importance of these texts of the Old Testament. There is important historical information we can know, but there is so much more to ask. For those who love only quiet museum tours of "certainties" enclosed in glass cases so that the masses can be enlightened, biblical studies in the contemporary world is not for them. The marketplace is teaming, ebullient, and alive.

Works Cited

Ahn, John. 2010. *Exile as Forced Migrations: A Sociological, Literary, and Theological Approach on the Displacement and Resettlement of the Southern Kingdom of Judah*. Berlin: de Gruyter.

Albertz, Rainer. 2003. *Israel in Exile: The History and Literature of the Sixth Century* B.C.E. Atlanta: Society of Biblical Literature.

Avalos, Hector. 2007. *The End of Biblical Studies*. New York: Prometheus.

Bailey, Randall, Tat-siong Benny Liew, and Fernando F. Segovia, eds. 2009. *They Were All Together in One Place? Toward Minority Biblical Criticism*. Atlanta: Society of Biblical Literature.

Barr, James. 2000. *History and Ideology in the Old Testament: Biblical Studies at the End of a Millennium*. Oxford: Oxford University Press.

Boase, Elizabeth. 2006. *The Fulfillment of Doom? The Dialogic Interaction between the Book of Lamentations and the Pre-Exilic/Early Exilic Prophetic Literature*. London: T&T Clark.

Brueggemann, Walter. 1997. *Theology of the Old Testament: Testimony, Dispute, Advocacy*. Minneapolis: Fortress Press.

Callahan, Allen Dwight. 2006. *The Talking Book: African Americans and the Bible*. New Haven: Yale University Press.

Chalcraft, David. 2006. *Social-Scientific Old Testament Criticism*. London: T&T Clark.

Collins, John J. 2004. *Does the Bible Justify Violence?* Minneapolis: Fortress Press.

Cone, James H. 1970. *A Black Theology of Liberation*. Maryknoll, NY: Orbis.

———. 1992. *The Spirituals and the Blues: An Interpretation*. Maryknoll, NY: Orbis Books.

Craigie, Peter. 1979. *The Problem of War in the Old Testament*. Grand Rapids: Eerdmans.

Craven, Toni, and Mary Jo Kaska. 2011. "The Legacy of Creation in the Hebrew Bible and Apocryphal/Deuterocanonical Books." In *Spirit and Nature: The Study of Christian Spirituality in a Time of Ecological Urgency*, edited by Timothy Hessel-Robinson and Ray Maria McNamara, RSM, 16–48. Eugene, OR: Pickwick.

Cuellar, Gregory L. 2008. *Voices of Marginality: Exile and Return in Second Isaiah 40-55 and the Mexican Immigrant Experience*. New York: Peter Lang.

Davies, Eryl. 2010. *The Immoral Bible: Approaches to Biblical Ethics*. London: T&T Clark.

Deane-Drummond, Celia. 2008. *Eco-Theology*. London: Darton, Longman & Todd.

De La Torre, Miguel. 2002. *Reading the Bible from the Margins*. Maryknoll, NY: Orbis.

———. 2007. *Liberating Jonah: Forming an Ethic of Reconciliation*. Maryknoll, NY: Orbis.

Dennett, Daniel. 1996. *Darwin's Dangerous Idea*. New York: Simon & Schuster.

Dever, William G. 2001. *What Did the Biblical Writers Know and When Did They Know It?* Grand Rapids: Eerdmans.

———. 2003. *Who Were the Early Israelites and Where Did They Come From?* Grand Rapids: Eerdmans.

Edwards, James. 2009. *A Biblical Perspective on Immigration Policy*. Washington, DC: Center for Immigration Studies. http://www.cis.org/ImmigrationBible

Egerton, Douglas R. 1999. *He shall go out free : The lives of Denmark Vesey*. Madison, WI: Madison House, 1999

Eichrodt, Walter. 1961. *Theology of the Old Testament*. Translated by J. A. Baker. Vol. 1. London: SCM.

———. 1967. *Theology of the Old Testament*. Translated by J. A. Baker. Vol. 2. London: SCM.

Elsmore, Bronwyn. 1985. *Like Them That Dream: The Maori and the Old Testament*. Wellington, New Zealand: Tauranga Moana Press.

———. 1989. *Mana from Heaven*. Auckland: Reed.

Enz, Jacob. 2001. *The Christian and Warfare: The Roots of Pacifism in the Old Testament*. Eugene, OR: Wipf & Stock (reprint).

Fanon, Frantz. 1963. *The Wretched of the Earth*. New York: Grove.

Felder, Cain Hope, ed. 1991. *Stony the Road We Trod*. Minneapolis: Fortress Press.

Feyerabend, Paul. 2010. *Against Method*. New York: Verso.

Foskett, Mary F., and Jeffrey Kah-jin Kuan, eds. 2006. *Ways of Being, Ways of Reading: Asian American Biblical Interpretation*. St. Louis: Chalice.

Frend, W. H. C. 1984. *The Rise of Christianity*. Minneapolis: Fortress Press.

Gabler, Johann P. "An Oration on the Proper Distinction between Biblical and Dogmatic Theology and the Specific Objectives of Each." In Ollenburger, *Old Testament Theology*, 497–506.

Gafney, Wilda C. 2008. *Daughters of Miriam: Women Prophets in Ancient Israel*. Minneapolis: Fortress Press.

González, Justo L. 1996. *Santa Biblia: The Bible through Hispanic Eyes*. Nashville: Abingdon.

Gottwald, Norman. 1979. *The Tribes of Yahweh*. Maryknoll, NY: Orbis.

Grabbe, Lester. 2007. *Ancient Israel: What Do We Know and How Do We Know It?* New York: T&T Clark.

Habel, Norman. 1993. *The Land Is Mine: Six Biblical Land Ideologies*. Minneapolis: Fortress Press.

Hallman, David G. 1994. *Ecotheology: Voices from South and North*. Maryknoll, NY: Orbis.

Hayes, John H., and Frederick Prussner. 1984. *Old Testament Theology: Its History and Development*. Atlanta: John Knox.

Hopkins, Dwight N., and George C. L. Cummings, eds. 2003. *Cut Loose Your Stammering Tongue: Black Theology in the Slave Narratives*. Louisville: Westminster John Knox.

Janzen, David. 2012. *The Violent Gift: Trauma's Subversion of the Deuteronomistic History's Narrative*. LHB/OTS 561. London: T&T Clark.

Jenkins, Philip. 2002. *The Next Christendom: The Coming of Global Christianity*. New York: Oxford University Press.

———. 2006. *The New Faces of Christianity: Believing the Bible in the Global South*. New York: Oxford University Press.

Kelle, Brad. 2013. *Ezekiel*. New Beacon Bible Commentary. Kansas City: Beacon Hill.

Kuhn, Thomas. 1996. *The Structure of Scientific Revolutions*. 3rd ed. Chicago: University of Chicago Press.

Levine, Lawrence. 1977. *Black Culture and Black Consciousness.* New York: Oxford University Press.

Linzey, Andrew. 1995. *Animal Theology.* Urbana: University of Illinois Press.

———. 2009. *Creatures of the Same God.* New York: Lantern.

Mandolfo, Carleen. 2007. *Daughter Zion Talks Back to the Prophets.* Atlanta: Society of Biblical Literature.

Meyers, Carol. 1988/2013. *Rediscovering Eve: Ancient Israelite Women in Context.* Oxford: Oxford University Press.

Middleton, J. Richard. 2005. *The Liberating Image: The Imago Dei in Genesis 1.* Grand Rapids: Brazos.

Miller, David. 2011. *Animal Ethics and Theology.* New York: Routledge.

Muir, Lynette R. 1995. *The Biblical Drama of Medieval Europe.* Cambridge: Cambridge University Press.

Niang, Aliou. 2009. *Faith and Freedom in Galatia and Senegal.* Leiden: Brill.

Nichols, Aiden. 2007. *Lovely Like Jerusalem: The Fulfillment of the Old Testament in Christ and the Church.* San Francisco: Ignatius.

Niditch, Susan. 1993. *War and the Hebrew Bible: A Study in the Ethics of Violence.* Oxford: Oxford University Press.

Ngan, Lai Ling Elizabeth. 2006. "Neither Here nor There: Boundary and Identity in the Hagar Story." In Foskett and Kuan, *Ways of Being*, 70–83.

O'Connor, Kathleen. 2002. *Lamentations and the Tears of the World.* Maryknoll, NY: Orbis.

Ollenburger, Ben, ed. 2004. *Old Testament Theology: Flowering and Future, Sources for Biblical and Theological Study.* Winona Lake, IN: Eisenbrauns.

Overholt, Thomas. 1992. *Cultural Anthropology and the Old Testament.* Minneapolis: Fortress Press.

———. 2003. *Channels of Prophecy: The Social Dynamics of Prophetic Activity.* Eugene, OR: Wipf and Stock.

Perdue, Leo. 1994. *The Collapse of History: Reconstructing Old Testament Theology.* Minneapolis: Fortress Press.

Plantinga, Alvin. 2009. "Two (or More) Kings of Scripture Scholarship." In *Oxford Readings in Philosophical Theology*, vol. 2, *Providence, Scripture, and Resurrection*, ed. Michael C. Rea, 266–301. Oxford: Oxford University Press.

Pulido, Laura, Laura Barraclough, and Wendy Cheng, eds. 2012. *A People's Guide to Los Angeles.* Berkeley: University of California Press.

Raboteau, Albert J. 1978. *Slave Religion: The Invisible Institution in the Antebellum South.* New York: Oxford University Press.

Rogerson, John. 1984. *Old Testament Criticism in the Nineteenth Century: England and Germany.* London: SPCK.

———. 2010. *A Theology of the Old Testament.* Minneapolis: Fortress Press.

Roberts, Nathaniel. 2012. "Is Conversion a 'Colonization of Consciousness'?" *Anthropological Theory* 12:271–94.

Ruiz, Jean-Pierre. 2011. *Readings from the Edges: The Bible and People on the Move.* Maryknoll, NY: Orbis.

Said, Edward W. 1979. *Orientalism.* New York: Vintage.

Schüssler Fiorenza, Elisabeth. 2009. *Democratizing Biblical Studies.* Louisville: Westminster John Knox.

Segovia, Fernando F. 2000. *Decolonizing Biblical Studies: A View from the Margins.* Maryknoll, NY: Orbis.

Segovia, Fernando F., and Mary Ann Tolbert, eds. 1985. *Reading from this Place*, vol. 1, *Social Location and Biblical Interpretation in the United States.* Minneapolis: Fortress Press.

Smith-Christopher, Daniel. 2002. *A Biblical Theology of Exile.* Minneapolis: Fortress Press.

———. 2007. *Jonah, Jesus, and Other Good Coyotes: Speaking Peace to Power in the Bible.* Nashville: Abingdon.

Sommer, Benjamin, ed. 2012. *Jewish Concepts of Scripture: A Comparative Introduction.* New York: New York University Press.

Soyinka, Wole. 2003. *Samarkand and Other Markets I Have Known.* New York: Methuen.

Stanovich, Keith. 2004. *The Robot's Rebellion.* Chicago: University of Chicago Press.

Sugirtharajah, R. S., ed. 2006. *Voices from the Margin: Interpreting the Bible in the Third World.* 3rd ed. Maryknoll, NY: Orbis.

Summers, Harry G. 1984. "What Is War?" *Harper's*, May, 75–78.

Toly, Noah J., and Daniel I. Block, eds. 2010. *Keeping God's Earth: The Global Environment in Biblical Perspective.* Downers Grove, IL: IVP Academic.

Thompson, Thomas L. 1974. *The Historicity of the Patriarchal Narratives: The Quest for the Historical Abraham.* Berlin: de Gruyter.

Trible, Phyllis. 1984. *Texts of Terror: Literary-Feminist Readings of Biblical Narratives.* Minneapolis: Fortress Press.

Trimm, Charles. 2012. "Recent Research on Warfare in the Old Testament." *Currents in Biblical Research* 10:171–216.

Rad, Gerhard von. 1962. *Theology of the Old Testament.* Vol. 1. New York: Harper & Row.

———. 1965. *Theology of the Old Testament.* Vol. 2. New York: Harper & Row.

Warrior, Robert Allen. 1996. "Canaanites, Cowboys, and Indians." In *Native and Christian: Indigenous Voices on Religious Identity in the United States and Canada*, edited by James Treat, 93–104. New York: Routledge.

Weems, Renita J. 1991. "Reading Her Way through the Struggle: African American Women and the Bible." In Felder, *Stony the Road We Trod*, 57–77.

———. 1995. *Battered Love: Marriage, Sex, and Violence in the Hebrew Prophets.* Minneapolis: Fortress Press.

White, Lynn, Jr. 1967. "The Historical Roots of Our Ecological Crisis." *Science* 155:1203–7.

Wimbush, Vincent L., ed. 2000. *African Americans and the Bible: Sacred Texts and Social Textures.* New York: Continuum.

Yadin, Yigael. 1963. *The Art of Warfare in Biblical Lands.* London: Weidenfield & Nicolson.

Yee, Gale A. 2003. *Poor Banished Children of Eve: Woman as Evil in the Hebrew Bible.* Minneapolis: Fortress Press.

———. 2006. "Yin/Yang Is Not Me: An Exploration into an Asian-American Biblical Hermeneutics." In Foskett and Kuan, *Ways of Being*, 152–63.

THEMES AND PERSPECTIVES IN THE HISTORICAL WRITINGS

Norman K. Gottwald

Introduction

The so-called historical books of the Hebrew Bible provide a sweeping view of ancient Israel in the period from circa 1225 BCE to circa 400 BCE. These books form a continuous series in the Christian canon, extending from Joshua through Judges, 1–2 Samuel, 1–2 Kings, 1–2 Chronicles, Ezra-Nehemiah, and concluding with Esther. In the Jewish canon, Joshua through Kings are called the Former Prophets, 1–2 Chronicles and Nehemiah are included in the Writings, as is Esther, which is grouped with four other shorter books connected with Jewish festivals (the Megilloth). Joshua through Kings are probably named Former Prophets because they contain traditions about prophets who preceded Hosea (the first book listed in the Latter Prophets, also known as the Writing Prophets), and there is major attention to the prophets Elijah and Elisha in 1–2 Kings.

The flow of Israelite life begins with Joshua's conquest of Canaan and continues with the leadership of "judges" before recounting the fortunes of the united and divided kingdoms in 1–2 Samuel and 1–2 Kings. Interestingly, 1–2 Chronicles covers in part the same ground as Kings but does so by repeating much of Samuel-Kings, to which it adds traditions of its own, producing a decidedly more religious view of the monarchy than the former. Oddly, the period of the exile is omitted and the story line jumps to the postexilic return to Palestine (Ezra-Nehemiah) and ends with the outlier short story about a Jewess who rises to the status of queen of Persia (Esther).

Authorship and Date

The author or authors of the historical books are unknown, and in this respect they differ from the works of Herodotus and Thucydides of Greece, widely regarded as the first historians in the

Western world, who composed roughly at the same time as Joshua-Kings. The Greek histories are clearly written by identifiable individuals. By contrast, with an unknown author and a division into six books that differ greatly in design and style, the books of Joshua, Judges, 1–2 Samuel, and 1–2 Kings might easily be judged to constitute three separate books. The transition from Joshua to Judges and from Judges to 1 Samuel is abrupt, whereas the four volumes of Samuel and Kings flow seamlessly into one another. Chronicles stands apart as a briefer reinterpretation and supplement to the longer work.

Nonetheless, in Joshua-Kings, there is a continuity of viewpoint expressed in a common language at key junctures in all six books, demonstrating that the overall composition is the work of a single hand, or of a company of like minds. This unknown author, or joint authors, has been given the clumsy moniker of "the Deuteronomist" (hereafter as Dtr) because these historical books share a common vocabulary, style, and theology with the book of Deuteronomy. In fact, the book of Deuteronomy is the actual introduction for Dtr, even though it has been separated from the historical books and is counted as the last book of the Law in Jewish and Christian canons. For this reason, Joshua to Kings has been described as the Deuteronomistic History (hereafter as DH).

Apart from the common language and theology spanning the six volumes of DH, the contents of these historical books are sufficiently different that they pose the question: Is Dtr an author or an editor-compiler? We make the best sense of the literary data if we understand Dtr as both editor-compiler and author. Clearly DH has been composed of varied traditions differing greatly in genre and often reaching back in time, so that they constitute a veritable depth-dimensional anthology of Israel's historical and cultural memories. Consequently, the loosely connected stories of the judges read very differently from the smoothly rendered narratives about Samuel, Saul, and David, and the accounts of the so-called conquest of Canaan are far less likely to give us material for a history of Israel than information from Kings on the divided kingdoms of Israel and Judah. It almost goes without saying that a poem like the Song of Deborah (Judges 5) needs to be approached with quite another sensibility and mind-set than the tribal allotments. In short, scattered sources of varying age and provenance have been assembled and edited to form the contents of Dtr (the editor-compiler function) and stamped with an emphatic, even dogmatic, explanation of why Israel's history transpired as it did (the author function).

Likewise, Chronicles lacks an authorial identity, and the author is called simply the Chronicler (hereafter Chr). His compositional practices differ from those of Dtr in that there is a single, well-known primary source in 1–2 Chronicles, namely, the books of Samuel-Kings, which serve as the backbone of the work. In this dependence on a single published source, Chr operates in much the same manner as the New Testament Gospels of Matthew and Luke, whose authors employ Mark as the ground plan of their Gospels. The unique materials in 1–2 Chronicles include long genealogies that preface a glowing, almost rapturous account of David and his dynasty. These books have a compelling interest in the glorious dynasty of David, especially the religious practices in the temple prepared by David and built by his son Solomon. The names of priests and musicians who minister at the temple are recited. The northern kings are ignored except at points where they interact with the Davidic dynasty. Nonetheless, surprisingly, Chr issues an invitation for the apostate northern tribes to rejoin Judah, submit to the Davidic dynasty, and adhere to worship at the Jerusalem temple.

The date of the historical books is as uncertain as the identity of their author(s). Nevertheless, some clues to date appear within the documents. The narratives in DH and Chronicles stop abruptly with the fall of Jerusalem and the deportation of its upper class to Babylonia (the so-called exile). The sole exceptions are a reference by Dtr to the favor shown by a Babylonian ruler to the captive king Jehoiachin (2 Kgs. 25:27-30) and by Chr's inclusion of the proclamation of Cyrus the Persian in 538 BCE to return the deportees to Jerusalem and to rebuild the temple (2 Chron. 36:22-23). As a result, the critical fifty years between the eclipse of the political and religious sovereignty of Judah (586 BCE) and the proclaimed restoration of Judah as a province of the Persian Empire (538 BCE) are virtually a blank slate in the biblical historical record. It also means that the terminal stage in the composition of Joshua-Kings was later than the favor shown Jehoiachin in 561 BCE. Likewise, the finished composition of 1–2 Chronicles was later than the proclamation of Cyrus in 538 BCE. However, it is persuasively argued by some scholars that Joshua-Kings went through two editions, the first during the reign of King Josiah (640–609 BCE), celebrating a sweeping religious reform, and the final edition explaining why the kingdom of Judah was totally destroyed in spite of its promising future under Josiah. As a consequence, DH contains both the promise to David of an eternal dynasty and the nullification of that promise by the destruction of state and temple and the decimation of Judah's religious and political leadership. Chronicles softens the blow of exile by symbolizing exilic Judah as a land enjoying a Sabbath rest for seventy years, and little is made of the eclipse of the Davidic dynasty.

The books of Ezra and Nehemiah present yet a different picture. Past scholarship commonly understood Chr to be the author of these two books, but that attribution is now generally denied on stylistic and ideological grounds. The books tell of a period in the history of restored Judah, dated in the fifth century BCE, when the priest Ezra headed a sizable group of deportees returning to Judah and the layman Nehemiah served as governor of the province of Judah under Persian imperial rule. The two leaders are presented as contemporaries, but a close study of the disordered narrative suggests that Nehemiah came first and laid the foundation for the political and economic restoration of Judah that Ezra subsequently capitalized on in securing commitment of the populace to reforms that purify religious belief and practice. The sources of Ezra-Nehemiah include actual or allegedly Persian political documents, lists of returnees, and portions of first-person memoirs by Nehemiah and Ezra.

In contrast, Esther is a piece of historical fantasy telling how a young Judahite woman became queen of the Persian Empire and saved her people from a plot to annihilate them. The story reflects the known practice of Judahites serving at times in foreign administrations, but its descriptions of the Persian royal court and empire are distorted and exaggerated. It features a lurid account of how the table is turned on those who plan to massacre all Judahites in the kingdom, with the result that the nefarious plotters are visited with the fate that they intended for Esther's people. The book is connected to the festival of Purim, a late Jewish holiday of unknown origin. The intense hatred exhibited between Jews and gentiles appears to reflect the late Hasmonean dynasty, when Judah was briefly independent and a power-wielding player in Palestinian politics that pitted Jews against Hellenists, and even traditional Jews against Hellenized Jews. Esther is likely the latest book included in the Hebrew Bible, written between 180 and 80 BCE.

Clues to Reading the Historical Books

When we pick up a work of nonfiction, we often scan the introduction and conclusion in order to orient ourselves to the content, often to decide whether we want to read the whole book. The biblical historical books give us little such help. They plunge into their stories immediately, Dtr with "after the death of Moses," and Chr with the genealogy of David, who is unspecified until the end of its catalog of names, "Adam, Seth, Enosh . . ." The conclusions trail off with Dtr's "a regular allowance was given him [King Jehoiachin in Babylonian captivity] by the king [Evil-merodach, king of Babylon], every day a portion, as long as he lived," and Chr ends with the voice of Cyrus, king of Persia, speaking to the captive Judahites: "Whoever is among you of all his people, may the LORD his God be with him. Let him go up." Even the opening line of Deuteronomy, which is the first book of Dtr, is terse, "These are the words that Moses spoke to all Israel beyond the Jordan." Chr does not even offer a prefatory sentence but plunges into the story with a lengthy genealogy running from the first human to King David. In short, we must read some distance into the historical books, certainly beyond a speech by Moses (in Deuteronomy) or the alleged ancestry of David (in Chronicles), to get a sense of what they are about. Similarly, Nehemiah and Ezra require guidance to unravel the order of events in the two books, since they provide neither preface nor concluding summary.

Because the historical books are normally read individually according to the interests that scholars and ordinary readers bring to the biblical text, it is easy to overlook the great differences among them. For one thing, with the exception of Ezra and Nehemiah, the principal characters receive unequal space. A long narrative in DH recounting the reigns of Saul, David, and Solomon is spread over two and a half books, namely, 1 Sam. 1:1—1 Kgs. 11:43. This account of the first three kings of Israel is a developed narrative, with plot, connected episodes, and vivid characters, whereas Joshua, Judges, and the remainder of post-Solomonic kings (1 Kings 12—2 Kings 17) are described by single stories, clusters of stories, or excerpts from royal archives, either unconnected or only loosely connected. As the kingdom of Judah nears its end, however, Dtr provides a more integral narrative from Hezekiah to Zedekiah (2 Kgs. 18–25). Some of the sources of Dtr are cited in the text: the Book of Jashar (Josh. 10:15; 2 Sam. 1:18); the Book of the Acts of Solomon (1 Kgs. 11:41); the Book of the Acts of the Kings of Israel (beginning with 1 Kgs. 14:9, et passim); the Book of the Acts of the Kings of Judah (1 Kgs. 14:29, et passim). The poems of Hannah, David, and Deborah may derive from liturgical usage. Accordingly, the known and likely pre-Dtr writings are clusters of written, possibly oral, traditions, recounting the activities of a colorful cast of characters both political and religious.

Thus the first three kings of Israel receive as much press as all the remaining kings of Israel and Judah! Most of the kings are treated in brief cameos, with the fullest attention given to Jeroboam I, Ahab, Jehu, Jehoshaphat, Jehoash, Hezekiah, and Josiah, as well as extended legends about the prophets Elijah and Elisha, who interact critically, and less often supportively, with the northern house of Omri. Most of the monarchs are presented hurriedly, with the briefest of comments on their reigns. Unmistakably, David is the prime personage for Dtr, and even more so for Chr. All the action and energy in Joshua and Judges points toward the coming house of David, but after

Solomon, the dynasty of David is in decline and is finally extinguished by the Neo-Babylonians. Dtr presents David as the acme of royal popularity, piety, and virtue (in spite of his glaring shortcomings). Solomon receives great wisdom, but squanders the political unity of the kingdom achieved by David. In short, the reader must approach DH aware of the literary habits and notions about "history" typical of ancient Israelite narration of past events, as they impinge on and give shape to the present time of the author.

Sources and Composition

Dtr employs several structural and rhetorical devices that underscore the leading themes and signal the important stages and turning points in the story. Attention to these compositional features enhances appreciation of the challenges Dtr faced in composing his lengthy history from seemingly incompatible materials. Dtr not only unifies his work with transitions that link era to era but also employs several devices to link individual texts within each segment of history and spanning two or more segments. These thematic and rhetorical devices are editorial maneuvers that show DH to be a single document, forged from many documents and oral traditions and sprinkled with editorial comments and connections that show a consistent religious ideology. The architecture of this literary tour de force, like centuries-old cathedrals, is in no way diminished if, as seems likely, it has been worked on by several editors with shared understandings.

Grand Design

It is fairly easy to identify the principal theme of Dtr as the momentous clash between two versions of the Israelite story: the conditional terms of the Mosaic covenant and the unconditional terms of the Davidic covenant. The more challenging task is to bring to light the literary means by which that clash is represented. What makes the movement from Joshua to Kings so engaging is that we see at each point in the history a clash between the two covenants, but in different guises and with a constantly changing cast of characters. Assuming that Dtr aimed to show how the two covenants played out through the centuries after Moses, the big challenge was to decide what sources to use, how to arrange them, and how to link the sources into a continuous story from Joshua to the collapse of the two kingdoms.

Dtr had in hand several blocks of material, each dealing with a segment of that long history: taking of the land of Canaan; judges arising in a tribal system; the united kingdom under three successive kings, Saul, David, and Solomon; splitting into two states, one in the north (Israel) and one in the south (Judah), followed by the sequence of the kings in each monarchy and the loss of independence for both. It is crucial to realize that Dtr was not writing six books but one segmented history only later divided into six books within the canon. The four segments of Dtr's work are sewn together with transitional links:

> **Era of the Occupation of Canaan**
> with a link to the era of judges: Joshua's death and burial (Josh. 24:29-33)
> repeated in the introduction to the judges (Judg. 2:6-10)

Era of the Judges
with a link to the united kingdom: annual festivals at Shiloh provide the setting for the last episode about judges (Judg. 21:16-23) and the first episode about the United Kingdom (1 Samuel 1)

Era of the United Kingdom
with a link to the divided kingdoms: episodes of Jeroboam and Ahijah before the death of Solomon (1 Kgs. 11:26-31) and after the death of Solomon (1 Kgs. 12:15)

Era of the Divided Kingdoms
ends with destruction of the two kingdoms, deportation of Judahite officials to Babylon, and an open-ended note about the favor shown to captive King Zedekiah by a Neo-Babylonian ruler.

The era of the united kingdom is told in a continuous narrative, by far the most cohesive segment of Dtr. In fact, many interpreters have treated the so-called Court History of David as an eyewitness account, so vividly and artfully is it fashioned (2 Samuel 9–20; 1 Kings 1–2). However, the sources for the other eras were not as cohesive, so that Dtr had to find a way of shaping them into an ongoing narrative. With the era of Joshua, the stories and lists are framed by his introductory and farewell speeches. With the era of the judges, Dtr linked episodes by means of an artificial cyclical framework with a repeated pattern: Israel does evil by abandoning the covenant, YHWH punishes the people by oppression at the hand of enemies, the oppressed Israelites cry out for deliverance from oppression, YHWH rescues the Israelites by raising up a military judge, and at the death of the judge the Israelites revert to their evil ways. Then the identical cycle is repeated several times. For the final phase of his history, Dtr tells the story of the divided kingdoms by drawing information about each king from royal archives, and using a formula that includes length of the reign and a verdict of good or bad on the king's performance. Dtr inserts into this scheme a cycle of stories about the northern prophets Elijah and Elisha, largely folk traditions that venerate them as YHWH loyalists and defenders of the people.

Programmatic Texts

Lacking introduction and conclusion, the dominant themes of Dtr have to be ferreted out in the course of its narrative. Set in motion by Moses' command to observe the law (Deuteronomy 1–4), interpretive passages at strategic points throughout the history describe and explain how the unfolding course of events is shaped by Israel's failure to adhere to that law. Counting Deuteronomy as the fountainhead and pacesetter for the historical books, these programmatic texts are presented in the form of speeches and prayers by the leaders of Israel and discourses or notations by the author. Among the most important of these programmatic texts are the following:

Parting speech of Moses (Deuteronomy 29–30)
Inaugural speech of Joshua (Josh. 1:10-15)
Speech of God introducing the covenant (Josh. 24:1-13)
Speech of Joshua at the making of the covenant (Josh. 24:14-28)

Discourses on the Judges (Judg. 2:6—3:6; 10:10-16)
Speech of Samuel about kingship (1 Samuel 8)
Parting speech of Samuel (1 Samuel 12)
Speech of Nathan and prayer of David (2 Sam. 7:4-29)
Blessing of the temple, prayer, and speech of Solomon (1 Kgs. 8:14-61)
Speech of God to Solomon (1 Kgs. 9:1-9)
Speech of Ahijah to Jeroboam (1 Kgs. 11:29-40)
Message of the Assyrian general to Hezekiah (2 Kgs. 18:19-25; 19:8-13)
Speech of the Assyrian general to the Jerusalemites (2 Kgs. 18:28-35)
Discourse on the fall of the northern kingdom [Israel] (2 Kgs. 17:7-23, 34-40),
Discourse and speech on the fall of the southern kingdom [Judah] (2 Kgs. 21:2-16)

When these pivotal texts are read together, it becomes abundantly clear that the central motifs in DH are the binding law of Moses and the promise of an everlasting dynasty to David. While both themes are of immense importance, they stand in radical contradiction to one another. This series of texts is as close as Dtr comes to explicitly disclosing his own interpretation of the story he composes. In the end, obedience to the law trumps the promise to David. The stunning consequence is that the dynasty of David is cut off with the fall of Jerusalem. Nevertheless, the outcome of the conflict between the law of Moses and the dynasty of David is so skillfully delayed by Dtr that the reader is kept in suspense until the final years of the kingdom of Judah.

Lists of Names

While the programmatic texts of Dtr give a measure of coherence to the history, there is another type of text favored by Dtr that militates against narrative coherence, at least for today's reader. Contemporary readers are easily intimidated by the lists of the names of persons and places that disturb, even interrupt, the narrative flow, most grievously so in Chr. These personal names are identified as ancestors, officials, and priests with specified duties and privileges, or deported leaders. The named places are variously tribal regions, monarchic territories, or political and religious sites. In DH, these recitals of the names of people and places occur frequently and at times bridge the gaps between narrated events:

Conquered and unconquered kings and territories in Canaan (Josh. 12:1—13:6; 23:1-13)
Land allotments of the tribes (Josh. 13:6b—19:51)
Minor judges (Judg. 10:1-5; 12:7-13)
David's officials (2 Sam. 8:15-18)
David's mighty warriors and bodyguards (1 Sam. 23:8-39)
Solomon's officials (1 Kgs. 4:1-19)
Details of Solomon's palace and temple (2 Kgs. 6—8)
Ahaz's alteration of temple worship (2 Kgs. 16:15-18)
Assyrian deportation of Israelites replaced by foreign captives (2 Kgs. 17:6, 24)

Foreign gods accepted by Samaritans (2 Kgs. 17:29-31)
Officials of Judah deported to Babylon (2 Kgs. 24:10-17; 25:11, 18-21)

Some of these are lists in freestanding form, while others have been more or less integrated into the narrative. In a modern history, much of this sort of information would be relegated to footnotes or appendixes. Nevertheless, some of these narrative "asides" preserve informative details of historical value, especially the data from state archives. In 1–2 Chronicles, in addition to the lists, the author also attaches names to each of the many sources he cites. Some of these sources, if not all, seem to be modeled on the less frequent naming of sources in DH:

In 1 Chronicles (samples)
Lineage of David and the tribal heads (1–9)
David's mighty men (11)
David's Levitical musicians (15:16-24)
Priests and officials in court of David (24–27)

In 2 Chronicles (samples)
Solomon's building projects and chief officers (8:1-10)
Solomon's riches (9:13-28)
Rehoboam's fortified cities (11:5-12)
Jehoshaphat's princes and Levites' instruction of people in the law (17:7-9)
Levites cleanse the temple and restore the utensils Ahaz discarded (29:12-19)
Officers collect offerings for the temple (31:11-15)
Workmen repair and restore the temple (34:8-13)

The books of Ezra-Nehemiah give census-like lists of names that seek both to describe and to authenticate the return of the exiles to Judah. The whole assembly of returnees is said to consist of 42,360 priests and laity, plus 7,337 of their servants (Ezra 1–2). Of course, these figures cannot be verified, but they are strikingly less than the hundreds of thousands elsewhere in DH. Furthermore, the rebuilders of the walls of Jerusalem are identified by name and the section of the wall they worked on (Nehemiah 3).

The effect of these lists is to break the momentum of the story line, or at least to slow it down dramatically, especially so if the reader pauses to dwell on the names listed. Truth be told, these lists contribute to the impression that DH is a miscellany of traditions held together by a chronology of questionable merit. Since most of the lists appear to be collected by Dtr and Chr, rather than composed by them, their original life settings are a matter of conjecture. Many were excerpted from governmental or temple documents. It is debated as to whether the name lists actually belonged to the historical settings to which Dtr and Chr assign them or rather were derived from later historical contexts and reassigned to Joshua, David, Solomon, or a later king. One thing seems abundantly clear: both author and original readers found delight in punctuating narrative texts with lists of this sort. It is conceivable that it was a matter of pride that the narrator could confidently produce such details to embellish and authenticate the narrative.

Chronological Schemes

For long stretches of DH, there are no temporal indicators, but at certain points the narrative is punctuated, even organized, by temporal considerations. These markers are often simply given in round numbers. The most elaborate temporal scheme in round numbers is the forty-year periods of rest secured by several judges who delivered Israel from foreign oppressors (Othniel, Deborah, Gideon, and Samson, with an eighty-year [2 × 40] rest for the land secured by Ehud). Forty years seems to be an idiom for "a very long time," also claimed as the length of rule by both David and Solomon. This amplitude of time is contrasted with the ill-fated Saul, whose reign of two years is cited in a broken text (1 Sam. 13:1), which speaks for his failure as king, even though he is estimated to have ruled for as much as twenty years. On the other hand, the so-called minor judges are assigned periods of office in an irregular pattern along a spectrum from six years (Jephthah), to seven (Ibzan), eight (Abadon), ten (Elon), twenty-two (Jair), and twenty-three years (Tola). It is not always clear whether the specified years were already in Dtr's sources or were introduced by him.

When Dtr reaches the divided kingdoms, instead of rounded numbers, we encounter precisely calibrated periods of time for the reigns of all the kings of north and south. Dtr informs us that this chronological information is derived from the royal annals of Israel and Judah. The reigns in the two kingdoms are staggered, switching back and forth in an ingenious method that confuses readers, because the account does not move forward in a straight line but doubles back to catch up on events that occurred earlier in the other kingdom. This method is a way of emphasizing the point that the two kingdoms have a common religious heritage, enduring even when they are political enemies.

There is no reason to doubt the authenticity of the records, especially since at the points where events in Kings are also recounted in extrabiblical texts, the biblical numbers are accurate enough in terms of an absolute chronology. The split into two kingdoms can be dated to 930 BCE, plus or minus no more than ten years, and narrowing to a one-year difference for the fall of the northern kingdom in 722–721 BCE and the destruction of Judah in 587–586 BCE. This of course is not to claim that everything Dtr says about particular kings is factual or that the court records praised or maligned kings as Dtr does. It does, however, strengthen the hypothesis that kings with the biblical names did rule in north and south within the time spans indicated, and that claims Dtr makes about what happened during their reigns must be given serious consideration, which is not the same as validating Dtr's interpretations of events.

Confounded by the early death of Josiah and the subsequent collapse of Judah so soon after the sweeping reforms of Josiah, Dtr resorts to blaming the decline and fall of Judah on Manasseh, "because of all the provocations with which Manasseh had provoked [the LORD]" (2 Kgs. 23:25-27). This is strange since Manasseh preceded Josiah, whose reforms proceed on the assumption that the heartfelt repentance and zealous reforming program of Josiah totally reversed the apostate policies of Manasseh his predecessor. Adding to the confusion is the promise to Josiah that "you shall be gathered to your grave in peace" (2 Kgs. 22:20), an assurance immediately shattered by Josiah's untimely death (2 Kgs. 23:29-30). Even more anomalous is the report by Chr that when Josiah sallied forth to confront Neco, the pharaoh advised him not to attack his Egyptian forces. Speaking in the unexpected role of a prophet, the pharaoh warns Josiah, "Cease opposing God, who is with me [Neco], so that he will not destroy you [Josiah].... He did not listen to the words of Neco from the mouth of God" (2 Chron. 35:20-24). This jumbling of events, both propitious and ominous, represents groping attempts by Dtr and Chr to find causal relationships between Judah's apostate past, its sudden radical renewal, and its precipitous decline and downfall after the reign of Josiah.

Predictions/Commands and Their Fulfillment

Dtr pictures the word of God as often delivered by prophets who predict future events that unfailingly occur or who issue peremptory commands not to be questioned. Even before prophets begin to appear at the dawn of monarchy, Joshua utters an oath declaring that anyone who even starts to rebuild Jericho will do so "at the cost" of his older and younger sons (Josh. 6:26), and this curse is activated during the reign of Ahab, when Hillel of Bethel loses both of his sons upon laying the foundation stone and erecting the gates of Jericho (1 Kgs. 16:33-34). Ahijah prophesies the split into two kingdoms and later announces that the house of Jeroboam will be wiped out because of his idolatry (1 Kgs. 11:29-31; 12:12-5; 14:17-18; 15:29). When an old prophet of Bethel discovers a second prophet has lied, he announces that the lying prophet will not be buried in his family tomb, which proves to be the case after he is killed by a lion (1 Kgs. 13:20-32).

Shemaiah, by the word of the Lord, forbids Rehoboam to try to quell the rebellion of the north: "You shall not go up or fight against your kindred the people of Israel," so Rehoboam doesn't (1 Kgs. 12:22-24). Jehu ben Hanani announces the overthrow of the house of Baasha (16:1-4, 7). Elijah declares a three-year drought in the land (1 Kgs. 17:1) and ends it by defeating the prophets of Baal (1 Kgs. 18:1, 45). Elijah specifies that Ahab will die in Jezreel, the very place where he seized Naboth's vineyard, and he does (1 Kgs. 21:17-19; 22:37-38).

The most awesome of these predictions is made by an unnamed "man of God" who not only declares that the altar at Bethel where Jeroboam worships will be destroyed, but actually names Josiah as the future king who will destroy the profane altar (1 Kgs. 13:1-2). In this instance, the prophet is described as foreseeing an action by a ruler who will not ascend the throne until nearly three hundred years later and will indeed destroy the altar at Bethel as prophesied (2 Kgs. 23:15-20). Isaiah, on hearing that God will spare the life of Hezekiah, declares that the sick king will be healed and add fifteen years to his life (2 Kgs. 20:1-7). Sometimes the prophet not only announces what is to come but also serves as the agent of fulfillment, as when Elisha incites Jehu to overthrow the house of Ahab because of the wickedness of Jezebel, the Baal-worshiping queen, who killed the prophets of God (1 Kgs. 9:1-3, 6-10). And Isaiah becomes the agent for Hezekiah to live on by applying a poultice of figs to the king's boil (2 Kgs. 20:7).

These close engagements of prophets in the unfolding history emphasize that God determines the course of events in response to Israel's fitful commitment to the covenant with YHWH. The prophetic words and actions underscore the thoroughly religious evaluation of the history of the two kingdoms. The literary effect of these prophetic interventions is to move the story forward, to compensate as it were for the interrupting name lists and to give implementation to the programmatic texts. In this way, God's guidance of the history is implemented through persons who are active in the story, but whose authority is independent of the established political and religious leadership, and who as "outsiders" are able to anticipate the outcome of Israel's adherence to or violation of its covenant with God.

Book by Book

One searching for a plot in DH might summarize it on this order: It is the story of a tribal people in covenant with God who, after long bondage, acquire a homeland with great effort in the face of opposition from outside and conflicts within, and who transition from tribal life to a monarchic form of government that, in spite of its pomp and prosperity, splits into two states. Increasingly, these states are dominated by foreign powers, against whom they rebel and are defeated, their leadership deported, and their political and religious independence lost. This downfall of the kingdoms is repeatedly explained as the punishment of God for the people's abandonment of the covenant.

Summarized in this manner, however, the story feels abstract and colorless, lacking the vivid force of the stories about judges, kings, priests, and prophets—brilliant narratives that have earned the praise of Jewish, Christian, and secular readers. Moreover, such a plot summary fails to capture the overarching tension between adhering to or departing from prescribed religious practice that Dtr asserts to be the determining factor in Israel's history. It is a "tragic" tale, but a course self-chosen by the people who nevertheless should have known better, having been warned of the consequences of disobeying the law of Moses (Deuteronomy 27–28). So one of the abiding attractions of DH consists in the way it introduces its readers to religious and political leaders around whom political and religious forces swirl with an uncertain outcome: led by such leaders, will this people live on or die off?

A more detailed book-by-book account of Joshua through Kings reveals the events of Israel's past that Dtr counts as of importance in understanding how and why its initial achievements are cut short by the demise of the kingdoms of Israel and Judah.

Book of Joshua

The book of Joshua is the first chapter in the centuries-long story Dtr records. It begins with Moses handing off leadership of Israel to Joshua with the charge to conquer the land of Canaan. This follows directly on the final verses of Deuteronomy. The significance of Deuteronomy for understanding Dtr is that it presents a body of laws incumbent on Israel to observe (Deuteronomy 12–26), and it is precisely by these laws that Dtr passes judgment on the priests, prophets, and kings of Israel. He gives each of them a "thumbs up" or a "thumbs down" depending on whether or not they have complied with the laws.

To be sure, Joshua purports to be obeying the laws, but he himself fails to fully obey the divine command to annihilate all the inhabitants of Canaan. Joshua aggressively attacks Jericho, Ai, and

Hazor, but he exempts Rahab (Joshua 2; 6:22-25) and the Gibeonite cities (Joshua 9; 10:1-6) from destruction, even though the latter have tricked Joshua into entering a treaty with them. So, although the laws are to be kept in their totality on pain of death (Deuteronomy 28), the first generation after Moses is already knowingly breaking them. Israelites have joined Canaanites in marriage and in worship, which is tantamount to breaking faith with the God of Israel. Much as Joshua has tried to conquer the entire promised land, large parts of Canaan and Transjordan remain unconquered. The stated reason for this failure is that the conquerors have broken divine commands and must accept partial victory as their punishment. However, a bit later in DH, a different reason is given for the continued resistance of Canaanites: they are allowed to stay on in the land in order to train Israel in the arts of war (Judg. 3:1-2).

Book of Judges

The most striking feature of the book of Judges is the dramatic change in the protagonist of the story. In Joshua, as throughout the Torah, the subject of the story is a united people, Israel, under the leadership of Joshua, in continuity with the united people under Moses. Suddenly in the stories of Judges, the single entity Israel breaks into its tribal components who act alone or in combinations as they choose. The largest of these intertribal actions is celebrated in the Song of Deborah, where six tribes fight together and four tribes are condemned for failing to show up for battle (Judges 5). This presupposes that Israel consists of tribal units that ought to act in unison but may not do so. In the other episodes in Judges, the actors are single tribes, or at most two or three together, with charismatic military leaders who arise from time to time: Othniel, Ehud, Deborah, Gideon, Jephthah, and Samson. Dtr presents these leaders of the moment as the best Israel can muster to carry on the work of Moses and Joshua, yet most of them show no knowledge of the Mosaic law by which Dtr judges them!

Only in the last episode of the book are all the tribes united, save one, to punish the tribe of Benjamin because it is held responsible for the rape and murder of a Levite's concubine (Judges 19–21). The book ends with a detailed account of this horrific crime, which the narrator insists demands a king, who would presumably prevent such deplorable behavior (21:25). It appears that Dtr wants to conceive of Israel as a unity, but is pressured by his sources into drawing the picture of a seriously fragmented people who repeatedly breach the law of Moses. Only the long-suffering lenience of YHWH allows the story of Israel to continue. The last word of Judges, "In those days there was no king in Israel; every man [tribe?] did what was right in his [its?] own eyes (21:25)," clearly anticipates the kingdom of David, as it also embraces the implicit understanding that the deeds condemned in the book are not only divisive of community but also stand in blatant violation of the law. However, which deeds are condemned? Only those of the Gibeonites, or also of Micah and the Danites (Judges 17–18), as well as the idolatry that leads to the cycles of oppression and deliverance? What about the behavior of the judges who deliver Israel but also engage in actions inimical to the laws? Abimelech, the would-be king, dies in retribution for the murder of his brothers, and the Shechemites who follow him perish as the just punishment for their folly (Judg. 9:56-57), but there is no claim that he is a judge, even a lapsed judge.

Books of Samuel and Kings: The United Kingdom

The history of the united kingdom of David and Solomon is told in one long stretch in 1–2 Samuel and 1 Kings 1–11. Dtr accords so much space to telling the story of the establishment of the monarchy in part because his sources were especially abundant for this era, but also because he wants to describe the historical roots of the Davidic dynasty and the Jerusalem temple, the two institutions that rival the law of Moses in importance, which are not necessarily in conflict, but become so as the post-Solomonic rulers undermine the moral foundations of dynasty and temple. Extended attention is given to tracing the rise of David to the kingship, with the intention to exonerate him of all suspicions that he conspired against Saul. The reported decline of Saul is intertwined with the ascent of David as his rival and eventual successor. Once established on the throne, serious conflicts erupt within David's family following his murder of Uriah in order to acquire Bathsheba as wife. These family conflicts are intertwined with his struggle to retain the throne against rebellions, one being led by his own son, Absalom. Although David is rebuked by Nathan the prophet, and David even "repents" of the Bathsheba affair, he is not required to give her up (2 Sam. 12:1-25), and it is Bathsheba's cunning advocacy that secures the throne for her son Solomon (1 Kgs. 1:11-21, 28-31).

The achievements of David as king, beyond his military successes against the Philistines and Transjordanian kings, are lightly touched on. His rule over his subjects is pictured as being much less onerous than that of Solomon. David aspires to build a permanent temple for YHWH in Jerusalem, but is prevented from doing so by the prophet Nathan, who declares God's extreme displeasure with "a man of blood" honoring the deity in this fashion (2 Samuel 7). David proves very indulgent of his adult sons and seems to have been lax in his duties as chief justice in the system of criminal law. All in all, David is portrayed as remarkably human in showing his failings as well as his accomplishments. The David described here is far from the paragon of virtue and piety elsewhere venerated as preeminent psalmist (2 Sam. 23:1) and the very model of the messianic ruler to come (Isa. 9:1-7; 11:1-9). Solomon becomes successor to David after a bitter dynastic fight in which he forcibly suppresses a powerful faction backing his brother Adonijah.

Opening his reign with an iron fist, Solomon is emboldened to launch an ambitious program to increase the wealth and extend the power of his kingdom. His basic resources were heavy taxation on the agricultural surpluses of his peasant subjects, supplemented by income from tolls on caravans in transit, as well as shrewd commercial deals as middle man for the arms sales of Anatolian horses and Egyptian chariots to other states. In order to secure his booming economic empire, Solomon reaches for military superiority by building massive fortifications and equipping large chariot forces. With his newfound wealth, he builds the temple in Jerusalem that his father had been forbidden to build, along with a palace that greatly exceeds the temple in size. This temple would have been little more than a royal chapel rather than the national shrine that Dtr anachronistically envisions as the sole legitimate place of worship in Israel.

To facilitate state administration, Solomon redistricts his kingdom and appoints officials in each of the new districts, centralizing his command structure to secure delivery of taxes and to forestall rebellion against his regime, such as the rebellions David had to put down (1 Kgs. 4:1-28). In short, Solomon is pictured as hugely successful in securing a luxurious and privileged life for a small upper class in government and trade, but only with contradictory policies that threaten agricultural production by pulling peasants off the land to form labor battalions for his pet building projects (5:13-18; 9:10-21). He overspends to the point that he has to pay off a debt to the king of Tyre by surrendering a sizable area of his kingdom (1 Kgs. 9:10-14).

One would think that the enhancement of the power and wealth of his kingdom would have secured Solomon the unalloyed approval of Dtr. This, however, is not the case. It is true that the king's successes are attributed to wisdom bestowed on him by God (1 Kgs. 3:3-28; 4:29-34). Moreover, the lavish adornment of the temple and its appointments and the pomp of its dedication are reported in great detail, because for Dtr the building of the temple is Solomon's principal achievement (1 Kings 5–6; 7:9-51). In fact, Dtr insists that this Jerusalem temple is the sole site where YHWH worship can henceforth be carried out, and it becomes the litmus test by which Dtr judges all later kings: Did they or did they not restrict worship to Jerusalem? In glaring contrast to his noble start, Solomon eventually falls into idolatry by adopting the gods of the many wives he has acquired in diplomatic alliances with other countries (1 Kgs. 11:1-13)

A further contradiction arises when it becomes evident that Jeroboam, the leader of the northern labor battalions, rebels against Solomon, not because of idolatry in the narrow religious sense, but because of the heavy social and economic burdens Solomon's policy of forced labor has imposed on the north (1 Kgs. 11:27; 12:1-20). To further complicate Dtr's account, the split of the kingdom approved as divine punishment on Solomon automatically consigns all northern worship of YHWH to idolatry, since the northerners no longer recognize the religious legitimacy of the Davidic dynasty in Jerusalem and will henceforth have nothing to do with worship in what has now become a foreign state (12:25-33). In effect, Jeroboam is damned if he does separate from Judah and damned if he doesn't!

Book of Kings: The Two Kingdoms

It is axiomatic for Dtr that Solomon built a temple intended to be the sole place of worship in his kingdom and in the reigns of all his successors. In his account of the two kingdoms, Dtr holds fast to this prohibition of worship at any other site than the Jerusalem temple. This immediately means that any and all worship practiced in the northern kingdom is condemned by Dtr, even though the northern prophets (Elijah and Elisha and later Hosea), while lambasting their rulers for infidelity to YHWH, do not include failure to worship at Jerusalem as one of these infractions. It also means that every subsequent ruler in Judah is judged by a religious requirement that did not come into force until centuries later under Kings Hezekiah and Josiah. Consequently, even when Dtr has some good things to say about particular kings, he counts their rule as a failure if they allow worship at any other place in the kingdom (characteristically, "on the high places" of false worship).

In spite of this grossly contradictory and flagrantly anachronistic religious criterion that Dtr has applied to the post-Solomonic rulers of both kingdoms, his account provides a considerable body of information about social, political, and religious conditions. Much of this information appears to have been drawn from court documents cited as "the Book of the Records of the Kings of Israel," paired with a similar source for the kings of Judah. Where the chronology of the royal reigns intersects with events also reported by Assyrian and Babylonian texts, its dates are confirmed. There is also information about religious developments in both kingdoms, which disclose practices outlawed by Deuteronomy. In addition, there is a sizable body of traditions about the northern prophets Elijah and Elisha, who worship apart from Jerusalem without Dtr's censure. These inconsistencies in the criteria in the historical books for valid worship are indicative of a document that tells us the views of Dtr and his several sources without much of an attempt to reconcile them.

Instead of recounting the two histories one after the other, or interweaving their fortunes so as to emphasize certain phases or aspects of the two histories, Dtr treats political events in Israel and Judah in self-contained literary panels devoted to each ruler. Moreover, the sequence of these panels switches back and forth between north and south. The result is a staggered recital of the two kingdom histories, entailing some repetitions and a certain amount of chronological "backtracking." Into this synchronic framework are inserted annalistic accounts of diplomatic maneuvers, battles, political coups and purges, deeds of prophets, and religious reforms. Chronicles follows the same regnal formulas for Judah as does 1–2 Kings but lacks the latter's synchronisms, since it does not recount the full history of the north but only episodes involving Judah.

Ingenious as is this interweaving of the northern and southern histories, it fails to give a balanced, coherent account, broken as it is into brief glimpses of the reigns of a majority of the kings, but alternating with fuller accounts of others. This creates a pronounced disproportion in coverage, such that we have in effect two styles of presentation, one consisting of little more than a chronicling of events and the other going into greater detail about rulers who initiated religious reforms centered on the Jerusalem temple (Jehoash, Hezekiah, Josiah) or who interacted with prophets (Ahab, Hezekiah), while saying surprisingly little about kings whom we otherwise know or suspect to have been major political figures (Omri, Jeroboam II, Manasseh).

Why did Dtr resort to such a tortuous manner of recounting the histories of the two kingdoms? He did so, it seems, in order to underscore his belief that the history of the two kingdoms was actually the history of one people with a common religion. Politically, there were two kingdoms, but they spoke the same language, shared the same culture, and practiced the same religion, albeit in regional variations. Following the acclaimed reigns of David and Solomon, the rulers of the two kingdoms, with a few exceptions, are described as a sorry lot, unacceptable to YHWH because of the political corruption, social injustice, and religious apostasy they practiced or permitted. The exceptions are Hezekiah and Josiah, who undertook religious reforms that cleansed the Jerusalem temple of foreign accretions and reestablished it as the sole legitimate place of worship. The reforms of Josiah so closely correspond to the religious demands of Deuteronomy that the book on which Josiah is said to have based his actions is generally taken to be Deuteronomy or some version thereof. The reforms of Hezekiah manage to spare Jerusalem from destruction by the Assyrians, but in spite of Josiah's laudable, more extensive reforms, they do not prevent Josiah from execution by the Egyptians or the eventual destruction of Jerusalem and its temple by the Neo-Babylonians. These political catastrophes following earnest reforms are so troubling to Dtr that he explains them as due to the evil deeds of King Manasseh, which outweigh the reformers' achievements.

Fact-Checking the Historical Books

Are the "historical books" an accurate account of the early history of Israel? Yes and no.

No, in the sense that they are not word-for-word transcripts of events that occurred long ago, and they misjudge the time when worship at the Jerusalem temple was mandated as the sole place of worship for all Israelites. The events recorded and the time and place of those doing the recording are so far removed from one another—often by many centuries—that the very capacity of Dtr and Chr to know the past in great detail is thrown into doubt, and the sources at their disposal lack no more than scraps of eyewitness testimony. The sources they depended on mostly showed so little interest in doing history as we know it that we do them an injustice to measure them against the practices of present-day historiography.

Both "historians" certainly had an urgent reason for writing as they did. Their overwhelming concern was to describe the past as best they could in order to lay a foundation for rebuilding a new "Israelite/Judahite" community after the destruction of Jerusalem. They differ, however, in what they conceive that "foundation" to be. Writing after the temple is rebuilt, Chr asserts that the future of Israel lies in faithful worship at the restored temple led by priests and Levites according to the arrangement prescribed by David and Solomon. Writing before the restoration of Judah, Dtr has in mind that the society prescribed in the book of Deuteronomy should be the basis of the restored community. However, Deuteronomy's laws had been so infrequently observed in the history that it seemed unthinkable for Dtr to anticipate an independent Judah. That would require the dubious return of the dynasty of David, not to mention permission and support from the imperial overlord, Neo-Babylonia or Persia. He is so deeply uncertain about Israel's future that he can offer no more than the hint of the future by relating the favor accorded to the captive king of Judah by the Neo-Babylonian king. Concerning the condition of the survivors of the fall of the northern kingdom, Dtr and Chr seem to have no knowledge and little historical interest.

Yes, Dtr writes a trustworthy "history," provided we allow a fairly broad conception of history-writing and correct for anachronisms. However, when Chr introduces material not in Dtr, it is of uncertain worth. The genre in which Dtr and Chr have cast their narratives is sometimes called "history-like tradition." In short, they are works of the historical imagination, employing the sources at hand but shaped by the imaginative vision of the writer. Dtr presents an amazing array of portraits of the past, some being better anchored historically than others. Chr presents a monochromatic view of the past, single-mindedly focused on the ascent and triumph of David and erection of the temple by Solomon, with no more than a glance at other aspects of Israel's past. Chr's account is narrowly and unrelentingly religious, with no interest in Joshua, Judges, or events in the life of David before he ascends the throne.

In assessing the accuracy of Dtr, it is essential to understand his mind-set. Dtr is primarily interested in the religion of ancient Israel. He traces the fortune of the belief and practice of Yahwism, reaching heights under David, Solomon, Hezekiah, and Josiah but lapsing into idolatry and prohibited behavior for long stretches of time under judges and kings. Sadly, a majority of the populace of both kingdoms has abandoned the cult of YHWH or clings to corrupt forms of worship. In Dtr's view, God has tolerated this faithlessness and corruption for centuries. In exasperation, God finally abandons both kingdoms and delivers them to conquest by the Assyrian Empire and the Neo-Babylonian Empire. Over the centuries, the erring people of Israel and Judah have become so apostate that God delivers both kingdoms into the hands of the great empires, who not only defeat them militarily but destroy their political and religious institutions as well, leaving them bereft of resources to rebuild community. The troubled and agitated mind-set of Dtr is preoccupied with this tale of the cataclysmic end of both kingdoms.

As he writes, Dtr knows that these terrible events have left the people in despair. YHWH has warned Israel through Moses and subsequent leaders that it risks annihilation if it abandons exclusive worship of the deity. The defecting populace has no excuse, but they have come to overly rely on the promise to David of an eternal kingdom. Surely, out of his love for David, God will not break his promise and the line of David will continue to give the people confidence in God's forbearance and shelter from foreign aggressors. Surely, they reasoned, God would not cut off the dynasty of David or permit desecration of the holy sanctuary. But Dtr, the leaders, and the people were wrong. So, even though it is difficult to establish the facticity of many of the details in these history-like traditions, the overriding "fact" is the threatened demise of stateless Israel, which the author is seeking to forestall by telling the amazing story of the people through multiple generations.

Three Zones of Political Economy

Dtr and Chr focus on the political and religious histories of Israel, but give far less attention to the social and economic facets of life in the periods they cover. To get a more fully rounded picture of the terrain Dtr covers, we must shift our inquiry into an entirely different register by calling on the social sciences to help us grasp the society-wide context *in* which and *about* which Dtr and Chr wrote.

Political economy is the way goods are produced and distributed in a society under prevailing forms of social and political power. When analyzed, this process yields an answer to a key question about any society: *Who* gets what, *how* do they get it, and, if possible, *why* do they get what they do get? In its long history, ancient Israel passed through three zones or modes of production (hereafter MP).

1. The Communitarian Tribal MP (reflected in Joshua and Judges and evident in some of the tribal rosters in 1 Chronicles)
2. The Native Tributary MP (1–2 Samuel; 1 Kings as far as 2 Kgs. 23:30 // 1 Chron. 10:1—2 Chron. 35:16)
3. The Imperial Tributary MP (2 Kgs. 23:31—25:30 // 2 Chron. 35:20—36:23)

Now, for ancient Israel, the primary production of the necessities of life—namely, the agrarian and pastoral yields of grains, fruits, olives, milk, wine, and occasional meat—continued more or less the same over its entire history. What marked the difference between these modes is the allotment of what is produced. In the Communitarian (or Household) MP the people who produce are those who garner their product directly without payment to or permission of third parties. In the Native Tributary MP, what is produced is subject to onerous loans, taxation, and forced labor imposed by a central government and an elite class, and the remainder is allotted to the producers. In the Imperial

Tributary MP, what is produced is "taken off the top" by the imperial elite, secondly by the native elite, and finally the remainder of the product, such as it is, is allotted to the producers.

The Communitarian MP

Early Israel was born as an anti-imperial resistance movement that broke away from Egyptian and Canaanite dominion to become a self-governing community of free peasants who emerged in the central highlands of Palestine toward the close of the thirteenth century BCE. Israelite subsistence lay in the cultivation of crops that they enjoyed, freed from the double taxation of tribute in kind to nearby city-states and to the Egyptian Empire. Instead of their surplus production being taken to support national or imperial elites, as was the case among peoples living around them, it was directly consumed or bartered or shared in a system of mutual aid characterizing the Communitarian MP. Israelites controlled their own lives, labor, and produce with an enhanced sense of dignity and self-worth. Loans in kind to assist impoverished farmers were offered without interest. Owing to difficult growing conditions, theirs was not an easy life, but it compared favorably with peasants subject to state and empire.

The marks of the Communitarian MP are everywhere exhibited in the first Israelite MP. Their society is without centralized government. They are a loose association of tribes with common interests in livelihood, domestic peace, defense, and religion. Tribal elders in consultation decided on major issues within the tribe, and deliberated on external matters that affected the whole tribe, such as joining other tribes in self-defense. There was room for charismatic leaders (so-called judges) to rally the tribes to battle. A covenant linked the tribes in worship to YHWH, but other forms of religion were practiced, probably viewed in many cases as manifestations of YHWH or at least permitted, since YHWH was not believed to be the only deity—just the most powerful as well as the special god of the Israelites.

The antipathy of early Israelites to centralized political structures is dramatically highlighted by their repeated mockery of the brutality, incompetence, and misrule of kings, expressed in narratives about the king of Jericho (Josh. 2:1-4), the Canaanite ruler Adonizedek (Judg. 1:5-7), the Moabite king Eglon (Judg. 3:5-25), and the rise and fall of Abimelech, who aspired to kingship in Israel (Judges 9). The crowning blow against the arrogance and self-inflation of rulers is brilliantly etched in Jotham's fable about the "trees" that set out to anoint a king over themselves. Three trees are invited in succession to become king: the olive tree, the fig tree, and the grapevine. All three scornfully reject the offer because they do not want to abandon their socioeconomic role as providers of Israel with food and drink. However, the nonproductive bramble readily agrees to serve as king and ludicrously offers refuge to the trees in its shade, which of course the scraggly bramble does not possess (Judg. 9:7-15). The patent lesson of this satirical fable declares that kings are socially and economically worse than useless, since they make false promises to their subjects and in the end bring destruction on those who rely on them. The military leader Gideon is said to have erred in making an image for worship, but he is credited with refusing to accept the role of king that some of his troops propose. As he succinctly puts it, "I will not rule over you, and my son will not rule over you; YHWH will rule over you" (8:23).

The fragile unity of the tribes is illustrated by six tribes responding to the muster of troops for a major battle against Canaanite kings (Judges 4–5). When four tribes are condemned for not responding, the only sanction that can be imposed on the offending tribes is a religious curse. Using primitive weapons and guerrilla tactics, and with the help of a flash flood, the tribes achieve victory by immobilizing the Canaanite chariots. The victory is attributed to YHWH, but the agency is credited to the peasant warriors of Israel. So it is throughout the Hebrew Bible that the acts of God claimed to guide Israel's history are nearly always enacted by humans.

The Native Tributary MP

There is a great gulf in social organization between "the regulated anarchy" of tribes without rulers and the hierarchic state organization that restructures society with priorities, powers, and values that befit the rule of elites who consume what the lower classes produce. Tribes do not "evolve" into states. In fact, they resist the state as both unnecessary and invasive. Always some factors "push" the tribe toward statehood. By far the primary pressure arises from states that threaten to overwhelm tribes and incorporate them into the invasive state, even when such a manufactured political status is cast as a vassal state. In our time, this has been the reality of the so-called third world, where tribe after tribe has fallen under the control of invasive states eager to build empires on the contention that "might makes right." But the pressure from outside is often preceded or accompanied by internal forces of two kinds: weak or corrupt leadership from within the tribe or collaboration of some tribesmen who encourage or hasten state control, often because they are rewarded by the enemy state.

In early Israel, the tribes resisted the Philistines, a powerful league of city-states eager to turn the Israelite highlands into a "breadbasket" to deliver the cereals that were in short supply in the Philistine coastal plain. Samuel, a priest and seer—and in many ways the last of the judges—managed to keep the Philistines at bay for some time. But, as the situation darkened, the cry went up for a warrior-king who would overcome the Philistines and secure domestic tranquility.

With their tunnel vision, most tribesmen did not realize what else went with kingship. Samuel warns them that along with the military strength of kingship come transformations of society so far-reaching that they spell the loss of tribal life and the Communitarian MP, precisely the social and economic institutions that most Israelites cherish, even the very folk now demanding a king. "You shall be his [the king's] slaves" (1 Sam. 8:17). In short, these measures taken together strike at the integrity and viability of village life, where at least 85 to 95 percent of Israelites continued to live.

Samuel's warning rejected, Israel set forth on the road to statehood. The first three kings were assertive leaders, each of them taking steps to introduce and tighten the structures of state rule, precisely as Samuel had predicted. Saul operates as "a glorified judge," who lacks most of the powers that a king exercises while he seeks in vain to secure a dynasty. David operates as a crafty chieftain who holds the loyalty of the tribes for a time, long enough to make Jerusalem his state capital, lay down the rudiments of state organization, and begin a long-lived dynasty. Solomon increases the powers of state by introducing systematic taxation and forced labor, lives extravagantly, connects diplomatically with other states, builds the elegant temple. His displays of wealth and power backfire on him as he runs into debt and pushes his forced labor battalions until they rebel, and the northern tribes withdraw from his rule altogether, forsaking Judah and Jerusalem to found their own state. This new state eventually falls prey to the same Tributary MP against which it has revolted, replacing Solomon with the autocratic house of Omri and subsequent kings. Kingship, centralized rule, was anathema to the tribes, even when they were compelled to come to terms with the state. It is perhaps more correct to say that the sentiment of many tribesmen was to adopt the state, while others abhorred adoption or submission to statehood. Israelite attitudes toward the state continued to reflect this ambivalence.

The Imperial Tributary MP

At the level of the production of goods, the Imperial Tributary MP sustains the same shape it took under the Native Tributary MP, but the distribution of agrarian wealth escalates, flowing to the upper class as it weakens the cultivators and herdsmen who produce what wealth the nation possesses. It was characteristic of the empires to retain the mode of production of the conquered and to retain some of the former royal staff to supervise the producing class below them, and even on occasion appoint a puppet "king." Empires tended to have two stages in the absorption of foreign lands. At first, the conquered states, still intact, were given the status of "vassal kingdoms." The former ruler may have been retained as administrator if judged to be loyal and competent. Hezekiah and Manasseh apparently held this status when the Assyrians overpowered Judah and ruled until Josiah broke free as the Assyrian Empire declined. In the second phase, vassal states were turned into provinces of the empire and governed by imperial appointments. In some cases, the officers of vassal states were deported, this being the case with Judah. On occasion, whole populations were deported and replaced with captives transferred from abroad, as was the fate of Israel, the northern kingdom.

It is the conviction of Dtr and Chr that obeying or disobeying the law of Moses determines the course of Israel's history. Granted that a people's religion may be an important factor in its corporate life, nonetheless the biblical account is a gross simplification. It ignores, downplays, or does not recognize the interplay of economic, social, and political factors that shape the context of Israel's religion. Simply put, the course of Israel's experience from tribal life to statehood, and on to eventual extinction by more powerful states, was much the same course followed by other small states in the ancient Near East. Even had Israel and Judah kept the law of Moses in its entirety, it is not likely that either kingdom would have been able to withstand the juggernauts of Assyria, Neo-Babylonia, and Persia or the depredations of their ruling elite.

What *is* different about Israel is that it preserved an extensive national literature that contains abundant indications of the trajectory from tribal life through independent statehood to foreign domination. For instance, we may safely say that nearby Moabite, Ammonite, and Edomite states took shape as stateless societies that practiced the Communitarian MP, and then advanced to kingship and the Native Tributary MP before being extinguished by the Assyrian Empire in much the same way that Israel was conquered. Also, it is known that these peoples worshiped national deities thought to control their destinies, much as Israel conceived of YHWH's role amid his people Israel.

We tend to treat Israel's history as distinctive and its religion as superior to other religions, overlooking Israel's immersion in ancient Near Eastern culture, because the religion of ancient Israel developed without a break into rabbinic Judaism and Christianity. In short, Dtr's and Chr's views on the history and the religion of ancient Israel have been "saved" by their canonization as Scripture, not because they are adequate sociohistorical accounts. The point is that just as the religion of other small states was interwoven with their economy, society, and politics, so exactly was the religion of ancient Israel bound up with its economic production, social structure, and political order. In this way, judicious use of the social sciences can facilitate our understanding of the origins of the religions we practice. Because the secular and religious dimensions are so closely related, we shall misconstrue the religion by isolating it from all the other aspects of life. Quite the contrary, if we are to see the religion of ancient Israel in the depth and detail that its impact on our lives categorically merits, we must come to terms with how it has been shaped by the enduring structural effects of political centralization, social stratification, shifts in land tenure, and the transformation wrought by international trade, diplomacy, and warfare. In brief, in ancient Israel, materiality and spirituality are not only joined but also inextricably intertwined.

The Historical Books over the Centuries

The historical books have undergone (one is inclined to say "suffered") the same range of interpretation as the rest of the Bible. In what sense are they true? Do they tell us what to do? Some say no and some say yes.

Literalists, on the one hand, say that every (or nearly every) word of the historical books is accurate. If the biblical text says that the sun stood still at Gibeon, the sun certainly did stand still (Joshua 10). If 1 Kings reports that Solomon spoke 3,000 proverbs, wrote 1,005 songs (4:13) and had 1,000 wives and concubines (11:3), those are the exact numbers, no more and no less. When 2 Kings reports that an angel of the Lord killed 185,000 Assyrian soldiers in one night, both the angelic agency of the slaughter and the huge number of casualties are accepted without question (2 Kgs. 19:35).

Nonliteralists, on the other hand, view the sun standing still as symbolizing the determination of Joshua's troops, with the help of the heavens, to finish off the Canaanites in short order. The writer, overawed by the grandeur of Solomon's reign, piles up claims about the volume of his productivity in sealing diplomatic marriages and in creating proverbs and songs. The huge number of Assyrians slain by the messenger of God dramatically underscores the miraculous delivery of Jerusalem from Sennacherib's tightening siege.

Thus, for some readers, the words of the Bible, spoken by the mouth of deity, are the very Word of God, while others, without prejudice to their religious value, believe that the Bible is subject to the same rules and practices of interpretation as all other books. Flowing from these differing hermeneutics, readers reach divergent conclusions regarding the applicability of biblical texts in today's world. Are the historical books a proper source for Jewish and Christian ethics? If so, in what sense and with what consequences?

For example, Joshua's murder of all Canaanites and the seizure of their land has been "a bone in the throat" of innumerable readers, while others relish it. Is it simply a recital of past events or does it in some way reinforce, even legitimate, the aggressive policies and practices of nations today? All we need to do is cite the brutal record of Western colonialism, in the course of which "inferior" peoples have been plundered, their land seized, and literally millions on millions of them have been killed without compunction. Other similar instances are worldwide: the treatment of Native Americans by transplanted Europeans; the dispossession of South Africans by British and Boer settlers; the murder of Chinese by Japanese invaders; the murder of Jews, gypsies, and homosexuals by Germans; and we could continue the litany. Moreover, some Jews and Christians consider Joshua's taking over Canaan as outright biblical support for the state of Israel's occupation and settlement of Palestinian land, regardless of international rules of warfare to the contrary. All these atrocities are justified by the right of nations to wage war, the policy of "might makes right," and the dehumanization of whole populations.

Do nations commit these atrocities because they have been motivated by reading Joshua? No, the will to colonize was already there, but in the eyes of many Jews and Christians, Joshua's deeds excuse their own nation's aggression by giving it religious sanction. It does not greatly help to argue historically that the first Israelites were actually themselves native to Canaan and that such killing as occurred was directed chiefly against city-state rulers and officials, not the general population. It matters little to most readers that the Israelites were colonists under attack by colonial Egypt and their Palestinian allies, since most readers know only the Joshua account as fantasized by Dtr. However, Joshua aside, the other historical books teem with violence, and it would be an impossible task to eliminate all violence-laden texts. If we did, it would be something like Jefferson's shortened Bible!

Yet another questionable use of the Bible is to cast an aura of authority and invincibility around rulers in Christendom, ever since Christianity became the official religion of the Roman Empire. The key text in the historical books is 2 Samuel 7, which promises David an everlasting dynasty, a promise brilliantly confirmed by the wealth and power of his son Solomon. Since it is in the nature of political leadership to hold on to power as long as possible, this assurance of divine appointment and longevity of the head of state has been tempting consolation to rulers and a warning against rebellion by those ruled. Ever since Christianity was adopted as the official religion of the Roman Empire, heads of state have happily laid claim to similar divine endorsement. "The divine right of kings" has been the bulwark against any who would threaten the emperor, king, or prince of the moment. Of course, little attention has been given to the caveat buried in the Davidic promise, "when he commits iniquity, I will chasten him with the rod of men" (7:14 RSV), much less to the unholy conduct of a succession of kings following Solomon who are roundly criticized by Dtr as well as by the Latter Prophets. It is not surprising that postbiblical monarchs and their ecclesiastical minions have failed to follow the whole narrative of kingship throughout the historical books. Of course, as monarchy has waned and democracy has prospered, appeal to the Davidic promise is largely an empty gesture, even if retained ceremonially with the trappings of religious sanctity. Nonetheless, it is arguable that the substance of the promise has transmogrified into its secular equivalent by claiming the unshakable foundation of the state, any state, through all changes in its leadership, even when corrupt or incompetent.

Nevertheless, while the present heads of state and their regimes bask in the confidence that God will uphold their power, there are others who go beyond 2 Samuel 7 to read all of the historical books and prophets and, in doing so, notice how the majority of rulers have broken faith with the lofty terms of their installation, so seriously that the line of David falls, along with all the political, social, and religious institutions of Judah. Some of these contemporary readers are severe critics of the conduct of their own state, which is allegedly securing justice at home and peace abroad. In fact, some of the political critics have turned the Davidic promise on its head by affirming the right of rebellion against unjust rule, citing the rebellions of Absalom and Shebah against David, Jeroboam against Solomon, and Jehu against the House of Omri. Indeed, in the historical books, Dtr provides numerous examples both of kings worthy of support and those deserving of severe criticism, even death.

Taking the historical books in their wider biblical context, we see that the legacy of ancient Israel provides no distinctive politics and no template for translating culture and religion into viable social programs and polities. The historical books have been mined not only in support of the divine right of kings (or of any autocratic rulers) but also in support of the countervailing right of revolt against unjust authorities. Additionally, the historical books have been used to give support to a wide spectrum of political systems, such as covenanted commonwealths, liberal democracy, nationalism, capitalism, anarchy, and socialism. This search for a biblical warrant for particular political systems is due in part to the scriptural and cultural authority vested in the Hebrew Bible, repeatedly tempting proponents of sociopolitical systems to claim biblical legitimation. This problematic basing of politics on biblical warrants is further encouraged by the unsystematic and unreconciled political structures, practices, and values expressed in the Hebrew Bible, containing elements thought to have affinities with one or another modern political system. The best governance and social order are the province of history, social ethics, and political science, not the historical books of the Hebrew Bible.

Works Referenced

Berrigan, Daniel. 2008. *The Kings and Their Gods: The Pathology of Power*. Grand Rapids: Eerdmans.

Gottwald, Norman. 2001. *The Politics of Ancient Israel*. Louisville: Westminster John Knox.

Grabbe, Lester L., ed. 2005. *Good Kings and Bad Kings*. New York: T&T Clark.

Hawk, Daniel L. 2010. *Joshua in 3-D: A Commentary on Biblical Conquest and Manifest Destiny*. Eugene, OR: Cascade.

Horsley, Richard, ed. 2008. *In the Shadow of Empire: Reclaiming the Bible as a History of Faithful Resistance*. Louisville: Westminster John Knox.

Jobling, David. 1998. *1 Samuel*. Berit Olam. Collegeville, MN: Liturgical Press.

Lasine, Stewart. 2001. *Knowing Kings: Knowledge, Power, and Narcissism*. Atlanta: Society of Biblical Literature.

Polzin, Robert. 1993. *David and the Deuteronomist: 2 Samuel*. Bloomington: Indiana University Press.

JOSHUA

Pekka M. A. Pitkänen

Introduction

The book of Joshua, following on the narrative of the Pentateuch, describes how the Israelite people, having been liberated from slavery in Egypt and made a covenant with YHWH at Horeb in the wilderness of Sinai and at the plains of Moab, now move on to conquer and settle the land of Canaan. Joshua 1–5 describes the crossing of the River Jordan, and 6–12 portrays the main Israelite conquest. Joshua 13–21 then describes the allotment of the land, with some short, conquest-related interludes. Joshua 22–24 describes a number of events after Israel has settled, with Joshua in chapters 23–24 exhorting the Israelites to follow YHWH, just before his death. Hendrik Koorevaar succinctly describes this four-partite division as follows: 1:1—5:12 *avar* ("cross"), 5:13—12:24 *laqah* ("take"), 13:1—21:45 *halaq* ("divide"), and 22:1—24:33 *avad* ("serve") (Koorevaar, 283).

As Joshua 1–9 and 13–24 ultimately describe just a few events, the book of Joshua really appears to be about the allotment and settlement of the land in a larger context and over a longer period of time. This is mostly achieved by war, but also relatively peacefully in parts (e.g., 17:12-13), and large swathes of land are still classified as unconquered (esp. 13:1-7). The book's literary style has affinities with other extant ancient Near Eastern conquest accounts (see esp. Younger). A number of comments interspersed throughout the book imply a date of writing already at least somewhat removed from the time of the events portrayed (e.g., 6:25; 7:26; 13:13; 15:63).

The Masoretic text (MT) of Joshua differs from that of the Septuagint (LXX) to some extent, but not radically. The main divergences are found in connection with 5:2-9 (circumcision at Gilgal), 6:1-15 (the circling of Jericho), the placement of 8:30-35 (Ebal incident) and 20:1-6 (establishment of the towns of refuge), and there are a few extra verses at the end of the book in Greek. There is also variation between the MT and LXX in the town and boundary lists of Joshua 13–21. For simplicity, this commentary will mostly follow the MT, noting some of the main divergences and some possible implications (for more detailed treatments, see, e.g., Butler; Nelson; Meer; Tov).

The book of Joshua incorporates various sources, such as the poem in 10:12-13 (note the Book of Yashar mentioned in the verse) and the town and territorial lists in chapters 11–21. In the larger context, since the birth of modern biblical criticism, the book of Joshua was generally seen as part of the Hexateuch (Genesis–Joshua), with Joshua completing the story of Israel from creation to conquest. However, since the publication of Martin Noth's *Deuteronomistic History* in 1943 (for the ET, see Noth 1991), Joshua has generally been seen as part of the Deuteronomistic History, which spans from Deuteronomy to 2 Kings, incorporating earlier sources into a Deuteronomistic framework and then also some post-Deuteronomistic Priestly additions. Recently, a number of scholars have rejected the idea of a Deuteronomistic History and essentially returned to the Hexateuch theory (see, e.g., Westermann; Carr; Otto 2000; 2012; Dozeman, Römer, and Schmid), and this basic concept is followed here (see also Pitkänen 2010, 2013a).

It is recognized that Joshua and Deuteronomy are closely connected. As modern biblical criticism has generally dated Deuteronomy to the seventh century BCE (see, e.g., Otto 2012, 62–230), Joshua, too, has been dated to the same time, even though it is seen to have possibly incorporated earlier traditions (see Noort). With the rise of the discipline of archaeology, scholars since the latter part of the nineteenth century (see, e.g., Moorey; cf. Levy for the present status) have generally viewed events described in the Bible from the period of the judges on as reflecting actual history, but events earlier than that became suspect. In addition, some recent, more "radical," or minimalist, scholars have argued that biblical Israel is a scholarly construct from the Persian period (see, e.g., Lemche; T. L. Thompson) and that nothing can really be known about preexilic Israel based on biblical documents. Historically, there have been three main models for the Israelite conquest and settlement (see Dever for a summary). First, the conquest model argued for the general veracity of the biblical record, even though it moved the date of the conquest from the thirteenth century to the fifteenth century implied by the biblical chronology. Second, the peaceful infiltration model suggested that the Israelites were nomads who peacefully immigrated to the land from outside. Third, the peasant's revolt model proposed that the Israelites were Canaanites who revolted against the existing socioeconomic structure and withdrew to the highlands to form a new society. All three of these models have been subjected to criticism. Most recently, the indigenous origins of the Israelites has often been held (see, e.g., Dever), with some allowance for an external influx of people as well (e.g., Faust). In terms of diversity of opinion, presently the so-called maximalists tend to date the book early and to see it largely as reflecting actual history, with a modified form of the original conquest model that does not exclude peaceful immigration and assimilation (e.g., Kitchen; Pitkänen 2010; 2013a). Proponents of more mainstream approaches lean toward peaceful immigration and Canaanite origins (see, e.g., Miller and Hayes; Dever). The minimalists, for whom the history of ancient Israel is largely postexilic fiction, again go with the peaceful transformation models, mostly based on the indigenous origins of the Israelites (see, e.g., Liverani; T. L. Thompson).

The view taken in this essay, on which readers are invited to reflect critically, is that an external group of Semites escaped from slavery in Egypt (see Hoffmeier 1997; 2005) and brought with it memories of its founding fathers the patriarchs and a belief in YHWH. This group then somehow gained a foothold and overall control of the Canaanite highlands and subsequently reproduced and assimilated indigenous and possibly other exogenous elements to form Israel (see Pitkänen

2010; 2013a). Arguably, the archaeological evidence can be seen to support the possibility of such an idea, even when it is not easy to verify a number of the related details directly. The change from the Late Bronze culture to the Iron Age hill country culture happened first in the central highlands and expanded on from there over the next two to three hundred years (e.g., Finkelstein, 324–30; Junkkaala, esp. 308–9). Much of this process was peaceful, but some violence could easily have been involved. A process of that type can be compared with processes known from the more modern world that have recently been labeled and analyzed as settler colonialism (see Veracini 2010; Day; see Pitkänen 2013a for considerations of how modern settler-colonial theory can be applied to the ancient world). Settler-colonial societies are "autonomous collectives that claim both a special sovereign charge and a regenerative capacity" (Veracini 2010, 3–4). Settlers are founders of political orders who carry their sovereignty with them, as opposed to migrants, who are suppliants seeking to fit into an established political order (Veracini 2010, 3). As David Day suggests, a related "process of supplanting" involves three often overlapping stages: Establishing a legal or de jure claim to the land; making a claim of effective or de facto proprietorship; and setting a claim of moral proprietorship over the territory (Day 2008, 7–8). In a broad sweep and keeping in mind that the Late Bronze Canaanite societies somehow became Israelite, in Genesis–Joshua, the patriarchal promises reflect the first claim, the conquest and settlement the second, and recourse to Yahwism as an exclusive ideology, together with the constitution of the new Yahwistic society, the third, moral claim (see, e.g., Deuteronomy 7 in contrast to the previous inhabitants). Settler colonialism aims to effect a dissolution of native societies and erect a new society on an expropriated land base (see Wolfe, esp. 103), with the eliminatory aim typically involving a "genocidal imperative" (see Day, 176–97), but not limited to it (see esp. Veracini 2010, 16–52). For the ancient Israelites, this genocidal imperative is reflected in the concept of *herem*, though one must keep in mind that it has a wider scope, encompassing objects also in cultic use (e.g., Lev. 27:28; Num. 18:14).

Arguably, then, the main problems for interpreting Joshua in today's contexts relate to the violence portrayed in the book. This problem has much to do with the book's relation to actual history. While reading the book as a mythical narrative of a distant past would undoubtedly reduce the problem of its apparently violent character (see, e.g., Earl), at the same time, denial of the problems can also be compared with disavowal, cognitive dissonance, and screen memories identified in modern settler-colonial studies (see Veracini 2010, 95–116). These reactions try to deal with trauma that results from seeing violence committed by one's own community (see ibid.). From an explicitly theological angle, as Eryl Davies points out, there are five main possible responses to acknowledging the violent and hence problematic character of the book. In the so-called evolutionary approach, the text represents primitive thinking that has now been superseded. The cultural relativists' approach sees the text in terms of an ancient and therefore different culture and therefore less relevant for moderns. Canonical approaches in practice exclude the text from the canon. The paradigmatic approach extracts acceptable general principles from the texts. Finally, the reader-response approach accepts the problematic nature of the texts and tries to respond to them accordingly (Davies).

This commentary is broadly in agreement with a reader-response approach, which does not seek to disavow the violence. Such an approach, in fact, builds on an already-existing biblical mode of questioning God and his actions, for example, by the book of Job and a number of the Psalms (cf., e.g., M. E. W. Thompson 2011), without necessarily jettisoning belief in him. The apostle Paul also touches on this issue in Romans 9, though without questioning God. Finally, we do well to remember that the ostensible promotion of violence in the Bible is not confined to Genesis–Joshua; other examples include the imprecatory psalms and the book of Revelation. The book of Joshua, then, encourages Christians to reflect on theodicy and the role of violence in human history as a whole, seen from the perspective of salvation history and, importantly for Christians, the first-century Christ event. Politically, a reader-response approach is generally in line with postcolonial approaches. Any material in the book that can be read theologically in a reasonably straightforward and "nonproblematic" way as reflecting courage, trust in YHWH, and so on must arguably be read against the backdrop of postcolonial readings.

Joshua 1–5: Transitions and Memory

■ THE TEXT IN ITS ANCIENT CONTEXT

The beginning of the book of Joshua describes a people in transition. Israel is at the plains of Moab, and their great leader Moses has just died. Joshua takes on the leadership, and people move over into the promised land in preparation of the conquest. Joshua 1 describes how Joshua receives his orders from YHWH himself (1:1-9) and then commands the rest of the people (1:10-18). Importantly, the Transjordanians who settled East of Jordan (Numbers 32) are required to help the rest of the people in their conquest of Cisjordan (land west of the Jordan River), which they again commit to do (1:12-18). Joshua 2 describes the reconnaissance of Jericho, in preparation of its conquest, which is related in chapter 6. Joshua 3 and 4 describe the crossing of the Jordan and setting camp at Gilgal, mirroring the wider Hexateuchal narrative of the crossing of the Sea of Reeds in Exodus 14. In Joshua 5, after a note about the worry of the indigenous peoples concerning Israel's entrance (5:1), the Israelites are circumcised (5:2-9; cf. Genesis 17; Exod. 12:43-48) and subsequently celebrate the Passover (5:10-12; cf. Exodus 12). Joshua then meets a commander of the army of YHWH (5:13-15; cf. Exod. 3, incl. v. 5).

For Noth, Joshua 1 as a whole should be seen in the context of the wider Deuteronomistic History (Noth 1953, 27). However, while it is true that Deuteronomic ideology is prominent in the chapter, such ideology is also tied to broader ancient Near Eastern ideologies. YHWH's reassurances in Josh. 1:5-6 in a Deuteronomistic style can be compared with the Zakkur stele (e.g., lines 11–15: "But I lifted my hands to Baalshamayn, and Baalshamay[n] answered me, [and] Baalshamayn [spoke] to me [thr]ough seers and through visionaries, [and] Baalshamayn [said], 'F[e]ar not, for I have made [you] king, [and I who will st]and with [you], and I will deliver you from all [these kings who] have forced a siege against you!'"; see Nissinen, 204–6). In Joshua 1, and the book as a whole, Joshua can in some respects be seen to reflect a royal figure (Nelson, 29), with links with Josiah suggested (Nelson, 29); however, there is no royal succession with Joshua, and the names Joshua and Josiah appear to derive from different Hebrew verbal roots.

Previous academic discussion on chapter 2 has mainly centered on its provenance, purpose, and literary prehistory, including sources (Noort, 131, 135–43). Commentators have generally thought in essence that the story of Rahab was originally self-standing and that the author only later picked it up and tied it to its present context of the conquest of Jericho (Noort, 131–32; cf. Noth 1953, 29; Nelson, 41). Such a conclusion is not necessary, however. Biblical parallels to the chapter include Judges 1:23-26 and Genesis 19:1-23. Such parallels extend beyond the Bible (Noort, 132). The story as a whole has generally been seen as etiological, giving a rationale for the existence of the family of Rahab in the midst of Israel (Noort, 131), thus accounting for the story's inclusion. The spying motif can also be compared to other accounts of spying in the Israelite conquest tradition (see Nelson, 45).

The literary form of Joshua 3–4 has been subject to much discussion. Above all, the narrative appears to be uneven, and the text seems to present a number of inconsistencies, even contradictions (see Nelson, 55, 65 for details). However, if it had an oral existence or was meant to be read to audiences, one can read the material as having a purposeful structure and as having been constructed fairly well (see Pitkänen 2010, 129–32). The material has often been seen as stemming from a cult center at Gilgal (see Noth 1953, 11–12), which appears to have had an important role in Israelite history. That there was a sanctuary of some kind at Gilgal seems warranted, but fuller details are unknown, including that the site has not been identified. In any case, in the book of Joshua, the stones set up there serve as a memorial and as a sign for the future generations.

The similarities between the crossing of the Jordan and the crossing of the Sea of Reeds in the book of Exodus are significant (see Ottosson, 79) in the overall Hexateuchal narrative. The crossing of the Sea of Reeds starts the period of wilderness wanderings, and the crossing of Jordan ends it. Both stories also involve a miraculous dividing of the waters. The related children's questions in the chapter (4:6-8, 21-24; cf. Josh. 22:24-28) are paralleled with Deut. 6:20-25. The cultic procession of the ark, with YHWH's presence at the ark, is reminiscent of Priestly material in Numbers (similarly also Ottosson, 54).

As with Joshua 3–4, the link to what has happened before Joshua's time is strong in chapter 5. Joshua 5:1 certainly links back to Deuteronomy's promises about a fear that will fall on Israel's opponents (Deut. 2:25; 11:25). Joshua 5:2-9 explicitly links back to Egypt and the wilderness, as does the reference to manna in verses 10-12. The story about the commander of YHWH's army reminds one of Exod. 3:1-5 (cf. esp. Josh. 5:15 with Exod. 3:5). Importantly, the appearance of the commander is in line with ancient Near Eastern motifs of gods fighting with the troops as a divine vanguard (see Mann, 40–41). Chapter 5 also contains two etiological comments, on Gilgal (v. 9), and, even if not stated completely explicitly, on the Hill of Foreskins (v. 3). The MT and LXX of 5:2-9 differ, primarily in the clarification that unleavened bread was eaten on the day following the start of Passover, which is included only in the MT. This brings it in line with Lev. 23:4-8, whereas the LXX suggests eating unleavened bread on the eve of the Passover, more in line with Deut. 16:1-8 (see Nelson, 72–73, 78–80).

■ THE TEXT IN THE INTERPRETIVE TRADITION

The beginning of the book of Joshua opens the story from the perspective of salvation history. This salvation history is referred to in Stephen's speech in Acts 7, which also refers to Joshua (v. 45).

Hebrews 4:8 implies that the rest achieved in the time of Joshua was not a true rest, suggesting that such a rest is achieved in Jesus under the new covenant. Hebrews 11:31 and James 2:25-26 praise the faith of Rahab as exemplary in her welcoming the spies, with the latter passage also drawing out a spiritualized lesson for salvation.

Patristic and later Christian commentators continued along similar lines, considering themes of transition and spiritual rest and spiritual battle instead of physical battle (see description in Earl, 111–15). As for Rahab, commentators have asked how her deception should be viewed and also how she relates to *herem* (Earl, 116). Postcolonial literature sees her as a traitor instead of a hero (see Earl, 48). As for *herem*, Rahab's example, in contrast to Achan, transfers her into an "insider," which saves her from death, whereas Achan becomes an "outsider" through his transgression and is thus destroyed (Hawk 2000, 20 and passim; cf. Hawk 2010, 79 and passim).

Crossing the Jordan in Joshua 3–4 can easily be equated with new life, and indeed, Gregory of Nyssa links the story with baptism (Earl, 122–23), even if the connection relates much to the symbolism of the Jordan in the biblical tradition otherwise. In Joshua 5, the fullness of new life begins to manifest itself, with the gifts of the new land instead of the manna that was eaten in the wilderness (Earl, 126, referring to Brueggemann). Origen also saw the wilderness as representing the present Christian life under instruction of the word of God, which is equated with manna, and the implication of the promised land representing the hereafter (Earl, 126–27). In a preliminary sense, with the physical being spiritualized, early Christian commentators did not give much attention to the problem of violence in the book, but it is also true that a fair bit in these chapters can be interpreted in such a spiritualized way.

▮ THE TEXT IN CONTEMPORARY DISCUSSION

The considerations in the section directly above are entirely valid for modern Christian communities. Here attention will be drawn to a few further aspects of possible contemporary reflection.

In all life, humans often experience change, in leadership and in other areas, and people may have to "cross the river" to new things. Such situations are often a time of uncertainty, sometimes even great uncertainty. But they can also be a time of new beginnings. At these times, Christians can think of the words of YHWH to "be strong and courageous" (1:6-7, 9), especially when they are taking a leadership position; but, equally, Christians can also trust in God for the future, even under new leaders. Trust in God and in God's presence is an important consolation and comfort, even in the tightest of situations.

Joshua 1 (esp. 1:18) raises an interesting dilemma in a wider context. How should a Christian react to a war (or comparable societal actions) that he or she does not approve of? For example, one might be a member of a society that moves to invade the lands of another society. In such situations, the resulting ethical dilemma can be a vexing one, and refusing national service for reasons of pacifism can already in itself bring a great stigma in societies that have a general draft. The effects of this stigma have affected and continue to affect Christians who also rely on their surrounding societal structures for their life and survival.

The ark of the covenant features prominently in Joshua 3–4 as the locus of YHWH's presence. In the Priestly material of Genesis–Joshua, it belongs in the tent of meeting, where it is housed and where YHWH dwells in the midst of his people; and in Deuteronomy, people are required to assemble in YHWH's presence three times a year and make sacrifices only there (Deuteronomy 12, 16). In contrast, for Christians, an ark or a temple (see the tabernacle in Josh. 18:1; see also 22:9-34) is no longer necessary as a place of God's presence. Their bodies are now the temple of God (1 Cor. 3:16; 2 Cor. 6:16). Of course, attending church with other people is a partaking of the body of Christ, and this has a special significance. But the concepts of holy objects and holy places are now less important in themselves. While most people would feel something special about a building that has been dedicated to God, fundamentally, the place of worship is no longer crucial from the standpoint of Christianity, and this may help in the Western context when people see worship buildings sold and converted into the "secular" realm.

One of the emphases of Joshua 3–4 is the remembrance throughout the generations of the crossing the Jordan. As for Christians, they also have items for remembering God. Many people have crucifixes hung on the walls in their homes, or they wear them as pendants. Catholic and Orthodox believers have traditionally used icons, or images of Christ and the saints. Some Protestants in particular have objected to such pictorial representations, worrying that they might become objects of worship. Here the issues are surprisingly similar to Joshua 3–4 and the use of standing stones. The stones are to serve as memorials, but in the ancient world, people also frequently made such stones objects of worship. Perhaps it can be said that Christians can also be encouraged to use memorials, as long as they do not elevate them to a status where they become objects of worship. Along these lines, Christians may also travel to holy places and consider church buildings as inspirational objects, but really only so that seeing such places might help them remember the great deeds of God.

Chapter 5 looks to the past (5:4-7), to the present (5:8-11), and into the future (5:12-15). Transition from old to new usually involves both looking back at old things and seeing the changes that are taking place and are likely to take place with the transition. For a people of faith, this may involve meditating on the great deeds of God for them, and remembering in faith God's guiding hand and presence in preparation for things to come. And, just as YHWH fought for Israel, Christians can trust God's presence in times of need, even if one should not expect that this will involve physical violence.

Joshua 6-9: Insiders and Outsiders

■ THE TEXT IN ITS ANCIENT CONTEXT

Joshua 6–9 describes a number of events taking place at the initial stages of the conquest. Joshua 6 describes the conquest of Jericho, in conclusion to the story in chapter 2. Joshua 7–8 describes the conquest of Ai. Joshua 8:30-35 describes the building of an altar on Mount Ebal. Joshua 9 describes the Gibeonite deception, and as a result the Gibeonites make a covenant with the Israelites that protects them against extermination based on the concept of *herem*.

The literary form of Joshua 6 resembles a Ugaritic entry ritual (Pitkänen 2010, 158), suggesting that the account does not necessarily need to be taken in a literal manner in all its details, also considering that, according to the narrative, it is the first locality in Canaan to be conquered (Pit-känen 2010, 162–69). Nevertheless, allowing that the story is being creatively retold, a conquest of a modest Late Bronze Age town is historically possible. The conquest of Ai, however, is extremely difficult to verify archaeologically (Pitkänen 2010, 182–84), and its historicity must be left open. The Ai narrative has parallels with Judges 20 and 1 Samuel 14–15. The building of an altar on Mount Ebal in Josh. 8:30-35, which is placed slightly differently in certain manuscripts, is tied to Deuteronomy 27 and can also be compared with the altars built by the patriarchs in Genesis, including those by Abraham at Shechem in Genesis 12. The Gibeonite treaty is mentioned in 2 Sam. 21:1-14, and Gibeon acts as a cultic center in the time of Solomon (1 Kings 3:4; cf. 1 Chron. 16:39; 21:29). The archaeological data from Gibeon is somewhat equivocal in terms of the question of the potential historicity of the related events in Joshua (Pitkänen 2010, 214–16).

An important issue in these chapters is the question of insiders versus outsiders, a theme pointed out most notably by L. Daniel Hawk (2000; 2010). The basic idea of the book of Joshua is that those outside the Israelite community may in certain circumstances become members of the community (Rahab in Joshua 6, Gibeonites in Joshua 9). Conversely, those not following YHWH can be excluded from the community and may even fall under *herem* (Achan in Joshua 7). Again, subjecting these issues to a postcolonial analysis can help elucidate the text. We may first note the complexity of colonial situations. As Maria Aubet summarizes, "Colonialism cannot be studied only from the dominator's point of view nor only from that of the dominated," as has often been the case until now, "because the relationship between domination and resistance changes in the course of a colonial situation" (2013, 76). "The colonised do not form a homogenous group; some are dominant over others and there are internal conflicts, so it is necessary to contextualise the colonial process" (Aubet, 76, quoting Gledhill). A dichotomy between the dominators and the dominated "in fact masks highly complex practices of interaction" (Aubet, 76).

Anthropologists and archaeologists "have started to study the mixed character of some colonial situations, that on occasion actually constitute new and hybrid cultural entities" (Aubet, 77). These comments apply to Rahab and Gibeon in that her relationship to Israel is complex, both before and after their encounter with the Israelites. In addition, one may note here the basic tripartite settler-colonial dynamic between the settler collective and indigenous and exogenous others in settler-colonial situations (Veracini 2010, 20–32). While indigenous others are a threat to the existence and legitimacy of the settler collective, there can be a selective inclusion of exogenous others, as there is the possibility of collaboration (Veracini 2010, 26). However, there can also be undesirable exogenous others who may be subject to deportation or segregation (Veracini 2010, 27), and abject others who are permanently excluded from the settler collective and have lost their indigenous or exogenous status. In the case of ancient Israel, the Israelite *qahal/edah* corresponds to the settler collective (Josh. 8:30-35; 22:9-34). The Canaanites who—according to the Israelite view—are to be destroyed (Deuteronomy 7) are the indigenous others. The *ger* are the exogenous others (e.g., Exod. 12:38 [mixed multitude]; Josh. 8:33). Abject others might include people who have been subject to the *karat* punishment of being cut off from the people (e.g., Lev. 7:20-27; 17:4-14; 18:29). As Lorenzo Veracini suggests, a "successful" settler society "is managing the orderly and progressive emptying of the indigenous and exogenous others segments of the population economy and has permanently separated from the abject others" (Veracini 2010, 28; see also Deut. 23:1-8).

We can now see what is happening with Rahab, Achan, and the Gibeonites. Rahab is transferred away, defining *transfer* as "cleansing" the settler body polity of its indigenous and exogenous alterities, whether by violence or by some more subtle conceptual means from the indigenous other category, and she is no longer under *herem*, a transfer by killing. As to her new status, it is unclear whether she is considered as part of the *qahal* or as equivalent to a *ger* ("resident alien"), at least initially. As for Achan, whose desire of prestige goods was typical of those belonging to ancient societies, if not also modern ones (Aubet 2013, incl. 98–99), he is transferred away from the Israelite collective by execution, which is close to the *karat* command, but apparently not the same.

As for the Gibeonites, they are transferred away from being Canaanites under *herem* into a servant class (see also 2 Samuel 21), which, however, is closely connected with Israelite worship (1 Samuel 7, where the ark is at Kiriath Jearim, a Gibeonite town). Later on, the Gibeonites seem to be considered as Israelite; this generally seems to be achieved by a transfer of assimilation by incorporating them into Israelite genealogies (1 Chron. 2:50-52; Neh. 7:25-30), as is done with Caleb at an early stage, at least in the narrative world (Num. 13:6; 32:12; Josh. 14:6-14; 15:13). At the same time, the responses to Rahab and the Gibeonites can also be considered as "unintended consequences" of colonialism (Dietler, 18).

Similar processes of incorporation into a genealogy can be detected in the Iron Age Aegean world, probably dating back to the Late Bronze Age (Finkelberg, 24–41) and in the more modern world (Horowitz, 78). The "transfers" of Rahab, Achan, and the Gibeonites therefore represent the larger number of transfers happening in early Israel according to the biblical texts. In these transfers, the Israelite society of settlers is expanding its scope and influence under a complex dynamic between the Israelite society and the natives. This process takes centuries and in many ways can be seen to have been completed by the postexilic time (e.g., 1 Chron. 2:50-53; Ezra 2:25; Neh. 7:25, 29; vs. Josh. 9:17).

The building of the altar on Mount Ebal is tied with the Israelites' staking a legal claim to the land. It can be compared with the practices of the modern English, Spanish, Portuguese, Dutch, and French colonialists. For example, Columbus erected in "every harbour which his ships entered and on every suitable promontory 'a very large cross in the most appropriate spot'" (Day, 13). Or Vasco Balboa, when reaching the Pacific Ocean in the Americas, ordered his escorts to kneel and sing the *Te Deum* and then waded in the waters of the sea, claiming in the name of his king all the lands whose shores would be washed by this sea. The Portuguese typically erected a *padrão*, or stone pillar topped with a cross, together with an inscription, to mark their discoveries and accompanying claims, and providing markers for navigation on sea routes for the future. Tasman, the Dutch explorer, erected a flagpole in the southern Australian island that came to bear his name "as a memorial for those who shall come after us, and for the natives of this country" (Day, 18). On the main island of New Zealand, Cook erected a cairn, inside which he placed some coins and musket balls (Day, 22). The Israelite ceremony in Joshua then harks back to the actions of the patriarchs in Genesis. Especially Abraham, who is described as building his first altar at Shechem (esp. Gen. 12:6-7), which is in the vicinity of Mount Ebal (Deut. 11:30; see Moreh in this verse and Gen. 12:6).

■ THE TEXT IN THE INTERPRETIVE TRADITION

As indicated above, many of the indigenous peoples were sooner or later integrated into ancient Israelite society. In the New Testament, the scope of ancient Israel is explicitly extended to include all nations of the world (Acts 2; 10–11; Galatians) as the new Israel (Romans 11). Only faith in Christ, not any national association, is required. Yet a type of insider-versus-outsider distinction still remains in the New Testament, but it centers on faith and on no other characteristic. There is to be no real difference in status among those belonging to the Christian community (Gal. 3:28).

Origen spiritualized the destruction of Jericho into an idea of the destruction of evil (Earl, 135). A main point of the Achan narrative is that one must follow YHWH's instructions, and it is particularly emphasized that one should not violate what has been devoted to him. However, in terms of the Christian community, whereas Achan had to die, Christians do not need to, as Jesus has borne their transgressions. In this respect, it is true that Ananias and Sapphira died because of their attempted deception against God (Acts 5:1-11), but this seems to be somewhat of an extraordinary exception. It is perhaps true that God also chastises God's children, but this can be understood to be for developmental purposes, and the nuance is different from that in Joshua. Christians are not to have a spirit of fear but of sonship (Rom. 8:15). Achan has been seen as a type who confessed his or her sin, even if Achan himself did not seem to benefit from such confession (Earl, 144–45). Emphasis on the law in 8:30-35 has been seen as pointing to Christ (Earl, 146).

■ THE TEXT IN CONTEMPORARY DISCUSSION

In actual practice, churches and other human communities do set rules, whether implicitly or explicitly, of who is an "insider" and who is to be an "outsider." Issues such as race, wealth and social status, religion, and sexual orientation may be determining factors. Even dressing differently from others can be a reason for exclusion. For example, a church consisting of middle-aged, middle-class people might find it difficult if a "goth" were suddenly to sit in the pews. Similarly, while present human rights legislation speaks for diversity and inclusion in wider society, there is still work to be done. One area is integrating foreigners and people of different ethnic origin and religion into societies as equal participants. The situation can be fairly good in this respect in Britain and in many ways in the United States and Australia, to a degree, but can presently be problematic in certain countries in continental Europe, Russia, and Asia, not to mention Israel—at least in terms of practical life, if not in a legislative sense. As for women, despite feminism, there are still many areas where their rights and equality need further work. LGBT rights is a further issue to reflect on, both at a societal and church level; debates are currently taking place as to what extent they should be considered equal in churches.

Today's settler-colonial societies have provided and continue to provide special challenges (Veracini 2010, 95–116). For example, in American history, the original settler collective consisted only of whites, with blacks as slaves, essentially abject others, and with newly entering whites and Asians as exogenous others, though with a better status for whites. In time, the settler collective has uplifted the status of the blacks and Asians. It nevertheless still sees Native Americans as indigenous others, having transferred them by killing, displacement, and forced or voluntary assimilation (see Stannard; see Hawk 2010 for a number of parallels between the book of Joshua and the North American conquest). The natives living in reservations are still oppressed. Even today, a person coming from outside who commits a crime in reservation territory cannot be tried by the Native Americans, and in practice, US law enforcement is tardy in pursuing such cases. It is no wonder that Native Americans are still experiencing a continued terrible trauma of the past (Tinker 2004; 2008). Other indigenous peoples around the world still experience similar traumas. For them, the issue is not so much inclusion to the new society but regaining their past freedom, land, and property. Decolonization would include such issues as an apology by the colonizer and restitution of land, property, and dignity to the victims, but this has proven extremely difficult in settler-colonial situations, such as with the United States, Australia, and New Zealand (see also Veracini 2010, 95–116).

In South Africa, with the whites never constituting a majority of the population, after a period of apartheid, blacks have regained power. In modern Israel, a settler-colonial process against the indigenous Palestinians continues unabated (Veracini 2006). The recent UN Declaration of the Rights of Indigenous Peoples (2007) is a step in the right direction in the global context, but much work remains to be done.

Joshua 10–12: Conquest and Genocide

▮ THE TEXT IN ITS ANCIENT CONTEXT

Joshua 10–12 describes the main conquests Joshua and the Israelites achieve in Canaan. In Joshua 10, the Israelites defeat a southern coalition of indigenous forces, and in chapter 11 they overcome a northern coalition led by the king of Hazor. Joshua 12 summarizes these and other conquests, together with conquests already previously achieved by the Israelites, including in Transjordan, as described in Numbers and Deuteronomy.

Joshua 10 follows on from the story of the Gibeonites. The southern coalition attacks Gibeon on hearing about their treaty with the Israelites. The Gibeonites call for the help of the Israelites, who respond and then achieve victory aided by a miraculous hailstorm and celestial portents (10:11-13). The kings of the coalition are then executed in verses 16-28. From here, Joshua attacks further towns in the South. In Joshua 11, the scope widens toward the north, which then leads to a yet fuller scope in chapter 12. At this point in the narrative of Joshua, what had started at the crossing of the Jordan and the conquest of Jericho and Ai now branches out to cover the whole land, to be followed by the allotment of the land in Joshua 13–19. While one can see the author's logic in framing Joshua as part of the wider Genesis–Joshua narrative, in which the Israelites move in from Egypt and the wilderness, the narrative should be seen as at least a partially artificial creation. There could have been a unified campaign by a leader of a main exodus group, but in reality it is more likely that a number of conflicts with locals occurring at various times have been telescoped together into a narrative and attributed to Joshua as the military leader par excellence of the Israelites (see 12:7, which mentions Joshua *and* the Israelites). A number of these battles and conquests can be difficult to verify archaeologically. For example, 11:14 suggests that Joshua and the Israelites did not normally burn the conquered towns. If so, and if towns were not demolished otherwise, few traces would be likely to have been left in the archaeological record (cf. 24:13; Deut. 6:10-11).

In Josh. 10:11, a hailstorm caused by YHWH settles the score for the Israelites. Hailstorms are not uncommon in Israel, especially between October and May. The size of hail can be considerable and can cause damage (Pitkänen 2010, 224). In terms of the Joshua narrative, above all, the timing is providential. The storm is sent by YHWH to help the fighting Israelites. It should also be noted that no Israelites are reported to have been harmed, even though the point may simply be that, even if there were Israelite injuries, as a whole, the storm resulted in an advantage to the *Israelites*. That in itself could already be seen as a miracle.

A bigger miracle is then described in Josh. 10:12-14. The heavenly bodies stop their travel in the sky until the Israelites are victorious. Understood according to a modern scientific worldview, the implication is that the earth's rotation slowed or stopped altogether. This would of course be stupendously miraculous, and many commentators have accordingly sought to explain the comments in some other way. Joseph Blenkinsopp suggests that the narrative references local understandings of the sun and the moon as deities, which should be seen to be under YHWH's control during the battle. Whether or not this was the case, it is true that the sun and moon were considered divine throughout the ancient Near East at the time (Blenkinsopp, 44–50). However, it appears that the Israelites were not to think in this way, or at least not worship these deities (Deut. 4:19).

In the context of this passage, then, it cannot be said with confidence whether any divine implications are intended. Richard Hess has summarized other attempts to solve the meaning of the passage, including an eclipse and an interpretation of the position of the constellations as an omen, but he notes that none of the suggested solutions is "entirely satisfactory" (197–99; cf. Younger, 211–20). Richard Nelson (145) suggests that "these two heavenly bodies were being called upon to stand frozen or fixed, or perhaps silent, in stunned reaction to an awe-inspiring victory," and the (apparently Deuteronomic) redactor then directed the speech through the accompanying prose section "*away from sun and moon and towards Yahweh*." Whatever one thinks about the matter, the narrative itself states that what happened was something very special and something that has never happened before or since the time of Joshua (10:14). The occurrence of the miracle is also attested in the "book of the righteous" (*sefer hayyashar*), and the writer here appears to call on the book in support of the authenticity of what he is saying, as a kind of ancient footnote (cf. 2 Sam. 1:18; possibly 1 Kgs. 8:53 LXX).

■ THE TEXT IN THE INTERPRETIVE TRADITION

There is little reference to the conquests in Joshua 10–12 throughout the rest of the Bible. Until the rise of postcolonial analysis, subsequent commentators appear to have had little problem with the violence portrayed in these chapters. The following comments from John Calvin are instructive (1854, on Josh. 10:40).

> Here the divine authority is again interposed in order completely to acquit Joshua of any charge of cruelty. Had he proceeded of his own accord to commit an indiscriminate massacre of women and children, no excuse could have exculpated him from the guilt of detestable cruelty, cruelty surpassing anything of which we read as having been perpetrated by savage tribes scarcely raised above the level of the brutes. But that at which all would otherwise be justly horrified, it becomes

them to embrace with reverence, as proceeding from God. Clemency is justly praised as one of the principal virtues; but it is the clemency of those who moderate their wrath when they have been injured, and when they would have been justified, as individuals, in shedding blood. But as God had destined the swords of his people for the slaughter of the Amorites, Joshua could do nothing else than obey his command.

Similarly, the New England Puritans could see the destruction of the indigenous peoples as a result of divine providence (see Guyatt, 178) that was tied to their identification with the Israelite foundation story (see Waswo). The text allowed Cotton Mather to say in a 1674 sermon at the eve of a (brutal) war with Metacom and the Wampanoag Indians (quoted in Guyatt, 48),

> The Lord will not as yet destroy this place: Our fathers have built Sanctuaries for his Name therein, and therefore he will not destroy us. The Planting of these Heavens, and the laying the Foundations of the Earth, is one of the Wonders of this last Age. . . . God hath called out a people, even out of all parts of a Nation, which he hath also had a great favour towards, and hath brought them by a mighty hand, and an out-stretched arm, over a [sic] greater than the Red Sea, and here hath he planted them, and hath caused them to grow up as it were into a little Nation; And shall we think that this is to destroy them within forty and fifty years.

Presumably Joshua could have expounded a similar message to his troops before the battle with the southern coalition, or any other battles with the indigenous peoples. While the Puritans were slightly different in that they also had a missionary inclination toward the natives, the genocidal disposition prevailed as a whole, as can be seen in the extent of native dispossession on the North American continent since then. Broadly similar stories apply to Australia and parts of South Africa. While there were those among Christians who spoke against the Western genocidal colonial advance (e.g., Bartolomé de las Casas), their arguments could not stop the colonial tide. In addition, many Zionists, including the first prime minister of Israel, David Ben-Gurion, looked back at the stories of Joshua as legitimation for the Zionist project of conquest and dispossession of the Palestinians, even if this has been dampened by the relatively recent challenges against the historicity of the biblical narrative (Sand 2010, 74–75).

▌THE TEXT IN CONTEMPORARY DISCUSSION

The main problem for modern readings of Joshua 10–12 is that the material attests a genocide ideology. While it is not always entirely easy to define genocide, we may reproduce the UN definition of genocide here as an indicative statement.

> In the present Convention, genocide means any of the following acts committed with intent to destroy, in whole or in part, a national, ethnic, racial or religious group, as such:
>
> (a) Killing members of the group;
> (b) Causing serious bodily or mental harm to members of the group;
> (c) Deliberately inflicting on the group conditions of life calculated to bring about its physical destruction in whole or in part;
> (d) Imposing measures intended to prevent births within the group;
> (e) Forcibly transferring children of the group to another group.

We can see that items (a) through (c) are clearly attested in Joshua. Items (d) and (e) do not seem to apply, even though the Israelites themselves are described as suffering something like (d) and (e) in Egypt (Exod. 1:15). These examples show the role of power in genocide. The relative power portrayed is what changes the Israelites from victims to perpetrators. In Egypt, they are the weaker party and thus become the victims of the Egyptians. In Canaan, they are, or at least aspire to be, the stronger party and wish to found a perfect society, into which the Canaanites do not fit. Thus the Israelites intend and partially implement genocidal policies. This does not all go according to plan, as Judges shows the Israelites intermixing with the indigenes. However, battles and killing are only an aspect of the actual settler-colonial process. There are other, more subtle ways to achieve control over the area, such as assimilation (see comments on Joshua 6–9). Of course, with the lack of modern communications and possibly largely oral nature of early Israel, together with the question of the dating of the biblical materials, it is unlikely that the Israelites had the effective organization that would have enabled them to carry out the orders of the Yahwistic purists in Deuteronomy 7 (see Judg. 2:6-13).

In this vein, modern communities may ask how to deal with those who do not fit with their plans, which ties in with the question of exclusivity. History shows how—time and again—a desire for uniformity, or the desires of one particular interest group followed at the expense of others, can lead to violence and genocide. Therefore, it is of vital importance for today's individuals, groups, and societies to acknowledge pluralism not only at the innersocietal level but also at the intergroup and intersocietal level. So, for example, powerful societies like the United States or the West in general, or powerful groups within them, should reflect on whose interests are being promoted in international economics and politics: those of merely their own, or those of humanity at large?

Joshua 13–19: Settler-Colonial Advance

■ THE TEXT IN ITS ANCIENT CONTEXT

Joshua 13–19 describes the allotment of land to the tribes of Israel. Together with chapters 20–21, the allotments make provision for everyone in the land of Canaan. These chapters begin a new, distinctive section in the book. Focus shifts away from conquest to allotments and settlement, to be continued with exhortation for a life according to the commands of YHWH in Joshua 23–24 in particular. Chapters 14–19 form a chiastic structure, as pointed out by Koorevaar (289).

<pre>
a   14:6-15   Beginning: Caleb's inheritance
  b   15:1—17:18   The lot for Judah and Joseph
    c   18:1-10   The tent of meeting taken to Shiloh
                     and the apportioning of the land
  b' 18:11—19:48   The lot for seven remaining tribes
a' 19:49-51   Ending: Joshua's inheritance
</pre>

In addition, Joshua 13, a passage that relates to the Transjordanian tribes, can probably be matched with the towns of refuge and the Levitical towns in chapters 20–21. These pertain to groups that have in some way a special status in Israel. The link, however, is perhaps somewhat more tenuous than with 14:6—19:51. The Greek text differs in a number of details for the boundary and town lists.

The above shows that the setting up of the tent of meeting at Shiloh and the apportioning of the land stands at the center of the allotments. This structure fits with the importance of the tent of meeting as the place where YHWH dwells in the midst of the people of Israel, perfectly in line with Priestly theology, including that of the Holiness Code (Exodus 25–40; Lev. 26:11). YHWH's dwelling in the tent amid the people is also broadly in line with Deuteronomistic theology, which is the primary framework of Joshua. Thus, together with the chapters as a whole, Priestly material has been incorporated into a Deuteronomistic framework.

In relation to the centrality of the concept of land here and throughout Genesis–Joshua (including the Holiness Code and Deuteronomy), again, we may make a comparison with settler-colonial studies. According to Patrick Wolfe (130n71): "settler colonialism has . . . two principal aspects—not only the removal of native society, but also its concomitant replacement with settler institutions. This latter, positive aspect involves the establishment and legitimation of civil hegemony." And, "eliminatory strategies all reflect the centrality of the land, which is not merely the component of settler society but its basic precondition" (Wolfe, 103).

There has been enormous discussion about the boundary and town lists in the past (see Pitkänen 2010, 252–53 for a summary). Even today, there is no agreement about their dating. However, it seems safe to suggest that Judah's town list dates from the late monarchy. Also, the boundary lists are more detailed for Judah and Benjamin, the two main tribes of the southern kingdom. At the same time, we know from Hittite treaties that boundary and town lists were in use already in the second millennium BCE. So it is entirely possible that, whatever way they were then incorporated into the book and possibly edited after their initial incorporation, the Israelite materials originate from an earlier time than their final form.

Joshua 14:6-15 and 19:49-51 and the emphasis on Caleb and Joshua tie back to the narrative in Numbers 13–14, in which the Israelites spy the land before their actual entrance into it. All the spies except Caleb and Joshua, representatives of the tribes of Judah and Joseph, bring back a bad report. These tribes, then, are portrayed as leading tribes here in Joshua. Joshua himself becomes the leader of the Israelites, and Caleb is given Hebron, an important town in the Israelite tradition, as it serves as both a town of refuge (Josh. 20:7) and a priestly town for the Aaronides (Josh. 21:11). It is also the town from where David rules initially, before the move to Jerusalem (2 Sam. 5:1-4). In addition, it is an important town in the patriarchal narratives and is the place where most of the patriarchs were buried (Gen. 13:18; 23; 49:31; 50:13; but cf. Gen. 35:19-20 for Rachel and Josh. 24:32 for Joseph). Thus, arguably, the North and the South are also represented by Shiloh and Hebron in Joshua 13–19 and in 20–21.

As already indicated, these chapters reflect a more peaceful process than that in Joshua 1–12, even though they also portray conquests, for example, with Caleb. In this respect, these chapters are more in line with Judges 1. They are also in line with how typical settlement processes work. As in early America—among other cases—such processes may include periods of apparently peaceful coexistence, and then extensions of the process of settlement that may include further fighting, killing, and expulsion (see Josh. 13:1-7; 15:63; 16:10; 17:12-18; 18:5-7; 19:47; Exod. 23:20-30), and may also include assimilation, or attempts to assimilate, indigenous peoples (see, e.g., Kakel; cf. Veracini 2010, esp. 16–52, which lists twenty-six different ways to "purge" a settler collective of indigenous elements).

In addition, visions of territory may include areas that have not yet been conquered (see Kakel, 130 for *two* differing visions of territory in Germany during the Second World War), and this seems to be the case with Joshua also (13:1-6). In Joshua 13–19, a settler-colonial "structure" (rather than an event; see Wolfe) has been put in place in which the Israelite polity is set to expand, and this actually seems to mirror what happened during Iron Age I, as archaeological evidence indicates that the Israelite settlement and control started from the central, eastern, and northern highlands and expanded out from there, to include lowlands in the later course of Israel's history (Finkelstein, 324–30; cf. Junkkaala, 308–9). Eventually, by the time the Israelite state(s) itself was conquered by the Assyrians and Babylonians, indigenous peoples had been assimilated into the Israelite community (1 Chron. 2:50-53; Ezra 2:25; Neh. 7:25, 29; vs. Josh. 9:17), and Solomon is said to have incorporated non-Israelites as slaves at the early stages of the ancient Israelite monarchy (1 Kgs. 9:20-23). The daughters of Zelophehad may actually represent one group of indigenous peoples that had been assimilated early and incorporated in the Israelite genealogies, as many of their names correspond with localities in Samaria (Josh. 17:3-4; cf. Numbers 36).

▮ THE TEXT IN THE INTERPRETIVE TRADITION

Stephen's speech in Acts 7:45 refers to the tabernacle and the taking of the land from the indigenes as part of the salvation history described, which can be compared with the allotment of the land and the setting up of the tabernacle at Shiloh in Joshua 13–19 in particular. The passage exhibits no criticism of the process of dispossession, and, again, it is only postcolonial criticism that really has started to ask questions about the legitimacy of what is depicted here. That said, the apostle Paul touches on the matter in Rom. 9:6-24. Paul acknowledges the problem of theodicy but nevertheless puts it aside under the explanation that it is a mystery of God that humans cannot understand.

At the same time, the Old Testament describes how the focus of Josiah's reform on the destruction of non-Yahwistic religious objects and any killing is marginal (as pointed out by Moberly), and the book of Ezra only advocates separation from the people of the land (Ezra 9–10), not the extermination of those peoples. Also, according to 1 Kgs. 9:20-21, while the destruction of non-Israelites should have taken place during the time of the conquest, such an attitude did not prevail any more during the time of Solomon. Thus one can suggest that the destruction of the Canaanites during the early history of Joshua was part of a unique situation as part of God's plan of salvation that is not to be repeated otherwise, which is how many recent commentators have tended to approach the subject. Some also see the violence that is portrayed as ultimately mythical (e.g., Earl), or only as a story (see Docker, 113–29). And yet, as also pointed out in the previous sense unit, settler-colonial processes have repeated themselves in world history and have sometimes been at least partially legitimated by recourse to the ancient Israelite conquest and settlement story through an identification with the conquering Israelites. This is unfortunate, as the concept of the promised land has been spiritualized in the New Testament, referring there to the eternal life for which Christians wait. It is true, too, though, that Origen did spiritualize the extermination of the Canaanites into the mortification of the flesh (see Earl, 166). And, more broadly, it was typical for the church fathers to interpret chapters 13–19 typologically and spiritually, with the new land signifying new Christian life (see Franke, 71–87).

◼ THE TEXT IN CONTEMPORARY DISCUSSION

Recent postcolonial analysis has been critical of the overall ancient Israelite colonial and settler-colonial expansion into the highlands as described by Joshua 13–19, viewing it as a form of exploitation in an intercultural and intersocietal context where a stronger party dominates a weaker party and exploits that party for their own benefit (see Osterhammel, 15–22). Historically, texts have often drawn attention to exploitation by the powerful within society (e.g., Laws of Hammurabi; Deuteronomy and the widow, orphan, and alien; the Gospels). It is thus now time to draw increasing attention to intersocietal and international oppression and exploitation. The New Testament can be seen to support this.

According to the New Testament, greed is idolatry (Eph. 5:5; Col. 3:5). In the Old Testament, the second part of the Decalogue already also speaks against greed (Exod. 20:13-17; Deut. 5:17-21) after an explicit warning against idolatry. The New Testament extends the older covenant, which originally applied to the Israelite nation only, to apply to people from all nations instead of only one, and thus to international politics also. Especially those nations and people that are politically and financially powerful should thus reflect on their dispositions and actions so that the interests of humanity as a whole are served and not just those of one powerful interest group.

In light of the above, we can say that oppression and greed in these contexts is idolatry and should be avoided at all costs. While the explicit era of colonialism is now largely over, neocolonialism is still a reality in many parts of the world. Neocolonialism still includes occasional conquests—and even at least partial genocide—by powerful nations to exploit raw materials, such as the conquest of Iraq by the United States in 2003. However, exploitation by powerful multinational companies and financial institutions in the interest of excessive capitalism should also be included in this category, and the banking crisis of 2007–2008 and beyond has demonstrated that exploitation is not limited to non-Western peoples.

In terms of settler colonialism, the recent UN Declaration on the Rights of Indigenous Peoples (2007) is a step in the right direction for recognizing the rights of the weaker peoples. However, constant vigilance is still needed, especially in acknowledging the right of these peoples to determine their own destiny. In addition, those societies that have oppressed and in many ways destroyed and taken land from indigenes should acknowledge what they have done and offer restitution to those indigenous people that have survived their onslaughts. This is an issue for humanity as a whole, and settler-colonial studies has shown how resistant settler-colonial societies are to this and other related types of decolonization (Veracini 2010, 95–116).

There are also societies that continue their assault on indigenous peoples, sometimes under the full gaze of the world. These include powerful nations such as the United States and the modern state of Israel. In the United States, most of the settler-colonial process was completed by the second half of the nineteenth century, but the Native American communities still live in often destitute situations (Tinker 2004; 2008). In modern Israel, the settler-colonial process of taking land from the indigenous Palestinians that started some one hundred years ago is currently in full swing (see Veracini 2006). In this case, some modern Israelis may legitimate their actions by recourse to the ancient biblical texts, including Joshua. From an ideological perspective, except for Jewish Zionism, Christian popular eschatology has caused many Christians to support Israel (see Sand 2012, esp. 119–253, for the history of Zionism). As part of this, those who take a so-called dispensationalist premillennial view on the Scriptures (see Clouse for a basic exposition; and Court, 123–24 for its origins in nineteenth-century America) argue that Israel should still be considered as a literal concept, that the return of the Israeli(te)s to Palestine is foretold in the Bible, and even that the temple will be rebuilt in Israel, if only to administer sacrifices that serve as memorial for Jesus. However, the dispensationalist view is by no means the only one available.

So-called historical premillenialists, amillenialists, and probably postmillennialists all see, in the light of the New Testament, the promises to Israel as now applying to the church (Romans 9), even if the "literal" Israel still has some kind of role (for the basic positions, see Clouse; for a historical dimension to millennial movements, see Court). In this light, there is no need to interpret biblical material as foretelling a literal return of the Jews to Israel (the concept of Jews as more than ideological heirs—i.e., rather as descendants of converts than physical descendants of the ancient Israelites—has also been challenged; see esp. Sand 2009; cf. Sand 2012). Therefore, prophecies about Israel's return to the land can be received metaphorically (see Chapman). Interestingly, before Zionism's nineteenth-century rise—having been connected with the rise of European nationalism (Sand 2012)—Jews largely thought that they should not "go up the wall," that is, collectively migrate to the land. This view was based on a passage in *Ketubot* 13:11 in the Talmud. (There were also two other injunctions in the talmudic passage, that Israel should not rebel against the nations and that the idolaters, that is, the nations of the world, should not oppress Israel too much; see Sand 2012, 106–7.) Through this lens, we can see a strong argument for the support of Palestinians, who are losing their land to Israeli policies.

Joshua 20–22: YHWH's People—Unity, Right Worship, Justice, and Provision for All

▌THE TEXT IN ITS ANCIENT CONTEXT

Joshua follows on the great Deuteronomic vision of unity, right worship, justice, and provision for all in the land YHWH has promised to Israel's forefathers. There is unity in conquest, in that the Transjordanians take part in it rather than staying east of the Jordan (1:6-9; 3–4; 22:1-8). Joshua's altar at Mount Ebal (8:30-35) attests unity in worship in the promised land, as does the memorial altar in Transjordan (22:9-34), even if there are initial suspicions that the Transjordanian altar had been built in order to provide an alternative place of worship to that at Shiloh. After land has been allotted to the Israelite tribes (13–19), the institution of Levitical towns (21) helps take care of cultic functionaries; and the institution of towns of refuge (20) that cover the land as a whole, both east and west of the Jordan, helps to protect a person who has committed accidental manslaughter. The Greek text of Joshua 20 differs from the MT in that, for example, 20:4-6 is missing in LXX B. The Greek text also differs somewhat from the MT in the list of towns in Joshua 21.

The system of blood avenging seems to be attested in the ancient Near East, and already well into the second millennium. The victim's family generally had a chance to choose between killing the offender or to receive "blood money" in compensation (see Barmash, 20–70). The vassal treaties of Esarhaddon directly mention that, "just as a stag is overtaken and killed, so may the avenger overtake and kill you, your sons and daughters" (Barmash, 54). Also, cuneiform legal material stipulates for capital punishments in case of homicides (e.g., Barmash, 168–70). We may conclude from this that the system of towns of refuge had its grounding in ancient Near Eastern law and practice, but appears to have a specifically Israelite slant in the book of Joshua. In the present form of the text, the towns have been set up roughly evenly across the Israelite territory (comments by Zvi, 97–98 notwithstanding). This would enable one equally easy access to a town of refuge throughout the land (as observed by Barmash, 85; see also Boling and Wright, 447, for a rough map). The relationship of Joshua 20 to Exod. 21:12-14; Num. 35:6, 9-34; and Deut. 4:41-43; 19:1-3, which also deal with cases of accidental manslaughter, is a much-discussed issue (see Barmash, passim). For our purposes here, we may note that Joshua 20 seems to be based on both Deuteronomic and Priestly materials (Pitkänen 2010, 334–36; Barmash). The actual implementation of the towns of refuge as described in Joshua would suggest that this part of the Israelite legal provision was intended as realistic rather than theoretical, at least in the narrative world.

Apart from their first mention in Lev. 25:32-34 as something known, the Levitical towns are first "properly" introduced in Num. 35:1-8 in the canonical context (and order), and the passage here in the book of Joshua provides a fulfillment of the stipulations in Numbers. The Levitical towns are not directly mentioned in Deuteronomy proper. The legislation regarding the towns in Lev. 25:32-34 is in agreement with the corresponding legislation in Numbers and Joshua. Apart from Joshua 21, another list of the towns is provided in 1 Chron. 6:54-81 (Hebrew 6:39-66). The lists in Joshua and Chronicles differ somewhat, as do the Hebrew and Greek versions of Joshua 21. Much discussion has surrounded the Levitical towns (Kallai 1986; 2010; Hutton). By and large, they have been dated from the early monarchy to the postexilic period. Much of the discussion has also centered on the question of whether the system should be seen as programmatic (or idealistic, even "utopian") or as based on some actual historical reality during the history of Israel. The concept does, however, have parallels with land and town grants and property sales in second-millennium-BCE Ugarit and Alalakh (see Pitkänen 2010, 342).

Joshua 21:43-45 suggests that Israel achieved rest in the promised land during the time of Joshua, after the allotment of the tribal land. Commentators have often pointed out that this seems to contradict the rest of the book, which portrays fighting and incomplete settlement. However, recourse to settler-colonial studies can again help. Settler-colonial societies generally wish to "disavow" their violent origins. According to Veracini, as one part of such processes, "An anxious reaction to disconcerting and disorienting developments produces a drive to think about a pacified world that can only be achieved via voluntary displacement" (2010, 89). Also, while "settlers are natural men engaged in building a settled life in an ahistorical locale, recurring representations of settler original idylls insist on an immaculate foundational setting devoid of disturbing indigenous (or exogenous) others" (2010, 88). The contradictions in the book of Joshua can thus be understood in psychological terms. The cognitive dissonance between founding violence and desired idyllic peace is a contradiction that the author of Joshua was not able to completely resolve, and neither can the readers of the book. As Veracini (2010, 89) notes in terms of settler-colonial situations, "Ultimately, the fact that these images coexist with ongoing (explicit, latent, or intermittently surfacing) apprehension may actually suggest the activation of a splitting of the ego-like process, where two antithetical psychical attitudes coexist side by side without communicating, one taking reality into consideration, the other disavowing it."

Joshua 22 describes how the Transjordanians, having assisted their brothers in the conquest, are sent home (22:1-8; a passage in Deuteronomistic style) and how they then build an altar in the Transjordanian territory (22:9-34, a passage in Priestly style, with a plotline similar to Numbers 32). After achieving rest, sacrifices are to be made only at the central sanctuary (22:19, 23, 27; cf. Deut. 12:10-11). The Transjordanians explain to the representatives of the Western tribes that the altar is to only serve as a monument, and a civil war over the cultic matter is averted (22:26, 28, 33).

▌ THE TEXT IN THE INTERPRETIVE TRADITION

The application of the institution of towns of refuge does not receive a lot of discussion in other parts of the Old Testament. The flights of Joab and Adonijah to the tent of YHWH (1 Kgs. 1:50-53; 2:28-34) have often been seen as related to the matter but in reality are more likely based on political asylum (Barmash, 72–80). The concept does not carry over to the New Testament except for its general principle of justice. In modern democratic societies, perhaps the idea of a trial by jury can be taken as a safeguard against unreasonable response to capital cases.

The Levitical towns are also not mentioned in the New Testament. However, their basic principle of taking care of cultic functionaries carries over quite strongly in the New Testament. Jesus was supported financially by a number of people (Luke 8:2-3), and Paul states it as the right of a church worker to be supported financially (1 Cor. 9:7-10), also referring back to the cultic system of the Old Testament (1 Cor. 9:13-14), and surely the system of Levitical towns is at least implicitly included here. Paul himself, however, relinquishes that right (1 Cor. 9:15) and supports himself through his own means, apparently by his tentmaking skills (Acts 18:1-3).

Hebrews 4 speaks about rest for God's people. According to the chapter, the rest achieved by Joshua was not yet a real rest (4:8), and the author quotes Psalm 95 in support, especially 95:7-8. That is, had Joshua already been given that rest, the psalm would not have spoken of yet another day, as per 95:7-8, 11. On a broader canvas, certainly, the later history of Israel showed that the nation was not able to follow YHWH and ultimately fell to the Assyrians and the Babylonians, only to be restored partially in the postexilic and intertestamental times. Instead, for the writer of Hebrews, the rest to be achieved by Christians is the real rest (4:9-11), and apparently eternal life is its ultimate realization (4:11), emphasizing the "already and not yet" thematic typical of the New

Testament. Interestingly, Joshua's rest is also compared to and at least partially equated with the Sabbath rest in the Hebrews passage, another Old Testament concept that relates to the founding stories of the Israelite nation.

Questions about the right way to worship YHWH permeate the New Testament. Jesus' ministry challenged established practices, and this was the main reason for his crucifixion. The new Christian worship continued to define its ways of worship against internal challenges (e.g., 1 Chronicles 11–14) and external threats, such as those coming from the Jewish community (Acts 8:1-3; 21:27—26:32; Galatians) and gentile community (Acts 16:16-40; 19:23-41). Both the Roman persecutions of Christians and the various factions and churches within Christianity, including those resulting from the Reformation, demonstrate the continuing importance of religious matters and the right worship of God.

The early church fathers again spiritualized the cities of refuge and the Levitical towns. Jesus is the high priest in a city of refuge (Ambrose), and the lots were drawn in order, referring to the orderliness of the resurrection and also the orderliness of the heavenly power (Origen; see Franke, 88–90). The dismissal of the two and a half tribes indicates the mystery of the fullness of the nations, and the Transjordanian altar is a type of the true altar that is with Jesus (Origen; see Franke, 91–92).

▍THE TEXT IN CONTEMPORARY DISCUSSION

As with the ideal presented in Joshua, today's communities should strive to provide the best possible environments and institutions in order for people to flourish and so that justice and provision might be available for all. One should also ask what the role of religion should be in society. In the Old Testament, religion was part of the society, much in line with other societies of the time. Judaism, however, was not a dominant religion in Roman society, even though it was a religion with some special privileges from the state. Christianity diverged from Judaism in the Roman Empire, was initially persecuted, and then became an accepted religion and shortly thereafter in the fifth century the only allowed religion. The concept of Christendom was carried over in Europe by the successors of the Roman Empire, and Christendom's hold started to weaken only after the Enlightenment. In most countries outside the West, however, churches have usually not been connected with political power. The history of colonialism has shown the abuses that can take place when Christianity allies itself with political power.

Perhaps the way forward for Christians is to continue acting as leaven (see Matt. 13:33) and lobby political powers (some Christians may themselves be in high positions in society) in order to achieve both societal and intersocietal justice and provision for all. In this, they can ally themselves with secular organizations that have similar goals. For example, the great social movements of the nineteenth and twentieth centuries that achieved universal health care for those who would not be able to have it otherwise should be seen as one good example of the types of programs that Christians can advocate in wider society. In the international context, Christians can lobby for such issues as political and economic justice, as well as equality for weaker nations and the rights of indigenous peoples. As one specific example, Western Christians can work toward moving past the continuing disavowal of the recognition of the rights of indigenous peoples in such countries as the United

States, Canada, Australia, and New Zealand. With the expansion of the new covenant to include all peoples, the welfare of all of humankind should be considered, and not only that of one nation or interest group. Care for the environment and for the creation of God as a whole can also be included in this category.

In terms of the Christian church, the end of Christendom in the West and the lessening or withdrawal of state support from the church in Europe is changing the role of how those in Christian ministry should be supported. These texts from Joshua can be used to encourage people to offer freely from their own in order to support churches. Perhaps the principle of the Old Testament tithe is no more directly applicable, but it can provide a good, broad guideline in a number of cases. It is important that churches trust in the provision of YHWH and not seek to present their message in a "market-oriented" manner, as is the case with the so-called success theology, or the "prosperity gospel."

The spirit of unity promoted in Joshua 20–22 could speak to religious communities that struggle with worship styles. While working to find their right way of worship, they might do well to recognize diversity of opinion and peacefully seek to resolve their differences, rather than heading toward schism. This may be of particular use for faith communities that struggle with contemporary-traditional divides.

Joshua 23–24: Looking into the Future

▎THE TEXT IN ITS ANCIENT CONTEXT

As with the beginning of the book of Joshua, the last two chapters describe a people in transition. Joshua is about to die, and the people are again in a situation where they have to manage on their own, without their great leader. The two chapters constitute a kind of "double ending" for the book. Broadly speaking, Joshua 23 is more concerned with Deuteronomistic themes, and chapter 24 more with overall Hexateuchal themes. However, the fact that the book of Joshua as a whole already mirrors Genesis–Joshua, and that Joshua 24 is presented in an overall Deuteronomistic style, speaks against an easy detachment of this chapter from the rest of the book.

The structure of Joshua 23, while slightly difficult to delimit, can be described as follows (partly based on Nelson, 256).

> Joshua summons Israel in his old age (23:1-2a)
> Joshua's speech (2b-16)
> Joshua's note about his old age (2b)
> Review: YHWH's victory and land allotment (3-5)
>> YHWH's faithfulness (3)
>> Overview of conquest and settlement thus far, and promise of driving out remaining nations in the future (4-5)
> Exhortation to follow the law of Moses and not to join with the remaining nations and their gods (6-8)
> Review: YHWH's victorious fighting for Israel (9-10)

Exhortation to love YHWH and conditional threat in regard to alien nations, with special mention against intermarrying (11-13)
Joshua's note about his impending death (14a)
Review: fulfillment of all of YHWH's promises (14b)
Conditional threat about covenant violation (15-16)

Nelson helpfully notes the increasing severity in the threats as the chapter progresses—see 23:6-8, 13 and 15-16 (Nelson, 256). The word "peoples" is used six times (23:3-4, 7, 9, 12-13.) The expression "good land" is important at the end of the passage (see Nelson, 256–57). In other words, the chapter uses a strategy of rhetorical persuasion.

The structure of Joshua 24:1-28 can be described as follows:

The covenant renewal at Shechem (24:1-28)
 Joshua assembles Israel at Shechem (1)
 Joshua's first speech: YHWH's message (2-16)
  Historical recital (2-13)
   Call of Abraham (2-3)
   Isaac, Jacob, Esau, and going down to Egypt (4)
   Moses and Aaron and the exodus (5)
   Miracle at the Sea of Reeds (6-7a)
   Wilderness wanderings (7b)
   The conquest of Transjordan (8)
   Balaam incident (9-10)
  Conquest of Canaan with YHWH's help (11-13)
  Exhortation to serve YHWH (14-15)
 Response by the people (16-18)
  Denial that the people will serve other gods (16)
  Acknowledgment of YHWH's work (17-18a)
  Promise to serve YHWH (18b)
 Joshua's second speech (19-20)
  People cannot serve YHWH (19a)
  Threat of punishment (19b-20)
 Response by the people promising to serve YHWH (21)
 Joshua's response, making people witnesses (22a)
 Response by the people, acknowledging that they are witnesses (22b)
 Joshua's exhortation to put away foreign gods (23)
 Response by the people, promising to serve YHWH (24)
 Summary about making a covenant (25)
Joshua writes the words of the covenant in a book of the law of God (26a)
The stone of witness (26b-27)
 Setting up the stone (26b)
 Joshua's summary about the role of the stone (27)
Joshua sends the people back to their homes (28)

The overall purpose of verses 1-28 strengthen Joshua's overall rhetoric in exhorting the Israelites to follow YHWH exclusively. The forming of a covenant (see Koopmans for this aspect, including comparisons with ancient Near Eastern treaty formats; but note also the *misharum* acts in Babylonia, which were basically minor legal edicts addressing specific situations, meant to be understood as additions to existing legal or legal-related practice), examples from past history, and various exhortations throughout serve to reinforce this objective. As Nelson notes, repetition serves to "impel the reader to go along with the assembled Israel and to concur with the text's agenda" (268). The means of pleading, setting an example, and using accusatory speech are part of the rhetorical means of persuasion in 24:14-21 (Pitkänen 2010, 396).

The location of the covenant ceremony and of charging the people to remove all foreign gods and consider YHWH only heightens the symbolism of the occasion, as this is *the* place (24:25-26) where Jacob, the grand patriarch of Israel *in actuality* threw away *his* foreign gods (Gen. 35:1-5). Thus the whole point of the ceremony in this chapter is to emphasize total commitment to YHWH, a decisive point of no return in the life of the new Israel in the land of their forefathers, where they have now returned after a long absence. Just as Jacob was to purify himself of foreign gods after his stay away in Paddan Aram and YHWH's gracious granting of return and prosperity to him (Genesis 35), so is Israel to do also. Of course, the reader (or hearer) of the book of Joshua is expected to take note accordingly. Chapters 23–24 are generally in line with the idea that religiopolitical ideology is often driven by political elites, even if it can be helped by popular support or even partially also driven by it (see Kakel, 213–14). Religious diversity in ancient, preexilic Israel is confirmed by known archaeological evidence, and it would appear that the idea that the people followed YHWH in the time of Joshua should be seen as a more or less idealized concept (see the comments on 21:43-45 in the Joshua 20–22 sense unit).

Joshua 24:28-33, which is followed by a few lines of extra material in Greek manuscripts, describes the death and burials of Joshua and Eleazar, together with the burial of Joseph's bones, tying the material explicitly to Genesis. The additions in the Greek attest connection with the book of Judges, and such a connection must have been done at a suitable time, as Judges in its present form follows on from the book of Joshua relatively seamlessly. This is true even when Judges, at least arguably, is clearly a separate book (even though, for Noth and those following him, both Joshua and Judges are part of a unified historical work of a Deuteronomistic History).

▌ THE TEXT IN THE INTERPRETIVE TRADITION

The Bible itself shows that the ideology of following YHWH as advocated by Joshua 23 and 24 did not fare well in the wider societal setting. This is the overall conclusion of the writer(s) of 1–2 Kings (e.g., 2 Kgs. 23:26-27; cf. Ps. 78:56-64) and many of the Old Testament prophets, and of course the Pentateuch shows that the Israelites already did not follow YHWH wholeheartedly in the wilderness from Exodus on either (see also Ps. 78:8-57).

The New Testament, of course, exhorts Christians to follow God wholeheartedly. The concept is so pervasive that hardly any additional commentary is required on the principle itself. And yet, the question of what is the right way to follow God is equally alive in the New Testament. The New

Testament includes many descriptions about internal debates already at the time of the first apostles. Even the apostles themselves could be of differing opinion (Acts 6:1-15; 15:36-40) and could also rebuke each other in case of perceived inappropriate practice (Gal. 2:11-14; cf. 1 Cor. 11:18; 1 Thess. 5:21). Of course, Christian history shows many debates about what is the right way to follow YHWH, as attested by the great church councils of the first few centuries of the Common Era and by the Reformation in Europe.

The early church fathers generally understood chapters 23–24 less typologically than usual with the book of Joshua (see Franke, 93–98), probably simply because these chapters lend themselves more easily to a straightforward theological interpretation from a post–New Testament perspective. But Cyprian saw the stone of witness in Joshua 24:26-27 as Christ (Franke, 97). Interestingly, Jerome assumed that Joshua had no children and was not married since they are not mentioned, and thus argued for celibacy as a better status than marriage (see Franke, 97–98). Jerome also suggested that the fact that there is no mention of the Israelites' grieving Joshua (as they did with the death of Moses) symbolizes our not needing to grieve in the face of death, since we have put on Christ (see Franke, 98).

◼ THE TEXT IN CONTEMPORARY DISCUSSION

Christians, when thinking about their covenant ("treaty") with God, can also reflect on their past history with God. Such history consists of YHWH's acts through history as expressed in the Bible (both the Old and the New Testaments), in church history, and in remembrance of YHWH's acts in their personal lives (and also in the lives of others they may know [about] in their communities). Such memory and understanding serves as a vital basis for one's faith. If one wishes, one may also write down one's experiences in a book and arrange for some kind of object (e.g., some like to wear a crucifix) to commemorate such events and experiences. Christians may also reflect on other aspects of the (new) treaty that was established through the sacrifice of Christ on the cross. They may draw attention to Joshua's call to his hearers to choose between YHWH and other gods. This call to follow YHWH is also reflected in Jesus' call to "follow me!"

However, for Christians in a post-Christendom and postcolonial world, this exhortation to follow ought to be tempered by a caution against desiring a form of political power tied to religion, and it ought not include any violent inclination toward those who think differently, even when differences of opinion and their testing are appropriate (see 1 Cor. 11:18; 1 Thess. 5:21). In addition, in general, Christians are exhorted to reflect humbly on the role of violence in the development and history of their own religion and its relation to questions of theodicy, rather than disavowing that violence (see Davies, 120–47). In an eschatological sense, while portions of the Gospels and the book of Revelation may be viewed as predicting eschatological violence, Christians should refrain from being instigators of such violence. And, while in some cases the attainment of justice and protection of others would seem to require the use of violence, one should always consider its use as the last resort after all other possible means have been exhausted.

A related issue in following YHWH is the question of what one should do when life does not seem happy or worth living even when one is following YHWH wholeheartedly (e.g., the book of

Job). One may be struggling to earn a living, be ill or grieving, or persecuted because of one's faith. Such situations can often also make one reflect on the concept of theodicy. As with the question of violence, it may not be that a rational theodicy of the Old Testament—and often not one of the New Testament either—seems attainable. Instead, when thinking of the past, present, and the future, the only option for Christians is often to make an existential leap of faith, trusting in God and God's goodness, that everything will ultimately go well with those who do so, exactly whatever this "going well" may entail (see M. E. W. Thompson 2011).

Works Cited

Aubet, M. E. 2013. *Commerce and Colonization in the Ancient Near East*. Cambridge: Cambridge University Press (Spanish original 2007).

Barmash, Pamela. 2005. *Homicide in the Biblical World*. Cambridge: Cambridge University Press.

Blenkinsopp, Joseph. 1972. *Gibeon and Israel: The Role of Gibeon and the Gibeonites in the Political and Religious History of Early Israel*. Cambridge: Cambridge University Press.

Boling, R. G., and G. E. Wright. 1982. *Joshua: A New Translation with Introduction and Commentary*. AB. Garden City, NY: Doubleday.

Butler, T. 1983. *Joshua*. WBC. Waco, TX: Word.

Calvin, John. 1854. *Commentaries on the Book of Joshua*. Translated by Henry Beveridge. Edinburgh: Calvin Translation Society (Original 1564).

Carr, David M. 2011. *The Formation of the Hebrew Bible: A New Reconstruction*. New York: Oxford University Press.

Chapman, C. 2005. "God's Covenant—God's Land?" In *The God of Covenant*, edited by Alistair I. Wilson and Jamie A. Grant, 221–56. Leicester, UK: Inter-Varsity Press.

Clouse, R. D., ed. 1977. *The Meaning of the Millennium: Four Views*. Downers Grove, IL: InterVarsity Press.

Court, J. M. 2008. *Approaching the Apocalypse: A Short History of Christian Millenarianism*. London: I. B. Tauris.

Davies, E. W. 2010. *The Immoral Bible: Approaches to Biblical Ethics*. New York: T&T Clark.

Day, D. 2008. *Conquest: How Societies Overwhelm Others*. Oxford: Oxford University Press.

Dever, W. G. 2003. *Who Were the Early Israelites and Where Did They Come From?* Grand Rapids: Eerdmans.

Dietler, M. 2010. *Archaeologies of Colonialism: Consumption, Entanglement and Violence in Ancient Mediterranean France*. Berkeley: University of California Press.

Docker, J. 2008. *The Origins of Violence: Religion, History and Genocide*. London: Pluto.

Dozeman, Thomas B., Thomas Römer, and Konrad Schmid, eds. 2011. *Pentateuch, Hexateuch, or Enneateuch? Identifying Literary Works in Genesis through Kings*. Ancient Israel and Its Literature 8. Atlanta: Society of Biblical Literature.

Dozeman, Thomas B., and Konrad Schmid, eds. 2006. *A Farewell to the Yahwist? The Composition of the Pentateuch in Recent European Interpretation*. SBLSymS 34. Atlanta: Society of Biblical Literature.

Earl, D. S. 2010. *Reading Joshua as Christian Scripture*. PhD diss., Durham University. Available at *Durham E-Theses Online*: http://etheses.dur.ac.uk/2267/ (also published in slightly revised form as *Reading Joshua as Christian Scripture*. Journal of Theological Interpretation Supplement 2. Winona Lake, IN: Eisenbrauns, 2010).

Faust, A. 2006. *Israel's Ethnogenesis: Settlement, Interaction, Expansion and Resistance*. London: Equinox.

Finkelberg, M. 2005. *Greeks and Pre-Greeks: Aegean Prehistory and Greek Heroic Tradition*. Cambridge: Cambridge University Press.

Finkelstein, I. 1988. *The Archaeology of the Israelite Settlement*. Jerusalem: Israel Exploration Society.

Franke, J. R., ed. 2005. *Joshua, Judges, Ruth, 1–2 Samuel*. In Ancient Christian Commentary on Scripture, Old Testament 4. Downers Grove, IL: InterVarsity Press.

Fritz, V. 1994. *Das Buch Josua*. HAT I/7. Tübingen: J. C. B. Mohr.

Guyatt, N. 2007. *Providence and the Invention of the United States, 1607–1876*. Cambridge: Cambridge University Press.

Hawk, L. D. 2000. *Joshua*. Berit Olam. Collegeville, MN: Liturgical Press.

———. 2010. *Joshua in 3D: A Commentary on Biblical Conquest and Manifest Destiny*. Eugene, OR: Cascade.

Hess, R. S. 1996. *Joshua: An Introduction and Commentary*. TOTC. Leicester, UK: Inter-Varsity Press.

Hoffmeier, J. K. 1997. *Israel in Egypt: The Evidence for the Authenticity of the Exodus Tradition*. Oxford: Oxford University Press.

———. 2005. *Ancient Israel in Sinai: The Evidence for the Authenticity of the Wilderness Traditions*. Oxford: Oxford University Press.

Horowitz, D. 2000. *Ethnic Groups in Conflict*. Berkeley: University of California Press, 1985. Reprint.

Hutton, J. 2011. "The Levitical Diaspora (II): Modern Perspectives on the Levitical Cities Lists (A Review of Opinions)." In *Levites and Priests in Biblical History and Tradition*, edited by Mark Leuchter and Jeremy Hutton, 45–82. Ancient Israel and Its Literature 9. Atlanta: Society of Biblical Literature.

Junkkaala, E. 2006. *Three Conquests of Canaan: A Comparative Study of Two Egyptian Military Campaigns and Joshua 10–12 in the Light of Recent Archaeological Evidence*. Turku: Åbo Akademi University Press. https://oa.doria.fi/handle/10024/4162.

Kakel, C. P. 2011. *The American West and the Nazi East: A Comparative and Interpretive Perspective*. Basingstoke, UK: Palgrave Macmillan.

Kallai, Z. 1986. *Historical Geography of the Bible: The Tribal Territories of Israel*. Jerusalem: Magnes Press; Leiden: Brill.

———. 2010. *Studies in Biblical Historiography and Geography: Collection of Studies*. BEATAJ 56. Frankfurt am Main: Peter Lang.

Kitchen, K. 2003. *On the Reliability of the Old Testament*. Grand Rapids: Eerdmans.

Knauf, E. A. 2008. *Josua*. ZBK 6. Zürich: Theologischer.

Koopmans, W. T. 1990. *Joshua 24 as Poetic Narrative*. JSOTSup 93. Sheffield: Sheffield Academic Press.

Koorevaar, H. J. 1990. *De Opbouw van het Boek Jozua*. Heverlee: Centrum voor Bijbelse Vorming Belgie v.z.w. (Dutch, with an English summary).

Lemche, N. P. 1998. *The Israelites in History and Tradition*. Louisville: Westminster John Knox.

Levene, M. 2005. *Genocide in the Age of the Nation State*. Vol. 1, *The Meaning of Genocide*. London: I. B. Tauris.

Levy, T. E., ed. 2010. *Historical Biblical Archaeology and the Future: The New Pragmatism*. London: Equinox.

Liverani, M. 2005. *Israel's History and the History of Israel*. London: Equinox (Italian original, 2003).

Mann, T. W. 1977. *Divine Presence and Guidance in Israelite Traditions: The Typology of Exaltation*. Baltimore: Johns Hopkins University Press.

Meer, M. N. van der. 2004. *Formation and Reformulation: The Redaction of the Book of Joshua in the Light of the Oldest Textual Witnesses*. VTSup 102. Leiden: Brill.

Miller, J. M., and J. H. Hayes. 2006. *History of Ancient Israel and Judah*. 2nd ed. London: SCM.

Moberly, R.W.L. 1999. "Toward an Interpretation of the Shema," in *Theological Exegesis: Essays in Honor of Brevard S. Childs*, ed. by C. Seitz and K. Greene-McCreight. Grand Rapids: Eerdmans.

Moorey, P. R. S. 1991. *A Century of Biblical Archaeology*. Cambridge: Lutterworth.

Nelson, R. D. 1997. *Joshua*. OTL. Louisville: Westminster John Knox.

Nissinen, M. 2003. *Prophets and Prophecy in the Ancient Near East*, with contributions by C. L. Seow and Robert K. Ritner. SBLWAW 12. Atlanta: Society of Biblical Literature.

Noort, E. 1998. *Das Buch Josua: Forschungsgeschichte und Problemfelder.* Darmstadt: Wissenschaftliche Buchgesellschaft.

Noth, M. 1953. *Das Buch Josua.* 7th ed. HAT, series 1. Tübingen: Mohr Siebeck.

———. 1991. *The Deuteronomistic History.* 2nd ed. JSOTSup 15. Sheffield: Sheffield Academic (German original: *Überlieferungsgeschichtliche Studien.* Vol. 1. Halle: M. Niemeyer, 1943).

Osterhammel, J. 2005. *Colonialism: A Theoretical Overview.* Translated by Shelley L. Frisch. 2nd ed. Princeton: Markus Wiener.

Otto, E. 2000. *Das Deuteronomium im Pentateuch und Hexateuch: Studien zur Literaturgeschichte von Pentateuch und Hexateuch im Lichte des Deuteronomiumrahmens.* FAT 30. Tübingen: Mohr Siebeck.

———. 2012. *Deuteronomium 1,1–4,43.* HTKAT. Freiburg: Herder.

Ottosson, M. 1991. *Josuaboken: En programskrift för davidisk restauration.* Acta Universitatis Uppsaliensis, Studia Biblica Uppsaliensia 1. Stockholm: Almqvist & Wiksell.

Pitkänen, P. M. A. 2010. *Joshua.* AOTC 6, Leicester, UK: Inter-Varsity Press.

———. 2013a. "Pentateuch-Joshua: A Settler-Colonial Document of a Supplanting Society." *Settler Colonial Studies.*

———. 2013b. "Ancient Israel and Settler Colonialism." *Settler Colonial Studies* 4, no. 1.

Sand, S. 2009. *The Invention of the Jewish People.* London: Verso.

———. 2012. *The Invention of the Land of Israel.* London: Verso.

Stannard, D. E. 1992. *American Holocaust: Columbus and the Conquest of the New World.* Oxford: Oxford University Press.

Thompson, M. E. W. 2011. *Where Is the God of Justice? The Old Testament and Suffering.* Eugene, OR: Pickwick.

Thompson, T. L. 1992. *Early History of the Israelite People: From the Written and Archaeological Sources.* Leiden: Brill.

Tinker, G. E. 2004. *Spirit and Resistance: Political Theology and American Indian Liberation.* Minneapolis: Fortress Press.

———. 2008. *American Indian Liberation: A Theology of Sovereignty.* Maryknoll, NY: Orbis.

Tov, E. 2012. *Textual Criticism of the Hebrew Bible.* 3rd ed. Minneapolis: Fortress Press.

Veracini, L. 2006. *Israel and Settler Society.* London: Pluto.

———. 2010. *Settler Colonialism: A Theoretical Overview.* New York: Palgrave Macmillan.

Waswo, R. 1997. *From Virgil to Vietnam: The Founding Legend of Western Civilization.* Hanover, NH: Wesleyan University Press.

Westermann, C. 1994. *Die Geschichtsbücher des Alten Testaments: Gab es ein deuteronomistisches Geschichtswerk?* ("The Historical Books of the Old Testament: Was There a Deuteronomistic History?"). Gütersloh: Chr. Kaiser/Gütersloher.

Wolfe, P. 2008. "Structure and Event: Settler Colonialism, Time and the Question of Genocide." In *Empire, Colony, Genocide: Conquest, Occupation and Subaltern Resistance in World History*, edited by D. Moses, 102–32. New York: Bergahn.

Younger, K. L 1990. *Ancient Conquest Accounts: A Study in Ancient Near Eastern and Biblical History Writing.* JSOTSup 98. Sheffield: Sheffield Academic Press.

Zvi, E. ben. 1992. "The List of the Levitical Cities." *JSOT* 54:77–106.

JUDGES

Victor H. Matthews

Introduction

Since the time of Martin Noth, the book of Judges has been included by scholars in the Deuteronomistic redaction (Deuteronomy–2 Kings). However, portions of the book, especially chapters 1 and 17–21, do not readily fit the theological pattern of obedience/success and disobedience/punishment (Greenspahn, 389–95). Like the book of Job, the book of Judges is characterized by a sandwich structure. The introductory materials in 1:1—3:6 and the judge-less narratives in 17–21 envelop the collected tales of the judges as they are presented within the context of the framework cycle (compare Genesis 1 and Exod. 7:14—12:32 for similar literary frameworks). In this middle portion of the book, a succession of individuals, both male and female, are portrayed in a variety of contexts. Each (excluding the minor judges, who function simply as literary pauses between the tales of major figures), however, must deal with a crisis precipitated by Israelite apostasy.

Interspersed within the narratives are small vignettes, often depicting physical humor, that point to individual heroes operating in a time when violence is common. For instance, the stories of Caleb and Othniel (Judg. 1:11-21) set the stage for later, more developed episodes like those of Gideon and Samson (Judges 6–8 and 13–16). Perhaps they serve as oral reminders of the body of tales in the storyteller's repertoire or a way to portray aspects of life and the difficult land the Israelites have come to inhabit. In sum, the stage is set for future tensions with neighboring peoples that appear more graphically in the framework-bound stories in Judges 3–16.

In what appears to be an addendum to the book of Judges, the last five chapters are remarkable for their gross violations of the covenant with God and for their gratuitous violence and are therefore a fit conclusion to a text that shows the Israelites to be their own worst enemy (McCann, 117). They are reminiscent of the unsettling events recounted in the fourteenth-century-BCE Egyptian El Amarna tablets that describe Canaan as filled with lawlessness men (*'apiru*) and political opportunists.

Even though the conclusion to Judges does not follow the structure of chapters 3–16 and does not include the activities of a judge, it achieves the goal of showing that social, religious, and political chaos are prone to exist in the absence of a central government and a king (Judg. 21:25). That is not to say that they are entirely promonarchy. After all, the Deuteronomistic Historian is a politico-religious voice that generally promotes the house of David. It is therefore not surprising to find in these final chapters some poorly disguised political polemics (Leuchter, 438). Thus the house of Saul is tied to the setting (Gibeah) and atrocities in the story of the Levite's concubine (cf. 1 Sam. 11:4-7 and Judg. 19:22-30), and Jeroboam's placement of a golden calf and shrine in Dan (1 Kgs. 12:28-30) finds it origins in the story of Micah's idol (Judg. 18:27-31).

It is still unclear how the Israelite tribes entered Canaan and coalesced into an identifiable people (Niditch, 6–8). Archaeological evidence indicates a large number of new settlements in the central hill country after 1200 BCE, but they may be tied to the collapse of the Canaanite city-states after the sea people's invasion or to a synthesis of refugees and new peoples. Judges, with its stories that range from a set of ancient "battle-story accounts" (Younger) to a theodicy of the Israelites' failure to conquer the promised land, diverges from the triumphalist conquest account found in Joshua. Its narratives present a mix of victory and defeat, with the Israelite tribes continually falling short of their obligations under the covenant and then "crying out" for divine assistance. In fact, the accounts are closer in tone to the ninth-century-BCE Moabite inscription of King Mesha, with its acceptance of divine wrath of their god Chemosh (see Judg. 2:14; 11:24), and a subsequent return of divine grace that leads to military victory and an end to oppression (compare 2 Kings 3).

When stories are so "over the top" in their depiction of characters and their antisocial activities, modern audiences come to see them as either satire or as a gross form of comedy. Who could believe anyone or any group could possibly do the things described in these final chapters in Judges? And yet, news reports are filled today with incredible statements or violent acts in the name of religious piety. Mass murders, rape, and mayhem are a part of civil wars around the world. It may be that shock literature such as this in Judges or portrayals of the dark side of human nature are necessary to make the point that it takes more than identifying a problem to cure it. Conscious intent to work with and ease the pain of those who have been broken in spirit and body is needed far more than taking revenge on the culprits. When everyone does what is "right in their own eyes" (Judg. 21:25), there is no justice except by force; and there is no peace when self-interest overrides the well-being of the community.

Judges 1:1—3:6 Introductory Narrative

Post-Joshua Conquest Attempts (Judges 1:1—2:10)

▌ THE TEXT IN ITS ANCIENT CONTEXT

There are two distinct beginnings to Judges, although both reference the end of Joshua's life and career (1:1 and 2:6-10). The first, stating "Judah is to go up" first to fight against the Canaanites provides justification (linked to later political realities) for the emergence of the tribe of Judah as one of the two most important tribes in Israel's later history (1:2). The second introductory passage begins with a divinely heralded proclamation of the Israelites' failure to obey the covenant. Therefore, they will be unable to drive out the Canaanites (2:1-6), who will subsequently become a test of Israel's faithfulness and a means of sharpening their skills in war (3:4).

Despite Judah's initial success, more realistic references to differences in material culture (i.e., use of more sophisticated weapons) are injected into the text that explain why the tribes are bottled up in the hill country (1:19). The Joseph tribes (Manasseh and Ephraim) do achieve mixed success, but the rest of the tribes are listed in a litany of failures in other areas of the land (1:21-36). This section also includes the ironic fate of King Adoni-bezek (Judg. 1:5-7), who suffers the same mutilation as the seventy kings he had defeated. It serves as a reminder that the proud, Canaanite or Israelite, can also fall. His scuttling about under the table without thumbs or big toes punctuates the rough humor of a frontier society often quick to laugh at the misfortunes of a former oppressor.

▌ THE TEXT IN THE INTERPRETIVE TRADITION

The third-fourth-century Christian historian Eusebius of Caesarea traces Judah's emerging prominence among the tribes (1:1-10) as an indicator of the tribe's future role in producing leaders like David, Zerubbabel, and ultimately Jesus. Another church father, Jerome, the translator of the Vulgate, sees the reference to the tears shed by the disobedient Israelites at Bochim (Judg. 2:1-5) as an allegory for the "vale of tears" imposed on all humankind after their expulsion from Eden. In this way, humanity had the opportunity to wrestle with vice and obtain merit through its righteous labor.

▌ THE TEXT IN CONTEMPORARY DISCUSSION

These narratives represent the struggles faced by pioneers in their effort to exploit the resources of the land while fighting to maintain their hold over the land and its resources in order to survive. It is, of course, possible for North American audiences to identify with the settlers as part of their own pioneering history. The push to conquer or eliminate the indigenous population from territory assumed to be given to the settlers as their Manifest Destiny is also familiar.

It is also apparent that these shocking tales contain little that is uplifting or admirable. However, when seen in the light of how oppressed or marginalized people depict themselves, Judges emerges in its original context as a way of coping with oppression. These first two chapters make it clear that obtaining ownership of the land will not be an easy task. The pluralistic and polytheistic environment in which the settlers find themselves becomes a major stumbling block. At the same time, these chapters demonstrate that people do not live in a social vacuum and that hard choices must be made continually. Interestingly, the Israelite tribes in these introductory chapters do not adequately recognize cause and effect. They simply know that they have either succeeded or failed, and occasionally they acknowledge the role of God in this process. It is their unsteady relationship with Yahweh that is highlighted in these texts. The stories show God's persistence in upholding the covenantal agreement in the face of a "stiff-necked" and disobedient people. They also demonstrate that the benighted Israelites do keep crying out for relief, a sign that they have not abandoned their hope in Yahweh.

Disobedience, the Judges Cycle, and Testing (Judges 2:11—3:6)

▮ THE TEXT IN ITS ANCIENT CONTEXT

In a tightly reasoned theodicy, the Deuteronomic editors of the Judges material lay out a clearly defined cycle of disobedience, divinely sanctioned oppression by neighboring peoples, divine redemption (rising up of a judge), and a return to disobedience. A more explicit tone of repentance by the Israelites is injected in the actual accounts of the judges (3:9), but in this initial version they are simply described as being "in distress" (2:15). A similar pattern is reprised in the prophetic materials in which God responds to idolatrous behavior with foreign invasions, drought, and plague, and then raises up prophets to call on the people (usually just a righteous remnant) to return to proper compliance with the covenant (see Jer. 26:4-6; Hag. 1:2-11). However, in Judges the cycle also functions as a sort of literary glue holding together a disparate collection of narratives.

The use of a collective "Israelites" (*bᵉnê yiśrāʾēl*) throughout the book (sixty-one times) might be compared to the hieroglyphic determinative for a people attached to the ethnic name Israel in the Egyptian Merneptah Stela (1208 BCE), at least in the sense of assigning collective guilt. However, there is no real effort at chronological progression in these stories, and their settings never encompass all of the Israelite tribal allotments. It is enough to say that disobedience to the stipulations of the covenant, and in particular idolatry (2:19), provides sufficient justification for divine anger and action.

The injection of a divinely appointed hero/champion is an interesting story element and does seem to preshadow the introduction of the earliest anointed kings (Saul and David) when the monarchy is established (see Nathan's reference to the judges period in 2 Sam. 7:11). Of course, the hero archetype is as old as the third- and second-millennium-BCE Gilgamesh legends of ancient Mesopotamia. These figures are often aided by deities and demonstrate greater than human abilities. Where the archetype differs in the biblical account is in the stated purpose for the judge's appearance. Each is to function as a temporary deliverer whose job is to remove the current form of oppression inflicted on the Israelites. While some do display feats of strength, skill, and courage, they are different enough in their methods and character to escape too much stereotyping.

God's response to the recurrence of disobedient behavior following the death of each judge is to set aside divine protection so that the indigenous inhabitants of Canaan remain in the land (Judg. 2:20-23). Conflict with these enemy nations functions as a live classroom for the Israelites to learn the arts of war while testing their allegiance to the covenant (3:1-4). Unfortunately, the presence of these foreign peoples simply entices the Israelites to intermarry with them and to worship their gods (3:5-6)—a socio-theological situation that provides the spark to begin the cycle and the raising of the first judge, Othniel.

▮ THE TEXT IN THE INTERPRETIVE TRADITION

In his recounting of the Judges narrative, Josephus cites the Israelites' refusal to fight against the Canaanites, preferring to indulge themselves with luxuries obtained from their cultivation of the land (*Ant.* 5.132–35). He then demonstrates their corruption by appending the stories of the Levite's concubine (Judges 19–21) and the migration of the tribe of Dan (Judges 17–18). The church fathers drew comparisons between unbelievers in the time of Christ and those who bent the knee to Baal (Origen—third century), and saw the testing of the Israelites (Judg. 3:1-4) by the nations left in the land as part of God's plan to teach humility (John Cassian—fifth century) and to develop perfection through trial (Isaac of Nineveh—sixth century).

■ THE TEXT IN CONTEMPORARY DISCUSSION

It is tempting to see these introductory sections of the book of Judges as part of the "apology" of David and thus a political treatise arguing for the establishment of the monarchy as an alternative to anarchy. But that sets aside the Deuteronomistic Historian's focus on the need for religious fidelity (Block 1988, 46). At the heart of these stories is the temptation faced by the Israelites to assimilate to a wider culture and to set aside allegiance to their tribal god and what may be considered less sophisticated customs. In a pluralistic society (then and now), it is easy to lose focus on what really matters and be drawn to the dominant culture or the latest craze or religious movement. Is it possible to say that we are "tested" by God in our own society, as the Deuteronomist believed the Israelites were tested in theirs? A complementary issue has to do with human recidivism and divine patience. A divine patron who saves once is not remarkable, but one who repeatedly forgives is. The Judges cycle does not end with just a single revolution of its elements. God is shown to be patient and willing, after getting the people's attention through very harsh measures, to provide them yet another chance; and that is indeed remarkable and worth taking seriously.

Judges 3:7—16:31 Collected Tales

■ THE TEXT IN ITS ANCIENT CONTEXT

What becomes quite evident after the judgeship of Othniel is that a literary framework provides a narrative vehicle to highlight the personal flaws of each successive judge, ultimately overshadowing their accomplishments. While Othniel succeeds with the help of God's infusing spirit and without any comment beyond his total success, other judges will not be as successful. There is always something about their character (tricksters like Ehud and Gideon) or the degree to which they can call on the allegiance of other tribes (Deborah and Jephthah) that suggests matters are just not quite right. In the end, the last of these divinely appointed figures (Samson) is portrayed as an utterly self-centered, self-indulgent womanizer, and much closer to the stereotypical ancient hero typified by Gilgamesh or Hercules.

Perhaps this downward progression is part of a larger editorial plan designed to set up the audience for the political statements in 18:1 and 21:25 that blame a lawless society on the lack of a king to rule the tribes. However, that may be too narrow a view given a similar pattern of stubborn disobedience to God's commands found elsewhere in the Deuteronomistic History (see 2 Kgs. 17:7-20) and in the Psalms (78; 81) and in the Prophets (Jeremiah 5; Hosea 4; Zech. 7:8-14). The judges, like the kings in a later period, have to deal with real-world situations and yet will also have to work within a structure in which they are the servants of a god. The mixture of secular situations and crises, and divine assistance/interference is a favorite device of ancient authors. (The Sumerian sage Adapa, for example, is offered the "bread of life" by the gods, but is counseled by his patron deity Ea to refuse to eat, and thus loses the chance for personal immortality.)

▇ THE TEXT IN THE INTERPRETIVE TRADITION

The need for humility and the expunging of a prideful and destructive spirit were self-evident to the church fathers, who used the text of the book of Judges to call on Christians to recognize God's active concern in current difficulties. Just as the Israelites were handed over to enemy nations because of their wickedness, those who call on God in repentance can expect that they will be lifted up by "throngs of archangels" and restored to their inheritance of salvation (Origen; cf. Eph. 2:1-2). In that way, it is possible to interpret the succession of judges as divine deliverers, brought to the people because of the Israelites' tendency to become "tepid" in their faith and thus need more than a single lesson in humility (Cassian).

▇ THE TEXT IN CONTEMPORARY DISCUSSION

Among the questions that can be asked about these texts is how they relate to our perception of leadership today, and whether it makes a difference if the Bible does not present the judges as perfect heroes. Given the fact that some of today's leaders are shown to be flawed and unethical in their dealings with their constituents and others, does the book of Judges simply excuse such behavior as "simply human"? Are the obvious narrative cues and a host of incidents that contain social gaffes to be taken as social criticism or humor? To be sure, modern literature is filled with these types of characters, and it is almost a comfort to be introduced to less-than-perfect protagonists with whom it is possible to identify. There is also a clear sense in these stories of divine redemption apart from the merit of those to be redeemed. Biblical characters are thus released from the unreasonable expectation that they must always be perfect role models.

Othniel (Judges 3:7-11)

▇ THE TEXT IN ITS ANCIENT CONTEXT

The story of the first judge, while it sets a precedent , tells little more than the fact that Othniel of the tribe of Judah "went out to war" and with God's help defeated King Cushan-Rishathaim, most likely a king of Edom (Sadler, 812–13; Judg. 3:10). Such a bare-bones account of the unvarnished steps of the cycle format may have been intended to set the proper tone for the behavior of judges. It does resemble the initial presentation of Abram, who answers God's call to immigrate without question (Gen. 12:1-4), and shows unquestioning loyalty to God's command through his willing-ness to sacrifice his long-desired son Isaac (Gen. 22:1-19). However, it would be impractical to think that the storyteller would choose to present every other judge in the same shorthand manner. In fact, the editors do not, resorting instead to the Deuteronomist's theme of social and religious disintegration.

Curiously, there is a similar story in Judg. 1:11-15 in which Othniel successfully, and without any narrative elaboration, captures the city of Kiriath-sepher. More interesting here is the inter-change between Othniel's new wife Achsah and her father Caleb. It provides a human-interest story that includes a tone of barely disguised, disrespectful dissatisfaction over the dry dowry lands provided as part of her wedding contract. Caleb's quiet acquiescence to Achsah's request for springs to water their given section of the Negev acknowledges that she is in the right (1:14-16; compare Judah in Gen. 38:25-26).

■ THE TEXT IN THE INTERPRETIVE TRADITION

Both Josephus (*Ant.* 5.182–83) and his first-century contemporary Pseudo-Philo (*L.A.B.* 26–28) have recounted Othniel's story, ascribing his accomplishments to his father Kenaz/Cenaz. Josephus focuses more on the political crimes of the Israelites rather than their covenantal failures as the cause for the crisis that leads to God's revealing to Kenaz what he must do. Pseudo-Philo grants Kenaz a larger role than in either the Bible or in Josephus, expanding his leadership efforts to include interrogating sinners and punishing those who question his authority (Begg, 334–35).

■ THE TEXT IN CONTEMPORARY DISCUSSION

The editors of Judges have created a sliding scale of effectiveness in their portrayal of the deliverers, which requires the first judge to be an unsullied paragon and the last to exhibit total self-interest and disregard for the needs of the community. Modern society publicly sets a high standard of ethical leadership for its officials, but few actually measure up to that ideal. The twenty-four-hour news cycle and the ability to delve into every aspect of a leader's life put extreme pressure on them and sometimes leads them to make foolish decisions. The pattern of decline in Judges does allow for a more realistic view of leadership while warning society against letting bravado and demagoguery replace substance. Many would appreciate a conscientious public servant like Othniel, but we often settle for someone who simply gets things done.

Ehud (Judges 3:12-30) and Shamgar (Judges 3:31)

■ THE TEXT IN ITS ANCIENT CONTEXT

The second judge, Ehud, is a successful leader, and he serves in that capacity for eighty years, longer than any other judge/deliverer. His narrative also begins the downward spiral that will take the judges from the pinnacle represented by Othniel to the lawless egotism of Samson. In many ways, these stories echo the character types among Homer's heroes in their struggle before Troy. Some, like Achilles, are able to achieve remarkable feats of strength, usually with the assistance of a patron deity; some are trickster figures (Odysseus); and some are willing to make incredible bargains with the gods to gain a victory (Agamemnon). Ehud falls into the trickster category, a favorite character in Israelite tradition (cf. Jacob).

Ehud's tale begins with an indictment of the Israelites for their unfaithfulness (3:12). An affronted God then allows an alliance of traditional foes led by Eglon, king of Moab, to take possession of portions of the land for eighteen years (3:13-14). The audience is then provided with a series of narrative cues and puns. Ehud is a Benjamite (Saul's tribe; 1 Sam. 9:1-2), and the seat of power chosen by Eglon is the "city of Palms" (probably Jericho), a reference to the partial dismantling of Joshua's conquests (Joshua 6). The fact that Ehud is left-handed, possibly ambidextrous

(3:15), and carries a specially designed dagger on his right thigh (3:16) foreshadows Ehud's means of assassinating Eglon. The play on Ehud's name ("Where is majesty?") and Eglon's name ("calf" or "bull") plays into the contest-between-gods motif in which Yahweh challenges the power of Baal, who is often represented as a bull or astride a bull (Keel and Uehlinger, 144–46; see 1 Kings 18). For comic-relief purposes, it is possible that a phonetic pun on Eglon's name may be stretched to include the "round" nature of the king's ample belly fat (3:17b, 22; Butler, 69).

Ehud's trickster nature emerges in his fabrication of a sleek, double-edged dagger, which he hides under his right thigh. A right-handed man would normally draw from his left side, and it is not surprising the guards miss the weapon when they search his person (cf. Joab's assassination of Amasa in 2 Sam. 20:9-10). Extending the trickster theme, Ehud first tempts Eglon's cupidity with the promise of a "secret message" (3:19), and then expands this to a "message from God" (3:20) in order to get the king alone. Given the opportunity, Ehud thrusts his dagger into Eglon's belly and the fat completely envelops the blade (3:21-22). In what may be the first "locked-room mystery," Ehud foils any likelihood of quick discovery of the king's body by locking them both into Eglon's private toilet and escaping through the opening to the cesspit (3:23-26; Halpern, 43–46). The victory over the leaderless Moabites, completing the narrative framework, is almost an anticlimax (3:27-30).

Susan Niditch (57–58) compares Eglon's murder to the emasculation of enemy soldiers in the *Iliad* and to the surprising narrative shift when Jael's tent peg penetrates Sisera's skull (Judg. 4:21). Certainly, that does fit into the type scene of an unlikely victory against great odds (see David and Goliath in 1 Sam. 17:31-54).

The single verse describing the exploits of Shamgar ben Anath (3:31) serves, like the listing of other minor judges (10:1-5; 12:8-15), as a literary interlude separating the tales of the major figures. Since his name includes the name of a Canaanite goddess, it is unlikely that Shamgar is an Israelite. However, because he is able to slay six hundred Philistines with a weapon generally used to herd cattle, he fits into Israelite tradition as a heroic ally (like Jael the Kenite in Judg. 4:17-22).

▮ The Text in the Interpretive Tradition

The church fathers seem to have been impressed with Ehud's ambidextrous abilities. However, because the left hand is often associated with "unfortunate" purpose or occurrence, they style the ability to use both hands for righteous purposes a divine gift that guides him to proper uses and "turns both into a right hand" (Cassian). Jerome also refers to Ehud as having "two right hands" because he was "a just man." Origen, who appears to be enthused by Ehud's story, labels his actions as a "praiseworthy deception," a remark that reinforces the view that many acts are justified if they are done in battle for God and the right. Later thinkers had mixed views of Ehud's assassination of King Eglon. Voltaire (*Philosophical Dictionary*, 1764) decried regicide as a sign of fanaticism, while John Milton used Ehud's example to justify the regicide of King Charles I in England (Gunn, 38–39, 45).

▮ The Text in Contemporary Discussion

In current political discourse, there is a fine line between the recording of freedom fighting that includes acts of extreme violence for a just cause, and criminally minded insurgents, whose fanatical and bloody deeds are decried by other nations and by their victims. Since stories are composed for particular audiences, it is unlikely that all will share the same viewpoint on the matter any more than the Moabites would have appreciated Ehud's heroics. In modern parlance, it remains to be seen, for instance, how suicide bombers and political assassins will be viewed in the future, both within their own social context and by outsiders. Perhaps it is possible to laud Ehud's desperate act as a model of bravery for a subject people. However, because the story contains raw details and comic asides, it is difficult, as Heb. 11:32 seems to indicate, to include it in the litany of heroes of the faith.

Deborah (Judges 4–5)

■ THE TEXT IN ITS ANCIENT CONTEXT

There are a number of remarkable aspects to the dually presented story of Deborah. The narrative version in Judges 4 helps to fill some of the gaps left in the "song" in Judges 5, which concentrates more on the theme of blessings and curses (Butler, 133). The most obvious point is that Deborah is the only female judge ("a mother in Israel," 5:7), the only figure in the book to be given the label of "prophetess," and the only person to actually participate in legal mediation (4:4-5). Her role as prophet places her in company with Moses' sister Miriam (Exod. 15:20) and Huldah in Josiah's time (2 Kgs. 22:14). As an arbitrator of the law, Deborah, unlike Samuel who worked a circuit of sites (1 Sam. 7:16-17), has a recognized location in the Ephraimite hill country beneath a palm tree where the people come for justice. From her seat of authority, Deborah summons the Naphtali war chief Barak and exercises her prophetic office to call on him in God's name to lead his men against the Canaanite general Sisera at Mount Tabor (4:6-7; cf. Samuel in 1 Sam. 15:1-3).

While Barak's request that Deborah accompany his army suggests a lack of faith on his part (cf. Saul in 1 Sam. 13:8-10), it was not unusual for an army to include prophets as an intermediary for divine presence (see Elisha in 2 Kgs. 3:9-20). In this case, Barak's reluctance becomes a narrative catalyst for gender reversal, substituting a female champion whose "hand" would bring the ultimate victory (4:9). The battle in which Sisera's forces are defeated is barely mentioned (4:12-16), although the "song" in Judg. 5:19-23 does contain elements of the divine warrior's intervention ("mountains quaked," 5:5; "stars fought from heaven," 5:20). More important is the praise for the faithful tribes who joined the campaign (4:10; 5:13-15a, 18) and the sarcastic remarks made against those who stayed away (5:15b-17). In this chaotic period, it will take more than the call of a prophet and her war chief to unite the tribes in a common cause (cf. Saul in 1 Sam. 11:5-7). Deborah's only fault, then, is an inability to unite the people.

Of central interest here is the role of the Kenite woman Jael, who is called "most blessed of women" (5:24) while performing horrific acts that would under normal circumstances violate hospitality protocols (Matthews, 66–74). Serving as a narrative surprise, it is Jael's "hand" rather than Deborah's that will dispose of Sisera and the Canaanite threat (4:17-22; 5:24-27). Demonstrating that this is a world without the normal social constraints, Jael takes on the male role by playing host, inviting Sisera chaperoned into her tent, and then playing the vengeful angel (perhaps echoing God's angel in 5:23) by driving a tent peg through his skull (a sexual innuendo that would not have been lost on the ancient audience).

The "song" then supplies a poignant and stinging satire comparing Jael's heroic act to the greedy anticipation of Sisera's mother, who looks in vain for the plunder she expects will accompany the return of her son (5:28-31). For a people so often oppressed by their more powerful neighbors, there is great satisfaction found in the ability to say "so perish all your enemies" (5:31).

▌ THE TEXT IN THE INTERPRETIVE TRADITION

There is much praise in the church fathers for Deborah, the "mother" who provides prudent advice, exhorts Barak to victory, and saves the nation by directing men to do their duty (Chrysostom). Jael the Kenite becomes for Ambrose the model of the righteous gentile, who is quicker than the Jews in accepting the doctrines of the church. Origen agrees by saying Jael, the foreigner, "symbolizes the church, which was assembled from foreign nations" (Franke, 117). Artistic representations of Jael's act range from a graphically pinned Sisera to more subtle depictions (Gunn, 78). While ancient and medieval commentators subordinate the role and accomplishments of women in the bible, in the nineteenth century Elizabeth Cady Stanton (*The Women's Bible*) hails Deborah's self-reliance and heroic virtues as "worthy of their imitation," and demonstrating women's ability to take a more active role in society. However, she is more reserved in her treatment of Jael, noting the Kenite must have at least "imagined herself" called by God to commit an otherwise fiendish act (Gunn, 64–65, 83).

▌ THE TEXT IN CONTEMPORARY DISCUSSION

There is an interesting mixture in this tale of decisive purpose, prophetic anticipation of divine intervention in warfare, and personal triumph made possible by taking incredible risks. For once in Judges, it is possible to identify with women who are positive role models. Deborah can easily be compared to other powerful female figures (cf. Abigail in 1 Sam. 25:2-42) whose actions drive the narrative and who often overshadow their husbands, just as Deborah overshadows Barak. However, even the celebration of her as a "mother" in Israel, usually a nurturing, life-giving role, is used by the narrator to remind us that rape and the exploitation of women is a factor in the male ideology of war (Judg. 5:30; Exum, 73–74).

Jael may be more difficult for modern audiences. Her remarkable fortitude and courage is matched by her bloody-handedness. Is she to be compared to women today who are used as suicide bombers to kill crowds of people? Is her encounter with Sisera an example of collateral damage in wartime, or just another instance of the blasé attitude about the rape of women in a war zone (see Sisera's mother's musing in 5:28-30)? While the editors' narrative shell enclosing Sisera's encounter with Jael is built around how God uses unlikely vehicles to achieve victory, there is also an internal drama centered on Jael's choices. She is engaging in risk calculation designed to uphold the honor of her household and to preserve her body from the potential of rape and death at Sisera's hands. Does that, then, justify her deception and Sisera's murder? Can today's "castle doctrine" apply here, allowing her, like us, to protect herself against an unfriendly invader?

Gideon (Judges 6–8)

■ THE TEXT IN ITS ANCIENT CONTEXT

Despite the heavy-handed oppression of the Midianites (Judg. 6:1-6), Gideon is the only judge who actively campaigns against his own appointment. In that sense, his call narrative is similar to that of Moses (Exod. 3:7—4:17), Isaiah (Isa. 6:5-8), and Jeremiah (Jer. 1:4-10; Habel, 287–305). Like these reluctant prophets, Gideon shows his temerity by claiming to be too insignificant (Judg. 6:15), and prior to battle with the Midianite coalition he twice requests that God provide an oracular sign that Gideon will be able to deliver Israel (Judg. 6:36-40). The comparison breaks down, however, because Gideon never manages the ability to truly trust God or to grow into his potential as a leader (Butler, 199–200).

Intertwined with Gideon's vacillating allegiance to God's command and his own desire to gain fame for himself is another theme, the contest between Yahweh and Baal for worshipers (Bluedorn, 69). Both themes appear when Gideon is required to tear down the Baal altar that his father had built in their village (Judg. 6:25-27). Lacking the courage to perform this ritually cleansing act, Gideon dismantles the altar in the dark of night and then only escapes the wrath of the villagers when his father asserts that it is up to Baal to take vengeance, if the Canaanite god can (Judg. 6:28-31). There is a clear parallel here to Elijah's challenge of Baal's divinity on Mount Carmel (1 Kgs. 18:21), but again Gideon is in the shadows. He benefits from his actions, but he is not the one to assert Yahweh's preeminence.

In a similar manner, the battle narrative against the Midianite host contains an element of resignation on God's part about the people's and Gideon's trust. Almost with a divine shrug of the shoulders, it becomes necessary to radically diminish the size of Gideon's army so that the victory can only be attributed to God's intervention (compare the fight against the Amalekites in Exod. 17:8-13). Thus only three hundred men, all of whom have shown their lack of vigilance by lapping up water from a stream (Judg. 7:4-7), are mustered for a night attack. Still Gideon has doubts, and once again God gives him the chance to pluck up his courage by a secret foray into the enemy camp, where he hears a dream interpreted (Judg. 7:9-15). What is remarkable is that Gideon's battle call, "For the Lord and for Gideon," allows him to share credit with God, a strategy Shakespeare echoes in *Henry IV*: "'God for Harry, England, and Saint George!" (act 3, scene 1). Moses was denied the promised land for a similar lack of faith when he gave himself more credit than God for providing water in the wilderness (Num. 20:7-12). Gideon's action, however, is in tune with the growing egotistic tendencies of the judges.

His initial battle is won using trumpet blasts (compare the "battle" of Jericho in Josh. 6:15-16) and nocturnal brandishing of torches that frighten the enemy (Judg. 7:19-22). Gideon's hurled torches and smashed pots may have evoked the fear of divine lightning strikes or might associate him with shamanistic abilities to call down a fiery torrent (see Elijah's acts in 1 Kgs. 18:36-38) like Apollodorus's description of Salmoneus, who attempts to imitate Zeus (Brown, 385–86). Whatever the case, the aftermath is a chase to round up the enemy leaders.

Two facets of the narrative stand out here. First is the shrewd diplomatic speech employed to mollify the Ephraimites, who had entered the fray late and were angry that they did not share in the loot (Judg. 8:1-3). Gideon distinguishes himself, using flattery to prevent conflict between tribes. That magnanimity is not extended to the towns of Succoth and Penuel, who were reluctant to trust the Israelites' ability to achieve total victory. Gideon therefore takes heavy vengeance on those who had refused to assist his men (Judg. 8:4-21). His savage treatment of the elders and the enemy chiefs shows no hint of forgiveness and serves to enhance his role as a commander, who is to be feared by all who oppose him (Judg. 8:16-21).

At the height of his popularity, Gideon refuses the offer of hereditary kingship, saying that the people will be ruled by God alone (Judg. 8:22-23). However, he spoils what could have distinguished him as a servant-leader by presenting the people with an ephod made from the spoil taken from the Midianites (8:24-27). This trophy, a memorial to Gideon's successes, later becomes a cult object, drawing the people away from Yahweh after Gideon's death (8:33-34). In the end, Gideon earns a sad epitaph, in that the people exhibit no loyalty to either God or him. It foreshadows the editorial comments about the kings of Israel, who continue the "sins of Jeroboam" and "caused Israel to sin" (1 Kgs. 22:52-53; 2 Kgs. 13:2).

▌THE TEXT IN THE INTERPRETIVE TRADITION

Setting aside any concern over the existence of a Baal altar in Gideon's village, Ambrose focuses on the analogy between Gideon's sacrifice of a bull (making an end to all gentile sacrifices) and Jesus' crucifixion as the true offering for the people's redemption. In like manner, the church fathers pass over Gideon's lack of faith in asking for a sign and instead see the dew (Judg. 6:36-40) as the divine word sent down from heaven (Ambrose), Christ as the "sweetness of the dew" (Augustine), and the fleece as Mary, who in her conception of the Lord "absorbed him with her own body" (Maximus of Turin, fifth-century bishop in Franke 127). Gregory the Great (sixth-century pope) styles Gideon's army as "glittering martyrs, who willingly exposed their bodies to their opponents' swords" (Franke, 131–32).

▌THE TEXT IN CONTEMPORARY DISCUSSION

What kind of role model can Gideon the reluctant judge be for modern audiences? The degree of divine hand-holding necessary to get him in motion throughout his career may be taken as either indecisiveness or dependence. Some leaders today justify their inaction by constantly seeking out new polling data or going on endless fact-finding excursions. Are today's leaders turning a blind eye to "Baal's altar" in their town square while decrying the community's failure to erect a monument to the Ten Commandments? Do we prefer flashy, if temporary, victories or vengeful attacks to seeking out the causes of cultural differences and discontent? While Gideon was a successful general, with God's assistance, he did not pave the way to stable leadership, and he left a legacy of idolatry and divided loyalties. For modern audiences, that may raise the question of how leaders should be chosen and what long-term expectations we have for their accomplishments.

Abimelech (Judges 9) and the First Minor Judges Interlude (Judges 10:1-5)

■ THE TEXT IN ITS ANCIENT CONTEXT

The contrast between Gideon's refusal to accept the kingship (Judg. 8:22-23) and the striving by his son Abimelech to obtain that office is symptomatic of a society that desires stability but is not yet ready for the full implications of centralized government (Amit, 111). Plus, the association with Shechem may be another Deuteronomic, political polemic against northern-based leaders (Schneider, 136). Other interesting facets of this narrative include the importance placed on kinship in elevating Abimelech (Judg. 9:2-3) and the extensive use of direct speech (Judg. 9:2, 16-20, 28-29, 31-33) and dialogue (9:36-38) at crucial points in the political drama, drawing the audience more closely into the action.

What is bloodily begun when Abimelech murders his seventy brothers (Judg. 9:5; cf. Saul's slaughter of eighty-five priests at Nob) ends with Abimelech's bloody demise (9:54). Between these two events is a frenzy of activity resulting from a change of heart by the "Lords of Shechem," who had originally supported Abimelech's rise to kingship. They make the roads unsafe, robbing travelers (9:25), and support Gaal (9:26-29). Gaal's challenge, "Who is Abimelech?" (9:28), calls his legitimacy into question (cf. Nabal, who defames David's right to the throne, saying, "Who is David?"; 1 Sam. 25:10). His brief venture into Shechem's vacillating politics concludes with many of his supporters killed, the city captured, and its ruins "sowed with salt" (cf. eighth-century Aramaic vassal-treaty of Sefire's curse imposed on covenant-breakers, "Hadad will sow salt thereon"; Fensham, 49). Abimelech's escalating rampage finally comes to a conclusion when he is struck by a millstone thrown by a woman from the walls of Thebez (Judg. 9:53). Rather than die at her hands (like Sisera in 4:21), he orders his armor bearer to slay him (9:54). Abimelech's mistake of going too near the wall becomes a military maxim cited by Joab when he sends David a report that Uriah the Hittite has been slain (2 Sam. 11:20-21).

Embedded in the narrative is a fable recited by Jotham, the only surviving son of Gideon (Judg. 9:7-15). His fable is a political metaphor cautioning the "Lords of Shechem" to consider the type of ruler they have chosen for themselves, which will likely "backfire" on them (Butler, 241–42). The comical selection process and the subsequent curse predicting a fiery ending to these events matches the tone of the overall narrative (9:56-57).

Abimelech's death forms a bridge to two minor judges, Tola and Jair. The only information contained here (Judg. 10:1-5) is the number of years they served as a judge and in Jair's case the symmetry of thirty sons, thirty donkeys, and thirty towns. These brief remarks may be based on an annalistic style more typical in the monarchy period (cf. 2 Kgs. 17:1-2). While they may have served as local leaders, the lack of a formal call from God diminishes their importance except as representatives of a brief period of stability between two violence-prone judges, Abimelech and Jephthah (Block 1999, 337).

■ THE TEXT IN THE INTERPRETIVE TRADITION

The church fathers had to stretch to find anything uplifting in the tale of Abimelech. Augustine chose to defend the value of fables to achieve understanding through metaphor, and Methodius, a fourth-century bishop of Olympus, sees Jotham's parable as a prediction of the future reign of chastity, viewing the story of trees meeting to appoint a king as a representation of humble penitents who approach God asking to be governed by his pity and compassion.

■ THE TEXT IN CONTEMPORARY DISCUSSION

Considering the problems created throughout history by persons whose ambitions have led them to take power by violence, Abimelech's story does not sound all that unusual to modern audiences. The damage to lives and property caused by political purges, wars of conquest and retribution, and the brutalizing of society can be ascribed to poor political choices and rampant ambition (e.g., Hitler's rise to power first through constitutional means and then by force and fiat). The question is always how long societies that accept high levels of everyday violence can last. And, is there a higher dictum to question and if necessary remove leaders who foster tyranny?

Jephthah (Judges 10:6—12:7) and the Second Minor Judges Interlude (Judges 12:8-15)

■ THE TEXT IN ITS ANCIENT CONTEXT

Jephthah's narrative is sandwiched between two lists of minor judges (Judg. 10:1-5; 12:8-15). Both lists recount individual leaders who are apparently quite prosperous and, more importantly, have numerous progeny. That alone provides a marked contrast with both Abimelech and Jephthah, who spent their lives in continual conflict and died childless.

Before Jephthah is introduced, the editors provide an extended review of the Israelites' apostasy comparable to Judg. 2:1-5, 11-23 (10:6-18; Block 1999, 344). The Ammonite oppression leads to a beseeching cry for deliverance by the Israelites. Before God relents, there is a caustic retort that the Israelites should turn to the gods they had chosen to deliver them (compare Joash's challenge to Baal in 6:31). Only after the Israelites cleanse themselves of their foreign worship can the search begin for someone to lead them in battle (10:17-18; cf. 1:2; 20:18).

What follows is a strange pedigree for a judge. Jephthah is an illegitimate son whose brothers have expelled him from his father's household. Operating as a bandit chief out of the Gileadite city of Tob (11:1-3), his experience compares with David's outlaw period (1 Sam. 22:1-2) and with the fifteenth-century-BCE king of Alalakh, Idrimi, who spent years living with the outcasts of society before regaining his throne (*ANET* 557–58). His outsider status and experience as a seasoned military leader make him a good choice as deliverer, and aids his negotiations aimed at being recognized as their legitimate leader (Judg. 11:6-10). Unlike Gideon, Jephthah is not a reluctant leader, but it is only when he is filled with God's spirit that it is made clear he has divine sanction as a judge (11:29).

Before the conflict begins, there is an interesting diplomatic exchange between Jephthah and the Ammonites (11:12-28). Using the ancient Near Eastern lawsuit form (O'Connell, 195), his messenger recites the Israelites' preconquest narrative of their dealings with the peoples of Transjordan (see Num. 21:21-31 and Numbers 22) while discounting Ammonite claims. Unable to find a diplomatic solution (cf. the failure to appease the Ephraimites in Judg.12:1-6), Jephthah attempts to negotiate with God to obtain a victory. He takes a rash vow promising to sacrifice the first member of his household to greet him after the battle (11:30-31). Some commentators have attempted to compare Jephthah's sacrificial offer to the classical story of Agamemnon's vow to sacrifice his daughter Iphigenia, but there are too many variations to make this conclusive (Marcus, 40–43). More important is the parallel to Saul's rash oath to execute anyone who eats during a battle with the Philistines (1 Sam. 14:24-45).

Jephthah does gain his victory, but it precipitates a poignant scene when his daughter rushes out to celebrate and he realizes he has condemned her to death. She demonstrates a stronger spirit than her father by insisting he must carry through rather than become an oath-breaker (Judg. 11:34-40). Thus Jephthah wins his battle and loses the chance to continue his line. Jephthah's final episode is equally tragic. Although he is victorious over the greedy Ephraimites, his dialectal strategy of demanding that each man crossing the fords of the Jordan River pronounce the word *shibboleth* costs the Israelites a staggering toll of 42,000 lives (12:1-6).

◼ THE TEXT IN THE INTERPRETIVE TRADITION

Most interpreters focus on Jephthah's vow and whether he actually sacrificed his daughter. Luther considers the text to be ambiguous, and Augustine argues against the possibility that an animal was meant. The *Midrash Tanḥuma* attempts to excuse Jephthah on the grounds that he was ignorant of the law allowing the substitution of payment for a human vowed to be sacrificed (Lev. 27:1-8; Marcus, 47). Josephus blames the daughter for "rushing out" to meet Jephthah and thus causing her father such distress (*Ant.* 5.265), but later interpreters see her in a more sympathetic light. Peter Abelard (twelfth century) considers her embracing of a sacrificial death a model for monastic women devoted to God, and Lord Byron (1814) portrays her as a cheerful martyr who wins her father's freedom from his vow (Stewart, 133–37).

◼ THE TEXT IN CONTEMPORARY DISCUSSION

The narrator of the story of Jephthah's unnamed daughter emphasizes her adherence to legal principles and her self-sacrifice (Judg. 11:37-40). However, that only serves the interests of the male-dominated society that approves her brave action while not questioning why God did not stop the sacrifice as in Gen. 22:10-12 (Exum, 74–77). Are children to be abused or used in this way when their parents make foolish choices or are governed by their own mental pathologies? Are they expendable resources, too weak to prevent becoming victims of their parents or other adults? The irony is that Jephthah must live on childless and be labeled as a fool, while his daughter's memory lives on among her more compassionate female friends (Judg. 11:39-40).

Samson (Judges 13–16)

◼ THE TEXT IN ITS ANCIENT CONTEXT

With a brief tip of the hat to the Judges structure (citing disobedience as the cause for Philistine oppression—Judg. 13:1), Samson's saga is launched with a remarkable birth narrative (cf. Moses in Exod. 2:1-10 and Samuel in 1 Samuel 1). The theophany and annunciation instruct Samson's parents three times to maintain a strict Nazirite discipline (Num. 6:1-8) while his mother is pregnant (Judg.

13:2-14; cf. Luke 1:8-15). That holy discipline imposed on mother and son (Bal, 200) becomes the ironic foil to Samson's decidedly un-Nazirite lifestyle. There is also an interesting dynamic between Manoah and his unnamed wife. The angel appears to her first, and she recognizes the messenger as a "man of God" with an angelic appearance (13:3-6). Manoah cannot simply accept her word and entreats God for further instructions. Lacking true perception (13:16), he is shocked to discover they have been in the presence of the divine and responds with frightened awe (13:22; cf. Jacob in Gen. 28:16-17), and has to be comforted by his wife's logic (13:23). The interplay between the sexes will become a subtheme in the stories, as Samson is entrapped by his dealings with a series of women throughout his life.

There is a curious juxtaposition between Samson's potential to accomplish great things (regular infusion of God's spirit: Judg. 13:25; 14:6, 19; 15:14) and his carnal appetite, which continually draws him into the company of dangerous, foreign women (14:2; 16:1, 4). His dual character plays into the hero archetype, which places him in the company of other flawed strong men whose superhuman passions include feats of courage and strength and the need to demonstrate their virility with women (Gilgamesh and Hercules).

Contests and trickery also play heavily in these tales (Niditch, 153–54). The riddle game during his marriage feast is fraught with cultural conflict and ends with Samson being deceived by his Philistine wife and his slaughter of thirty Philistines to pay off his debt (14:12-19). In a similar manner, Samson's taunting the Philistines by burning their fields leads to confrontation and slaughter (14:3-8) while demonstrating that he is merely acting alone without any consultation with tribal leaders (Wong, 178). The frightened elders of Judah are caught in the middle since they are under Philistine control and must turn him over to their masters (14:9-13). Samson plays both sides, using this opportunity to obtain a nonaggression pact with the Judahites and then breaking his bonds and killing a thousand Philistines with a donkey's jawbone (14:12-16; cf. the surprise encounter at Gaza's gate in 16:1-3). Like Ehud's deception (3:21-22) and Jael's slaying of Sisera (4:21), these bloody episodes appeal to the partisan, ancient Israelite audience and also provide some comic relief.

The final contest centers on Samson's relationship with Delilah, the Philistines' spy (16:4-21). Paid to discover the source of his strength, Delilah plays a fourfold game, cajoling and pleading with her lover and repeatedly frustrating the Philistines waiting in her back room to pounce on what they hope is a helpless victim. Samson appears to be enjoying both the game and Delilah's growing anger. But like his first wife, who also nagged him incessantly (14:17; Ackerman, 232), Delilah's repeated pleas for him to demonstrate his love by revealing his secret wears Samson down and he tells her the truth (16:16-17). It is not clear why Delilah believes him this time, although some structured folktales do have a limit on the number of times a deception can be spoken (Matthews, 160).

At the height of Samson's despair over his capture and blinding, the storyteller injects the seed for ultimate revenge and reversal: his hair begins to grow back (16:22). The Philistines' decision to display a potentially dangerous captive for their entertainment (16:23-25) is a match for Samson's own hubris when he does not mention God in his victory hymn (15:16; Crenshaw, 36). The text does not contain a direct answer from God to Samson's petition (16:18; cf. the etiological vignette in 15:18-19). Perhaps the regrown hair gave him the strength to pull down the Philistine temple, killing the celebrants and him in the bargain (16:28-30). Or, he may have been an unwitting participant in another contest between gods that gives Yahweh a victory over Dagon (cf. 1 Sam. 5:1-5). Samson's career had begun with such hope, but ends with a destructive gesture and a simple epitaph noting he was buried in his father's tomb (16:31). His story serves as a fitting metaphor for Israel's unfaithfulness and self-centered behavior.

▌THE TEXT IN THE INTERPRETIVE TRADITION

Most commentators have taken a more positive view of Samson's exploits. Pope Gregory the Great and the sixth-century bishop Caesarius of Arles even see his carrying away of the gates of Gaza (16:3) as a metaphor for Christ's breaking the gates of death and freeing the righteous souls from limbo. They are less kind to the women in his life, whose roles as temptresses or harlots lead Samson astray. Ambrose labels Delilah a prostitute and cautions that men should avoid marriages with those "outside the faith." Milton (*Samson Agonistes*) first portrays Delilah as a penitent, asking for forgiveness and offering to care for the blind Samson, but when he spurns her she becomes the spiteful Philistine attempting to sting him with verbal abuse. Modern film (Cecile B. DeMille's *Samson and Delilah*) romanticizes their relationship without offering much in the way of character development.

▌THE TEXT IN CONTEMPORARY DISCUSSION

Samson is neither an unredeemable character nor a fictionalized figure drawn from various folklore strands. His reckless enthusiasms for women, adventure, and violence provide the ancient and modern audience with the consequences of the destructive actions of fools and a contrast with the wise, thinking person, who can be instructed (cf. Prov. 11:29-31; 14:16-17; Greene, 54). Similarly, the women in his life are not just sources of temptation. They often become victims of Samson's appetites, being used and then cast away. Even the self-sufficient Delilah, who apparently makes her living without the benefit of a husband (Fewell, 73–74), serves as Samson's unwitting, comedic foil until he plays the gambit once too often. Seemingly, the outlandish behavior by caped superheroes (Superman, Batman) seems excusable when hope emerges in the form of a champion. However, it is always dangerous to put too much confidence in them to change the world.

Judges 17–21 Anarchy (Tales without Judges)

Micah, the Levite, and the Migration of Dan (Judges 17–18)

▌THE TEXT IN ITS ANCIENT CONTEXT

The Deuteronomic editors of the story of Micah's idol create a "morality play" focused on lawbreaking and indifference to covenant obligations in a time before the rule of kings (Mueller, 76–82). The tale begins with Micah's dishonorable theft of silver from his mother and his fearful return of the hoard to avoid a curse (17:2-3a; Amit, 324). She in turn "consecrates" the silver to the Lord so that it can be cast into an idol (17:3b). Like Aaron (Exod. 32:4) and King Jeroboam (1 Kgs. 12:28), neither Micah nor his mother can discern the difference between idols and Yahweh (McCann, 121). These three violations of the Decalogue (Exod. 20:4-5, 12, 15) provide the backdrop to Micah's creation of a house shrine for his newly minted cultic objects, including an ephod and *tĕrāphîm* (cf. Gen. 31:19; 2 Kgs. 23:24). Providing yet another insight into religious practices in the village context, Micah initially installs one of his sons as the priest (17:4-5). However, that will change when an itinerant Levite from Bethlehem arrives in search of his own "place," something not unusual prior to the establishment of the central shrine. Micah is quick to hire him to raise the social and cultic value of his shrine, and the Levite apparently has no qualms about serving before idols (Judg. 17:10; Niditch, 182).

Micah's prideful attitude in acquiring a Levite for his household takes an ironic turn in the next scene, when the scouts from the tribe of Dan stop at his house and encounter the household's live-in Levite. They ask for an oracle on the success of their mission to locate a new territory for their tribe (a further sign of Israel's political decline; Butler, 389). The Levite obliges with an ambiguous benediction, "Go in peace," noting that their efforts are "under the eye of the Lord," but not suggesting they have divine sanction (18:4-6; Schneider, 237). Once the scouts complete their mission by spying out the vulnerable northern city of Laish (Butler, 394), they return to Micah's house. Just as they later forcefully capture Laish and its lands, the Danites take the opportunity to steal Micah's sacred objects (violating Deut. 7:25), and they hire away his Levite. The Levite makes the best of the situation (Mueller, 71), matching Micah's avaricious nature and readily accepting the Danites' offer to become the "priest to a tribe and clan" (18:14-20).

The source of Micah's pride and boasting thus vanishes with these marauders (Judg. 17:13). Adding to the irony and the level of covenant disobedience is the creation of a tribal worship center at Laish (renamed Dan), with Jonathan son of Gershom, son of Moses, and his sons serving as priests for the tribe of Dan and its ill-begotten idols (18:30). Tying the Mosaic priestly line to what the Judeans would consider an illegitimate shrine serves as the editors' justification for Israel's destruction by the Assyrians in 721 bce (Niditch, 184). It also reiterates the Deuteronomic polemic against the northern kingdom's shrines at Dan and Bethel and its priests (1 Kgs. 12:29).

THE TEXT IN THE INTERPRETIVE TRADITION

Some rabbinic sources (midrash *Tanhuma, Yelammedenu* 1:100) tie Micah to the exodus story and especially to Aaron's construction of the golden calf (Exod. 32:4). Chapter 24 of the midrash *Exodus Rabbah* contends that Micah's idol was created in Egypt and passed with the Israelites over the Red Sea. The *Babylonian Talmud Sanhedrin* 103b, however, says only the metals crossed the sea and were later cast into an idol. Protestant commentators, including Milton, use Micah's idol as part of their polemic against the veneration of images in the Roman Catholic Church (Gunn, 234–35).

THE TEXT IN CONTEMPORARY DISCUSSION

One of the admonitions included in police investigations is "follow the money." If the audience follows the silver in Micah's story, it is possible to see how the covetous desire (Exod. 20:17) for this precious metal becomes the catalyst for crime and covenant-breaking. Micah's tale is not just about idolatry or the unfaithfulness of itinerant Levites or the migration of the tribe of Dan. From a single act of theft comes dishonor to one's parent, the casting of idols, suborning of a Levite to serve in a house shrine dedicated to cultic images and the personal pride of the owner, and then theft on a grander scale and the transference of the crime of idolatry from a single household to an entire tribe. The narrative provides a warning to modern hedge fund managers and investors (foundations and individuals) to beware of the corrupting influence of ill-gotten riches at the expense of the public and the economy.

Levite's concubine and civil war (Judges 19-21)

■ THE TEXT IN ITS ANCIENT CONTEXT

The editors of the final set of episodes in Judges recast the story of Lot in Sodom (Genesis 19; Lasine) using an unnamed Levite and his concubine as the narrative catalyst for a horrific tragedy. The Levite is presented as a failed husband (19:2), a traveler who exercises poor judgment (19:11-14), an ungrateful guest (19:16-20), and a coward who sacrifices the life of his concubine to preserve himself from a mob of lawless men in Gibeah (19:22-25). Hospitality protocols are turned upside down throughout the narrative (Matthews, 181–88). When the long night is over, the Levite shows no concern for his concubine's brutal gang rape, not even crying out after finding her body lying on his host's doorstep (19:27-28; Yee, 154–56). Instead, he bundles her onto his donkey, and when he arrives home he gruesomely carves her body into twelve pieces (cf. Saul's butchering his oxen in 1 Sam. 11:7). Then the Levite sends these grisly items "throughout all the territory of Israel" with the inflammatory message "Has such a thing ever happened? . . . Consider it, take counsel, and speak out" (19:29-30).

Without questioning the Levite's claims, all of the Israelite tribes gather at Mizpah, creating the only instance in the book when they are all gathered together (20:1; cf. 1 Sam. 7:5-7; 10:17). The Levite uses this opportunity to condemn Gibeah and the tribe of Benjamin while painting himself as a helpless victim. Similarly, the Benjaminites, when asked to "hand over those scoundrels in Gibeah" in order to "purge the evil from Israel" (20:13; cf. the stoning of Achan's household in Josh. 7:16-26), absolutely refuse to comply and proceed to gather their own army (20:14-15). There is a mad dash to judgment and intemperate action on both sides. The result is a series of three battles, none of which need have occurred if wiser and cooler heads had intervened (cf. the negotiations in Josh. 22:10-34).

Two military defeats lead to the sole appearance in Judges of the ark of the covenant and a cameo appearance by Phinehas, a contemporary of Joshua, as the Levite in charge (see Num. 25:7-11; 31:1-12; Josh. 22:13-34). However, the Israelites' desperation and the editors' efforts to draw the combatants back to proper cultic procedures require the tribes to seek God's help through proper channels (Judg. 20:19-25; cf. Num. 14:39-45; Butler, 445–47). Duly chastised, they receive not only the command to "Go up" but also the divine assurance that this time "I will give them into your hand" (cf. Josh. 7:8-9).

In the end, the tribe of Benjamin is decimated and is only able to survive through an artful avoidance of the stipulations of the tribal oath and the capture of women from Jabesh-gilead and Shiloh (Judges 21). These female captives, unable to protect themselves from the desperate Benjaminites who pursue them, form an inclusio with the Levite's concubine, whose rape served as the cause célèbre for this destructive civil war (Keefe, 85–86).

■ THE TEXT IN THE INTERPRETIVE TRADITION

Josephus, explaining why Israel needed to call on God for deliverers, places the Levite's concubine incident prior to the rise of individual judges rather than after that sequence had begun (*Ant.* 5.2.8). The church fathers are less condemning of the Levite than modern commentators. The fourth-century bishop of Alexandria Athanasius merely describes this crime against the Levite's concubine as an affront to her husband, and then points to her death as a small thing compared to the atrocities committed against the church. Milton saw the rape as a sign of civil unrest that could not go unpunished. However, the seventeenth-century cleric Robert Gomersall, facing the prospect of civil war and political chaos in England, argued against the type of inflammatory political rhetoric used by the Levite to stir up intemperate violence (Gunn, 260–61).

■ THE TEXT IN CONTEMPORARY DISCUSSION

Contemporary readings of this text have most often centered on the theme of sexual violence against women and spousal abuse. Rape, damaging to the psyche as well as the body, must be addressed openly without transforming the victim into a harlot who provoked the attack. Perhaps by using this story as a pedagogical tool, it will be possible to strengthen the ability to confront the crime and its consequences publicly (Scholz, 7). Also contained here is an argument for mediation rather than unthinking, precipitate action (see Prov. 15:18). A reasoned approach that avoids the self-serving, shallow arguments of demagoguery can lead to reconciliation and a cooling of tempers (Prov. 7:27). Plus, a husband who sees his wife as an equal rather than as a sex object or as a trophy to his success is less likely to cause her to be harmed by inaction or inattention.

Works Cited

Ackerman, Susan. 1998. *Warrior, Dancer, Seductress, Queen: Women in Judges and Biblical Israel*. New York: Doubleday.

Amit, Yairah. 1999. *The Book of Judges: The Art of Editing*. Leiden: Brill.

Bal, Mieke. 1988. *Death and Dissymmetry: The Politics of Coherence in the Book of Judges*. Chicago: University of Chicago Press.

Begg, Christopher. 2006. "Israel's First Judge According to Josephus." *NedTT* 60:329–36.

Block, Daniel I. 1988. "The Period of the Judges: Religious Disintegration under Tribal Rule." In *Israel's Apostasy and Restoration: Essays in Honor of Roland K. Harrison*, edited by Avraham Gileadi, 39–57. Grand Rapids: Baker.

———. 1999. *Judges, Ruth*. NAC 6. Nashville: Broadman & Holman.

Bluedorn, Wolfgang. 2001. *Yahweh versus Baalism: A Theological Reading of the Gideon Abimelech Narrative.* JSOTSup 329. Sheffield: Sheffield Academic Press.

Brown, John P. 1981. "The Mediterranean Seer and Shamanism." *ZAW* 93:374–400.

Butler, Trent. 2009. *Judges.* WBC. Nashville: Thomas Nelson.

Crenshaw, James L. 1978. *Samson: A Secret Betrayed, a Vow Ignored.* Macon, GA: Mercer University Press.

Exum, J. Cheryl. 2007. "Feminist Criticism: Whose Interests Are Being Served?" In *Judges and Method: New Approaches in Biblical Studies,* edited by Gale A. Yee, 65–89. 2nd ed. Minneapolis: Fortress Press.

Fensham, F. Charles. 1962. "Salt as Curse in the Old Testament and the Ancient Near East." *BA* 25:48–50.

Fewell, Dana N. 1987. "Feminist Reading of the Hebrew Bible: Affirmation, Resistance, and Transformation." *JSOT* 39:77–87.

John R. Franke, ed. 2005. *Joshua, Judges, Ruth, 1-2 Samuel.* Downers Grove, IL: InterVarsity.

Greene, Mark. 1991. "Enigma Variations: Aspects of the Samson Story, Judges 13-16." *VE* 21:53–79.

Greenspahn, Frederick E. 1986. "The Theology of the Framework of Judges." *VT* 36:385–96.

Gunn, David M. 2005. *Judges.* Malden, MA: Blackwell.

Halpern, Baruch. 1988. *The First Historians: The Hebrew Bible and History.* San Francisco: Harper & Row.

Keefe, Alice A. 1993. "Rapes of Women/Wars of Men." *Semeia* 61:79–97.

Keel, Othmar, and Christoph Uehlinger. 1998. *Gods, Goddesses, and Images of God in Ancient Israel.* Minneapolis: Fortress Press.

Lasine, Stuart. 1984. "Guest and Host in Judges 19: Lot's Hospitality in an Inverted World." *JSOT* 29:37–59.

Leuchter, Mark. 2007. "'Now There Was a [Certain] Man': Compositional Chronology in Judges–1 Samuel." *CBQ* 69:429–39.

Marcus, David. 1986. *Jephthah and His Vow.* Lubbock: Texas Tech Press.

Matthews, Victor H. 2004. *Judges and Ruth.* New Cambridge Bible Commentary Cambridge: Cambridge University Press.

McCann, J. Clinton. 2002. *Judges.* IBC. Louisville: Westminster John Knox.

Mueller, E. Aydeet. 2001. *The Micah Story: A Morality Tale in the Book of Judges.* New York: Peter Lang.

Niditch, Susan. 2008. *Judges.* Louisville: Westminster John Knox.

Noth, Martin. 1981. *Deuteronomistic History.* JSOTSup 15. Sheffield: Sheffield Academic Press. [2nd ed. first published in 1957]

Redditt, Paul L. 2007. "Themes in Haggai–Zechariah–Malachi." *Int* 61, no. 2:184–97.

Sadler, Rodney S., Jr. 2006. "Cushan-Rishathaim." *New Interpreter's Dictionary of the Bible,* 1:812–13. Nashville: Abingdon.

Schneider, Tammi J. 2000. *Judges.* Berit Olam. Collegeville, MN: Liturgical Press.

Scholz, Susanne. 2010. *Sacred Witness: Rape in the Hebrew Bible.* Minneapolis: Fortress Press.

Stewart, Anne W. 2012. "Jephthah's Daughter and Her Interpreters." In *Women's Bible Commentary,* edited by Carol A. Newson et al., 133–37. 3rd ed. Louisville: Westminster John Knox.

Wong, Gregory T. K. 2006. *Compositional Strategy of the Book of Judges: An Inductive, Rhetorical Study.* Leiden: Brill.

Yee, Gale. 2007. "Ideological Criticism: Judges 17–21 and the Dismembered Body." In *Judges and Method: New Approaches in Biblical Studies,* edited by Gale Yee, 138–60. 2nd ed. Minneapolis: Fortress Press.

Younger, K. Lawson, Jr. 1994. "Judges 1 in Its Near Eastern Context." In *Faith, Tradition, and History: Old Testament Historiography in Its Near Eastern Context,* edited by Alan R. Millard et al., 207–27. Winona Lake, IN: Eisenbrauns.

RUTH

Gale A. Yee

Introduction

In the Christian Old Testament, the book of Ruth is located after the book of Judges and before 1 Samuel, most likely because it is set during the time of the judges (Ruth 1:1), but before King David comes on the scene in 1 Samuel. In the Tanak, the Jewish Bible, the book is found in its third canonical section, known as the Writings, and is part of the five Megillot (Scrolls) that are read at different times during the Jewish liturgical calendar. Ruth is read during the feast of Shavuot (Feast of Weeks), fifty days after the feast of Passover.

The book narrates the story of Ruth, a foreign woman from Moab who journeys with her widowed mother-in-law Naomi to Judah, where she meets her future husband Boaz and becomes the ancestress of the great King David. The book was written either as an apology for the Moabite ancestry of David (c. tenth century BCE) or during the time of Ezra and Nehemiah (fifth century BCE), when intermarriages between Judeans and the indigenous peoples of Yehud (Judah) became an acute concern. Although often read as a tender love story between a man and woman, the book covers a greater range of social relationships: husband/wife, mother/son, mother-in-law/daughter-in-law, owner/overseer/laborers, resident/foreigner, native/immigrant, and so forth. How one reads Ruth depends on one's context and social location. For example, readers in cultures such as China, where mother-in-law/daughter-in-law relations are quite conflicted, will have different readings of the book of Ruth than those in which this relationship is more harmonious.

The book of Ruth has a rich interpretive history (Koosed), especially in music (Leneman). For an imaginative retelling of the Ruth, Orpah, and Naomi story that takes into account the various interpretations of biblical scholarship, see Brenner 2005.

Ruth 1:1-22: To Moab and Back

▋ THE TEXT IN ITS ANCIENT CONTEXT

The book of Ruth begins with a spare report of the who, what, where, when, and why. During the time of the judges, a famine in the land compels Elimelech from Bethlehem to take his wife Naomi and two sons, Mahlon and Chilion, to live in Moab, where the sons marry Moabite women. After ten years Elimelech and his two sons die, leaving Naomi with her two daughters-in-law, Ruth and Orpah. Hearing that Judah has become fertile again, Naomi decides to return to Bethlehem. She encourages her daughters-in-law to return to their "mother's house." Although Orpah leaves, Ruth declares her desire to remain with Naomi. Both return as widows to Bethlehem during the barley harvest.

The Genesis ancestral narratives record several migrations to foreign lands because of famine (12:10; 26:1; 41:57; 42–43). Elimelech's family thus become strangers in a strange land, just as Ruth will become a foreigner in Judah as the story progresses. The choice to emigrate to Moab would have provoked negative associations in the implied reader. According to Gen. 19:37, its people can be traced back to an incestuous relationship between Lot and one of his daughters. Because of their incestuous origins, no Moabite shall be admitted to the assembly of the LORD (Deut. 23:3-4).

Although the preferred marriage in Israel was within one's family lineage and ethnic group (known as endogamy), Mahlon and Chilion espoused Moabite women. Marriages with foreign women were often disparaged in Israel, because they were thought to lead to idolatry (1 Kgs. 11; 18). Moabite women were especially censured for using their sexuality to lead Israel astray (Num. 25:1-5). During the Persian period, the marital policies of Ezra and Nehemiah condemned inter-marriage with foreign women (Ezra 9–10; Neh. 13:23-31). Some scholars think that the book of Ruth was written to counteract their strict interdictions, by highlighting a Moabite female convert to Israel, one who will be the ancestress to King David.

In 1:11-13, Naomi declares that she can no longer bear sons because of her age, and even if she could have sons, it would be foolish for her daughters-in-law to wait for them to grow up. These verses have been used to support the idea that the marriage between Ruth and Boaz was a levirate union, in which a levir, the closest male relative of a deceased husband, was duty-bound to marry the widow (Deut. 25:5-10). Naomi's main point, however, is that she is just too old to give birth to sons for Ruth and Orpah. She does not mention the possibility of levirs in Judah, who would be obliged to marry them as widows. This lack of disclosure is significant, raising questions about Naomi's motives for wanting her daughters-in-law to return to Moab.

The Hebrew verb used to describe Ruth "clinging" to Naomi in 1:14 is the same one used in Gen. 2:24 to describe a man "clinging" to his wife in marriage and becoming "one flesh" with her. Ruth declares her commitment in a well-known speech that culminates in her desire to die and be buried in the same land as Naomi (1:16-17). Although most scholars interpret these verses as a literary expression of fidelity, others suggest that they may refer to a contractual relationship in which Ruth works for Naomi in some capacity in Judah (Brenner in Brenner 1999; Yee).

▌▌ THE TEXT IN THE INTERPRETIVE TRADITION

Even though there is no value judgment in the biblical text on Elimelech's migration to Moab, some rabbis have argued that Elimelech was a wealthy man who could have fed the whole country with food for ten years. However, he fled to Moab instead of helping the poor out of his own bounty and was justly punished (*Ruth Rabbah* 1:4; Rashi). While the text does not disparage the intermarriage between Elimelech's sons and Moabite women, the Targum on Ruth 1:4 says that they died because "they transgressed the decree of the Word of the Lord and took unto themselves foreign wives, of the daughters of Moab." Orpah herself is raped by "a hundred heathen" on the night when she separates from Naomi. She is also identified as the mother of the Philistine Goliath (*Ruth Rabbah* 2:20).

One of the main interpretive difficulties that confronted the rabbis was in dealing with a Moabite woman who, because of her ethnicity, was forbidden to enter the assembly of the Lord (Deut. 23:3), yet became a praiseworthy character and ancestor of King David. To explain these incongruities, the Targum on Ruth 1:4 and *Ruth Rabbah* 2:9 describe Ruth as the daughter of Eglon, king of Moab (see Judg. 3:12). David's line thus has royal blood on both paternal and maternal sides. Turning her back on Moab and embracing the God of Israel, Ruth becomes the exemplar of the perfect convert (see Targum on Ruth 1:16; 2:16, 11; 3:10), teaching Israel the true meaning of *hesed* ("loving-kindness": *Ruth Rabbah* 2:14).

Philip Hermogenes Calderon's painting *Ruth and Naomi* (1902) interprets their relationship homoerotically, by depicting a very feminine-looking Ruth passionately embracing a masculine-looking Naomi. The 1960 celluloid adaptation *The Story of Ruth* creates a backstory of Ruth as a Moabite princess who was sold by her parents to be raised in the temple of Chemosh.

▌▌ THE TEXT IN CONTEMPORARY DISCUSSION

Ruth's heartfelt speech to Naomi in 1:16-17 has become a popular reading in heterosexual Christian wedding services. Furthermore, because two women are involved in this intimate relationship, these verses have also been adopted in same-gender blessing and marriage ceremonies. In the movie *Fried Green Tomatoes*, the character Ruth sends her female "friend" the text of Ruth 1:16 to inform her of her desire to leave her abusive husband and live with her.

Even though the relationship between mother-in-law and daughter-in-law in the book seems to be amiable and collaborative, in Western cultures these relations can be strained, and in some Asian cultures, downright oppressive. Care must be taken in imposing Ruth and Naomi's relationship on present-day relations between mothers and daughters-in-law in exploitative ways.

Migration to foreign lands because of famine, drought, and poverty still occurs in many parts of the world today. The book of Ruth presents a positive picture of assimilation in the intermarriage between Judeans and Moabites and the devotion between mothers-in-law and daughters-in-law. Nevertheless, we must recognize that migrants often face intolerance and great hostility from the host country as they try to assimilate into new surroundings and cultures, and partake of their resources.

Ruth 2:1-23: In the Fields by Day

THE TEXT IN ITS ANCIENT CONTEXT

Chapter 2 opens with the detail that Naomi had a prominent wealthy kinsman on her husband's side whose name was Boaz, leading the reader to suspect that this character will play a major role in the coming narrative. Gleaning the land's leftovers was an institutionalized social practice to provide for the most vulnerable and impoverished in the community: the alien, orphan, and widow (Lev. 19:9-10; 23:22; Deut. 24:19). Entitled to glean as both a foreigner and a widow, Ruth obtains Naomi's consent to glean in the fields with the express purpose of finding a patron of some sort who will look favorably on her (2:2). And "as luck would have it" (JPS), Ruth ends up gleaning in the field belonging to the self-same Boaz, who takes notice of her and finds out from his overseer that she is the Moabite who returned with Naomi (2:3-6). Boaz tells Ruth not to glean in anyone else's field, but to keep close to his young women and to where they reap. He orders his men not to "bother" her, perhaps because female reapers were targets of sexual harassment, and instructs Ruth to drink water from the vessels the men have drawn (2:8-9).

Ruth prostrates herself before Boaz, wondering why she has "found favor" in his sight despite being a foreigner, recalling 2:2, where she hopes to encounter someone "in whose sight I may find favor." Boaz responds that he has heard of what she has done in leaving her native land and family to come with her mother-in-law to a strange land and people. He prays that the God of Israel, under whose wings Ruth finds refuge, will reward Ruth for her all her deeds (2:10-12). These divine maternal wings (*kanap*, see Deut. 32:11; Ps. 17:7-9; 36:6-8; Matt. 23:37) will have a human male complement in 3:9, when Ruth asks Boaz to spread his protective cloak (*kanap*) over her as her next of kin.

When Ruth returns home with a large stash of barley, an astounded Naomi asks where she gleaned and invokes a blessing on the man who took notice of Ruth. Upon discovering that Ruth's patron is Boaz, she tells Ruth that this man is a near relation, more precisely, a *go'el*, one with the right to redeem. Redemption in the Bible refers to the responsibility to assist impoverished relatives during times of hardship (Eskenazi, liii–liv). Because Naomi did not tell Ruth that there was a close male redeemer in Bethlehem and did not warn her about the dangers women faced in the fields during harvest, some interpreters think that Naomi was ambivalent about Ruth's welfare (Eskenazi, 29; Sakenfeld, 38–39; Nielsen, 64). In any case, Ruth continues to live with her mother-in-law and glean in Boaz's field, close to his young women until the end of the barley and wheat harvest (2:19-23).

THE TEXT IN THE INTERPRETIVE TRADITION

Why does Ruth catch Boaz's eye? Although the biblical text does not describe Ruth's appearance, later rabbis comment that Ruth was beautiful, modest, less greedy, and did not flirt with the reapers, compared to the other women in the field (Ibn Ezra, *Ruth Rabbah* 4.6; Rashi). The Targum to Ruth expands on Boaz's speech in 2:11 with the details that God's prohibition of Moabites entering the assembly of God affected only the men, not the women, and that Boaz had received a prophecy that kings and prophets will be Ruth's descendants because of the kindness she has shown to her mother-in-law.

Perhaps the most famous literary reference to Ruth gleaning in the fields is in John Keats's "Ode to a Nightingale," where the nightingale's song that Keats hears is "the selfsame song that found a path / through the sad heart of Ruth when, sick for home, / She stood in tears amid the alien corn" (65–67).

▌ THE TEXT IN CONTEMPORARY DISCUSSION

U.S. agriculture depends greatly on immigrant menial laborers, many of whom enter the country illegally. They are subject to poor working conditions, lack of medical benefits, sexual harassment, and the threat of deportation. Some feminists have interpreted Ruth from the perspective of migrant foreign workers and their lower-class status in their host country (Brenner in Brenner 1999; Yee).

The ancient biblical practice of gleaning still continues today, causing us to reflect on those who must resort to gleaning in our world in order to survive: the global poor and destitute. One major area of food waste in the United States is in fields where crops that do not meet top quality standards are left to rot on the fields or to be plowed under. Some 96 billion pounds of food are wasted each year, according to some statistics. A number of humanitarian organizations, such as the Society of St. Andrew, coordinate thousands of volunteers from many different social groups to glean the fields to deliver food to the hungry. Gleaning not only occurs in agricultural fields but also appears in the heartrending face of urban dumpster diving, as depicted in Agnès Varda's 2001 documentary *The Gleaners and I.*

Ruth 3:1-18: In the Fields at Night

▌ THE TEXT IN ITS ANCIENT CONTEXT

According to 2:23, the grain harvests are coming to an end, and so with them is Ruth and Naomi's economic livelihood. Naomi therefore suggests a daring plan to secure financial security for Ruth and, implicitly, for herself. Her instructions that Ruth wash, anoint herself, and don her best clothes can signify the end to Ruth's period of mourning (2 Sam. 12:20, a preparation for a wedding celebration (Ezek. 16:9-10), or even sexual seduction (Jth. 10:3-4). Ruth is then supposed to go down to the threshing floor secretly, mark where Boaz lies down after eating and drinking, and in an audacious act, uncover his feet and lie down (3:3-4).

The whole encounter between Ruth and Boaz is filled with sexual innuendo and ambiguity (3:6-16). The meeting occurs at night, the favorite time of many carnal assignations. The threshing floor is associated with illicit sexuality (see Hosea 9:10). Although it can simply mean to "lie down" to sleep, the verb *shkb* can also imply sexual intercourse (Gen. 19:33-35). Its eight occurrences in this chapter highlight the eroticism of the scene (v. 4, three times; v. 7, twice; vv. 8, 13-14). Ruth is instructed to *uncover* Boaz's *feet* and "lie down" (3:4, 7). The verb "uncover" (*glh*) evokes unlawful sexual intercourse (Lev. 18:6-18; Deut. 27:20); "feet" can refer to genitalia (Isa. 6:2; 7:20). Nevertheless, the text is completely silent about whether Ruth and Boaz actually had sexual intercourse that night, leaving it to the imaginations of many of readers and interpreters.

When Boaz awakens at midnight and blurts out "Who are you?" the woman lying at his "feet" informs him of her identity and bids him to spread his cloak (*kanap*) over her, because he is a *go'el*, a redeeming kinsman (3:8-9, JPS translation). Just as Boaz evokes God's blessing on Ruth, under whose wings (*kanapim*) she has come for refuge (2:12), so now Ruth requests the same patronage from Boaz. Because *kanap* as a "cloak" or "skirt" is spread over a woman who will become one's wife (cf. Ezek. 16:8), one can also say that Ruth is proposing marriage to Boaz, as well as asking for his protection.

Boaz responds by blessing Ruth, praising her for her acts of *hesed* (meaning "loyalty" in this instance), the first by accompanying her mother-in-law to Judah, and the second by choosing him as *go'el* over younger men, whether rich or poor. Ruth picks someone within Elimelech's line when she doesn't have to, thus reinforcing her kinship with Naomi. Boaz agrees to do what Ruth asks, but points out that there is "another kinsman more closely related" than he. If this kinsman will not agree to be a redeemer-kin for Ruth, Boaz will do so on her behalf (3:10-13).

Ruth remains the rest of the night "lying at his feet until dawn," leaving the reader to speculate what might have happened between the two during that interval. That Ruth's nocturnal appearance at the threshing floor was unconventional and perhaps even scandalous is evident when Boaz says, "It must not be known that the woman came to the threshing floor" (3:14). Boaz gives Ruth a significant supply of grain, which she carries back to Naomi. After relaying to Naomi what Boaz has done for her, she explains the gift of grain as Boaz's intention that Ruth not return to her mother-in-law empty-handed, even though this detail is not recorded in their interchange. This is the last time Ruth speaks in the book. Her fate now rests with the man who "will settle the matter today" (3:16-18).

▌ THE TEXT IN THE INTERPRETIVE TRADITION

Rashi has Ruth questioning Naomi's orders: "'If I go down all dressed up, anyone who meets me and sees me will think I am a harlot.' Therefore she went down in the first place to the threshing-floor and afterwards adorned herself as her mother-in-law had instructed" (Beattie, 107). To settle the problem of Ruth's uncovering Boaz's "feet," Salmon ben Yeroham says that Ruth really uncovers her face, which was covered to conceal her identity as she went through the threshing floor (Beattie, 47). The rabbis are thus at pains to exclude any possibility that Ruth and Boaz had sex that night. Commenting on 3:7, they highlight that when Boaz was "in a contented mood" (lit. "his heart was good"), "he occupied himself with the words of the Torah," and that he was looking for a wife (*Ruth Rabbah* 5:15), and that he "blessed the name of the Lord" (Targum on Ruth). According to the Targum on Ruth 3:8, when Boaz sees Ruth sleeping at his feet, he "subdues his evil inclination" and resists drawing closer to her, like Joseph who refused to sleep with Potiphar's wife, and Paltiel who put a knife between himself and Saul's daughter Michal. *Ruth Rabbah* 7:1 also highlights Boaz's virtue in not giving in to sexual temptation.

Several artists render Ruth sleeping at Boaz's feet literally: for example, an anonymous illustrator in the Wenzel Bible (Codex 2760); James Tissot, *Ruth and Boaz* (1900); and Marc Chagall, *Ruth at the Feet of Boaz* (1960).

While the biblical text is circumspect about the matter, many Western readers in the twenty-first century most likely will have no problem imagining Ruth and Boaz having sex on the threshing floor that fateful night. Explicit sexuality can be found in many aspects of Western culture, such as film, television, advertising, books, and so forth. However, this was not the case in ancient Israel and is not for a good part of today's world where sexual expression among the genders is strictly enforced and can have insidious undersides. We must never forget the desperate circumstances of poverty that compelled Naomi and Ruth to transgress the norms of their culture to carry out such a scandalous plan. Ruth, as a poor foreign woman, already a target for sexual harassment, secretly approaching an important landowner in the middle of the night, had the most to lose. For many destitute women today, marriage or concubinage to a wealthy man are their only sure routes out of poverty. Others must resort to or be forced to selling their bodies to men who sexually exploit them. While the book of Ruth ends "happily," it could have ended in humiliation, rejection, and sexual exploitation, which many impoverished women experience today in order to survive (Sakenfeld 2002).

Ruth 4:1-21: At the City Gate

■ THE TEXT IN ITS ANCIENT CONTEXT

In this chapter, Boaz cleverly maneuvers this nearer kinsman to decline his role as redeemer-kin for Ruth before the elders at the city gate. Precisely *how* Boaz negotiates the transaction is problematic. In the first place, Boaz tells the nearer kinsman that Naomi is selling a parcel of land that belonged to Elimelech. The land redemption laws in Lev. 25:25-28 specify that the next-of-kin (*go'el*) must buy the land of an impoverished "brother" to prevent its leaving the family lineage. However, why wasn't Naomi's piece of land mentioned earlier? Its economic value would have saved Ruth from the backbreaking work of gleaning. Second, why wasn't this nearer-kinsman mentioned earlier as a possible redeemer-kin for Naomi and Ruth? Was he simply a literary functionary brought in to create suspense in the "romantic" story of Ruth and Boaz? Third, although many interpret Boaz's coupling of land redemption with the obligation of a levir to marry the widow of the dead man (Deut. 25:5-10), the redemption of land does not require marriage with the widow of the deceased kinsman. These are two separate issues. Furthermore, the ritual of the sandal described in Deut. 25:9 is enacted between the rejected widow against the man who refused to be her levir, humiliating him by spitting in his face. The ritual in Ruth 4:7 is a more understated legal transaction between Boaz and the nearer-kinsman. Ruth plays no part in the negotiations.

Despite these and other difficulties, Boaz successfully declares before the elders and all the people that he has acquired the piece of land that belonged to Naomi's dead husband and sons (4:9) and has also acquired Ruth the Moabite as wife, in order to maintain the dead man's name on his inheritance (4:10). The elders and the people acknowledge the legality of the proceedings as Boaz's witnesses, blessing Ruth with the fertility of Rachel and Leah (the mothers of the tribes of Israel). The people's blessing concludes ironically with references to the house of Perez, whom Tamar bore to Judah (4:11-12). Tamar was a widow who disguised herself as a prostitute to seduce her father-in-law Judah, who had refused his levirate obligations by withholding her marriage with his surviving son (Genesis 38). Both Ruth and Tamar are widows. Both use socially unorthodox means to form an alliance with older men who will secure their economic and social future.

Although the "Moabite" designation is dropped from Ruth when she marries Boaz and conceives a son (4:13), one cannot presume that Ruth has been completely assimilated into the Judean community. She actually disappears from the story at this point, and the narrative turns to Naomi. The women bless God, who has provided Naomi with a redeemer-kin (*go'el*). Without naming Ruth, they praise the daughter-in-law who loves Naomi and is worth more to her than seven sons. It is significant to note that this praise of Ruth by the women appears only after she gives birth to a son (4:14-15). These women did not acknowledge Ruth when she returned with Naomi from Moab (2:19). It is Naomi, not Ruth, who becomes the child's nurse, and it is the local women, not Ruth, who names the child "Obed" (4:16-17). The book ends with the genealogy of Perez, concluding with Obed of Jesse, and Jesse of David. Although not specified as such, Ruth becomes the great-grandmother of King David.

▌ The Text in the Interpretive Tradition

The unnamed redeemer-kin in 3:13 and 4:1-6 is given the name Tob in rabbinic literature, where he is sometimes described as the uncle of Mahlon and Chilion, while Boaz is the son of another uncle, and thus cousin to Elimelech's sons. As an uncle, Tob takes precedence over Boaz in inheritance and redemption. Other rabbis argue that Tob and Boaz were brothers, but since Tob was older, he took precedence. Some rabbis speculate that Tob refuses to marry Ruth because he was poor and had his own children to support, and could not be saddled with another wife. Another view has Tob's wife threatening divorce if he takes another spouse (Beattie, 79–82). The Targum to Ruth 4:7-8 has Boaz taking off his right glove to seal the transaction. In the biblical text, the object of exchange is a sandal, not a glove, and it is unclear who removes it.

Matthew 1:5 places Boaz, Ruth, and Obed into Jesus' genealogy. Ruth joins four other women in the ancestral list: Tamar (Genesis 38), Rahab (Joshua 2), the wife of Uriah (Bathsheba, 2 Samuel 11), and Mary the mother of Jesus. Why these women? Perhaps because there is a whiff of sexual unconventionality surrounding these women. Tamar disguises herself as a hooker by the side of the road to seduce her father-in-law to fulfill his levirate obligations. Rahab actually is a prostitute. Bathsheba commits adultery with David, Mary is a pregnant unwed teenager, and Ruth places herself in a compromising position on the threshing floor with Boaz.

▌ The Text in Contemporary Discussion

In contrast to the Disney princess Snow White, who waits longingly for her prince to come, women in Western societies usually do not have to marry in order to become financially secure. They can acquire upper levels of education in order to make a living for themselves. They can inherit their family's resources. They usually do not operate under the social and sexual strictures that prohibited certain gender relations in ancient Israel. However, the story of Ruth supports attitudes regarding female dependence on men and the social necessity to marry in order to live in a financially safe environment. Naomi could not inherit the land owned by her husband, which had to be purchased by a male "redeemer." The Cinderella story of finding and seducing a rich man who will become her patron is often the hope of many impoverished women today in the third world. Their hopes are usually dashed when confronted with realities of sexual exploitation and human trafficking (http://facts.randomhistory.com/human-trafficking-facts.html). Although Ruth's story ends "happily" in that she "gets her guy" in the end and becomes upwardly mobile, this is not the case for many poor women today, thousands of years later, whose stories often end quite tragically.

Works Cited

Beattie, D. R. G. 1977. *Jewish Exegesis of the Book of Ruth.* JSOTSup 2. Sheffield: JSOT Press.

Brenner, Athalya, ed. 1999. *Ruth and Esther: A Feminist Companion to the Bible.* 2nd Series. Sheffield: Sheffield Academic Press.

———. 2005. *I Am . . . Biblical Women Tell Their Own Stories.* Minneapolis: Fortress.

Bush, Frederic W. 1996. *Ruth, Esther.* WBC 9. Waco, TX: Word.

Eskenazi, Tamara Cohn, and Tikva Frymer-Kensky. 2011. *Ruth: The Traditional Hebrew Text with the New JPS Translation and Commentary.* Philadelphia: Jewish Publication Society. [Cited as Eskenazi]

Koosed, Jennifer L. 2011. *Gleaning Ruth: A Biblical Heroine and Her Afterlives.* Columbia: University of South Carolina Press.

Leneman, Helen. 2007. *The Performed Bible: The Story of Ruth in Opera and Oratorio.* Sheffield: Sheffield Phoenix Press.

Matthews, Victor H. 2004. *Judges and Ruth.* NCBC. Cambridge: Cambridge University Press.

Nielsen, Kirsten. 1997. *Ruth: A Commentary.* Translated by Edward Broadbridge. OTL. Louisville: Westminster John Knox.

Sakenfeld, Katherine Doob. 1999. *Ruth.* IBC. Louisville: John Knox.

———. 2002. "At the Threshing Floor: Sex, Reader Response, and a Hermeneutic of Survival." *OTE* 15:164–78.

Yee, Gale A. 2009. "'She Stood in Tears Amid the Alien Corn': Ruth, the Perpetual Foreigner and Model Minority." In *They Were All Together in One Place: Toward Minority Biblical Criticism*, edited by Randall C. Bailey, Tat-siong Benny Liew, and Fernando F. Segovia, 119–40. Atlanta: Society of Biblical Literature.

1 AND 2 SAMUEL

Hugh S. Pyper

Introduction

The books of Samuel are treated in the Hebrew tradition as a single work. The division into two may well be a practical consequence of the conventional size of a scroll, and the death of Saul provided a convenient and appropriate breakpoint. These books cover the careers of the first two kings of Israel—Saul and David—and give an account of the reasons why this new institution arose in Israel and its effects. The Masoretic Hebrew text of the books has its problems, which are often explicable if reference is made to the different readings in the Dead Sea Scrolls and in the Greek translations, especially the so-called Lucianic tradition.

Critical scholarship on the text has been troubled by duplications of stories and inconsistent attitudes to the monarchy. This has been explained by postulating the combination of pro- and antimonarchic sources, either from different eras or perhaps originating in different circumstances. It has also been postulated that the text collects a number of originally separate works. Those identified include the Ark Narrative (4:1 to 7:1), concentrating on the history of the ark of the covenant; the History of David's Rise (16–31); and the Succession Narrative (2 Samuel 9–20; 1 Kings 1–2). In addition, the books of Samuel now form part of the great sweep of historical narrative that runs from Genesis to 2 Kings and are also included in the scholarly construct of the Deuteronomistic History, which includes Joshua, Judges, and the books of Kings. Such passages as 2 Samuel 12 do seem to accord with the language and theological concerns of the writers of Deuteronomy.

Without denying that there may be a complex history of accumulation and editorial revision behind the present form of these books, at some point the texts we have were accepted by some readers as at least an adequate representation of what they and their traditions had to say on the matters of David's kingship and its role in Israel's history. What may trouble some readers as inconsistency, both stylistically and ideologically, can also be seen as an acknowledgment of the complexity and messiness of human nature and human history, due to the residuum of the unknowable and unpredictable in any human transaction.

Literary scholars, most notably Robert Alter, have held up the characterization of David in these texts as an astonishingly rounded and subtle treatment of an endlessly fascinating and elusive personality. Indeed, he has been called the model of the ambiguity of what it is to be human (Frontain and Wojcik, 5). Rather than offering a simple stereotype of the hero and king, the books of Samuel present several Davids, public and private: father, son, lover, outlaw, and king. In the interplay of these Davids with each other and the other characters, there is a fascinating possibility for exploring the limits of these markers of identity.

Of course, there is a danger of over-reading here. Accidental and unintended juxtapositions may be just that, rather than precursors of modern and postmodern literary effects. Yet one thing is clear from reading these books. Those who handed on these traditions tell stories the whole point of which depends on the subtle ways in which language and power are related and the way history and story can be manipulated and reread in order to provoke particular responses from an audience. Time and again, it is David's ability to access, process, and manipulate the flow of information within the text that gives him his advantage; his failures occur when he is distracted or outwitted in this deadly game. It is surely not inappropriate to imagine that storytellers and writers who show their characters using and responding to complex communicative strategies would themselves be capable of using such strategies in their own work.

The message of works such as the books of Samuel resides, then, not so much in explicit accounts of actions, speech, and intention, but in the structure of the language, syntax, and narrative conventions that go together to make up this extraordinary work. The effort to match intention and effect is shown to be constantly thwarted. Speech and actions have unintended and unforeseen consequences. This implies that the attempt to reverse the process and deduce intentions from results is even more subject to error and misunderstanding (Frontain and Wojcik, 10).

Hence the importance of the promise and the oath, its divinely sanctioned refinement, in the narrative structure of Samuel 1 and 2 (Pyper, 131–55). Promises in the books of Samuel seem to bridge the gap between intention and action by invoking the divine but then compound it when they are broken or reinterpreted. Oaths are only necessary because plain statements do not bind people to a course of action.

This also emphasizes the paradoxical vulnerability of masculinity as a social category. Just as the spoken word always risks misinterpretation by its hearers, so the male has to entrust his seed to a woman, with no guarantee that a son will be forthcoming, or that any child will be his. The gap between intention and achievement that bedevils speech is structurally equivalent to the one between intercourse and childbirth.

Death and succession go together. It is because of death that a successor becomes necessary. This essential heir is also the paradoxical reminder of the inevitability of death and may in fact become the embodiment of that threat to the father. Death, however, is the ultimate downfall of human intention. No one can live forever simply by intending to. Human beings can bring about death, but cannot reverse it; they may bring death inadvertently or fail to do so when they try to.

This paradox is heightened when the political continuity of a community is tied to biological succession, as is the case in a hereditary monarchy. The books of Samuel explore the consequences of the move to a dynastic system in Israel. Questions as to how communities and individuals interact to preserve identity through time are at the heart of their concerns. If we take it that the form we now have of these texts is a product of a time no earlier than the latest incidents they relate, those who are transmitting them know also that the story of the monarchy ends in the defeat and destruction of the Davidic kingdom. They tell these stories to audiences that know the promises of peace and stability have proven to be untrue. How is this to be explained? What lessons can be learned from the past so that a meaning that has relevance to their present situation can be found?

These books also describe a crucial transition in the understanding of Israel as a political entity in the context of the conflicting power claims of the ancient Levant. They describe it, however, for the benefit of communities that are wrestling with the need to understand what Israel is in their own very different situation of defeat and the continued influence of powerful imperial forces. The model of communal identity put forward here has had persisting effects on the models of nationhood that shaped modern Europe and the ideology of colonial expansion, and in turn the complex issues around identity that underlie the struggle for independence from colonial rule (Hastings). The utopian dream of an independent and homogenous Israel united under one king and one God is presented and critiqued in the book in ways that can still inform and unsettle current political arguments.

For modern readers, they raise difficult questions about how identity is to be understood and how differences between genders, generations, and ethnic groups are to be dealt with. Although the cultural assumptions may not be ours and we need always to guard against importing our questions and our answers into ancient texts with different concerns, staying alert to the way in which these texts display the interchange of information and identity as the political and social systems of Israel develop and change can illuminate present dilemmas, often as cautionary tales.

1 Samuel 1–3: Samuel and the Promise to Eli

▌THE TEXT IN ITS ANCIENT CONTEXT

The first three chapters of the books of Samuel act as a prologue to the story of Israel and its kings up to the destruction of the temple, as told in Samuel and Kings. In many ways, they also foreshadow the key themes and dilemmas with which this longer history has to deal.

The extrabiblical evidence for the rise and fall of the Davidic kingdom is surprisingly scant as the archaeology of this period is contested and no accounts exist in other ancient literatures of the time. However, the period they cover marks a time when the two great powers of Egypt and Babylon—which lay to the south and the north of the area where these stories are set—were both undergoing internal convulsions. This left an unusual space for the various peoples of Palestine and Syria to assert their independence and indulge in local battles for supremacy. For the ancient reader, these books are one attempt to explain how and why the promises Israel saw as its heritage turned out so differently from what had been expected. A community that has experienced exile, the destruction of the temple, and the effective end to the Davidic monarchy needs to understand why this does not mean that the God whom the tradition says made promises of protection and enduring sovereignty has failed.

Read in sequel to the book of Judges, 1 Samuel 1 could easily be the birth story of the next judge. The repeated use of the verb "ask" in this story, which resembles the name "Saul" in Hebrew, has led to scholarly debate as to whether this was originally the birth story of Saul (McCarter 1980). Strikingly, neither Saul nor David has such a birth story in Samuel. The familiar story of a childless woman bearing a son through God's intervention has some twists, however. It is Hannah who takes the initiative in praying for a son, and the reassurance she needs is given by the priest Eli in the temple at Shiloh, rather than by a mysterious messenger. There is a further twist when Hannah vows to dedicate her son to God for life and in her song of praise.

A key theme that runs throughout Samuel and Kings is introduced in the discussion of the failures of Eli's sons. They are the presumptive heirs to hereditary priesthood of Eli, but their conduct is unacceptable. The narrative tensions develop around vows and their fulfillment, and around the related theme of the hereditary principle. A man of God comes to Eli and announces that despite God's much earlier promise that Eli and his family would be priests before him forever, now his sons are to be killed and a new order will come into force. This introduces a worrying principle into the narrative. God may rescind the promises he has made, even of an eternal priesthood. The unsatisfactory actions of sons may mean that a promised destiny is not fulfilled. Eli seems to have little influence over his sons but has less over the divine promise. As a model of the future prospects for kingship in Israel, this is sobering.

In another foreshadowing of the later story, Samuel has already entered the story as the one who will supplant Eli's sons as his successor, combining the roles of priest, prophet, and judge in an unprecedented synthesis. The young Samuel is inspired by the Lord to make this clear to Eli, whose response is the faithful acceptance of his fate. A pattern has been set, of sons who cannot be trusted, of promises, even divine ones, that turn out to be provisional or to have unlooked-for consequences, and of the rise of an unexpected successor.

▌ THE TEXT IN THE INTERPRETIVE TRADITION

The interpretative tradition has focused on the incident of Samuel's call and the rejection of Eli. For writers such as John Cassian and Basil the Great, it is a story that resonates with the issue of how and why God chooses people; in discussions of election, Samuel can be an important example (Franke). He is set aside from childhood, and the story does not argue that any particular gifts on his part set him aside. Eli as the representative of a failing priestly dynasty does, however, have the wisdom to understand that his own role in the story is to bow out graciously, giving what wisdom he can to Samuel.

▌ THE TEXT IN CONTEMPORARY DISCUSSION

For readers such as Donna Nolan Fewell and David Gunn (1993), the role of Hannah in this story has become a focus for attention. Her initiative and, particularly, the potentially revolutionary content of her song mean that she can speak for women who challenge any system that attempts to subjugate them. It resonates with the Magnificat in Luke 1:46-55 in its repeated praise of God as the one who reverses status, exalting the weak and humbling those with riches and power. Her song continues to be a challenge today, especially as the systems of power and privilege are constantly threatened in the story to follow, but often reestablish themselves in a new guise. Quite how radical a true expression of Hannah's sentiments would be is a continuing point of debate as the relationship between belief and political structures is negotiated.

1 Samuel 4–6: The Ark at Large

▌ THE TEXT IN ITS ANCIENT CONTEXT

In 1 Samuel 4–6, our attention is turned outward to the international and political environment of Samuel's new status in Israel. In a manner that becomes familiar through its repetition in the book of Judges, the test for the new political order is a Philistine invasion. Israel is reduced to playing its trump card when it brings the ark of the Lord into the camp, only for this to have the opposite effect of what was intended; the Philistines rally and capture the ark.

Scholars have speculated that a so-called Ark Narrative once formed part of an independently circulated cycle of stories (Gordon). This may be so, but one of the points of the books of Samuel is to account for the bringing together of the Davidic king and YHWH's temple in Jerusalem and to illuminate the tensions to which this juxtaposition gives rise. In these early chapters, neither the future king nor the ark—as the nearest thing to a physical embodiment of YHWH—are in Jerusalem, and the separate—and sometimes apparently random—stories of the ark and the king are juxtaposed rather than linked. How these two stories come to run together without becoming inseparable is the point of the narrative. In the end, the fate of the kings and the fate of YHWH will be very different. The human institution fails and is transformed, while YHWH's position continues undiminished despite the fate of the ark, at least within the ideology of the texts.

Even at this point in the story, what in an ancient context might seem to be the defeat of Israel's God turns out to be quite the opposite. In a series of comic accidents, the Philistine god Dagon is overthrown and the people are plagued with mice and hemorrhoids. The trouble is, however, that no one seems to be able to control the ark, and the story evolves into a sort of hot-potato game as various communities try to get rid of it until it finally comes to rest in Kiriath-jearim. There it waits until much later in the story when David is in a position to bring the ark into the orbit of his growing power.

▌ THE TEXT IN THE INTERPRETIVE TRADITION

This story of the ark has led to a rich allegorical series of interpretations. As the sign of God's earthly presence with Israel, Christian interpreters tied it to the incarnation of Christ (so, for instance, Bede) or to Mary as the vehicle of that incarnation (Jeffrey). In less concrete terms, it becomes a focus for meditation on the reconciling work of God in Christ, drawing on the understanding of the ark as God's mercy seat. Again, it is the point of encounter. Typically, the history of interpretation comes late to recognizing the satirical bent of the tales.

The Text in Contemporary Discussion

Theologically, these stories, which have a strong resemblance to folktales, remind the modern reader that these texts are well aware of the uncanniness and the unpredictability of the God they bear witness to. This story is as near as the Bible comes to comic writing. Its message is a serious one for modern readers. Whatever is powerful is also dangerous; whatever can protect us can also be a threat. Any tendency to treat God as a possession or, indeed, to use him as a weapon or as a threat against others is likely to have consequences that no one will enjoy. The unpredictability, allure, and danger of what is, after all, a wooden box on an oxcart, reminds readers that none of the human characters is in control of the story. Those in contemporary political discourse who claim divine support for their policies might well remember this. Humor and irony are appropriate in discussing God's dealings with humanity. The downside of this is that the opponents of God and of Israel are at times depicted as caricatures and figures of fun in a way that can, if unchecked, seem to justify a stereotypical response that risks forgetting their humanity. How biblical texts portray those who are alien and the proper response to them is a complex question. We do need to note the moments when the Philistines show unexpected courage and those when the people of Israel react through fear or prejudice.

1 Samuel 7–8: Samuel and His Sons: The Case for a King

The Text in Its Ancient Context

First Samuel 7 shows that Samuel has succeeded in the way that counts for a judge. Under his leadership, the Philistines are defeated. He does this, however, not by military power, but by exercising his priestly office and offering a sacrifice. Now, once more, there is a problem of succession. Samuel is in the same situation as Eli. His sons are worthless, yet, despite this, he names them as his successors. At this, the people protest and ask for a king "like other nations" (8:4).

Samuel takes his resentment at this to God, who agrees to the demand, but with a warning. The warning in 8:8-18 is Samuel's, however, not God's. This passage is often read as reflecting a later Deuteronomistic view of the inevitable failure of the monarchy and as being a definitive statement of the antimonarchical trend in these texts. Read in context, however, is it quite the condemnation that Samuel seems to think? After all, what he warns the people is that the king they are seeking will organize the army, give their sons a proper military training, and even find occupations in his palace for their daughters. After the years of uncertainty and chaos that are depicted in the book of Judges, when Israel had no clear leader or any mechanism for appointing one until they had suffered defeat, this is surely just what the people are asking for. Samuel is no longer able to lead them, and his sons offer no prospect of being able to provide stability.

◼ THE TEXT IN THE INTERPRETIVE TRADITION

Traditionally, this reading has led to a suspicion of kingship that has not always helped relationships between the church and the state. In response to the Geneva Bible's questioning of royal legitimacy in the footnotes to passages such as this, based on its endorsement of the Calvinist position that the people have the right to depose a tyrannous ruler, King James decreed that the new version of the Bible produced under his sponsorship should have no footnotes.

◼ THE TEXT IN CONTEMPORARY DISCUSSION

In a contemporary reading, we can recognize the same questioning of what constitutes legitimate power in the complex politics of identity that surrounds the call for independence among former colonies, which has led to the establishment of current political boundaries around the world. These issues are the topic of postcolonial studies. A key topic in such studies is the role of mimicry: the way in which the colonized take on the customs and institutions of the colonizer. Paradoxically, a colonized group can only be taken seriously if it shows itself to meet the colonizers' criteria for nationhood. Here, the people of Israel encapsulate the paradox in a phrase. To maintain their distinctive identity, they need to become "like the other nations." In particular, they need a king who will provide both a point of union and a continuity of leadership not available under the judges and who will be recognized by their enemies as a legitimate leader. The kind of decisive leadership and economic coordination of society that Samuel warns the people to expect from their king may actually be exactly what they feel they have been missing.

These texts give us an insight into the paradox that by seeking to establish the distinctiveness of our identity, we almost always have to reformulate and even compromise it. Whose criteria do we use? Religious groups fall prey to the same paradoxes as nation states. It also reminds us that any claim, even from a recognized authority, to speak in the name of God needs to be examined.

1 Samuel 9–13: Samuel and the Promise to Saul

◼ THE TEXT IN ITS ANCIENT CONTEXT

First Samuel 9 begins by introducing a new character who literally stands out in contrast to the rest of Israel: Saul, son of Kish. He arrives full-grown in the story, with no birth narrative. In fact, the obscurity of his ancestry is made a point. In the wake of 1 Samuel 8, the question—Is this character the new king?—comes to mind, but clearly nothing can happen unless Saul comes to Samuel's attention. In a story that almost seems to parody the way narratives need to get their protagonists to meet, Saul finds Samuel by accident as he seeks his uncle's lost asses and is directed to a seer whose words always come true. Samuel anoints him as ruler of Israel (note, however, that the word "king" is never mentioned at this juncture), an unprecedented act in Israel's story. There follows a promise, but only in the Greek translation. The Hebrew text does not specify what being a "ruler" entails.

Samuel does tell Saul of a sign that will show he has God's favor. This is an encounter with a band of prophets that throws him into a trance. In itself an intriguing glimpse into the prophetic culture as the writer understood it, this story leaves some doubt as to whether Saul's experience is seen as creditable.

The narrative recounts two further episodes where Saul is in fact declared king, rather than ruler, although it is the people and the narrator who use the word, not Samuel. In addition to prophetic anointment (10:1), he must be seen to be God's chosen by lot (10:21) and he must be acclaimed as king by the people (10:24). Again, this may represent the combination of different traditions, but it also emphasizes the fact that Saul's role is a new one. He is no one's successor but at the same time embodies a number of leadership roles, and then demonstrates his fitness for office through a military victory over the Philistines (11:11-15). Even so, his rule is challenged from the outset, and no sooner is he acclaimed than Samuel is given a speech—markedly Deuteronomistic in tone—that makes no bones about the fact that the kingship shows the people's wickedness. Not long after that, Saul takes it upon himself to undertake a sacrifice in the absence of Samuel. On his arrival, Samuel tells Saul that he has broken a divine command, although it is not easy to see from the text just what specific command is meant here (13:13). It is only at that point that we learn of a potential promise to Saul that has now been rescinded. He would have been promised an eternal kingdom, but now his kingdom is already superseded. Another has already been appointed ruler in his stead, although the reader is in the dark as to who this is.

In addition, the final verses of 1 Samuel 13 show that by this stage the vaunted independence of Israel is rather hollow. The nation may have a king, but it is still harried by Philistine invasion and indeed seems to be entirely dependent on the Philistines for any ironwork, as Israel is forbidden to have blacksmiths.

▌THE TEXT IN THE INTERPRETIVE TRADITION

Saul is mentioned only once in the New Testament, but at a crucial moment in the book of Acts, where his namesake, Saul, becomes known as Paul. In Acts 13:21, Saul is mentioned as the first king, but as one supplanted by David. Here Saul becomes the example that explains how those who are legitimately chosen by God can be replaced. Paul's speech is part of his argument that the rise of the new Israel of the church does not mean that the chosen status of Israel is to be questioned. Saul is legitimately king, even if his kingship passes to David.

▌THE TEXT IN CONTEMPORARY DISCUSSION

To modern eyes, Saul may seem a tragic figure (Exum). He resembles a number of modern leaders whose military prowess and charisma in their struggles for national independence did not equip them to deal with the infighting and political maneuvering that ensued once independence was won, and whose responses typically become increasingly arbitrary and dictatorial. Plucked unwillingly from obscurity, he carries out his key responsibility, to lead the people to military victory, with notable success. However, his status remains undefined and his kingship depends on the assent of the people and the continued support of God. He is then placed in the dilemma of risking loss of loyalty among the people because of the unrest caused by Samuel's failure to come when he had promised. He makes his decision, only to find that he has lost everything and faces an unknown rival who is destined to supplant him. Given Samuel's attitude to the kingship, what is his role in the whole story? How is Saul to know what God's commands are and what comes from Samuel himself? The real crisis of his story is that he loses all communication with God, which is a personal and political disaster. This is something that may speak to rulers of Egypt, Tunisia, and other countries that have experienced upheaval during and after the "Arab Spring."

1 Samuel 14: Saul and His Son

▊ THE TEXT IN ITS ANCIENT CONTEXT

We now encounter Saul's son Jonathan. His appearance in the story may remind us that we have been told nothing up to now of Saul's domestic life. Jonathan simply arrives in the story as a fully grown warrior. Given the move in these narratives toward hereditary succession, at this point in the narrative the question might arise, Is this the already-designated successor to Saul?

What follows is another story that revolves around an oath. One small detail sets up the unfolding disaster that will eventually destroy Saul's household. Jonathan goes out to fight the Philistines with just his armor-bearer, "but he did not tell his father" (14:1).

This lack of information becomes crucial. Throughout the books of Samuel, the importance for a ruler to control and master the flow of information in his court and kingdom is a recurrent theme. Because of Jonathan's omission, Saul has to find out who it is that is missing from the army, has managed to storm the Philistine garrison, and has caused the panic that leads to a full-scale Philistine retreat. We then learn that Saul commits what the Greek text describes as a "very rash act" (14:24). He swears an oath that no one is to eat anything before evening. Jonathan, who has not heard the oath, eats some honey. Things begin to go wrong quickly, culminating in YHWH's refusal to answer Saul's question as to whether he should attack the Philistines. Another vital channel of communication seems to be severed.

Saul's response is to declare that whoever has sinned shall die, even if it is Jonathan. Traditionally, this is seen as yet another rash oath. Yet Saul knew that the only people who were not around when he proclaimed his first oath about the fast were Jonathan and his armor-bearer. Is this second oath an innocent piece of folly, or is it made with that knowledge in mind?

When Jonathan returns, he is subjected to the lot but already seems to have been singled out by Saul. Jonathan owns up to his deed when the lot falls on him and is condemned to die until a unique event in the Hebrew Bible occurs. The people counter Saul's oath by a directly opposing oath, both invoking the name of YHWH, and thereby save Jonathan, but at the expense of the credibility and prestige of Saul (14:44). He is the only character in the Hebrew Bible who makes an oath in YHWH's name that is not fulfilled. This outcome also reinforces the growing separation and indeed hostility between Saul and YHWH. Yet despite all this, Saul continues to be a successful war leader, and we are finally told further details of his family. He has several sons and therefore several potential successors. His cousin is now serving as his general.

■ THE TEXT IN THE INTERPRETIVE TRADITION

In rabbinical discussion, this text stands with the story of Jephthah in Judges 11, where another child is put in mortal danger because of the unthinking oath sworn by her father. The warnings against oaths in the Hebrew Bible and the New Testament prohibitions of oaths (Matt. 5:33-36; James 5:12) are defended in later Christian writings with reference to these episodes. Saul's reputation is further besmirched in the tradition by these words. This is tempered by the interest in later Christian writers, including Tertullian and Bede, in the discipline of fasting. In that context, Saul's imposition of punishment for a breach of the rules of fasting without fear or favor is viewed favorably (Franke).

■ THE TEXT IN CONTEMPORARY DISCUSSION

This story can certainly stand as a warning against rash oaths, but there seems to be something deeper at work here that is a recurrent theme in biblical texts, with troubling repercussions for modern readers. It concerns the dynamics of the relationship between fathers and sons in the ancient world. On the one hand, a son is essential to ensure that the memory and legacy of the father are maintained, but on the other hand, he is a potential rival.

This tension is heightened when it comes to a royal family. Why would a royal son and heir wait for his father to die in order to succeed? A similar fear has prevented many contemporary dictators from nominating a successor until too late, resulting in the collapse of their regime on their death. The fate of Yugoslavia after Josip Broz Tito's death is one example among many.

Jonathan's military success and independence suggest that the day may come when he can supplant his father. Is Saul's oath, consciously or unconsciously, an expression of what in psychoanalytic terms could be a "Laius complex"? This is named after the father of Oedipus, who exposed his infant son in response to a prophecy, later fulfilled as we know, that his son would kill him. This will not be the only time Saul makes an attempt on his son's life.

1 Samuel 15: Saul's Broken Promise

■ THE TEXT IN ITS ANCIENT CONTEXT

There is an odd disconnection between the preceding chapters and 1 Samuel 15. Samuel reappears and this time seems to be about to anoint Saul as king, yet he has already declared that God's favor has passed to his successor. The episode suggests that, after all that has happened, Saul is not yet king. It is also the first time Samuel has brought himself to utter the word in Saul's presence (15:1). This renewal of Saul's kingship, if we read it in this way, brings with it a new test. Saul must eradicate the Amalekites in revenge for their ancient insult against Israel. Not only are the people to be killed, including the infants, but their livestock—even including the donkeys—are also to be wiped out, in accordance with the biblical law related to holy war.

Saul then takes it on himself to warn the Kenites, traditional allies of Israel, to leave the city. Saul and his army then carry out their task, but spare the Amalekite king and the best of the livestock, destroying "all that was despised and worthless" (15:9), a category presumably including the Amalekite women and children. Samuel, once more absent at a crucial juncture, returns, having heard directly from YHWH that he has repented of making Saul king because of his failure to obey divine commands (15:10). The prophet confronts Saul with the fact that he can hear the sounds of animals, and Saul explains that he has spared them in order to offer sacrifice to God.

Samuel rejoins that obedience is better than sacrifice, provoking Saul to a plea for forgiveness and for a restoration of the crucial communication between him and God. This Samuel refuses, which leads to a scene where Samuel expressly denies that "the Glory of Israel" can repent, despite the fact that he has earlier had an explicit message from God that he has indeed repented (15:29). This disparity is highlighted by the end of the chapter, where Saul and Samuel part for good, thus removing Saul's only remaining connection to God. We are left with a picture of the three in their separate spheres; Saul in Gibeah, Samuel in Ramah, grieving over Saul, and YHWH, explicitly sorry that he made Saul king.

■ THE TEXT IN THE INTERPRETIVE TRADITION

This passage raises for the interpretive tradition some complex moral dilemmas and philosophical quandaries. Obedience may be better than sacrifice, but are there commands that ought not to be obeyed? The problem is compounded in this case because the command is represented as the command of a God who can repent of his previous decisions. For patristic commentators such as Tertullian and Augustine, the implication that God might have been in error is inconceivable, and they explain at length why any language that seems to impute such human qualities to God is to be interpreted allegorically (Franke, 258). This complicates the sort of argument that would defend such genocide on the grounds that whatever God commands is by definition good. If God can change his mind, then what is good today may be bad tomorrow.

■ THE TEXT IN CONTEMPORARY DISCUSSION

Using this story and its cognates in the Bible as any sort of guide to contemporary political action poses acute difficulties. We have to rely on the authority of a human interpreter to find out what God's will may be. Can that ever be certain enough to justify such blind obedience? Can it ever involve the demand for complete annihilation of a people? In our contemporary context, where acts of terrorism and the use of overwhelming violence in response to these have both been justified by appealing to divine judgment, these stories have a troubling relevance.

Some glimmer of redemption of this text comes from the fact that, by the end of this chapter, apparently all the Amalekites, including the king, have been eradicated. Yet throughout the rest of Samuel, Amalekites continue to turn up, often in quite influential roles in the text. The text does not support its own claim of total annihilation. Do the writers know that such rhetorical claims are almost impossible to achieve and that they say more about the needs and anxieties of the text's writers many hundred years later than they do about God's actions in the context of Saul's reign?

1 Samuel 16: Samuel and the Promise to David

▉ THE TEXT IN ITS ANCIENT CONTEXT

First Samuel 16 begins with God's rather peremptory call to Samuel to stop grieving for Saul and to find the new king from the family of Jesse in Bethlehem. This begins a block of material running from 1 Samuel 16 to 2 Sam. 1:27, which has been called "the History of David's Rise." In this case, there is no ambiguity about the use of the word "king." Samuel rather unexpectedly hesitates for fear of what Saul will do to him, not having shown much fear of him before (16:2). Once in Bethlehem, he inspects all the sons who attend the sacrifice to which he invites them. At first, he is impressed by the physical appearance of the oldest son, in the way that Saul was impressive, but is told only to pay attention to the heart. All the sons prove not to be the chosen one, so Samuel asks if there is another, even younger son and is told that there is, but that he is out tending sheep. This reflects the common folktale motif of the successful younger son.

When David finally arrives, he ironically turns out to be good-looking as well. Samuel anoints him, and the spirit descends on him. We are then transported back to Saul's dwelling, where an evil spirit replaces the spirit of YHWH (16:14). He calls for a musician to be found to dispel the effects, and David is recommended in glowing terms as both a skilled player and a mighty warrior (16:18). David is thus installed in the royal entourage.

▉ THE TEXT IN THE INTERPRETIVE TRADITION

In the tradition of interpretation, David's lowly status as shepherd boy and his obscure origins give a particular focus to the metaphor of the shepherd in the subsequent history of interpretation. His musical skills are also at the heart of both Jewish and Christian understandings of the use of music in worship. This also is linked to his association with the Psalms and with the inauguration of the temple services in Chronicles. His role in the liturgy is a large part of his enduring significance in the spiritual life of the communities that look to these works as part of their heritage.

▉ THE TEXT IN CONTEMPORARY DISCUSSION

Modern interpreters may see here a common trope of the poor boy made good in many folktales. David is not the third son, or the seventh, as is often the case in such tales, but the eighth: a status pointing to both his marginality and his exceptionality. The role of music in alleviating Saul's suffering is also intriguing, foreshadowing much modern research on music as therapy.

The instruction to Samuel not to look at the outward appearance to judge who is the man fit to take on the kingship but to look at the heart is often held up as an example to condemn superficial judgments. The story, however, may complicate what is being meant. What exactly is it that Samuel sees in David's heart? Does he see the qualities that will lead to David's downfall as well as those that will allow him to rise to the kingship in the first place? The narrator of Samuel almost never gives us a glimpse into David's inner thoughts and motivations, although other characters are laid open to us at times. It is this that gives him his core of mystery, which is both alluring and at times disturbing and which has made him a character that different generations have been able to rewrite to fit their notions of what kingship might be (Josipovici).

1 Samuel 17–20: David, Saul, and Jonathan: The Transfer of the Promise

▌THE TEXT IN ITS ANCIENT CONTEXT

What follows in 1 Samuel 17 is one of the few cases in the Bible where seemingly discrepant elements in the Hebrew traditions of the story correspond to the fact that the Greek translations omit sections of the narrative and thereby read more coherently. The story of David and Goliath is so well known that the discrepancies get overlooked. At the beginning of 1 Samuel 17, David seems to be once again living in Bethlehem and is visiting his brothers on the battlefield with the Philistines, in a very inferior position. His questions and his brothers' responses do not square easily with the picture of the celebrated warrior introduced to Saul in the previous chapter. Indeed, the way in which they dismiss him seems to show that he has caused tension in his own family previously by his precocious self-confidence.

There seem to be at least two stories combined, one in which David is already Saul's squire and a respected warrior and one in which his first encounter with Saul is when he is brought to him because of his brash boasts about dealing with Goliath. First Samuel 17:13 seems to imply that he needs introducing to the reader, and Saul shows no knowledge of him when he is brought to him; the Greek versions omit much of this material (McCarter 1980, 306–9).

The felling of Goliath is a key moment. Goliath's height recalls the stories of giants in Num. 13:32-33 and Deut. 2:10-11, but also harks back to the description of Saul in 1 Sam. 9:2. Yet, what is stopping Saul and Jonathan, who elsewhere have shown both skill and courage as leaders of Israel, from taking on this challenge? In David, a new champion emerges who wins by cunning and skill rather than by strength or force of numbers. When the victorious David is brought to Saul, he asks a strange question: "Whose son are you?" (17:58). Again, this seems incongruous, given that in 16:19 Saul had dealt with Jesse himself. Historical criticism may explain this as an effect of the editing together of different accounts. However, that does not explain why such an obvious discrepancy has been left in the text. Another way of dealing with this text is to concentrate on the effect of this puzzling question. It highlights the key question of succession and the future of the kingship. The next king should be Saul's son. In the following chapters, David not only takes on the role of Saul's son and successor but also founds his own dynasty.

The celebrity of this story and its message that the plucky underdog can, with God's help, overcome the most intimidating and dangerous enemies has led to David and Goliath becoming part of a cliché. This story of victory against the odds may, however, be less clear-cut than it seems. In ancient warfare, the tactical advantage of the agile sling-bearer against an infantryman weighed down with heavy armor was clear.

However it happens, by the end of 1 Samuel 17, David has undoubtedly come to Saul's attention. We know, though most of the characters do not, that David has already been chosen as Saul's replacement. The next section can be read as a remarkable narrative achievement in that David, the chosen successor, exchanges roles with Jonathan, the presumed heir to Saul, in a way that means he can be at the same time the first Davidic king, but not the first king. Jonathan's soul is bound to David's at their first meeting, and he clothes David in his own princely garments and gives him his weapons (18:1-2). Saul also takes him into his own house and sets him over the army. Saul becomes a surrogate father to him. This also brings into play once more the Laius complex, the father's fear of the son who will supplant him and who is the reminder of his own mortality. The song the women sing that compares Saul unfavorably to the new young hero bespeaks a threat to Saul's position (18:7).

Problems quickly arise, which will repeat throughout the rest of the books of Samuel. Kingship is linked to military prowess. Almost inevitably, a successful king's territory and army will expand to the point where no one man can lead it. Yet appointing a general means risking the possibility that he will outdo the king in gaining victories, thus becoming a rival, just as Jonathan had been.

David's popularity rises, and Saul sees a threat to his position. In a dark reversal, the Philistine enemies become a potential solution to this problem if David can be induced into foolhardy attacks against them. Saul also uses his daughters to set up traps for David using the promise of marriage as bait in a way familiar from folktales around the world.

What Saul does not reckon with is his children's loyalty to David, which allows his rival to escape a series of plots against his life. Both his daughter Michal and Jonathan relay Saul's plans to David and enable him to evade their father (19:11-17; 20:35-42). In this situation, Saul may have the political power, but David has the crucial advantage when it comes to information. Through Jonathan, David can learn what Saul is doing and interpret it more astutely than Jonathan himself. Saul's anger against David extends thereafter to Jonathan, cementing the bond between the two younger men. Jonathan becomes the target of his father's spear as David had before him (18:10; 20:33). Both are united against "the enemies of David" (20:16), chief among whom is Jonathan's own father, Saul.

■ THE TEXT IN THE INTERPRETIVE TRADITION

Jonathan's relationship with David becomes a model for later writers to discuss the nature of friendship, often drawing on Greek models (Harding). Either the two are seen as an example of equal friendship, one soul in two bodies, or else they are seen as corresponding to the model of the friendship between an older mentor and the lad of promise. Insofar as David is seen as a type of Christ, Jonathan can be seen as the archetypal believer, content to renounce his own power and privilege in devotion to the church.

■ THE TEXT IN CONTEMPORARY DISCUSSION

The stories of David and Jonathan have been at the heart of recent discussions over biblical attitudes to same-sex relationships. The devotion of Jonathan to David is clear, but there is no unambiguous evidence as to whether this had a sexual component; the text will bear rather different interpretations (Harding). As is often the case in trying to answer contemporary questions from an ancient text, we risk applying alien categories to the ancient world. A good way of detecting this is to ask, Could I ask that question in Biblical Hebrew? If the answer is no, that should alert us to the possibility that our categories may be inappropriate. In any case, the word translated "love" in Hebrew is used in the contexts of covenant loyalty. David is never the subject of the verb in the books of Samuel; he is the one who is loved.

1 Samuel 20–23: Saul against David

▌ THE TEXT IN ITS ANCIENT CONTEXT

David is now a hunted man, and the next section depicts the lengths to which he will go to protect himself from Saul. Indeed, he becomes so implicated with the traditional enemies of Israel that the text has to go to improbable lengths to assure us that he was always at heart working in Israel's interests. Is this a later attempt to whitewash a murky series of tales? In any case, it resembles those in other cultures, such as the English tale of Robin Hood, featuring an outlaw who is really on the side of the oppressed and of justice.

David first flees to the temple at Nob (21:1). This is the first time we have seen David in the context of a temple and dealing with the priesthood. He asks for bread, but there is only holy bread available, hedged about with conditions. David claims to be on a secret mission from the king, but that does not convince the priest, Ahimelech. David declares that his men have obviously not been in contact with women, as they are on campaign (21:5), a declaration that will come to be ironic in the context of his later dealings with Uriah the Hittite (2 Samuel 11). Thus reassured, but also under duress, the priest allows him and his men to eat the bread.

David regains Goliath's sword (1 Sam. 21:9), although he is seen by one of Saul's servants, and then seeks refuge with the king of Gath, Goliath's own city, of all places. His reputation has gone before him, however, and only feigning madness saves the day. He then escapes to a cave, where he assembles the equivalent of Robin Hood's band of merry men from the marginalized people of Saul's kingdom, including his own brothers (22:1-2). Saul's servant, however, tells the king of David's doings at Nob, which leads Saul to order the slaughter of all the priests. David then moves to Keilah, where he is warned by YHWH that he will be given up to Saul.

Significantly, David now has the access to divine guidance that Saul has lost. The stories proceed through a series of near misses where the flow of information is all-important. David is informed against, but he always seems to be one step ahead through his own sources of information, crucially including divine guidance through his consultation of the ephod.

Toward the end of these stories, Jonathan and David meet again at Horesh (23:16-18). Jonathan for the first time explicitly states that David will succeed Saul as king, with Jonathan second in command. They make a covenant together once more, and David's position seems to be settled.

▌The Text in the Interpretive Tradition

The incident of David's eating the bread from the altar is recalled by Jesus in Mark 2:26 as part of his justification to the Pharisees for his disciples' act of plucking grain on the Sabbath. This has taken on a particular significance for subsequent interpreters in arguments over the authority of the Gospel. Jesus is represented as referring to Abiathar as high priest rather than Ahimelech as in 2 Samuel 21. Is Jesus mistaken? Is Mark mistaken? In order to avoid either conclusion, there is a body of literature that seeks to account for this difference with varied degrees of ingenuity. This may seem a rather small detail, but it has become a test case for belief in the historical reliability of the Gospels for certain groups. Others argue that the truths of the Christian message do not stand or fall by such textual details, and asserting that they do misconstrues the nature of these texts and the way in which the fallibility of communication is part and parcel not only of their message but also of their construction.

▌The Text in Contemporary Discussion

For the contemporary reader, the connections between religious institutions, political authority, and the control of information in this story has resonances with doubts about the implications for various political systems of the growth of surveillance, coupled with the possibilities for all sorts of groups, official and unofficial, to tap into supposedly confidential information. It is a useful reminder that, although the technology is vastly different, the moral issues around secrecy, spying, and disclosure were also of concern in the ancient world. Second Samuel 20–23 also raises issues as to whether the religious establishment and its rules should stand aloof from politics. Ahimelech is in an invidious position. Is his loyalty to David, to Saul, or to God? How is he to work out the alliances between them? Is complying with David's wishes going to please or offend either Saul or God? As so often, there is no clear answer in this complex situation. The story leaves us with a heightened awareness of the issues at stake, however.

1 Samuel 24–26: Saul, Nabal, and David

▌The Text in Its Ancient Context

First Samuel 24–26 forms an intriguing unit. The two outer chapters bear striking similarities, to the extent that they look like two versions of one underlying story. Between them is the apparently unrelated story of Nabal, the inhospitable rich man. Yet, read as a unit, these three stories shed light on each other.

In 1 Samuel 24 and 26, the basic premise is that Saul is in pursuit of David in the wilderness. David, by luck or cunning, is able to approach the unsuspecting Saul and take away part of his possessions. David then, brandishing his trophy, appears to Saul and his army (24:11; 26:16), allowing David to make the double point that he has had Saul at his mercy, but that he has chosen not to kill Saul because he is YHWH's anointed. As David is the new anointed leader, we might suggest that this is a good general principle for him to establish. Saul's response in both cases is, surprisingly, to acknowledge David's moral superiority. Nevertheless, his apparent acceptance of David's position proves to be short-lived.

There are significant differences in the stories and their results, however. In the first story in 1 Samuel 24, David cuts off Saul's robe as he is relieving himself. This harks back to the episode where Saul, clutching at Samuel's robe in despair, tears it, which Samuel interprets as a sign that the kingdom will be torn from his grasp (1 Sam. 15:27). Saul acknowledges explicitly that David will be king and in return exacts an oath from him that he will not wipe out Saul's name from Israel (24:19-20). This seems to be an acceptance by Saul that his line will go into decline.

In the second version of this encounter, in 1 Samuel 26, David takes Saul's water jar and spear—perhaps the very one hurled at David's own head in 19:10—from the midst of the army. David then reproaches Abner, Saul's general (and cousin), for not protecting the king (26:13-16). Intriguingly, this time Saul addresses David explicitly as his son (26:17), but makes no mention of his kingship, simply making a general statement that David will succeed in many things. After the apparent reconciliation of 1 Samuel 24, this is quite a contrast. David's reaction in 1 Samuel 27 is to see the lack of any specific pledge as the final confirmation that Saul will not rest until David is dead.

In between these two tellings, in 1 Samuel 25, is the story of Nabal, the man whose behavior is, at least from David's point of view, summed up by his name, which means "fool." In response to a request from David for food for his men, albeit with an implicit threat in his reminder that Nabal's wealth had remained untouched despite the presence of his band, Nabal dismisses David and his pretentions with scorn (25:10). David angrily orders armed reprisals but is forestalled by Abigail, Nabal's beautiful wife, who urges him not to incur the guilt of a rash blood revenge (25:24-31). In contrast to Nabal's characterization of David as a resentful ex-servant, she describes him as fighting the Lord's battles. David is mollified and accepts her gifts (25:35). She returns to the feasting Nabal and next morning tells him the news, which kills him. David is then free to marry Abigail himself.

In context, Nabal is a kind of surrogate Saul (Gordon). Here David is on the point of exacting satisfaction for an insult, which is much less dangerous to him than Saul's threats. Just as he has protected Nabal's herdsmen from attack, he has done more than any to preserve Saul's kingdom from Philistine attack. Saul in chapter 24 speaks in the conciliatory tones of an Abigail, but in 1 Samuel 26, his true feelings, which are much closer to Nabal's, seem to come to the fore. Yet the story of Nabal shows that restraint on the part of David leads to the outcome that favors him in the end while enabling him to avoid the charge that he is guilty of an inappropriate blood revenge. That would provoke a counteraction that would end in a general massacre, either of Nabal's men on one hand or of Saul's army on the other. A pattern that has already been set but that will recur throughout David's career is exemplified here. Anyone who is an obstacle to David tends to die unexpectedly and often violently, but in a way that allows David an alibi which, at least on the face of it, removes the suspicion of guilt from him.

▮ THE TEXT IN THE INTERPRETIVE TRADITION

Abigail is seen by early Christian interpreters such as Ambrose and John Cassian as exemplifying the virtues of wisdom, particularly in her skill both in her speech and in knowing when to keep silent (Franke, 310). As a particularly favored wife of David, who is often identified with Christ, she can also come to represent the church. As a type of the convert, she sees David's worth and throws in her lot with him. However, both the fact that she is still married and the fact of David's conduct have meant that this interpretation has some difficulties. That aside, she is an exemplar of the complex relationship between human initiative and divine purposes. By acting prudently to forestall a possible sin by David, she furthers God's purposes.

▌ THE TEXT IN CONTEMPORARY DISCUSSION

These stories show once again the psychological complexity of the books of Samuel. The inclusion of the story of Nabal can be read as an intriguing narrative device to reveal more than one side of David's character and to show the possibility of another response on his part to Saul. The respect he shows to Saul, and the respect he gains from Saul, may seem to point to the power of restraint to settle situations, but we would do well not to be carried away by the lofty sentiments of either Saul or David. Saul's words, however sincere, do not stop him from pursuing David. David's professed loyalty to the king, again whether sincere or not, turns to his advantage and sets a precedent for the treatment of the king that is to his benefit. The rapprochement between former enemies exemplified by such contemporary cases as the meeting between Egyptian president Anwar Sadat and the Israeli prime minister Menachem Begin in the late 1970s is essential at some stage if a protracted conflict is to find any resolution, but this story shows that overidealizing such a situation is rarely wise.

1 Samuel 27–28: Samuel and Saul's Final Meeting

▌ THE TEXT IN ITS ANCIENT CONTEXT

The result of the potential rapprochement between Saul and David is that David once again flees to the heartland of Saul's—and Israel's—enemies: the court of Achish, the king of Gath, the city of Goliath. He takes six hundred men and his wives to Gath and asks Achish for a city (27:5). He is given Ziklag. This seems extraordinary. The anointed king of Israel is installed as a vassal of the king of Gath, now allied with the enemy whose defeat gained him his fame.

It is also clear that Achish, for one, has taken David's final break with Saul to mean that he has also broken with Israel. The chapter explains how David practices an effective deception in this regard. He tells Achish that he is raiding Israel and its allies while in fact attacking other Philistine cities (27:10). He takes the precaution of following the practice that Samuel urged on Saul by massacring entire populations so as to leave no witnesses as to what had occurred. Note that the Amalekites, whom Saul supposedly wiped out, are among those mentioned. Again, David shows his adeptness at manipulating information. Achish takes this as meaning that David has burned his bridges with Israel (27:12). The arrangement works well until Achish decides that David will become his bodyguard and that he and his men will join Achish in a campaign against Israel at Shunem. This presents David with quite a dilemma. How will he maintain his double game?

The story then switches back to Saul. He is confronted by this powerful Philistine force and is now intimidated, in contrast to his younger self. He desperately seeks God's guidance, but fails to find any means of learning God's will in the matter (28:6). Samuel, who was one certain means of accessing God, has died. Saul resorts to seeking out a medium at Endor to summon Samuel's spirit even though he has himself ordered the expulsion of all practitioners of divination (28:7).

The encounter at Endor is an extraordinary passage. The Hebrew Bible contains repeated injunctions against those who have any dealings with the dead. Other ancient cultures in the region have no doubt that the dead have continued importance for the living and expend considerable resources placating them and consulting their wishes. Israel's traditions do not deny the possibility of such contacts, but forbid them (Lev. 20:6).

Saul, in stark contrast to David, is starved of information and sees no alternative but to break this taboo. Samuel indeed responds to the woman's summons and, ironically, simply confirms what Saul has already been told, rendering the consultation pointless. The kingdom has been given to David because of Saul's failure to carry out YHWH's instructions to annihilate Amalek. Saul collapses, partly because he has not eaten, which brings to mind his earlier rash injunction to his army in 1 Samuel 14. He initially refuses the woman's offer of food but relents, and she feeds both him and his men generously (28:22-25).

■ THE TEXT IN THE INTERPRETIVE TRADITION

This passage has, not unnaturally, been a source of a great deal of theological speculation on the nature of life after death and of the relation between the holy prophet Samuel and the abhorrent practices of witchcraft. Augustine and Tertullian both puzzle over this. King James VI of Scotland in his *Daemonology*, a dialogue on the reality of witchcraft, is one of those who uses this story to argue that witchcraft is a reality, not simply an illusion. In his case, this is used to justify his campaign to extirpate witches from his newly united kingdom, with appalling results for the next century.

What is it of Samuel that survives, and from what state has he been recalled? The text itself is not particularly interested in these details. It may well be that the ancient audience would have been familiar with the practices and beliefs of mediums. In any case, for the purposes of the story, an entirely consistent metaphysical account of the realm of the dead is not required. This story is also a source in the tradition for reinforcing the ban on witchcraft and for aligning witchcraft with necromancy. The effect of this on the sad history of witchcraft trials, such as the 1692 trials in Salem Village, Massachusetts, is well documented.

■ THE TEXT IN CONTEMPORARY DISCUSSION

Feminist commentators, in contrast to those who condemn the medium at Endor, have noted the surprisingly sympathetic treatment the text gives her (Frymer-Kensky 2002, 310). She shows genuine concern for the king, whose decrees have threatened her and her colleagues with banishment and death, providing him with food and with comfort. She represents a strand of female expertise and spirituality in ancient Israel that is otherwise suppressed. The books of Samuel, after all, are not written in order to give us an anthropological and sociological account of ancient Israel's religious practices. They have a clear ideology of their own. Yet we get glimpses in such passages of a religious situation in ancient Israel that is much more complex, and much more in line with wider cultural practices, than the texts are comfortable with. This could well enter into discussions pertaining to the persecution of those whose religious conventions do not represent a society's norm.

1 Samuel 29–31: Saul and Jonathan United in Death

▌ THE TEXT IN ITS ANCIENT CONTEXT

Chapters 29–31 of 1 Samuel bring Saul's story to a close and explain David's part in his death—or, rather, his alibi. After all, no one, on the face of it, stands to gain more by Saul's death, and David is now allied, in appearance at least, with Saul's enemies. We go back to the mustering of the Philistine forces. The army of Achish joins those of their fellow Philistine lords, and David and his men are obliged to follow on.

The song of the women about David's prowess compared to Saul's, which has followed David and has haunted Saul, now gives him an unexpected excuse. The other Philistine kings are highly suspicious of David and quote this song, pointing out to Achish that the coming battle gives David a good opportunity and motive for treachery against his new allies (29:5). By turning against them, he might hope to restore his damaged reputation in Israel. Achish defends David's record as a loyal servant but orders him to remain behind. David protests against the injustice of the accusation from the Philistine lords, and Achish repeats his high opinion of him, but again insists that David and his men part company with the Philistine army (29:9). The irony of Israel's hero pretending to be offended by the suggestion that he should be left behind in a Philistine assault on Israel is almost labored in this chapter. The upshot is that David goes back to Philistia while the Philistines go up to Jezreel (29:11).

On their return, David and his men discover that the Amalekites, who seem once more to have survived complete annihilation, have taken advantage of David's absence to subject his city, Ziklag, to the kind of destruction they themselves have suffered (30:1-2). Rather than slaughter all the inhabitants, as David would have done, however, they have captured and taken away the women and children. David's leadership is threatened as the people blame him for this catastrophe, but he takes swift action, with the Lord's support, to pursue the raiding party (30:10). An abandoned Egyptian slave directs them to the Amalekite camp, and they mount a successful rescue, killing all the Amalekites except for four hundred who escape on camels. On their return, the victorious party comes across those of their number who were too exhausted to follow them all the way, and a dispute arises as to whether they should share in the plunder (30:21-25). David makes it plain that the spoils are to be divided equally. He also begins the process of mending bridges with the people of Judah by sending them a portion of the spoil as well.

While this has been going on, the Philistine attack is continuing. Saul's sons are killed, including Jonathan, and Saul himself is surrounded (31:3). In extremis, he asks his armor-bearer to kill him so that he at least will not suffer the disgrace of being killed by the uncircumcised Philistines. The armor-bearer refuses, so Saul falls on his own sword. The news of his death leads to a wholesale flight by Israel, leaving the Philistines in occupation of the land (31:7). Saul's story is not yet finished. His body is found, his head cut off, and his body displayed on the wall of Beth-shan (31:10). Hearing of this, the people of Jabesh-gilead, the city Saul defended against Nahash as the first act of his leadership, make the journey to Beth-shan, rescue the bodies of Saul and his sons, and then burn and bury them with appropriate mourning.

▌THE TEXT IN THE INTERPRETIVE TRADITION

In marked contrast to the praise by many philosophers in the Greco-Roman world of the hero who shows mastery of his emotions and of his fate by taking his own life rather than face disgrace, the biblical tradition has been read as condemning any such act as a final rejection of God. Augustine is the most influential of the church fathers to write on the subject, and his views have shaped those of both Catholic and Protestant commentators in succeeding centuries (Augustine 1972). Rather than being seen as the final flaring of nobility for a tragic hero, Saul's suicide confirms his rejection by God. The text, be it noted, simply reports Saul's actions, offering no judgment.

▌THE TEXT IN CONTEMPORARY DISCUSSION

For the modern reader, there is a poignancy in Saul's desperation to maintain his relationship with God, which simply becomes yet another occasion for his inevitable fate to be reinforced. There is an uncomfortable message here about the possibility of coming to a point of no return in this relationship. Saul's culpability here is not easy to assess. After all, once he has become subject to the attentions of an evil spirit "from YHWH," is he morally responsible for his own actions anymore? If God is the source of the rebellion against himself, it is difficult to condemn Saul unequivocally. One message of the books of Samuel is that human judgment of others is deeply flawed. Achish and Saul both misjudge David, but he too is capable of misjudgment. The best result may be a due humility in judging others.

2 Samuel 1: The Amalekite Deception: A Pattern Set

▌THE TEXT IN ITS ANCIENT CONTEXT

Saul's death marks the transition to the second book of Samuel. The first chapter of 2 Samuel is typical of the ever-growing complexity of the book as David begins his rule. It begins with an extended incident that puts under the microscope the ability of the new king to assess and respond to information and to deal with the complex rivalries and loyalties of the various factions within the kingdom.

David is at Ziklag when a dirty and disheveled messenger arrives who does obeisance to David, the first person who has offered him such royal recognition (1:2). In answer to David's questions, the messenger reveals that he has escaped from the battle but that Saul and Jonathan are dead. Asked how he knows, he says that he came across the wounded Saul and, at his pleading, delivered a mercy blow. Picking up Saul's crown and armlet, he has brought them to David.

For the reader, this is, intriguingly, not the story we have just been reading in 1 Samuel 31. This messenger, who describes himself as an Amalekite, does not appear in that chapter; Saul killed himself (1 Sam. 31:4). Is this simply a contradiction caused by editing together different versions, or should we take seriously the fact that the earlier version has the authority of the narrator, whereas we only have the word of the Amalekite in 2 Samuel 1? Has he simply robbed the body of the dead king, seeking to curry favor with his successor?

Be that as it may, the king's first reaction is to order mourning for Jonathan and Saul (1:18). For all the enmity between them, the honor due to a dead king must be paid. David then questions the young man again and has him executed, not directly for killing the king, but for entertaining the idea of killing him (1:10). Very cunningly, David's judgment does not depend on deciding between the narrator's account of Saul's death in 1 Samuel 30 and the young man's version. His words, not his deeds, condemn him. Drastic as this is, it makes a clear point to anyone who might have problems with David's own rule.

We might also note that any other secrets the young man had have now died with him. More suspicious readers have even wondered if David engineered this whole scenario, as it all falls out remarkably well for him (McKenzie, 109). Saul and Jonathan, his key rivals, are dead, yet he is able to present himself as their chief mourner so as to begin to build bridges with his erstwhile opponents in Israel. He is also able to show the firmness of his rule and to reinforce the message that the person of the anointed king, no matter what he has done, is sacrosanct.

The last part of the chapter is taken up with a funeral lament for Saul and Jonathan (1:19-27). It is powerful and moving and yet distinctly at odds with the story we have read in the last few chapters. The elegy depicts Saul and Jonathan as "not divided." This ignores the accounts of their quarrels over David, not to mention Saul's attempts to kill his own son. David's lament for Jonathan, which stresses that his love was greater than the love of women, is a resonant line (1:26). Once again, though, we should note that there is no mention of David's love for Jonathan.

For all the emotional weight of this lament, the text could hardly be clearer that David is not simply giving vent to his private feelings but is making a public statement, one he orders to be taught to the people and recorded in the book of Jasher. Under the gaze of his people, he needs to reinforce the respect due to Israel's kings and to make it clear that the claims of the Saulide dynasty have ended in the regrettable death of Jonathan. As happens so often in 2 Samuel, David is not only the beneficiary of the deaths of his rivals but also in the position to lead the mourning and to condemn their killers. He is also, as we have seen, a master at using language through all the channels of communication at his command to turn events to his own advantage.

THE TEXT IN THE INTERPRETIVE TRADITION

In the history of interpretation, the lament for Saul and Jonathan has redounded to David's credit, being a sign of his prowess as a poet and musician and of his generosity of spirit. Many of its phrases have passed into the poetry of subsequent languages, and it remains a moving if enigmatic work, as evidenced by the variety of English translations. As such, it becomes part of the defense of religious poetry as a genre by Jerome and by Protestant writers after the Reformation (Jeffrey, 184).

THE TEXT IN CONTEMPORARY DISCUSSION

For modern readers, this chapter raises complex questions about David's motivations and the way in which the manipulation of perceptions about a ruler is a key part of any political system. Everything David is represented as doing here is part of a public display, and the reaction of his audience, first his own loyal followers and second the wider people of Israel, is firmly in view at all times. An attentive reading makes it hard to escape the conclusion that the text exposes in a sophisticated way some of the hidden workings of any political system. The release of state secrets after a period of embargo in the modern world often reveals that governments, even in democracies, have been routinely engaged in covert operations that were denied at the time.

2 Samuel 2: David at Hebron

■ THE TEXT IN ITS ANCIENT CONTEXT

David now begins to make his move to establish his rule in Judah, anchoring his claim to the kingship of Israel in the loyalty of his own tribe. He needs divine advice to work out his plan of action and is told that he should begin from Hebron. There the people anoint him as king of Judah. David is told that the people of Jabesh-gilead buried Saul and quickly sends a message of appreciation (2:5). This is necessary, because his claim to power is by no means unopposed. Abner, Saul's cousin and general, whom David had taunted, is sponsoring and protecting an alternative candidate, Saul's son Ishbaal, who is made king over all of Israel at Mahanaim. For seven and a half years, David is acknowledged as king only in Judah.

For reasons that are not made clear, this situation is destabilized by a contest between David's men and Abner's, drawn from Saul's tribe, Benjamin. David is not present, but is represented by his equivalent to Abner, his nephew Joab (2:12). In an oddly choreographic moment, the twelve champions from each side kill each other seemingly simultaneously and a fierce battle ensues. Abner is pursued by Joab's brother Asahel and is killed as he refuses to give up the chase (2:23). Joab and his remaining brother Abishai take up the pursuit until there is a standoff in which Abner asks how long this pursuit should last (2:26). Joab and Abishai break off their pursuit, but the damage has been done. Blood has been spilled on both sides. The Benjamites have lost 360 men, whereas Abner's men have only lost nineteen, but the loss of Asahel means that a potential cycle of vengeance is poised to restart at any moment.

■ THE TEXT IN THE INTERPRETIVE TRADITION

The continued success of the Saulides is one of the many aspects of this transition period between the two kings. It is completely passed over by the books of Chronicles. There, the transition from Saul's death to David's reign over all is accomplished by immediate general acclaim (1 Chron. 10:13—11:3). The tendency for the tradition to elevate David above the realpolitik of the books of Samuel clearly has begun early, which makes the depiction of David in Samuel all the more remarkable.

◼ THE TEXT IN CONTEMPORARY DISCUSSION

The modern reader is able, however, to see that the books of Samuel offer a picture of David that glosses over or explains away a number of potentially damaging incidents and decisions. How suspicious should we be of the books of Samuel as themselves products of royalist propaganda, or can we detect in them a hidden rhetoric of resistance that at various points in the history of these texts has been necessarily concealed? The most powerful message of this sort of biblical book, after all, may not be in what it explicitly states but the way in which it hints at the complex nature and motivations of any account of a national and political history. These dynamics are explored in a masterly way in Stefan Heym's novel *The King David Report*, which recounts the way in which Solomon ensures that the history of his father is written in such a way as to make his own succession inevitable. Heym, however, was writing under the Communist government of East Germany. Under the guise of a critique of the Bible, which suited the political censors, he was able to write a devastating attack on the manipulation of history by any oppressive regime, including the East German government.

2 Samuel 3–5: David and Saul's Successors

◼ THE TEXT IN ITS ANCIENT CONTEXT

In 2 Samuel 3, this incident proves to be the beginning of a long war for ascendancy between David and the descendants of Saul. In the meantime, we learn David has been fathering sons (3:2-5). This sets the conditions for a whole series of potential future conflicts between him, his sons, and his followers as the succession to the kingdom becomes an issue. At this point, however, David's own kingship over Israel is still far from established.

In Ishbaal's court, things are becoming complicated as well. Ishbaal accuses Abner of dalliance with one of his father's concubines, Rizpah, an act that could be construed as a bid for power on Abner's part and a claim to succession in his own right (3:7). Abner, who after all seems to have been the moving force behind Ishbaal's reign, is outraged and threatens to throw his weight behind David. In fact, he enters into negotiations with David, restores to him his former wife Michal, and communicates with the elders of Israel and Benjamin confirming that David is indeed the Lord's chosen ruler. This seems to imply that Abner and the elders have already been contemplating switching their loyalty from Ishbaal.

David then meets with Abner, and all seems to be arranged for Abner to deliver the loyalty of Israel to David (3:20-21). Joab learns of this and berates David for failing to realize that Abner is looking to his own advantage through learning David's plans (3:24-25). Is David this time the one who is on the receiving end of a political deception, or is Joab blinded by his personal vendetta against Abner? Joab solves the problem in a characteristically direct way. He arranges for Abner to be called back, without David's knowledge, and stabs him to death.

David is furious and curses Joab's household. He organizes a public funeral for Abner and himself offers a lament over Abner (3:33-34). As in the case of Saul, however, the narrative itself is clear that this mourning has an explicitly political purpose. All Israel is convinced that

David had no hand in Abner's murder, and David goes out of his way to praise Abner as a great man (3:37-38).

Once again, David has turned a situation to his own good. Abner—a much more formidable foe than the puppet Ishbaal—is dead, but the disastrous rift that the murder of Abner could have caused between David and Ishbaal's followers has been averted. Joab has conveniently taken the blame, and David has managed to establish an important precedent for any future problems (3:19). If things get out of hand, he can point to the distance between himself and Joab's actions even if they in fact benefit him. He has achieved what in political parlance would be called "deniability," an asset to any leader.

Ishbaal, not unnaturally, takes alarm at the loss of his mentor. In a rather piecemeal way, which may mirror the apparent disarray of Ishbaal's kingdom, the story proceeds. We are told that Ishbaal has two Benjamite raiders. Apparently inconsequentially, we then learn that Saul has another grandson, Jonathan's son, whom the text calls "Mephibosheth," a name that contains an element meaning "shame" (4:4). Chronicles preserves this name as Merib-baal (1 Chron. 8:34; 9:40), which seems more plausible and is in line with his uncle Ishbaal's name, although it carries the same problematic echo of the divine name Baal. The information that he is lame is introduced in a way that suggests this will become a significant plot element, but we hear no more of him at this juncture.

The two raiders kill Ishbaal in his own house, cut off his head, and bring it to David at Hebron (4:8). The reader may be struck by the similarity to the actions of the unnamed Amalekite in 2 Samuel 1, and this is confirmed when David makes explicit mention of the analogy as he condemns the two to death (4:9-11). Like the Amalekite, they had presumed that David would be pleased at the death of his rival. Like him, they learn how wrong that assumption was. They are killed, mutilated, and their bodies hung up.

At long last, in 2 Samuel 5, David is anointed king of all Israel after all the tribes come and declare their belief in him (5:1-3). His first act is to conquer the Jebusite stronghold of Zion (5:7). Politically, this is an astute move. Rather than elevate the Judahite capital of Hebron to the new seat of kingship or risk alienating his Judahite following by moving to an Israelite city, David marks a new beginning by establishing a new center for Israel. The rather odd byplay over David's apparent hostility to "the lame and the blind" remains mysterious (5:6-8), although the reminiscence of the lameness of Mephibosheth is clear (4:4). Zion is renamed the "City of David" (5:7), and David's international reputation is indicated by the fact that the king of Tyre sends him the materials and the craftsmen to build himself a house (5:11). More children are born to David in Jerusalem: twelve in all. The old enemy, the Philistines, make one final attempt to disrupt David's kingdom, but David defeats their army not once but twice (5:20, 25), the second time with the eerie aid of the Lord's army, signaled by the sound of marching in the treetops.

A pattern, however, has repeated itself. David's rival has met with his end in circumstances that, at least to the public eye, exonerate him from any possible blame. Any story to the contrary again has died with the perpetrators. David has succeeded in gaining the united acclaim of the people of Israel, but there are undercurrents of unsettled scores, potential rivalries, and stories that clearly admit of more than one interpretation. The rhetoric of kinship contains contradictions that can be managed but not eliminated.

■ THE TEXT IN THE INTERPRETIVE TRADITION

Ambrose of Milan speaks for many in the subsequent tradition who take David's integrity and piety as expressed in passages such as his mourning for Abner entirely at face value and hold him up as a model of conduct (Franke). It is incidents such as this that explain why God is prepared to forgive the sins of David and his sons, on this reading. Marcion, in his attack on the Old Testament, makes a point of the contrast between David's rejection of the blind and Jesus' healings to argue that Jesus is not David's son. This point is refuted by Tertullian, who finds the contrast in the faithfulness of the blind in the New Testament (Franke).

■ THE TEXT IN CONTEMPORARY DISCUSSION

For the modern reader, the books of Samuel are full of insights into these dynamics that can occur in any human organization: a school, a company, or a church, as much as in a kingdom. Once any organization grows beyond a certain size, its leader can no longer personally supervise every detail and so he or she needs trusted deputies. As we have seen, however, in David's own case, that deputy may begin to accrue the credit that the king depends on for his own popular success. Furthermore, there is a dangerous game to be played in relying on the loyal deputy to carry out the dirty work so as to leave the leader above suspicion. Inevitably, the deputy has knowledge that the leader cannot afford to make public. If relations become strained, this becomes a serious potential threat.

2 Samuel 6: The Ark Contained

■ THE TEXT IN ITS ANCIENT CONTEXT

Having disappeared from the narrative for many chapters, the ark of YHWH reappears as the topic of 2 Samuel 6. David leads a great procession of people down to the ark's resting place in order to retrieve it and bring it up to his new capital. A new cart is provided to move it, and as it travels David and the whole troupe dance and play musical instruments (6:5). Not all goes according to plan, however, and Uzzah, one of the drivers, is struck dead when he takes hold of the ark to steady it (6:7). The narrative strikingly tells us that David is both "angry" with God and "frightened" of him (6:8-9). This is something he cannot manage, and the presence of the ark in the royal city begins to seem a potential threat as well as an asset. The ark is left with a non-Israelite, indeed possibly a native of Achish's city of Gath, to see what will transpire. Its caretakers prosper, so David takes this as a good omen (6:11). In an even more elaborately choreographed procession, he and the people bring the ark to Jerusalem, sacrificing animals every six paces. David, wearing the priestly garment called the ephod, dances with all his might before it. Michal, Saul's daughter, watches him from the window and despises him (6:16).

The ark is brought to a tent, reminiscent of the tabernacle of the exodus stories, and David offers sacrifices, blesses the people, and distributes food to them, again carrying out typically priestly functions (6:17-19). He has succeeded in bringing into his own camp a potential source of division in his kingdom by avoiding any possibility that the ark and its attendant priesthood should become an alternative focus of the people's loyalty. He has also paved the way for his new capital to become the new center of Israel's religious life, trumping the claims of the ancient shrines such as Shiloh and Bethel.

One person is less impressed, his wife Michal, who scolds him for uncovering himself in the eyes of the people (6:20). His retort is stinging. The God before whom he danced is the one who decreed that he would supplant her father. She might not be pleased, but, as ever, David's concern is with his image among the people at large. If they honor him, his own sense of self-abasement counts for nothing. A brief phrase seals both Michal's fate and that of the Saulide dynasty. Michal bore no children; should any son of David succeed him, that son will not be a grandson of Saul (6:23).

▌THE TEXT IN THE INTERPRETIVE TRADITION

In the tradition, the coming of the ark into Jerusalem represents God's endorsement of the temple on Mount Zion. For early Christian writers such as Maximus of Turin, the ark, as the place where the Word was housed, becomes a type of Mary as she also bears the Word made flesh. David's dancing is, for Gregory the Great, an example of humility that Christian leaders should emulate (Franke).

▌THE TEXT IN CONTEMPORARY DISCUSSION

This story contains a number of disturbing elements for many contemporary readers. The apparent unfairness of the death of Uzzah is an unsettling reminder of the danger of any dealings with the divine, but the exchange between Michal and David is unsettling in another way. Michal's apparent snobbery is met with a curse on her, depriving her of children. In narrative terms, this is justified as we discussed above, but other readers have led us to consider the complex and difficult position of Michal in the story (Heym). Even without this, the story shows that the same events can have profoundly different interpretations depending on whose view we take. Reading with the eyes of the women in the story uncovers assumptions about the power relations in the story that may need to be questioned.

2 Samuel 7: The Promise of Eternal Kingship

▌THE TEXT IN ITS ANCIENT CONTEXT

Second Samuel 7 is one of the key chapters in the Hebrew Bible. In it, we see David at the peak of his powers, king of all Israel, at peace in his own city, which is both the political and religious hub of his newly established kingdom. We also see the first inklings of why this hard-fought and longed-for situation, which seems to be the fulfillment of the promise of a land and prosperity for the people of Israel, cannot last. Furthermore, it contains a clue as to how Israel manages to retain its sense of identity and of hope beyond the collapse of the kingdom that has just been established.

It begins with the king established in his palace and at peace with all his enemies, a description that chimes with the book of Deuteronomy (12:10-12) and its prediction that once peace has been established in the land, the Lord will choose a dwelling place. David remarks to the prophet Nathan that he now has a house, but the ark is still in a tent (7:1). Nathan expresses his agreement with whatever David has in mind. That night, however, YHWH speaks to Nathan. In an unprecedentedly long speech, clearly echoing the language and concerns of Deuteronomy, the deity points out that he has never asked for such a house in all his dealings with Israel (7:7). He further points out to David that he has raised him from obscurity and has established a place of safety and security for the people. Rather than David building YHWH a house, YHWH will build a house, in the sense of a dynasty for Israel. One of his offspring will be established forever in his kingdom, and it will be him who will build the house (7:11). YHWH explicitly refers to the cautionary tale of Saul and declares that this time the promise will not be rescinded even if the king commits sins against him. The house and the kingdom will be established forever. Nathan relates all this to David. The change in Nathan's message reminds the reader that his previous acquiescence with David's plan was not God's will; not everything a prophet says is from God.

David responds with an extended prayer (7:18-29), again an unusual feature in the books of Samuel. He does little other than repeat back to God his own promises and describe his deeds to him, acknowledging his own humility and his own dependence on God's favor.

∎ THE TEXT IN THE INTERPRETIVE TRADITION

Three crucial points come out of this declaration for later tradition. First, YHWH is in control of David's destiny. Second, YHWH is not tied to any temple, and so the destruction of any temple is itself of no eternal consequence. The third is the promise of an eternal kingdom with the possibility ruled out that God, as he has done in the past to Eli and Saul, will rescind the promise. For readers who have seen the destruction of Jerusalem and the failure of David's line, what can this mean? The reference in 1 Samuel 7 to the offspring of David who builds the temple is most easily attributed to Solomon, but his kingdom was irrevocably split under the reign of his son. The obvious rejoinder that this was due to the sins he and his heirs committed is not open to us, as that explanation is forestalled. If this passage is to mean anything, it can only be that it refers to a throne and a house that have as yet to be established and a kingship that is beyond the political exigencies of this world.

Christian readers have long interpreted this passage as a prophecy of the coming Messiah. Yet the New Testament seems to betray some uneasiness about aligning Jesus to the Davidic tradition. The genealogies have to reckon with the nature of Jesus' relationship to any Davidic line given that he is God's son, not Joseph's. Jesus is also depicted as reacting rather negatively to those who address him as "the son of David" (Mark 12:36-37) and as resisting some of the political and military expectations that seem to have become part of the expectations of a Davidic messiah. All the same, in Acts 13:34-36, Paul explicitly refers to the promises that were made to David being fulfilled in Jesus' resurrection, contrasting Jesus and David who, as a human being, "after he had served the purposes of God in his own generation, died" (Acts 13:36). This is followed up by a long tradition that reads allegorically David as a type of Christ, ruling, defeated, and restored, which idealized the king. Protestant commentators, uncomfortable with this type of hermeneutic, tend to lay more stress on his humanity and fallibility.

■ THE TEXT IN CONTEMPORARY DISCUSSION

For modern readers, especially those with some critical training, the tension between interpreting this passage as a much-edited failed prophecy of the eternal establishment of Solomon or some other successor's dynasty and responding to the tradition's verdict that it is a reference to a future messianic king is an acute example of the need for a sort of binocular reading of the text. Is it possible to hold such readings in tension without being justly accused of attempting to have one's interpretative cake and eat it? Again, however, is this not symptomatic of the inescapable dilemmas of any sort of revelation of a divine purpose in human affairs? It will always be possible to read the text differently, and the final option for the reader will always be a decision, not an inevitable conclusion. It is a decision that is always also aware of its provisionality. What the biblical text does do, however, is make that provisionality, and the need for decision, exceptionally clear. It also reminds us that such decisions depend on the context within which the text is read, whether the biblical canon or a particular interpretive tradition: Christian, Jewish, text-critical, or skeptical.

2 Samuel 8–10: Building Up Trouble

■ THE TEXT IN ITS ANCIENT CONTEXT

In the succeeding chapters, we begin to see that the picture at the beginning of 2 Samuel 7 is already shadowed by intimations of trouble ahead for the kingdom. David still has enemies who need to be subdued. He attacks the Philistines and the Moabites and reduces them to servitude (8:2). He attacks and cripples the army of Hadadezer of Zobah and defeats the Arameans, killing twenty-two thousand of them when they come to Hadadezer's aid, putting a garrison in place to subdue them and gain tribute (8:5). He gains such a reputation that Toi, king of Hamath, voluntarily offers him tribute (8:10). All this accumulated wealth is dedicated to YHWH. The Edomites are also defeated, losing eighteen thousand men (8:13-14).

Although these victories are presented as signs of the LORD's favor, we should also be aware that Israel is now in the situation of garrisoning the territory of powerful albeit defeated enemies. David may have won some new allies, but he has also created lasting resentments. He may be able to subdue any potential rebellion against his rule for now, but he is now ruling people who have not consented to his rule and who have no kinship to him. Unifying Israel was difficult enough. Will this new expanded kingship ever know peace?

Potential conflict is embedded in the list of David's administration at the end of 2 Samuel 8. We are assured that he rules justly over Israel (8:15), but does that term necessarily include these subject peoples? Do they now harbor the kind of resentments that Israel felt under Philistine rule? David is now dependent on an inner cabal. In charge of the army is David's nephew Joab (8:16). We already know the threat any general may pose, and in Joab's case, there is an explicit history of differences between him and his uncle (4:39). This circle contains priests who are named before the secretary (8:17), showing the importance of the mutual support of the religious and political establishments in Israel. There is also Benaiah, described as being in charge of the Cherethites and Pelethites

(8:18). These turn out to be elite troops whose loyalty is to the king. The fact that there is a need for such an imperial guard, which is distinct from the people's army, indicates a potential source of tension intrinsic in the kind of kingship David is establishing. A final note says that David's sons were priests. Not only is this at odds with at least the Deuteronomists' accounts of how priests are appointed (Deut. 18:5), it is worryingly reminiscent of the situation with both Eli and Samuel. Hereditary priesthood has proven to be an unreliable institution.

The persistence of potential points of resistance to David's rule in Israel is highlighted in 2 Samuel 9. Jonathan's lame son Mephibosheth reenters the story when David enquires whether any of Saul's descendants are left. The declared reason for this is his desire to show them favor in Jonathan's memory (9:1). This might be plausible but does not necessarily rule out the more practical point that David would do well to nip in the bud any possibility of Saul's heirs becoming a rallying point for disaffection from his rule. David brings Mephibosheth to his palace and feeds him at his table, having restored all Saul's lands to him. We should remember, however, that Saul protested that he came from the least of the families in the least of the tribes. What would his ancestral lands consist of? Not only that, but David's apparently generous gesture of feeding Mephibosheth is, it turns out, less than it seems. He instructs Ziba, an old servant of Saul, and his family to provide the food for Mephibosheth by their labor on Mephibosheth's own lands (9:9-10). David is thus not out of pocket, and Ziba's family now has a cause for resentment against him.

Further trouble ensues when the new king of the Ammonites treats David's ambassadors with disrespect and then hires men from a number of neighboring kingdoms, including the Arameans, to defend himself against reprisals from David (10:6). Joab and his brother manage to defeat the combined armies, but this spurs the Arameans into launching a concerted campaign on their own behalf (10:15). They in turn are defeated, and all the allied kings make peace with David (10:19), but once more, thousands have been killed and any ill-feeling against Israel has material to fuel it. The peace that prevails in the area is one based on fear and is therefore bound to be uneasy and volatile. Being "like other nations" is not a comfortable fate.

▌ THE TEXT IN THE INTERPRETIVE TRADITION

In the history of interpretation, the stress in this story has often been on the kindness and charity of David to his potential enemy Mephibosheth in loyalty to his dead friend. The tendency of the tradition to read David's actions favorably and to give him the benefit of the doubt means that it is taken as an example of the love of one's enemy that Jesus enjoins, but this may tend to reduce the disabled Mephibosheth to an opportunity for David's charity, with consequences for the view of disability in Christian tradition (Schipper).

▌ THE TEXT IN CONTEMPORARY DISCUSSION

For modern readers, 2 Samuel 8–10 has an uneasily familiar ring in an era where successive new countries and new governments seek to establish themselves, proclaiming peace and stability by repressing old injustices and then being led into reprisals against disaffected groups that simply add to a stock of resentment. Is the message that there is no political utopia and that even at its height, the Davidic empire, like all empires, contained the inevitable seed of its own destruction? An African proverb tells us, "You can't have the wood without the termites." The very processes necessary to build the kingdom import the justification and the means for others to tear it down or seek to rebuild it in their interests.

2 Samuel 11–12: Bathsheba: David's Plans and God's Purposes

■ THE TEXT IN ITS ANCIENT CONTEXT

The next chapter shows a kingdom that is not at peace but is now provoking wars on its own account. Second Samuel 11–12 is among the most extraordinary pieces of writing in the Hebrew Bible. Not only do they show a remarkable sophistication in their narrative technique, but they also tell a story that puts Israel's greatest hero in an uncompromisingly unfavorable light. Here is a king who will resort to deception, adultery, and murder involving loyal members of his entourage without any reference to his God but who apparently also believes himself to be the arbiter of justice.

The beginning of the chapter makes the point that David is now separated from his army. They are off fighting the Ammonites, while he is safe in his palace. A domestic drama ensues that is, tellingly, missing from the Chronicler's account of the same military campaign in 1 Chronicles 20. In short, David summons Bathsheba, the wife of Uriah, one of his loyal commanders, and makes her pregnant (11:5). When he learns of her pregnancy, he calls Uriah back and does all he can, including using alcohol, to induce Uriah to sleep with Bathsheba. This is all in contravention of the rule that active soldiers abstain from sex that he himself self-righteously invoked in 1 Samuel 21. When this fails, he notoriously sends a letter to Joab by Uriah's hand containing instructions for Uriah to meet his death (11:14). On hearing the news that he has died, David sends a subtle threat to Joab, who alone knows the whole story (11:25), and marries Bathsheba, ensuring that his child is part of his royal household (11:27).

In all this, David has reckoned without God. Nathan appears and traps him into condemning himself by leading him on so that he pronounces judgment against a fictional character who has stolen and killed a poor man's sheep (12:1-4). David's punishment is that the son born to Bathsheba will die. His response to the child's subsequent illness is flagged by the narrator as incomprehensible to his own courtiers. He mourns until the son dies and then ceases mourning (12:20). Readers are left with contradictory assessments of this behavior. Does it show David's faith in divine justice, or is it blatant cynicism? The upshot is that Bathsheba bears a second child, who turns out to be Solomon (12:24). What kind of a birth story is this for one of Israel's most prominent figures?

All this having occurred, Joab sends his own message to David, warning him that his reputation will be threatened unless he comes down to finish the siege of Rabbah himself (12:27-28). David is now the victim of his own concern with reputation. At the end of 2 Samuel 11, he seemed to have saved his own name and acquired a desirable new wife and child. On the contrary, he learns not only that he has offended God (11:26), whom he did not seem to consider before, but also that he has risked jeopardizing his standing with the army. His once unmatched awareness of and control over the important channels of information has lapsed. He forgot about what God knew, he took no account of the army's perceptions, and Joab now has damning evidence that he could use against him if occasion arises. It is Joab, who now has David and the kingdom's reputation in his hands, who has to recall David to his duty. For the time being, they are both better served by the continuance of David's rule—for the time being.

▌ THE TEXT IN THE INTERPRETIVE TRADITION

In the traditional interpretation of David, this scene sets the seal on the depiction of David as the archetypal penitent. Convicted by Nathan, he repents of his sins in a way that becomes a model for later generations of Christians. This reading is strengthened by the penitential psalms, such as Psalm 51, that are also attributed to him. He thus becomes an endorsement of the sacrament of confession in Catholic and Orthodox tradition, and of the use of the Psalms in self-examination by Protestant readers.

▌ THE TEXT IN CONTEMPORARY DISCUSSION

Contemporary readers may find it difficult to see a marked change in David's behavior after this episode, however. Readers have argued as to whether his apparent reconciliation with his son's death shows a mature spirituality or a cynical relief that the punishment has fallen on the child rather than him. Whatever may be true, his subsequent career is marked by the kind of swings between hostility and sentimentalism about his sons that are reminiscent of Saul. The tensions we have outlined throughout that beset any hereditary monarchy are explored here in a series of stories of great but disturbing power. David is shown to be much less astute in managing his own family than he has been in managing those around him on his way to the kingship. Political leaders worldwide are still beset by these problems, exacerbated by the prevalence of the media. The peccadilloes of a Bill Clinton and the complex relationship between Saddam Hussein and his sons are cases in point.

2 Samuel 13–18: Absalom, the Beloved Enemy

▌ THE TEXT IN ITS ANCIENT CONTEXT

The tension between father and sons, which is exacerbated in the case of a king and his potential heirs, has seldom been so well explored as in the following chapters of 2 Samuel. So far, we have heard nothing of his sons except for lists of their names and their mothers. Now they become the focus of the story in a series of interlinked masterpieces of the laconic narrative style of this book. In particular, they revolve around the glamorous but flawed figure of Absalom.

The first we hear of Absalom is in relation to his sister Tamar, who is the object of their half brother Amnon's passion. Deceived by his pretended illness, she visits his room only for him to rape her and then spurn her (13:14-17). With her life destroyed, as no one else will marry her if Amnon does not, she seeks refuge with her brother. David, we learn, is furious (13:21), but does nothing to Amnon, his favored firstborn. Absalom, enraged by his half brother's attack on his sister, bides his time for two years and then invites all his brothers and his father to a feast. It is here that he has Amnon killed and then flees to the king of Geshur's protection for three years (13:37).

Characteristically, the Hebrew is highly ambiguous about David's attitude to Absalom in a way that most translations cannot capture.

It is Joab, again, who takes the initiative in persuading David to invite Absalom back through an elaborate charade involving a wise woman and a story about a family where one son has murdered another and is now banished (14:5-7). She succeeds, as Nathan did, in trapping David into swearing an oath. The banished son should be allowed to return. David sees through the ruse too late and finds himself obliged to permit Joab to bring back Absalom (14:21).

Again, rather than a touching family reconciliation, there may be realpolitik at work here. Absalom in exile is a constant and uncontrollable potential rival and rallying point for dissent. Joab may be acting in the kingdom's interest in bringing him back where he can be watched, as David did in the case of Mephibosheth. More self-interestedly, Joab may be establishing himself in Absalom's good books against the day when David—who has forced Joab to put up with a great deal— becomes more of a liability than an asset to the kingdom.

David's subsequent refusal to meet Absalom simply fuels his son's resentment. Absalom cunningly begins to eat away at David's power by interrupting the flow of petitioners to the king and presenting himself as the only true hope for justice. After four years, he asks permission to go to Hebron (15:7), the place where finally the rest of Israel besides Judah had accepted David as king and has himself proclaimed as the new ruler of Israel. David's response is to call for the mass evacuation of the city (15:14). Only ten royal concubines are left. On the flight, there is a succession of encounters, the significance of which only becomes apparent on David's return. He meets Ittai the Gittite, another anomalous inhabitant of Gath, Goliath's hometown, who proclaims his loyalty. (15:21). He sends the ark back to Jerusalem (15:25), saying that its fate will show what God's will is. He learns that a trusted councilor, Ahitophel, is now advising Absalom and, in typical fashion, arranges for the elderly Hushai to spy on Absalom's court (15:34)

Old stories come back to haunt him. He meets Ziba, Mephibosheth's servant, who tells him that Saul's grandson is expecting the restoration of his kingdom. David rewards Ziba with the grant of Mephibosheth's property (16:4), reversing his earlier judgment. He meets another Saulide, Shimei, who abuses him roundly (16:7). David prevents his bodyguard from harming him, saying that if his own son has turned on him, he can hardly blame Shimei, who is doing the Lord's own bidding (16:11).

In the meantime, Hushai has persuaded Absalom that he has truly defected from David and proceeds to undermine the wise counsel of Ahitophel, who tells Absalom to sleep with the concubines left behind to signal the total break with his father (16:21). Hushai lets this pass, but then he opposes Ahitophel's advice that a swift targeted assassination of David would lead to the speedy end of the conflict. Instead, Hushai appeals to Absalom's vanity and counsels a pitched battle involving the whole army with Absalom at its head (17:11). Absalom agrees, and Hushai activates the network of informants that David has set up through the guise of the return of the ark. Ahitophel, seeing that he has been ignored and knowing what the outcome will be, hangs himself (17:23).

Sure enough, when battle is joined, David's forces under Joab defeat Absalom's. Absalom himself is caught in a tree by his much-vaunted hair, and Joab dispatches him, despite the public orders of David that Absalom is to be spared (18:14). An extraordinary account of the way in which the message of Absalom's death is brought to David ensues, playing on the reader's memory of the other occasions in which a messenger has brought David news of the death of someone whose actions have posed a threat to his kingship. Here this motif reaches an apotheosis as different messengers vie over how the news that David's son, who had become the embodiment of all that the so-called Laius complex so dreads, is now dead. The beloved son has been thwarted in his attempt to kill and supplant his father. David's reaction, as so often before, is public mourning for the one whom others might expect he would be glad to see removed from the scene. This time, however, there is no poetic outburst, denunciation of the killer, and protestation of royal innocence, only the broken repetition of his son's name and the wish that he had died in Absalom's stead (18:33).

THE TEXT IN THE INTERPRETIVE TRADITION

The theological appropriation of such stories has to reckon with the fact that God is generally absent throughout these chapters. It is the dynamics of the human family that are the focus of interest, as well as the way in which personal loyalties and feelings conflict with the necessities of statecraft. Absalom becomes a key example of the perils of pride and of personal vanity and extravagance, often at the expense of recalling the depth of his grievance against his father. Through the imagery of Absalom's death scene—a corpse hanging by the neck and entangled in branches—Cassiodorus likened his actions against his father David and subsequent fate to that of Judas Iscariot's betrayal of Jesus Christ (Franke, 383).

THE TEXT IN CONTEMPORARY DISCUSSION

The story of Absalom represents the tensions between father and son and the tension inherent between the human reactions of David as father and the political judgment of David as king. As in the episode with Bathsheba, David has to be recalled by Joab to his kingly duties and his responsibilities to the whole people. This is the nearest the Hebrew Bible comes to a story of patricide, and we may remember that Plato's main reason for banning poets from his Republic was that their stories are full of examples of sons killing fathers, something no government can risk encouraging. In this respect, the Hebrew tradition seems to have gone further in suppressing such stories. David's love for his son risks alienating the rest of his people; this story certainly encourages reflection on the difficulties of drawing the boundary between the personal and the political in any political system. An egregious example from British history is the short and inglorious rule of Richard Cromwell as Lord Protector in succession to his father Oliver, a role for which he had little inclination, aptitude, or training. The propensity for political systems that apparently have no place for the hereditary principle to throw up familial dynasties seems to continue unabated: the Nehru-Gandhi family in India, the Assad regime in Syria, and the Kennedy and Bush dynasties in the United States show that these issues persist in contemporary politics in a range of regimes.

Such close relationships can engender persistent tensions. At the time of this writing, the horrible revenge reportedly exacted by the North Korean leader Kim Jong-un on his uncle for alleged corruption, which extended to the killing of his family and associates, is a reminder that the personal and the political are intertwined in many political systems. Kim Jong-un himself only came to power because his elder brother fell out of favor with their father. Close family ties may mean that perceived betrayals lead to exceptional and drastic reprisals as personal hurt and family honor are brought into the equation and often override political considerations.

2 Samuel 19–20: Coming Home to Roost

■ THE TEXT IN ITS ANCIENT CONTEXT

Second Samuel 19–20 seems to show that the proverbial chickens are coming home to roost for David. First of all, this time the public act of mourning, instead of acting as a potential healing of the rifts in the kingdom and strengthening David's position, backfires. Once again, it is Joab who has to recall David to his duty to set aside his feelings as a father and act as king (19:5-7), bluntly pointing out that his days as king are over unless he reassures his followers that he would not prefer that they had all died so that Absalom could have survived. The rest of Israel is also in turmoil, knowing that they had thrown in their lot with Absalom and now fear David's reprisals.

David rallies by appointing Absalom's general Amasa as head of the army instead of Joab, straining the latter's loyalty yet again (19:13), and using Amasa to bring Judah back to their leader. Shimei reappears, and David appears to pardon him, swearing that he will not put him to death; he does not swear that his successor will be bound by this oath, however. More to the point, Mephibosheth reappears, alleging that the story Ziba had told was a fabrication designed to get hold of Mephibosheth's lands (19:27). The king, now apparently bereft of his former astuteness in dealing with deceptive characters, takes the easy way out by dividing the land between them, only for Mephibosheth to get the last word and renounce the land. A final encounter with the elderly Barzillai catches the ambivalent tone of this return. Barzillai refuses David's offer to become part of the court, but offers his servant Chimcham instead. Returning with David is not a reward he seeks.

This return, far from healing the rifts in the kingdom reopened by Absalom's appeal to the non-Judahites at Hebron, rubs salt in the wound. Judah and the rest of Israel are set at loggerheads as to which can claim David as their own. The problem is compounded by the actions of a Benjamite called Sheba, who persuades the other tribes that they have no stake in David anymore and should follow him instead, which they promptly do (20:2). David is apparently back where he was in 2 Samuel 2, king only of Judah. He calls on his new commander, Amasa, to muster the Judahite army, but Amasa, suspiciously, fails to return by the appointed time. David then turns to Joab's brother, instructing him to hunt down Sheba before he can consolidate his power (20:6). Joab joins his brother and in the process of the hunt meets and kills Amasa, concealing his body so that the troops are not distracted from their purpose. Sheba retreats to his ancestral city, which is then besieged (20:14). Through the intervention of a wise woman, the inhabitants are persuaded to kill Sheba and throw his head over the wall in return for the safety of the city (20:22).

The chapter—and the connected narrative of 2 Samuel—ends with a repeat of the list of David's chief men that is found at the end of 2 Samuel 8. After all that has happened, what has changed? Joab still commands the army, despite David's apparent attempts to discharge him; Jehoshaphat, Benaiah, Zadok, and Abiathar retain their roles. Two things are different, however. David now has an official in charge of forced labor. Significantly, there is no mention of his sons serving as priests (20:23-26). The relationship between ruler and ruled has changed, as has the succession to the king-dom. Both of these changes bode ill for the future stability of a kingdom that has already all but fallen apart and has only just been reconstituted.

It is quite striking how incidents from David's past now come back to haunt him and are read rather differently. It is clear from this material just how flimsy a construct the united kingdom of Israel under David has been. Matters that were thought to be settled turn out to be far from solved, and readers can legitimately wonder how subversive these texts are when it comes to the monar-chy. David here is hardly a hero. In one way of looking at it, all he has brought to Israel is to draw people into a series of deadly conflicts, which stem from the tensions in his own family. He has also installed the kingly response of forced labor.

▌ THE TEXT IN THE INTERPRETIVE TRADITION

Both Ambrose and Augustine account for the fact that David mourns for his treacherous son Absalom, but not for the innocent child in 2 Samuel 12, as a result of his knowledge that Absalom, deprived of the possibility of repentance, is lost to him forever in eternal punishment. David's seem-ing contrition and humility in the encounters that mark his progress to and from the city adds to the picture of him in later tradition as the archetypal penitent, although this masks the reality of the long revenge he later plans. In this context, his presumed authorship of the penitential psalms is also explained.

▌ THE TEXT IN CONTEMPORARY DISCUSSION

David serves here as a warning of the dangers of a charismatic leader whose personal ambitions and relationships spill out into the politics of his community. Contemporary history can supply all too many parallels. Where is the line between the private life and the public duty of a politician? How far should political careers be judged by private misjudgments and misdeeds? On the one hand, in France, the fact that President Mitterand maintained two families remained secret in a way that would be unthinkable in the United States or the United Kingdom and did not lead to his political downfall. On the other hand, in a later generation the marital misadventures of the later president Nicolas Sarkozy were a factor in changing public perceptions of his competence, although his suc-cessor François Hollande's own problems in this regard put this in a new perspective.

2 Samuel 21–24: Rereading David

▌ THE TEXT IN ITS ANCIENT CONTEXT

The final four chapters of the books of Samuel are anomalous. Rather than continuing the narra-tive sequence of the rest of the books, they seem to assemble a number of stories and poems that relate oddly to what has gone before. Second Samuel 21 tells the story of a famine, which YHWH announces is due to a continuing guilt on the house of Saul because he killed the Gibeonites. This seems rather strange in the context of the rest of Samuel, where the accusation laid at Saul's door is his failure to eradicate the Amalekites. Be that as it may, David agrees to hand over seven sons of Saul to be impaled by the Gibeonites as recompense (21:5). He spares the life of Mephibosheth (21:7), because of his loyalty to Jonathan his father, but the story makes no mention of the oath David swore to Saul that he would not cut off his progeny (1 Sam. 25:21-22). Perhaps he takes the typically evasive view that all he is doing is handing them over to the Gibeonites; what happens to them then is not his responsibility.

Once the sons are killed, however, the mother of two of them, Rizpah (the concubine over whom Ishbaal and Abner fell out in 2 Sam. 2:7), sits in vigil to protect their bodies from birds and animals (21:10). David takes that as a sign and retrieves the bodies of Saul and Jonathan from Jabesh-gilead and ensures them proper burial in Saul's father's tomb (21:12). Other names from previous chapters surface in puzzling ways. Both Merab and Barzillai are mentioned, prompting us perhaps to reflect on their motives in a new way.

Further material comes to light, recording a series of fights against giants. On each occasion, it is not David who kills the giant. Indeed, Elhanan is credited with the killing of Goliath (21:19). It is hard not to see a retrospective problematization of the picture of David as the brave young warrior confronting impossible odds on his own. Here David is surrounded by equally competent warriors. The key moment of the encounter between David and Saul is also thrown into question. If David did not kill Goliath, then what is the justification for his rise to prominence in Saul's court?

Second Samuel 22 is a psalm attributed to David on an occasion of his deliverance from his enemies. It is a fine example of the genre, but again contains material that sits uneasily with what we have read in the rest of Samuel. In particular, it represents David as claiming that he has been rewarded for his righteousness (22:21-25) as the singer harps on his blamelessness before God. Is there an irony here? Does the story of David not rather show that he has indeed been dealt with according to his righteousness, but that he has been far from blameless? His actions, intentional and unintentional, have led not to a serene monarchy in perfect accord with God, but to the fractious, unstable, and unjust kingdom depicted in 2 Samuel 20.

Second Samuel 23:1-7 contains what are presented as David's last words. This is surprising, as in the preceding narrative he is not yet dead and his story will continue into 1 Kings. Again, is there irony here? David is represented as having an everlasting covenant with God and as the just ruler in contrast to those who are wicked and who can only be touched by a spear. Yet spears abound in the stories of Samuel, most notably the spear David took from the sleeping Saul, which had been hurled at David and Jonathan. By that token, are David and Jonathan, whom Saul attempted to touch with a spear, to be counted among the wicked? How far is this text pointing to the contrast we have seen elsewhere between the pious David who traditionally lies behind the Psalms and the David we encounter in so much of Samuel who is far from a model of piety?

Chapter 24 recounts the brave deeds of David's champions. The main body of Samuel has kept silent about these for the most part. It commonly represents a military campaign by simply stating that "David went up" against a city and took it. Now we are reminded that he always, of course, went up in the company of mighty warriors whose exploits are not recorded in the books of Samuel but who have driven its story. It is surely not a coincidence either that the final name in the list is the one that haunts David's memory, then and now: Uriah the Hittite, here praised as a member of the band of thirty and thus one of the elite group of Israel's greatest fighters (23:19). Again, the contrast between what he deserved and what he received at the hand of David is reinforced.

The final chapter of this section, and thus of the books of Samuel, represents David as the instrument not of God's favor but of his anger. At YHWH's instigation, David numbers the people of Israel but then realizes that he has committed a grave sin (24:1). Through the prophet Gad, David is offered three choices: three years of famine, three months flight before his foes, or three days of pestilence (24:12-13). David prefers to fall in to God's hands than into human hands, and so the days of pestilence ensue, killing seventy thousand people.

This leads to an extraordinary encounter between David and the angel of destruction on a Jebusite threshing floor in Jerusalem, where David pleads for the punishment to be on him and his house rather than Israel (24:17). Nowhere in the rest of Samuel do we find such an incident, which could put a very different theological interpretation on the fate of the Davidic monarchy and how it relates to the survival of Israel. Is Israel's ultimate destruction explicable as a kind of transferred punishment for the shortcomings of David, just as his nameless son by Bathsheba dies for his sins? Or is the demise of the Davidic dynasty God's price for the survival of Israel?

The same incident also puts an odd twist into the story of the building of the temple as Gad instructs David to buy the threshing floor in order to set up an altar. The site of the altar is the site of David's confrontation with an angel of YHWH who is charged with the destruction of Jerusalem. If this is related to the temple, then it becomes not a home for God or a celebration of his bounty, but a mechanism by which the fatal intentions of God are averted.

■ THE TEXT IN THE INTERPRETIVE TRADITION

God's reaction to David's decision to take a census of the people has long consequences in the interpretive tradition. The book of Chronicles makes Satan the instigator of the census (1 Chron. 21:1). This adds a level of complication, in that Satan as a tempter is markedly absent in most of the Hebrew Bible. His role becomes prominent in the New Testament, however, and in subsequent Christian interpretation. The seeming disparity between the accounts in Samuel and Chronicles is thus fertile ground for subsequent reflection on the nature of human sinfulness and the role of demonic temptation in human ill doing.

■ THE TEXT IN CONTEMPORARY DISCUSSION

Put together, these anomalous final chapters cast a disconcerting retrospective light over the career of David and his significance in the books of Samuel. What other stories have we not heard, and what other motives have been hidden and suppressed? This peculiar "appendix of deconstruction," as Walter Brueggemann has called it (Brueggemann 1988), does not simply serve to throw open to question an otherwise straightforward story, however. Rather, it simply heightens the sense any attentive reader must grasp of how complex and enigmatic the story told in the books of Samuel really is. These final chapters also reinforce our sense of how aware these texts are of the intrinsic limitations and paradoxes of any human institution and any human communication. In doing so, they point for theologically minded readers to the way in which any communication between God and human beings is inevitably bound up in the same limitations. It is part of the power of the Bible's claim to be such a communication that it so subtly and clearly raises these issues, leaving the reader to make his or her decision as to how to respond.

Works Cited

Alter, Robert. 1999. *The David Story: A Translation with Commentary of 1 and 2 Samuel*. New York: W. W. Norton.

Augustine. 2007. *City of God*. Translated by Henry Bettenson. London: Penguin.

Brueggemann, Walter. 1988. "2 Samuel 21-24: An Appendix of Deconstruction?" *Catholic Biblical Quarterly*, vol. 90, 383–97.

Exum, J. Cheryl. 1992. *Tragedy and Biblical Narrative: Arrows of the Almighty*. Cambridge: Cambridge University Press.

Fewell, Danna Nolan, and David M. Gunn. 1993. *Gender, Power and Promise: The Subject of the Bible's First Story*. Nashville: Abingdon.

Franke, John, ed. 2005. *Joshua, Judges, Ruth, 1–2 Samuel*. Ancient Christian Commentary on Scripture, Old Testament 4. Downers Grove, IL: InterVarsity Press.

Frontain, Raymond-Jean, and Jan Wojcik, eds. 1980. *The David Myth in Western Literature*. West Lafayette: Purdue University Press.

Frymer-Kensky, Tikva. 2008. *Reading the Women of the Bible: A New Interpretation of Their Stories*. New York: Schocken.

Gordon, Robert P. 1986. *1 and 2 Samuel: A Commentary*. Exeter, UK: Paternoster.

Harding, James E. 2013. *The Love of David and Jonathan: Ideology, Text, Reception*. Sheffield: Equinox.

Hastings, Adrian. 1997. *The Construction of Nationhood: Ethnicity, Religion and Nationalism*. Cambridge: Cambridge University Press.

Heym, Stefan. 1984. *The King David Report*. London: Abacus.

Jeffrey, David Lyle, ed. 1992. *A Dictionary of Biblical Tradition in English Literature*. Grand Rapids: Eerdmans.

Josipovici, Gabriel. 1988. *The Book of God: A Response to the Bible*. New Haven: Yale University Press.

McCarter, P. Kyle. 1980. *1 Samuel: A New Translation with Introduction, Notes and Commentary*. AB 8. Garden City, NY: Doubleday.

———. *2 Samuel: A New Translation with Introduction, Notes and Commentary*. AB 9. Garden City, NY: Doubleday.

McKenzie, Steven L. 2000. *King David: A Biography*. Oxford: Oxford University Press.

Pyper, Hugh S. *David as Reader: 2 Samuel 12.1-15 and the Poetics of Fatherhood*. Leiden: Brill.

Schipper, Jeremy. 2006. *Disability Studies and the Hebrew Bible: Figuring Mephibosheth in the David Stories*. LHB 441. New York: T&T Clark.

1, 2 KINGS

Gale A. Yee

Introduction

Like the books of Samuel, 1 and 2 Kings was originally one book in the Hebrew canon, continuing the story of the monarchy's decline that was readily apparent from 2 Samuel 9, which recounted the dysfunctional family relations in King David's household, onward. The book of Kings narrates the stories about David's son Solomon, the division into two kingdoms after Solomon's death, the events leading up to the conquest of the northern kingdom of Israel by the Assyrians, and finally to the destruction and exile of Judah by the Babylonians.

Composition

Critical examination of the book of Kings was important for theories about the composition of a major portion of the Old Testament (for a fuller discussion, see Römer). In 1943, the German scholar Martin Noth argued that the final form of the books of Deuteronomy, Joshua, Judges, 1–2 Samuel, and 1–2 Kings was due to a single individual working during the Babylonian exile in the sixth century BCE. Because these books shared similar theological themes and concepts with the book of Deuteronomy, Noth referred to these books collectively as the "Deuteronomistic History" (DH), and called its author/editor the "Deuteronomist" (Dtr). As an editor, Dtr conscientiously incorporated older documents and traditions for his work, such as the stories about the prophets Elijah and Elisha. Dtr even named some of his sources: "the Book of the Acts of Solomon" (1 Kgs. 11:41); "the Book of the Annals of the Kings of Judah" (1 Kgs. 14:29); and "the Book of the Annals of the Kings of Israel" (1 Kgs. 16:27). However, as an author, Dtr shaped these sources and older traditions to compose a particular narrative history of the two kingdoms that articulates his own theological intents and purposes.

American scholar Frank Moore Cross built on Noth's theory by positing a "double-redaction" of the DH. Instead of a single individual working during the exile, Cross noticed an earlier version of the DH that concluded in 2 Kings 22–23, describing the achievements of King Josiah in the seventh century BCE. This first edition of the DH ended with 2 Kgs. 23:25: "Before [Josiah] there was no king like him, who turned to the LORD with all his heart, with all his soul, and with all his might, according to all the law of Moses; nor did any like him arise after him." This Josianic edition underscored two themes. The first was YHWH's promises to David's dynasty in Judah, in spite of the fact that some of the Judean kings kept some of the "high places" of worship. The second was the "sin of Jeroboam," worship at the illegitimate sanctuaries of Dan and Bethel that infected practically every northern monarch and precipitated the ultimate fall of Israel. These two themes converged with the stories about Josiah, who destroyed the altar at Bethel and purged the nation of its idolatrous gods and practices. This seventh-century Josianic edition was then updated in a Deuteronomistic school to form a sixth-century exilic edition of the DH. Other scholars have even posited further editions during the Persian period (late sixth–fifth centuries BCE). The Deuteronomists responsible for these editions were probably high officials of the scribal class in Judah that shared a particular ideology and rhetorical style (Römer, 45–49).

Sense Units

This commentary divides 1 and 2 Kings into the following sense units:

> 1 Kgs. 1:1—2:46: Solomon's Succession to the Throne
> 1 Kgs. 3:1-28: Solomon the "Wise" Man?
> 1 Kgs. 4:1—11:42: Solomon's Bureaucratic Rule
> 1 Kgs. 12:1—16:34: The Divided Kingdom
> 1 Kgs. 17:1—22:53: The Ministries of the Prophets Elijah and Micaiah
> 2 Kgs. 1:1—8:29: The Ministry of the Prophet Elisha
> 2 Kgs. 9:1—12:21: The Rise of the House of Jehu and the Demise of the House of Omri
> 2 Kgs. 13:1—17:41: Events Leading to the Fall of Israel
> 2 Kgs. 18:1—20:21: The Reign of Hezekiah
> 2 Kgs. 21:1—23:30: The Reigns of Manasseh and Josiah
> 2 Kgs. 23:31—25:30: The Final Days of Judah and Its Kings

Theological Framework

Beginning in 1 Kings 15, after the narratives regarding Jeroboam I, Dtr provides a specific theological framework to introduce each of the ruling monarchs that will continue to the end of 2 Kings. The kings of Judah are presented according to the following pattern:

- The date the king took office, correlated with the rule of his rival in Israel (15:1—"In the eighteenth year of King Jeroboam son of Nebat, Abijam began to reign over Judah.")
- His length of reign (15:2a—"He reigned for three years in Jerusalem.")
- The name of the queen mother (15:2b—"His mother's name was Maacah daughter of Abishalom.")

- Dtr's judgment on his rule (15:3-5—"He committed all the sins that his father did before him . . .")
- Other deeds, if any (15:6—"The war begun between Rehoboam and Jeroboam continued all the days of his life.")
- Citation of sources (15:7—"The rest of the acts of Abijam, and all that he did, are they not written in the Book of the Annals of the Kings of Judah?")
- Burial (15:8a—"Abijam slept with his ancestors, and they buried him in the city of David.")
- Name of successor (15:8b—"Then his son Asa succeeded him.")

For the kings of Israel, Dtr follows a similar pattern, but adds the city in Israel where the king had his capital and omits the name of the queen mother: "In the third year of King Asa of Judah, Baasha son of Ahijah began to reign over all Israel at Tirzah; he reigned twenty-four years. He did what was evil in the sight of the Lord . . ." (1 Kgs. 15:33-34).

The most important section in this framework is Dtr's judgment on the king's rule. A certain king may have been a very capable leader, economically and politically. Or the king may have been caught up in the larger imperial politics of the ancient Near East that may have influenced his religious policies. The Dtr, however, is only concerned with how faithful he was to God's covenant. For him, "evil" kings were those who worshiped other gods or allowed their worship in the land; those who allowed shrines and sanctuaries to YHWH, such as the "high places" outside of Jerusalem; those who did not listen to God's prophets; those who participated in religious rituals that Dtr regarded as illicit. According to Dtr, the ultimate destruction of both Israel and Judah was due to their infidelity to YHWH alone by worshiping foreign gods from the moment the people crossed the Jordan and entered the land promised to their ancestors.

1 Kings 1:1—2:46: Solomon's Succession to the Throne

▪ THE TEXT IN ITS ANCIENT CONTEXT

First Kings 1–2 provides a literary bridge from the end of 2 Samuel to 1 Kings. First Kings begins forebodingly, with the detail that old King David could not get warm. Instead of piling on yet another blanket, his servants search the land for a young virgin who will join his harem to be his attendant and share his bed. One of the hallmarks of a king's royal status is the number of his wives, concubines, and sons, and David accumulated many as he gained power (see 2 Sam. 3:2-5; 5:13; 16:20-23). Scholars have remarked on the different ways David's private relationships with his women reflect issues in his public life (Berlin). Because David is unable to "know" Abishag sexually in spite of her beauty, she becomes a signifier of the impotence of his leadership at the end of his rule. The biblical author, as is typical, does not provide access to Abishag's thoughts about being taken from her home to service the king sexually.

Because of his deterioration and the fact that he has not named an heir, David's sons jockey to replace him. Solomon's rival is his half brother Adonijah son of Haggith, who is not only next in line but good looking to boot. Adonijah presumptuously declares, "I will be king," and, like his older brother Absalom, who also had royal ambitions (2 Sam. 15:1-7), gathers a small band of chariots, horsemen, and fifty men to run before him. The declining David does not reproach him for his displays of royal privilege (1:5-6).

Adonijah has powerful people from the military and religious sectors of the kingdom supporting him: Joab, David's mighty general and son of David's sister Zeruiah, and Abiathar the priest. Solomon has his influential supporters as well: Zadok the priest, Nathan the prophet, Benaiah the leader of David's bodyguard, and his mother Bathsheba, the bathing beauty of 2 Samuel 11. Those supporting Adonijah go back to the time when David was king of Judah at Hebron. Those supporting Solomon only come on the scene when David moves his capital to Jerusalem. The parties thus represent the old guard versus the young "turks" in the dynamics of power (Ishida). The members of each party compete with each other for the same position in the realm: Adonijah and Solomon for the kingship; Haggith and Bathsheba as future queen mother; Joab and Benaiah as commander of the army; and Abiathar and Zadok as chief priest (1:7-8).

A sacrificial banquet, hosted by Adonijah, who invites all of David's sons and Judean officials but not Solomon or his supporters, becomes the catalyst for some harem politics to secure the throne for Solomon. Nathan the prophet exploits the jealousy and fears among royal wives to spur Bathsheba into action. He declares that the son of her rival Haggith has "become king" and gives her advice to save her own life and that of her son Solomon. He and Bathsheba cleverly maneuver an impotent, senile old king into proclaiming Solomon as his successor, and, with great fanfare, Solomon is anointed king at the spring of Gihon (1:9-40). When the news of this anointing reaches the banquet, Adonijah's guests abandon him and he himself flees to grasp the horns of the altar, its most sacred part. Solomon spares his life only on the condition that Adonijah "proves to be a worthy man" (1:41-53).

First Kings 2 begins with David on his deathbed giving his final instructions to Solomon. Exhibiting the hallmarks of Deuteronomistic redaction, David exhorts Solomon to adhere to God's covenantal demands as written in the torah/law of Moses in order to prosper in his rule (2:3). God's unconditional promise to David of an eternal dynasty (2 Samuel 7) now becomes conditioned upon the complete fidelity of his successors to God's commands (2:4). We will soon see that the rest of Kings narrates the failures of Israel and Judah to remain faithful to God, resulting ultimately in the destruction of the kingdom and the exile of the people at the end of the book. Solomon himself will initiate this falling-off by worshiping the gods of his many foreign wives (1 Kings 11). After his torah counsel, David instructs Solomon to assassinate Joab, David's right-hand man in military affairs, and Shimei, who had cursed him publicly (2:5-10). David then dies, ending a career riddled with murder by proxy (Halpern 2001).

In the next scene (2:13-46a), Adonijah, in either a shrewd or stupid move, asks Bathsheba to request from Solomon the hand of Abishag, David's last concubine, in marriage. Surprisingly or perhaps cleverly, Bathsheba agrees. The way Solomon behaves toward Bathsheba, rising up and bowing down in her presence and giving her a seat of honor, reveals the high position that Bathsheba achieves as mother of the king. This lends credibility to the notion that she understood very well the effect Adonijah's request would have on her son. Sexual relations with a woman from the former king's harem evoked strong responses in the male politics of gender (cf. 2 Sam. 3:7-8; 16:20-22). Solomon predictably interprets the request as a step to advance Adonijah's thwarted royal ambitions. He has Adonijah assassinated and then deals with Joab and Shimei according to his father's wishes. This unit concludes with the detail, "So the kingdom was established in the hand of Solomon" (2:46b).

■ THE TEXT IN THE INTERPRETIVE TRADITION

Much intriguing speculation exists on the voiceless minor character Abishag (Stahlberg). The Talmud records her saying to David, "Let us marry." When David replies, "Thou art forbidden to me," because he has attained his legal allotment of eighteen wives, she implicitly ridicules his impotence, at which point David shows that he still has what it takes in his old age and has sex with Bathsheba thirteen times (*Sanh.* 22a). Because she is from Shunem, Abishag is linked with the "black but/and beautiful" Shulammite, Solomon's beloved (Song of Sol. 1:5; 6:13). Jerome allegorically personifies Abishag as wisdom herself, "so glowing as to warm the cold, yet so holy as not to arouse passion in him whom she warmed" (*Letter 52 to Nepotian* 2–3). She is the subject of a number of poems that reconstruct her feelings and experiences of being taken from her home to nurse and sleep with a decrepit king (Baumgarten; Curzon). The aging Earl of Hauberk in Aldous Huxley's *After Many a Summer* (1939) records in his diary, "I have tried King David's remedy against old age and found it wanting." In Stefan Heym's novel *The King David Report* (1972), Abishag is given a prominent, if not flattering role, as "stupidest woman in Israel," a sexually ripe concubine whose torrid affair with Adonijah leads to his downfall. In Joseph Heller's novel *God Knows* (1984), David's first love was and still is Bathsheba, who won't have anything to do with David, but still gives Abishag friendly advice about David's personal hygiene and eating habits.

■ THE TEXT IN CONTEMPORARY DISCUSSION

Although royal males in their attempts to obtain the throne are the subject of 1 Kings 1–2, feminist scholars highlight the important roles that harem women play within these political dynamics. Abishag becomes a symbol of David's decline, and Adonijah's request for her hand in marriage leads to his murder. Bathsheba's collusion with Nathan successfully procures the throne for her son, and her sly request that Solomon approve Adonijah's bid for Abishag secures it.

In today's political arena, the wives of male politicians often exert tremendous influence on public policy, albeit informally and behind the scenes. Rosalind Carter and Nancy Reagan were First Ladies who had much influential sway on their presidential husbands. Only more recently have the wives of presidents, such as Hillary Rodham Clinton and Michelle Obama, assumed a more visible role.

1 Kings 3:1-28: Solomon the "Wise" Man?

■ THE TEXT IN ITS ANCIENT CONTEXT

Now that his rivals have been eliminated, Solomon sets about consolidating his state and securing his rule over it. The first and last details describing Solomon's reign—his marriage to Pharaoh's daughter (3:1) and his love for his many foreign wives (11:1-10)—form a bracket around

Solomon's story. Although his wisdom will be underscored throughout, the subtext of Solomon's narrative lays the blame for his decline on his unwise entanglements with foreign women, recurring Deuteronomistic specters thought to seduce Israel away from YHWH (Num. 25:1-3; Deut. 7:3-4; Josh. 23:11-13). His first foreign wife is the daughter of the Egyptian pharaoh, mentioned several times in this story (3:1; 7:8; 9:16, 24; 11:1-2). As a place of enslavement, genocide, and unrelenting oppression, Egypt occupies a significant negative site in the Israelite consciousness. And yet, Solomon seems to appropriate aspects of this empire in establishing his rule as his story unfolds: the large harem (beginning with the pharaoh's daughter), the procuring of "wisdom" (the province of the elite class, 4:30), the stratification of society into the haves and have-nots, the large building projects, the forced labor, the accumulation of wealth, and the brutal taxation. Although Solomon "loved the LORD" (3:3), eventually building YHWH a great temple, he simultaneously "loved many foreign women" (11:1). Even though the adverse consequences of empire building will eventually lead to Solomon's deterioration, what the reader remembers is his love for foreign women and their gods, which seems to displace its real causes.

This tolerance for foreign religions is hinted in the report that Solomon often sacrificed at Gibeon, "the principal high place" (3:4). In Deuteronomistic theology, worship at the high places is usually forbidden, because Jerusalem is the central and normative locus of worship (1 Kgs. 12:31; 15:14; 22:43; 2 Kgs. 14:13, et passim). That Solomon is sacrificing in Gibeon when the ark resides in Jerusalem is rather unsettling. YHWH appears to him in a dream, saying: "Ask what I should give you" (3:5). Because he is only "a little child," faced with the task of governing "a great people," Solomon requests "an understanding mind" and the ability to "discern between good and evil" (3:9). Solomon's dream and the self-deprecating allusion to his youth parallel that of Tuthmoses IV of Egypt (*ANET* 449) and other propagandistic accounts that supply divine legitimation of a king's rule. Because Solomon asks for "understanding to discern what is right" (3:10) and does not ask for riches or honor, God will also give Solomon riches and honor all his life (3:13). Nevertheless, this promise to Solomon of wisdom, riches, and honor is conditional. Solomon must walk in the ways of YHWH, keeping God's statutes and commandments (3:14), a condition that Solomon will not always keep, as we shall see. The narrative ends with Solomon waking up from his dream, returning to Jerusalem to stand before the ark of the covenant. He then offers sacrifices and a feast at the only legitimate place of worship, according to the Deuteronomist (3:15).

Although it originally may have been an independent folktale about the judgment of an unknown ruler, the familiar account of the two prostitutes before Solomon now provides an illustration of Solomon's newly acquired wisdom (3:16-28). Various reasons why the story has two *prostitutes* before the king have been proposed: perhaps the designation explains why these women live together with infants but no husbands; perhaps to highlight that all levels of social strata were able to find justice before the king; perhaps to foreground Solomon's dilemma in deciding between two women, who were considered disreputable and deceptive by nature because of their occupation.

The contours of the case are filtered through the eyes of the plaintiff. According to the plaintiff, the defendant gave birth to a son three days after the birth of her own. During the night when no one else was in the house, the defendant's son dies because "she lay on him" (3:19). While the plaintiff slept, the defendant allegedly took the plaintiff's son and replaced him with her own dead son at the plaintiff's breast. When the plaintiff awoke to nurse, she discovered that her son was dead, but in a closer look knew that the infant was not her son. The defendant refutes her accuser by declaring, "No, the living son is mine and the dead son is yours," arguing back and forth before the king (3: 20-22). The king resolves the conflict by commanding a sword be brought and slicing the infant in two. The true mother is revealed when, moved with compassion, she pleads to the king to not kill her son, but give him to the other woman. The other woman declares: "It shall be neither mine nor yours; divide it" (3:24-26). The Hebrew text is ambiguous regarding the true mother. English versions, for example, the NRSV and NIB, have the king respond, "Give *the first woman* the living boy," even though the Hebrew only says, "Give her the living boy" (3:27), without clearly designating either the plaintiff or the defendant. Biblical scholars have argued for one or the other as the true mother (Garsiel 1993; Wolde).

Although this story ostensibly reveals Solomon's wisdom after God grants him this gift, the process leading toward his judgment would not pass muster in present-day courtrooms. Solomon simply accepts the testimony of the plaintiff without question and does not ask for the defendant's version of the case. He does not probe more deeply how the plaintiff knew that the defendant switched babies in the middle of the night if she was indeed asleep. Why did she not wake up when the dead baby was put at her breast (3:20)? Solomon does not investigate the crime scene for any clues. Instead, he rather recklessly endangers the life of an infant to provoke a reaction from the true mother.

Scholars have pointed out intertextual contrasts between 1 Kings 3 and 2 Kgs. 6:24-31, which also involves two mothers wrangling before the king over one living son. One of these mothers demonstrates compassion for her son; the other, a lack. However, their case is much more gruesome than the one judged by Solomon. During a siege that has been starving the population, the plaintiff had made a pact with the defendant to cook and eat her son that day, and the defendant's son the next day. However, after the plaintiff's son was consumed, the defendant reneged on her side of the bargain and hid her son. The king, seeing no way to resolve this dispute, tears his clothes and irrationally seeks vengeance on the prophet Elisha. Second Kings 6 seems to provide a negative counterpart to the all-wise Solomon, a negativity that is already imbedded in 1 Kings 3 (Lasine; Pyper).

▐ THE TEXT IN THE INTERPRETIVE TRADITION

The story of Solomon's judgment over the prostitutes is perhaps the most well-known, interpreted, and even parodied of his narrative (Ipsen, 134–35). Ephrem the Syrian and Augustine interpreted the story as an allegory in which the two women represent the church and the synagogue, in which the Jews symbolized by the false mother kills her son Christ. Augustine also saw Jewish Christians who tried to enforce the law onto gentiles like the false mother (Conti, 15–21).

Because the text does not explicitly point out which woman is the true mother, the interpretive tradition had different ways to resolve the ambiguity. For example, Rabbi Joseph Kara (1065–1135 CE) thought one could distinguish between a day-old child and one who was three days old on the basis of the birth blood of each. Radbaz (1480–1574 CE) conjectured that Solomon noted the facial similarity between the living child and that of the plaintiff and between the dead infant and that of the defendant (Garsiel, 232–34).

In chapter 14 of Mark Twain's *Huckleberry Finn*, Jim provides a negative reading of this story, based on his experiences as an African American slave, to contradict Huck's understanding of Solomon as the "wisest man." Jim uses a dollar bill to substitute for the child desired by both women. A wise person would go around the neighborhood to find out to which of the two women the money belongs, and then hand it over to the right one. But Solomon would "whack de bill in *two*" and give the pieces to the two parties. Jim declares, "what's de use er dat half a bill?—can't buy noth'n wid it. En what use is a half a chile? I wouldn' give a dern for a million un um." Because Solomon had this large harem, he must have had "'bout five million chillen runnin' roun' de house." He does not value children as a man who only had one or two children. But Solomon, "*He* as soon chop a chile in two as a cat. Dey's plenty mo'. A chile er two, mo' er less, warn't no consekens to Sollermun, dad fatch him!" In the world of slavery, slaves are commodities that are bought and sold. Their intrinsic humanity to the slaveholder is of "no consekens." Jim thus comes off as a wiser man than Solomon in this chapter.

■ THE TEXT IN CONTEMPORARY DISCUSSION

Of the Solomon traditions, the common lectionaries only contain selections of his dream at Gibeon (3:5-15) and of his prayer at the temple's dedication (8:22-30, 41-43). These readings highlight Solomon's wisdom and piety, while omitting his ruthless elimination of his rivals (1 Kings 2) and his adoption of the oppressive trappings of empire. For the people in the pews, they thus present a one-sided picture of Solomon that supports the idealized traditional reputation as a wise and discerning leader, a reputation that should be counterbalanced with a more critical assessment of his rule.

One of the bitterest aspects of divorce proceedings is over the custody of children. These proceedings often take months, even years, of expensive litigation and emotional turmoil. Although dividing the family property down the middle can be a fair distribution between divorcing partners, "splitting the baby" according to Solomonic justice cannot be an option when it comes to their children. Determining the best interests of the child in our day and age takes much more wisdom than that demonstrated by Solomon in this text.

Feminist scholarship has highlighted the fact that the only narrated example of Solomon's wisdom was on behalf of prostitutes. Within the economics of the texts, one of the most vulnerable members of society, widows who have no male family members to support them may have to resort to prostitution in order to survive. When one focuses on the perspective of the women as prostitutes, one considers the systemic economic circumstances that force women into prostitution, in ancient times and modern, and what kind of justice they can appeal to when their rights are violated (Bird, 197; Ipsen, 134).

1 Kings 4:1—11:42: Solomon's Bureaucratic Rule

■ THE TEXT IN ITS ANCIENT CONTEXT

The different editorial and ideological layers in these chapters make it is difficult to determine their historical reliability about Solomon and his presumed tenth-century rule. Their narratives have analogues to eighth- and seventh-century-BCE Assyrian inscriptions, persuading scholars to regard them as later retrojections to create a magnificent past for Israel (see also Moore and Kelle, 244–57; Römer, 99). Although Solomon is depicted "in all his glory" (see Matt. 6:29 // Luke 12:27), there is a dark undercurrent revealing Solomon as just another dictatorial and oppressive king like those in other ancient Near Eastern empires. In order to secure his rule, Solomon reorganized his kingdom into twelve administrative districts that cut across tribal lines, staffing them with Judeans who had family or close ties with the Davidic dynasty (4:7-19). Through this redistricting, Solomon was able to constrain and exploit the powerful northern tribes through heavy tax burdens, from which his own tribe of Judah was exempt. First Kings 4:22-28 describes the exorbitant monthly demands from each of these districts, especially for luxury foods, such as meat, that go well beyond subsistence.

Solomon embarked on a number of expensive building projects to trumpet his successes and wealth, but these were realized at a heavy cost (1 Kings 5–7). He had to conscript thousands of his own people and foreigners into corvée labor groups to work on these buildings (4:6; 5:13-18; 9:20-21), taking them away from agricultural production, which was the major source of Israel's economy. The indigenous trees in Israel were not suitable for the great building projects that Solomon desired. In order to purchase and import the celebrated cedars of Lebanon, Solomon had to pay the foreign king Hyram of Tyre an enormous fee in wheat and fine oil (5:11), adding more to the people's tax burden.

The major and most famous building project was the Jerusalem temple (1 Kings 5–8). The three-part floor plan of the temple was similar to Canaanite temples that have been excavated from the same period. This is not surprising since Canaanite craftsmen were involved in the construction (see 7:13). The temple consisted of a vestibule, a nave, and an inner sanctuary, often referred to as the holy of holies (6:2-10). The construction reflected the stratification of the society. The three divisions marked the intensifying degrees of exclusivity, the vestibule having more public access; the nave, more limited; and the holy of holies, forbidden except to the most senior priests and only on special occasions. The rich latticework and carvings, the costly stones, the great bronze pillars and basins, the numerous vessels and accoutrements of gold and silver, and so forth (1 Kings 7) all have a flip side. This great extravagance for the few came at the cost borne by most of the population.

First Kings 6:1 notes that Solomon began this construction "in the four hundred eightieth year after the Israelites came out of the land of Egypt." Long after Israel was freed from Egyptian slavery, Israel ironically had to endure forced servitude and exploitation again under its own king. The building and its furnishings are described in all their opulence, but in the midst of these details of conspicuous consumption is an important condition in both the temple's construction and inauguration accounts: If Solomon obeys all of God's commandments, God will keep the promise made to David and dwell with Israel and not forsake them (6:11-13; cf. 8:56-61). Here the royal ideology of the monarchy that highlights God's promises to the Davidic dynasty stands in tension with the Mosaic covenantal demands that the people, including Israel's king, remain obedient to God's torah (Brueggemann, 88–89). We will soon see that Solomon was not successful in following God's commandments.

The section 1 Kgs. 9:10—11:42 narrates Solomon's downhill slide in his questionable dealings with foreign kings and foreign women, the slave labor of foreign peoples, his staggering greed, and his eventual idolatry. This decline is particularly evident when one compares 10:14—11:8 with Deut. 17:16-17, which stipulates that the king

- must not acquire horses for himself;
- must not return to Egypt in order to acquire more horses;
- must not acquire many wives for himself, or "else his heart will turn away";
- must also not amass silver and gold for himself in great quantity.

Solomon, however, commits all of these infractions in chapters 10–11, depicting a king who shaped his regime into the likeness of Egypt, who had oppressed their ancestors, sending his people back to Egypt to stockpile wealth and horses and adding women to his already substantial harem (Sweeney 2007, 146–47).

Solomon's rule, which began propitiously when Solomon "*loved* the Lord" (3:3), now comes to a shameful close because he "*loved* many foreign women," who turned his heart away from God to worship their own alien deities (11:1-8). Although a hint of disapproval exists, the Deuteronomist presents the negative economic aspects of Solomon's rule—the forced labor, his extreme taxation, his ostentatious materialism—rather neutrally, as opposed to the explicit censure of the king's economic exploitation found in 1 Sam. 8:10-18 and Dtr's advocacy for the most helpless in society (see Deut. 10:18; 24:17-22; 27:19). What comes under his unequivocal condemnation is Solomon's love of many foreign women, who persuade him to sacrifice to their gods. The reader is left with the lasting impression that Solomon's downfall was due to his sexual relationships with women and not to his material self-indulgence and economic oppression (Jobling, 61–64). Because of these marriages, God raises up three major adversaries against Solomon (Hadad, Rezon, and Jeroboam), whose rebellions sow the seeds for the division of the kingdom after Solomon's death (11:14-43). The most significant of these adversaries is Jeroboam, who was in command of Solomon's forced labor in the tribe of Joseph (11:28). After receiving a prophecy from the prophet Ahijah that God will "tear the kingdom from the hand of Solomon" and give to Jeroboam the "ten tribes" (11:31), Jeroboam flees to Egypt, only to return after Solomon's death to become the first king of the northern kingdom (12:20).

The Solomon narrative concludes with the Deuteronomistic citation of its source (the Book of the Acts of Solomon), Solomon's length of rule in Jerusalem, his death, and his succession by his son Rehoboam (11:41-21).

■ THE TEXT IN THE INTERPRETIVE TRADITION

The parallel account of Solomon in 2 Chronicles 1–9 omits the negative stories of Solomon's idolatry and revolts in 1 Kings 11 and foregrounds the temple in its exposition.

A number of early Christian allegorical interpretations of Solomon's kingdom and temple exist (Conti, 24–64). For example, according to Ephrem the Syrian (c. 306–73 CE), the twelve officials who administered Solomon's kingdom (1 Kgs. 4:7) foreshadowed the twelve apostles of Jesus. The Venerable Bede (c. 672–735 CE) believed that the three floors of the temple (1 Kgs. 6:6) reflected a hierarchical ordering of the lifestyles of the faithful: married people, those who practice continence, and virgins, "levels distinguished according to the loftiness of their profession but all belonging to the house of the Lord" (Conti 2008, 31).

Over the centuries, Jewish and Muslim traditions have presented the story of Solomon and Sheba (1 Kgs. 10:1-13) as a contest of body and mind between an independent and boundary-crossing woman and a man who is eager to keep her subservient. By the Middle Ages, the main focus of the queen's visit had shifted from international to sexual politics, so that in postbiblical and Islamic versions, the queen's sparring match with Solomon was depicted as a threatening attempt to subvert the traditional roles of gender. In the same vein, an Ethiopian legend in the *Kebra Negast* ("Glory of the Kings") records Solomon cleverly seducing the queen after she had made him swear that he not take her by force. They beget Menelik I, the first emperor of Ethiopia (Lassner 1993).

■ THE TEXT IN CONTEMPORARY DISCUSSION

The Solomon narratives reveal that the steep income disparity between the haves and the have-nots that we see so blatantly in our own day is not a new phenomenon. Solomon heavily taxed his rural population for both material and human resources in order to support the luxurious lifestyles of his court and build his grandiose monuments. Each month, the court received from one of the provinces not only the choicest grains and flocks but also exotic animals like deer, gazelles, roebucks, and fatted fowl (4:22-24). Similarly, in our day, meat is usually found only on tables in the so-called first world and especially in the United States. Our excessive consumption of meat is having disastrous effects on the environment globally. Moreover, Solomon's forced labor gangs have some analogues to the trade in human trafficking today. Although the former is state-run, while the latter is illicit, both involve coercion and much human suffering.

These narratives are also cautionary tales for us today. They raise serious questions about the abuse of power by a nation's leadership. Solomon's disproportionate wealth and exploitation of the people to obtain it would have enormous consequences. Resistance and protests plagued the last days of his rule. Nowadays, we have food riots over grain and water shortages as a result of the diversion of good farmland to feed cattle, not people. History has already shown us that indifference of the wealthier classes to the poverty and destitution of the people often results in armed conflict. With Solomon, as we will see, this indifference resulted in the division of his kingdom. These texts obligate us to attend to the most vulnerable in our midst so that our global world does not fracture any more than it already has.

1 Kings 12:1—16:34: The Divided Kingdom

■ THE TEXT IN ITS ANCIENT CONTEXT

Ahijah's prophecy in 11:31-40, that God will wrench the kingdom from Solomon and give to Jeroboam "the ten tribes," becomes fulfilled in this unit. After his father's death, Rehoboam goes up to be crowned in the important northern city of Shechem, perhaps as a positive gesture toward the northern tribes, or as a presumptuous declaration of his sovereignty over them (Seow, 100).

Having heard that Solomon has died, Jeroboam, his rebellious corvee overseer, returns from Egypt where he had fled from Solomon's wrath (11:40). Along with the tribes, he urges the new king to lighten the hard service and heavy yoke that Solomon had imposed on them. Recall the daily extravagant provisions that the northern tribes had to supply the Jerusalem court (4:22-28) and the corvée labor that built Solomon's building projects (5:13-18). Rehoboam first consults his father's seasoned advisors, who recommend that he "lighten the yoke" appointed by his father. However, rejecting their advice, he turns to a group of courtiers he grew up with, disparagingly described as "boys" to underscore their contrast with the elders. These middle-aged associates—Rehoboam was evidently forty-one years old when he ascended the throne (14:21)—encourage a reply that hints at Rehoboam's or perhaps their own "daddy issues": "My little 'thingie' [Sweeney 2007, 163] is thicker than my father's loins!" (12:10). Given the seemingly huge size of Solomon's own harem (11:3), this would have been an extravagant claim by his arrogant offspring. Rehoboam then declares that rather than lightening the heavy yoke, he will intensify the burdens that his father had laid upon the people (12:14). Predictably, the northern tribes reject Rehoboam as king and return back to their homes. Rehoboam foolishly tries to regain control by dispatching Adoram, his official in charge of corvée labor, to the northern tribes, who promptly stone Adoram to death. Their next victim possibly would have been Rehoboam had he not hastily jumped into his chariot and fled back to Jerusalem (12:16-18).

As the newly crowned king of Israel (12:20), Jeroboam is confronted first with a political problem with religious implications. The Jerusalem temple and its cult continue to be a significant focus of the people's worship, because it houses the ark of the covenant. The northern tribes venerate the ark because it resided in several of their sanctuaries before it was brought to Jerusalem (Judg. 20:26-27; 1 Sam. 3:3; 6:21—7:1). Even though Ahijah prophesied that if Jeroboam follows God's statutes and commandments his dynasty will endure (11:38), Jeroboam still fears that allowing pilgrimages to Jerusalem will turn the people's allegiance back to Rehoboam. To prevent the cross-border excursions, he establishes two shrines at Dan and Bethel, polar ends of his kingdom, installing two calves of gold, of which he declares, "Here are your gods, O Israel, who brought you up out of the land of Egypt" (12:26-33). While the calves themselves are not idols, but simply the beasts of burden that carry the invisible God, for the Josianic Deuteronomist they become reified as "the sin of Jeroboam" throughout his history (see 1 Kgs. 13:34; 14:16; 2 Kgs. 3:3; 10:29; 13:2, et passim). From his southern perspective, the only legitimate place of worship is the temple in Jerusalem. In the dangerous memory of Israel, the calves also conjure up the image of the idolatrous golden calf that Aaron made for the Israelites in the wilderness, underscoring the illegitimacy of Jeroboam's cult (Exodus 32; see Knoppers, 92).

In the next episode, the Deuteronomist continues to portray the competitors of the Jerusalem cult as illicit. While Jeroboam is offering incense at Bethel, a man of God from Judah directs a prophecy at the altar, proclaiming that Josiah, a descendant from the Davidic dynasty several hundred years later, will sacrifice on this altar the priests of the high places established by Jeroboam (13:2-3; cf. 12:31-32). Later in the DH, Josiah will eventually tear down this altar with its gruesome ashes and purge the land of its idolatrous cult (2 Kings 23).

Jeroboam's story ends tragically. When his son Abijah falls ill, Jeroboam tells his unnamed wife to disguise herself, go to Shiloh, and consult with Ahijah, the same prophet who had declared that Jeroboam would rule an enduring house like David's (11:38). However, because Jeroboam made for himself "other gods and cast images," provoking God to anger, Ahijah now proclaims that God will put an end of his dynasty (14:7-11). Ahijah then orders the wife back home, prophesying her son's death, which comes to pass when she crosses the threshold of her house. The seeming passivity of the wife prompts feminists to speculate whether the wife was a victim of domestic violence (Branch, 83–107).

From this point on, the Deuteronomist provides a particular theological frame for the rival kings of Israel and Judah (see the introduction). The most important part of his framework is his religious judgment on the rule, whether he obeyed God's law and banished idols, high places, and so on from the land or let them flourish. A particular king may have been an important political leader and good ruler, but is condemned by the Dtr for religious reasons. For example, given the propensity in Israel for regicide (assassination of kings; see 1 Kgs. 15:27; 16:9-10, 15-16), it is significant that the kings who had the longest reigns in Israel are censured by the Dtr: Jeroboam I (twenty-two years), Basha (twenty-four years), Ahab (twenty-two years), and Jeroboam II (forty-one years).

■ THE TEXT IN THE INTERPRETIVE TRADITION

A version of the LXX contains an alternative account that portrays Jeroboam more negatively (Sweeney 2007, 165–67). Although 12:26 describes his mother Zeruah as a widow (11:26), in this version she is a prostitute named Sarira. The unidentified wife of Jeroboam also receives a name. When Jeroboam flees to Egypt from Solomon's anger, the pharaoh Sausakim (MT Shishak, 12:40) gives him his sister-in-law, Ano, as wife, who bears him a son, Abijah. The version then recounts Jeroboam's gathering the Israelite tribes at Shechem and building fortifications there. At this point, Abijah becomes sick and Jeroboam directs Ano to seek God's counsel. Abijah dies, according to the prophecy Ahijah gives to Ano (see 14:12-13, 17-18). The LXX expansion highlights Rehoboam as an immature teenager and insinuates Jeroboam's role in instigating the revolt by placing him in Israel before the North's rebellion. Jeroboam's marriage into Shishak's royal family reinforces Jeroboam's culpability even more when Shishak later invades Judah after the division (14:25-28).

The Old Testament figure of Ahab was one of the biblical prototypes for Captain Ahab in Herman Melville's *Moby-Dick*. Because Jeroboam is Ahab's predecessor and the prophetic condemnation of the kings of Israel because of his "sin" (see 15:25) will determine the fate of Ahab, his story finds a particular analogue in Melville's tome. The ship *Jeroboam* in *Moby-Dick* becomes the forerunner of Captain Ahab's *Pequod*, and two members of its crew correspond to members of Jeroboam's household: the death of the shipmate Macey parallels Jeroboam's stricken son Abijah, and Gabriel parallels the prophet Ahijah (Bartel, 44–46).

■ THE TEXT IN CONTEMPORARY DISCUSSION

Lord Acton remarked in a letter to Bishop Mandell Creighton in 1887: "Power tends to corrupt, and absolute power corrupts absolutely. Great men are almost always bad men." Rehoboam's folly in not heeding the wisdom of his older advisors presents a cautionary tale about leadership and the abuse of power. In response to the people's request to ease up on the heavy burdens his father had laid on them, Rehoboam arrogantly responds: "Whereas my father laid on you a heavy yoke, I will add to your yoke. My father disciplined you with whips, but I will discipline you with scorpions" (12:11). History throughout reveals that tyrannical rulers and oppressive systems of power will face resistance when the subjugated will not take it anymore: from the slave rebellions against Rome, to the civil rights marches against racism of the last century, to the recent Occupy movement against corporate greed. The text raises questions about what it means to be a leader. Is it true that power corrupts and absolute power corrupts absolutely? How do we prevent or resist the corruption of power without becoming corrupt ourselves?

1 Kings 17:1—22:53: The Ministries of the Prophets Elijah and Micaiah

∎ THE TEXT IN ITS ANCIENT CONTEXT

These chapters highlight the ministries of the prophets Elijah (chs. 17–19, 21) and Micaiah (ch. 22) in their clashes with King Ahab of Israel (c. 873–852 BCE) of the powerful royal dynasty of Omri. According to 16:29-34, Ahab not only walked in the sins of Jeroboam but also angered God even more by marrying a foreign woman, Jezebel, daughter of the king of the Sidonians, and worshiping her gods Baal and Asherah. Recall that Solomon's marriages to foreign women and his apostasy led to his own deterioration (1 Kings 11). Also important in understanding these chapters is that both the kings of Israel and Judah continued Solomon's exploitative economic policy of extracting the surpluses from their agrarian subjects to support their building projects, wars, and extravagant lifestyles. This one-sided systemic extraction resulted in the impoverishment of the nation's peasant base.

In 17:1, Elijah appears out of nowhere to proclaim a drought in God's name that will afflict Israel. This declaration is a direct polemic against the worship of the Baal, the Canaanite god responsible for rain and fertility in the land. Although the veneration of Canaanite deities is expressly condemned in the Hebrew Bible, this represents only a part, though an important one, of the rich pluralism in Israelite belief and practice. The worship of Baal and even the goddess Asherah was accepted or at least tolerated in the early stages of Israel's religious development (Dever; M. S. Smith 2002). However, not only does 1 Kgs. 17–22 reflect the developing "Yahweh-alone" theology that belittled these deities (Lang, 13–56; M. Smith 1971, 34–37), but their worship is linked to a royal system of exploitation, in which the majority of the population suffered under the oppression of a small group of ruling elites (Brueggemann 2000, 202–3). Misery from the three-year drought particularly afflicted the marginalized classes of society, as is evident in Elijah's encounter with the starving widow and her malnourished son in Jezebel's own Phoenician hometown of Sidon (17:8-34). Meanwhile, Jezebel murders God's own prophets (18:4, 13), but hosts banquets for the 450 prophets of Baal and the 400 prophets of Asherah, while the rest of the nation starves (18:19). Ahab too seems more concerned about grass for his horses and mules than food for his own people (18:5).

According to the Kurkh Monolith, Ahab possessed enough horses to pull two thousand chariots in a campaign against the Assyrian king Shalmaneser III (Grabbe 2007, 131, 142–43). However, Obadiah's protection of God's prophets from Jezebel's persecution reveals that even some high-level members of the royal court resisted the oppressive policies (18:3, 13).

The confrontation on Mount Carmel between YHWH and Baal is about who can end the drought and bring rain to the land. It is also about the religio-political systems that undergird their worship (18:20-46). This narrative dramatically pits the 450 prophets of Baal against God's lone prophet, Elijah. Two altars for two bulls are prepared. The challenge is which god will answer by fire to consume his sacrificial altar. The Baal prophets go first, calling out to their god from morning till noon with no answer. Elijah taunts their efforts, and they set about gashing themselves, intensifying their raving until past midday with no response. Then, in some spectacularly theatrical moves, Elijah builds an altar with twelve stones symbolizing the twelve tribes of Israel and digs a large trench around it. He dismembers his bull and places the pieces on the wood of the altar. He commands four jars of waters be splashed on the altar three times. He prays one little prayer and immediately God answers with fire, consuming the whole altar and even the water in the trench. Elijah has all the prophets of Baal assassinated, and then tells Ahab to eat and drink, "for there is a sound of rushing rain" (18:41), proving that YHWH, not Baal, makes the life-giving waters flow.

The next clash between Elijah and Ahab, which occurs in 1 Kings 21, foregrounds the ruling elite's abuse of power over land ownership. Ahab wants a vineyard in Jezreel belonging to a man named Naboth, who refuses Ahab's offer of either a better vineyard or a reasonable price, because he regards the land as an inheritance that should not be bought or sold outside of the family to which it belonged (see Num. 27:1-11; Deut. 25:5-10; Jer. 32:6-12). Knowing Mosaic custom, Ahab reacts by pouting and refusing to eat, whereupon Jezebel admonishes him, saying basically, "Aren't you the one who rules Israel?" (21:1-7). Jezebel regards land as a tradable commodity to which the monarch has a privileged claim (Brueggemann 2000, 257–65). She instigates an illegitimate seizure of his land and engineers his death (21:8-16). God then orders Elijah to meet Ahab and prophesy his death sentence because of his wife's deeds: "Thus says the Lord: In the place where dogs licked up the blood of Naboth, dogs will also lick up your blood" (21:19). Jezebel also does not escape censure: "The dogs shall eat Jezebel within the bounds of Jezreel" (21:23).

Elijah seemingly disappears in 1 Kings 20 and 22, but Ahab does not. These chapters deal with Ahab's wars with the Arameans (present-day Syria; for the historical problems dealing with chs. 20 and 22, see Sweeney 2007, 237–58). Although a number of anonymous prophets interact with Ahab in 20:13-15, 22, 28, 35-42, the major prophet confronting Ahab in 1 Kings 22 has a name: Micaiah. Three years have passed since Ahab last fought, but then later made a peace treaty with, the king of Aram (22:1; see 1 Kings 20). Because of this ill-advised treaty, an unnamed prophet condemns Ahab to death (20:42), a sentence that will be fulfilled in 1 Kings 22. Ahab makes an alliance with Jehoshaphat, the king of Judah (c. 870–846 BCE), to recapture Ramoth-Gilead, a strategically important city near the border between Israel and Aram. Jehoshaphat first wants to consult the "word of YHWH" before entering into combat (22:5). Because war involved the participation of YHWH the Divine Warrior, it was a holy affair. Kings thus did not commence battle without consulting the prophets, who informed them about the divine will.

Ahab thus assembles four hundred court prophets and asks if he should go into battle. Though they guarantee his victory, Jehoshaphat still wants another prophetic opinion. Ahab replies that there is another prophet, Micaiah, who can be consulted, "but I hate him, for he never prophesies anything favorable about me, but only disaster" (22:8). Nevertheless, at Jehoshaphat's prompting, Ahab sends for Micaiah, while the court prophets continue to affirm Ahab's victory over the Arameans (22:9-12).

When Ahab asks Micaiah whether the army shall proceed against Ramoth-Gilead, Micaiah prophesies victory. Suspicious of this response in light of past experience, Ahab demands Micaiah to tell "the truth in the name of YHWH" (22:15-16). Micaiah responds with two visions, the first of Israel scattered like sheep without a shepherd, and the second of God in his heavenly court, who asks for a volunteer to be a lying spirit in the mouths of Ahab's prophets. The gist of these visions is that the Lord has decreed disaster for Ahab (22:17-23). Ahab indeed dies ignobly by the end of the chapter (22:29-36). His bloody chariot is washed by the pool of Samaria. Dogs lick up his blood, fulfilling Elijah's prophecy (21:19), and to add insult to injury, prostitutes also wash themselves in it (22:37-38). First Kings concludes with the ascension of his son Ahaziah to the throne, who not only continues the "sin of Jeroboam" but also walks in the way of his father and mother, citing both Ahab and Jezebel in their idolatrous worship of Baal (22:51-53).

▌ THE TEXT IN THE INTERPRETIVE TRADITION

According to the final verses of the book of Malachi, God will send Elijah before "the great and terrible day of the Lord" (4:5). Elijah thus will be seen as the harbinger of the Messiah in Jewish tradition. At Passover celebrations, a cup is usually left out for the arrival of Elijah. Elijah is included in Sirach's "praises of famous men" (Sir. 48:1-12). In the Christian ordering of the books of the Hebrew Bible, the book of Malachi is placed last in the canon, immediately before the Gospels, so that Elijah appears to herald the coming of Jesus. The Gospels describe John the Baptist, the forerunner of Jesus, in the manner of Elijah, a "hairy man, with a leather belt around his waist (2 Kgs. 1:8; cf. Matt. 3:4; 11:14; 17:10-13; Luke 1:16-17). Elijah also appears at Jesus' transfiguration on the mountain along with Moses (Matt. 17:1-13; Mark 9:2-13; Luke 9:28-36). Elijah is one of the prophets referred to in the Quran as a precursor of Muhammad. Martin Luther compared Elijah to the Reformers, and the prophets of Baal to the Roman Catholic Church. In some Jewish legends, the son of the widow of Zarephath, whom Elijah healed (17:17-24), will later become the prophet Jonah.

Ahab's wife, Jezebel, was most likely a very powerful woman in her time, part of the ruling class of an agrarian society, wielding considerable authority in her position as queen. However, she has been demonized even in the early developments of the tradition. The *zebul* of her original name, "Prince, nobility," was distorted into *zebel*, "dung" (Dutcher-Walls 2004; Yee, 848). In the New Testament, the book of Revelation depicts a strong woman "who calls herself a prophet" as a Jezebel, seducing her flock into fornication and idolatry (Rev. 2:19-23). Modern-day dictionaries have also nominalized her name to describe a shameless, scheming woman. This characterization can be found in numerous depictions of Jezebel and women like her in theological treatises, sermons, novels, poetry, and theater (Gaines; Snyder). She is perhaps most memorably embodied in the actress Bette Davis as a spoiled, conniving southern belle in the motion picture *Jezebel* (Warner Bros., 1938). (For a semifictional account of Jezebel by a biblical scholar that tries to rehabilitate her notoriety, see Beach 2005.)

■ THE TEXT IN CONTEMPORARY DISCUSSION

Prophets emerged in ancient Israel during the time of the monarchy to announce God's judgments regarding a particular king's wars, foreign agreements, religious allegiances, and domestic economic and political policies. They condemned a king's abuses of power. They were also described as performing miracles, healing the sick, and making fire come down from the sky.

The question these texts raise for us now is whether such prophets exist in our own time. The stereotype of a prophet is that of a fortune-teller, one who sees and predicts the future. A prophet should be regarded instead as one who sees and analyzes the *present*, one who reads the signs of the times and declares the disastrous future results if things do not change. Such a person must be knowledgeable of contemporary affairs and skilled in some sort of social analysis to critique any injustice or exploitation. Individuals, such as social activists, public policy makers, ecologists, artists, poets, and musicians can all be prophetic in their own way.

Ahab and Jezebel's seizure of Naboth's land has disturbing parallels throughout history in which colonizers from Europe seized lands in Asia, Latin America, and Africa, robbing their indigenous peoples of their rich resources. This colonization continues in our own global economy today, where big corporations exploit the so-called third world of its resources and cheap labor for money and profit. Land and its inhabitants become commodities that can be bought and sold. Where are the prophets today who will hold these corporations accountable?

Popular culture usually lists Jezebel as one of the "bad girls of the Bible." Such stereotyping affects all women who are powerful, competent, independent, and forceful. Qualities that are usually admired in men are depicted as "bossy, pushy, aggressive, and unfeminine" for women, especially those at high levels of authority. Such women may be threatening to men used to more obedient and submissive women. One must remember that the negative depiction of Jezebel arose out of a male-dominated society that served the religious and political interests of the author. Since then, social roles and attitudes regarding the genders have changed dramatically. When one reads or hears such descriptions for women of today, one must step back and consider the source.

2 Kings 1:1—8:29: The Ministry of the Prophet Elisha

■ THE TEXT IN ITS ANCIENT CONTEXT

Chapter 1 of 2 Kings begins with the detail that after Ahab's death, Moab rebels against Israel, a war that will be taken up in 2 Kings 3. This conflict may have some extrabiblical support in the Mesha Stele (Moabite Stone), which describes Omri's oppression of Moab before Mesha throws off his yoke (Grabbe 2007, 131, 144–46). Omri's dynasty is continued in Ahab's son Azariah (c. 852–851

BCE), who seeks the counsel of "Baal-zebub, the god of Ekron" after a bad fall from his house. The qualifier *zebub* is most likely a distortion of an original *zebul*, or "prince," which alters the god's name to "Lord of the flies." For inquiring of Baal-zebub, Elijah prophesies the king's death (1:1-18).

Wedged between the death of Azariah and the rise of his brother, Ahab's son Jehoram, as king of Israel (2 Kings 3) is the story of the transfer of prophetic power and authority from Elijah to Elisha in 2 Kings 2. It begins with the remarkable statement that God was about to take Elijah up to heaven in a whirlwind, but before this occurs, Elijah and Elisha travel to Gilgal, Bethel, Jericho, and finally to the Jordan River. At the Jordan, Elijah uses his mantle to divide the waters, and the two prophets cross over to the other side on dry ground, reminiscent of other stories where waters are miraculously parted (Joshua 3–4; Exodus 14). Elisha requests a "double share" of Elijah's spirit before he is taken away. According to Deut. 21:17, a double share is the inheritance claim given to the firstborn son of a family. A fiery chariot and horses then appear that separate the two prophets, and Elijah ascends upward in a whirlwind. The use of horses and chariots and whirlwinds may be linked to similar portrayals of ancient Near Eastern storm gods, such as Baal, riding through the clouds, to emphasize YHWH's superior control of the weather (see 1 Kings 18). Elisha declares his kinship with Elijah by crying out, "Father, Father" as the chariot and horses disappear. Elisha then takes up the mantle of Elijah, crosses through the parted waters of the Jordan again, and is joined by the company of prophets. Elisha thus begins his active prophetic ministry during the rule of the Israelite kings Jehoram, Jehu, Jehoahaz, and Jehoash.

Besides his introduction in 1 Kgs. 19:19-21, many of the stories of Elisha preserved in 2 Kings 2–13 have been described as legends and miracle stories, making their historicity suspect. Nevertheless, they provide clues to the social history that formed the context of Elisha's prophetic ministry amid the continued exploitation of the people by the Israelite governing classes (Rentería). For example, scholars think that the company of prophets is primarily composed of the peripheral lower classes and that several of Elisha's miracles are for their benefit (Petersen, 47–48; Schulte, 140). Second Kings 4:1-7 records the miracle of the jar of oil for one of the widows of this company, who, bereft of her husband perhaps because of war, famine, or accidental death in the king's building projects, is compelled to sell her children as debt slaves to pay off creditors. First Kings 18 describes the indifference of the royal court to the starvation of the people during famine. Similarly, the background for the miracle of the stew in 2 Kgs. 4:38-41 consists of the desperate attempts of the company of prophets to find food during famine, during which someone may unknowingly contribute a toxic plant to a shared pot of stew, poisoning the community. This episode is followed by one where Elisha feeds one hundred hungry people with only twenty barley loaves, with some left over (4:42-43). Behind the simple story of the recovery of the ax head from the Jordan (6:1-7) is the reality that the ax head was borrowed (v. 5), probably from one of the elite, who would have been able to possess and lend the expensive commodities necessary for farming like axes, plows, and sickles (cf. 1 Sam. 13:19-21). The average peasant or day laborer from this company would have had to become a debt slave to pay for the ax head.

As we saw in 1 Kings 20 and 22, significant features of monarchic rule are the wars and conflicts of kings. Such wars wreak havoc on the nation's fragile agrarian ecosystem, especially when springs of water are stopped up, fruitful trees are cut down, and the land despoiled (2 Kgs. 3:18, 25). All of these man-made disasters bring much physical and economic suffering to the rest of the population. Narratives of Elisha's prophetic ministry with those in the lower rungs of society, who have been tragically affected by these wars, are interwoven with his dealings with the kings and generals conducting the fighting in this global arena (see chart below). Indeed, the stories of the lowly servant (3:11), the female war captive (5:2-4), and the junior officer (6:12) reveal that the politically subordinate or disenfranchised know more than their masters about the prophetic and healing powers of Elisha (Brueggemann 2001, 52–56; Provan, 185).

> *The campaign of the three kings against Moab (3:1-27)*
> The miracle of the widow's oil, the Shunamite's son, the poisoned stew of the company of prophets, the feeding of the people (4:1-44)
>
> *The healing of the Aramean general, Naaman, of leprosy (5:1-27)*
> The recovery of the lost ax head for the company of prophets (6:1-7)
>
> *Elisha's adventures with the Arameans and the siege of Samaria (6:8—7:20)*
> The restoration of the Shunamite's house and land (8:1-6)
>
> *Elisha's "anointing" of the kings of Aram and Israel (8:7—9:13)*
> Adapted from Long and Sneed, 264

■ THE TEXT IN THE INTERPRETIVE TRADITION

Rabbinic tradition is filled with legends of Elijah's appearances on earth after his translation into heaven. He comes to the aid of the innocent victims and especially those who are impoverished. In one story, Elijah sells himself into slavery in order to provide funds for a poor man. He also cures diseases and helps couples with their marital problems. Rabbinic tradition also preserves legends of Elisha. In one of these, the husband of the widow who was compelled to sell her children into debt slavery (2 Kgs. 4:1-7) is the prophet Obadiah, the same official who hid one hundred prophets of YHWH from Jezebel's pogrom (1 Kings 18). Obadiah appears to his widow at his gravesite and directs her to bring a little cruse of oil to Elisha. The miraculous flow of oil not only sustains the widow through her financial difficulties but also the rest of her descendants (Ginzberg 1956, 589–94, 603–4).

Josephus seems to depict Elisha more positively than Elijah in his writings, perhaps because he does not want to be associated with a prophet thought to be the forerunner of the Messiah in his Roman imperial context. He composed a eulogy for the former and not the latter. He omits scenes that portray Elisha negatively, such as the cursing of the boys who called him "baldhead" (2:23-25) and greatly develops others, such as the curing of the waters of Jericho, just prior to the cursing of the boys (2:19-22). He eliminates or rationalizes many of Elisha's miracles, perhaps to counter gentile depictions of Jewish gullibility. Thus, while clearly preserving the popularity of Elijah for his Jewish audience and depicting Elisha as his subordinate, Josephus portrays Elisha's prophetic ministry in a greatly expanded way (Feldman).

Because prophets raised people from the dead (1 Kgs. 17:17-23; 2 Kgs. 4:32-36), cured lepers (2 Kgs. 5:5), multiplied loaves of bread (2 Kgs. 4:42-44; cf. 1 Kgs. 17:8-16), ascended into heaven

(2 Kgs. 2:11-12), and worked miracles for rich and poor alike, many thought Jesus was one of the prophets (Matt. 16:13-14; Mark 8:27-28; cf. Luke 4:24-27).

Aspects of Elijah's and Elisha's healings, horses and chariot, the passing of the prophetic mantle, and other elements form a biblical layer for Franz Kafka's short story "The Country Doctor" (Barzel). The African American spiritual "Swing Low, Sweet Chariot" is based on Elijah's ascension into heaven (2 Kgs. 2:11), and also to the angels that carried Lazarus to the bosom of Abraham (Luke 16:22).

■ THE TEXT IN CONTEMPORARY DISCUSSION

In 1879, General William Sherman declared "War is hell" to give a reality check to those in the graduating class of Michigan Military Academy who looked on war as all glamour and glory. Much of the background for the so-called miracles that Elisha performs is the hell of war: the death of a family's financial support and the danger of selling one's children into debt slavery (4:1-7); war captives (5:2); famine (4:38-39); starvation (6:24-25; 7:3-4); cannibalism (6:26-31); economic chaos (6:25); and ecological destruction (3:25). To counteract and militate against the trauma of war in its myriad guises, Elisha performs miracles at the local level, but does not critique the roots of war at the systemic level. His prophecy to the kings of Israel, Judah, and Edom deals with whether God will grant them victory over Moab (2 Kings 3), not whether they should engage in war in the first place. These texts encourage us to examine the systemic causes of war to eliminate the monstrous effects of war on the people and the land.

2 Kings 9:1—12:21: The Rise of the House of Jehu and the Demise of the House of Omri

■ THE TEXT IN ITS ANCIENT CONTEXT

For Ahab and Jezebel's abuses of power in illegally confiscating Naboth's vineyard in 1 Kings 21, the chickens finally come home to roost in 2 Kings 9–10. The great dynasty inaugurated by Ahab's father Omri is destroyed by Jehu's merciless assassinations of Ahab's son, relatives, and his formidable wife, Jezebel; the Baal cult sanctioned by their regime is purged from the land.

While Ahab's son Joram (c. 851–843 BCE; Jehoram in 3:1) recovers in Jezreel from a battle wound (8:28-29), Elisha sends one of the company of prophets to anoint Jehu (c. 842–814 BCE), a top-ranking military officer, as king over Israel (see 1 Kgs. 19:16). Jehu will "strike down the house of your master Ahab," thus fulfilling Elijah's prophecy against Ahab in 1 Kgs. 21:20-24. Furthermore, Jehu will wreak God's vengeance on Jezebel for the blood of the prophets (see 1 Kgs. 18:4; 19:10), so that "the dogs shall eat Jezebel in the territory of Jezreel, and no one shall bury her" (9:6-10). Jehu's military comrades proclaim him as king, and he embarks on the demolition of Ahab's house (9:13).

Recurring throughout 2 Kings 9 is the ambiguous question *hashalom*, literally, "Is it peace?" but better translated variously depending on the context: "Is everything okay?" "How goes everything?" "Are you well?" "Is all well [at the front]?" "Do you come in peace?" (9:11, 17-19, 22, 31; Olyan).

Accompanied by his nephew, Judah's king Ahaziah (c. 843–842 BCE; see 8:25-29), Joram ironically meets Jehu at the former property of Naboth the Jezreelite that was unlawfully seized by Jezebel. He asks Jehu, "Do you come in peace?" but Jehu replies, "What peace can there be, so long as the many whoredoms and sorceries of your mother Jezebel continue?" (9:22), alluding to her support of the worship of Baal. Joram then flees, warning Ahaziah of Jehu's treachery, but Jehu kills Joram and leaves him exposed without an honorable burial on the plot of land that belonged to Naboth. Ahaziah is also killed, but he at least gets an honorable burial in Jerusalem (9:27-28).

Jehu's next murderous stop in Jezreel is Jezebel's palace. If she is going to die, she will die looking like the royal queen she is, painting her eyes and adorning her hair. She is described as a "woman at the window," a conventional trope in ancient Near Eastern carved ivories. She too addresses Jehu sardonically, "Do you come in peace?" or "Is everything okay?" (9:30), and taunts him as a Zimri, who also killed his king but whose rule only lasted seven days (1 Kgs. 16:9-20). Her harem eunuchs, sensing a power change in the wind, obey Jehu's command to throw her down from the window, where her blood splatters the walls and horses trample her. Jehu, whose appetite seemingly is not affected by her gruesome death ("he went in and ate and drank"), begrudgingly orders a burial for "the cursed woman" since she is a "king's daughter." Unfortunately, all that remains of Jezebel's body is her skull, feet, and hands, fulfilling Elijah's prophecy over her. Jehu even adds a coarser adage to the prophecy by noting that her corpse will be like *dung* on the field in Jezreel (9:30-37), most likely an allusion to the corruption of her name from *zebul* ("prince, nobility") to *zebel* ("dung").

Jehu's brutal rampage continues with his slaughter of Ahab's seventy "sons" in Samaria. Just as the eunuchs desert Jezebel, so do the rulers, the elders, and the guardians of the descendants of Ahab in Jezreel deliver the decapitated heads of Ahab's male kin to Jehu. On the road to Samaria, Jehu encounters forty-two relatives of the assassinated Judean king Azariah, who are also members of Ahab's lineage, and has them massacred. Finally arriving in the royal capital Samaria, Jehu eliminates the remaining offspring of Ahab's line (10:1-17). He then "with cunning" exterminates the prophets, priests, and worshipers of Baal and demolishes his temple. Just as Jezebel's corpse will be like "dung in the field," Baal's temple is reduced to "a latrine to this day" (10:18-27).

The Deuteronomistic evaluation of Jehu's rule is equivocal. On the one hand, Jehu is praised for wiping out Baal worship from Israel. God promises that his dynasty in Israel will continue to the fourth generation, and indeed his is the longest and most prosperous one in the northern kingdom. On the other hand, it also points out that Jehu did not follow God's torah with his heart. He did not turn from "the sins of Jeroboam," the two golden calves installed at Dan and Bethel (10:28-31). His rule concludes with a detail that "the LORD began to trim off parts of Israel," in which Jehu loses the area of the Transjordan to the Arameans. Whether or not this territorial loss results from Jehu's disobedience to the law is left for the reader to decide (10:32-33). However, the ninth-century prophecy of Hosea is more explicit: God will "punish the house of Jehu for the blood of Jezreel" (Hosea 1:4).

The southern kingdom still has links with the newly destroyed house of Omri in the person of Athaliah, mother of the slain king Ahaziah, daughter of either Ahab or Omri, and wife of Judah's king Joram (Jehoram) (2 Kgs. 8:18, 25-26). When she hears about Jehu's massacre, she begins her own assassination of the Judean royal family, threatening God's promise of an eternal dynasty for

David. However, she is thwarted by her daughter-in-law Jehosheba, who hides Ahaziah's son Joash for six years, while Athaliah rules Judah (2 Kgs. 11:1-30). In the seventh year, the priest Jehoiada, Jehosheba's husband according to 2 Chron. 22:11, stages a coup to return the legitimate king of the Davidic line to the throne. Athaliah hears the noise of the coronation and cries "Treason, treason," but she is put to death outside the temple grounds (11:4-16). Jehoiada enacts a covenantal renewal ceremony "between the LORD and the king and the people," whereupon the people demolish the altars and priest of the cult of Baal, which evidently was instituted during the intermarriage of Judah's kings with the house of Omri. The threatened line of David is now restored in the installation of the seven-year-old Joash after this period of illegitimate female rule (11:17-20).

According to the Dtr's regnal formula, Jehoash (Joash) has a prosperous rule in Jerusalem of forty years, although this may include the six years of Athaliah (836–798 BCE). Under the tutelage of the priest Jehoiada, he is faithful to YHWH, even though he does not eliminate the high places (12:1-3). The narrative about Joash's rule deals with his attempts to repair the temple and arrange for the workers to be financially compensated (12:4-16). However, when the Aramean king Hazael threatens Jerusalem, Jehoash has to deplete the temple and royal treasury that had been built up by his royal predecessors in order to prevent Hazael's attack. The formula concludes with Joash's assassination by his servants (12:12:17-21). According to 2 Chron. 24:23-27, Joash is killed for having murdered the son of Jehoiada, his earlier co-regent (see below). His son Amaziah succeeds him. (For a comprehensive study of 2 Kings 11–12, see Dutcher-Walls 1996.)

■ THE TEXT IN THE INTERPRETIVE TRADITION

According to Ephrem the Syrian, Jezebel paints her eyes and adorns her head (9:30) in order to seduce Jehu and become one of his wives. He links the episode with the story of Adonijah, who requests Abishag the Shunamite as wife, so that he might be elevated to the throne (1 Kgs. 2:17). According to Ephrem, Jehu would want Jezebel as wife to pacify his troubled and agitated new rule. Ephrem also contrasts Jezebel's ignominious death with that of her husband, Ahab. While Jezebel is trampled by horses and eaten by dogs (2 Kgs. 9:33-37), Ahab receives an honorable burial (1 Kgs. 22:37), because he repents from his sins (1 Kgs. 21:27-29) and she does not (Conti, 185–86).

According to Jewish tradition, the prophet Jonah is a disciple of Elisha, who commissions him to anoint Jehu as king. Athaliah's reign of terror is God's punishment of the Davidic dynasty for the extermination of the priests of Nob (1 Samuel 22). Just as Abiathar is the only son of Ahimelech to survive this slaughter, so is Joash the only son of Ahaziah to survive Athaliah's pogrom. After Jehoiada's death, Joash sets up an idol in the temple, but Jehoiada's son and high priest, Zechariah, bars his entry to the temple on the Day of Atonement, which also happens to be the Sabbath. Joash has Zechariah killed, and his death remains unavenged until Nebuzaradan, captain of Nebuchadnezzar's army, destroys Jerusalem. Before his servants kill him, Joash falls into the hands of the Syrians, who "abused him in their barbarous, immoral way" (Ginzberg 1956, 609–10).

The advent of feminist criticism in the late twentieth century focuses critical attention on the queens, Jezebel and Athaliah, whose portrayals as wives and mothers in these texts belie their formidable power and authority in their husbands' kingdoms (Solvang; Bowen; C. Smith 1998).

■ THE TEXT IN CONTEMPORARY DISCUSSION

These texts describe a regime change through violent assassinations. Our own contemporary world is no stranger to such violence, as seen in the political assassinations of Abraham Lincoln, John F. Kennedy, and Martin Luther King. Each period after such murders is marked by much social instability. The killings by Jehu are depicted as particularly motivated by religious zeal: "to wipe out Baal from Israel" (2 Kgs. 10:28). These texts highlight the acute dangers that arise from intense religious passions, namely, the intolerance of other religions, leading to their persecution and extermination in God's name. History already provides many cautionary tales of this religious intolerance: the Crusades and the extermination of indigenous religions by Spanish colonizers in South America and Native American religions by white settlers. We can also include the terrorist attacks by Islamic fundamentalists today. Is violence at the root of the monotheistic faiths? Does religious fervor have to lead to violence? Where are the voices that resist and critique this violence and move beyond mere tolerance, to learn about and respect other religions in their comprehension of the sacred?

2 Kings 13:1—17:41: Events Leading to the Fall of Israel

■ THE TEXT IN ITS ANCIENT CONTEXT

According to 2 Kgs. 10:30, YHWH declares that Jehu's dynasty in Israel will last to the fourth generation. Second Kings 13 focuses on the second and third generation of the house: Jehoahaz (c. 817–800 BCE, 13:1-9) and Jehoash/Joash (c. 800–784 BCE, 13:10-19). Both are condemned for following in "the sins of Jeroboam son of Nebat." Both regimes are plagued by military confrontations with Aram/Syria. The prophet Elisha appears for the last time during Joash's rule. Hearing news of Elisha's imminent death, Joash goes to him, weeping and crying out, just as Elisha did at Elijah's departure: "My father, my father! The chariots of Israel and its horsemen!" (13:15; cf. 2 Kgs. 2:12). Elisha commands Joash to perform a sign act with a bow and arrow to symbolize "the arrow of victory over Aram" at the battle of Aphek (13:17). However, because Joash only strikes the ground with the arrows three times, instead of five (13:18-19), his victory over the Arameans will be incomplete, keeping Syria as an ongoing player in the politics of Israel and Judah (see the Syro-Ephraimite War below). Even in death, Elisha's miraculous powers live on, raising a dead man to life when his corpse touches the bones in Elisha's grave (13:2-21).

The narrative regarding Jehoash/Joash continues in 2 Kings 14, highlighting the rule of the Judean king Amaziah (c. 798–769 BCE). As soon as he gains power, Amaziah executes the two men who assassinated his father Joash (12:20-21), but spares their children according to law of Deut. 24:16 (2 Kgs. 14:5-6). He then engages in a successful campaign against his southeastern neighbor Edom (14:7). However, he foolishly challenges Jehoash of Israel, who responds with a parable of the thorn bush and the cedar, warning Amaziah that any military encounter will be disastrous (on Jehoash's fable, see Solomon 1985). Amaziah engages in battle with Jehoash anyway, but Jehoash not only defeats and captures him but also strips the Jerusalem temple and royal palace of its treasuries (14:8-14). Amaziah is killed after he flees to his stronghold in Lachish (14:17-20) and is succeeded by his son Azariah/Uzziah (14:21-22).

During the fifteenth year of Amaziah's rule in Judah, Jeroboam son of Joash (Jeroboam II, c. 788–747 BCE) rules in Samaria, representing the fourth generation of the Jehu dynasty (14:23-28). Although he follows in the sins of his namesake, Jeroboam son of Nebat (Jeroboam I), his rule is a prosperous one of forty-one years in Israel. Fulfilling the word of the prophet Jonah, Jeroboam expands Israel's borders from Lebo-Hamath (upper Syria) to the Sea of Arabah (the ideal boundaries of Solomon's kingdom, 1 Kgs. 4:21; 8:65). The reign of his Judean counterpart, Azariah/Uzziah, is also a long one of fifty-two years (c. 792–740 BCE, 15:1-7). Dtr only gives him a qualified approval, because he does not remove the high places. Second Chronicles 26, however, greatly expands on Uzziah's rule and provides a reason for God afflicting him with leprosy, which is missing in 2 Kgs. 15:5. The Deuteronomic focus on the religious aspects of their monarchic rule obscures the fact that Israel and Judah under Jeroboam II and Azariah/Uzziah witnessed dramatic political and economic growth (Premnath, 43–98).

Representing the fifth generation of Jehu's dynasty, Jeroboam II's son Zechariah (c. 747 BCE) is not covered under God's prophecy of 2 Kgs. 10:30. His rule therefore only lasts six months and he is assassinated by Shallum (c. 747 BCE, 15:8-12), beginning a series of unstable regimes that will eventually climax in Israel's destruction. After only one month of rule, Shallum is killed by Menahem (c. 747–737 BCE, 15:13-22), a violent king credited with ripping open the pregnant women of a city that refused to surrender to him (15:16; cf. Cogan). During this time, the powerful Assyrian king Tiglath Pileser III (Pul in the Bible, c. 745–727 BCE) begins his westward expansion to gain access to the economic and military possibilities provided by the Mediterranean Sea. Levying a steep tax on the wealthy, Menahem offers "a thousand talents of silver" to forestall King Pul from attacking Israel, tribute that is confirmed in Assyrian accounts (Grabbe 2007, 134). Menahem is able to hold on to power for ten years when his son Pekahiah (c. 737–735 BCE) succeeds him at his death. Pekahiah rules only two years, when he is assassinated by one of his officers, Pekah (15:23-26; regarding the problematic dating of Pekah's rule, see Na'aman, 74–82). During Pekah's rule, Tiglath Pileser captures the Israelite territories of Gilead, Galilee, and all the land of Naphtali, and activates the initial deportations of Israel to Assyria (15:27-29; Younger, 206–8). Pekah himself will eventually be killed by Hoshea (15:30-31), but his narrative will continue in the account of the Syro-Ephraimite War in 2 Kings 16.

During Pekah's rule in Israel, Jotham (c. 759–743 BCE, 15:32-38) begins his administration in Judah when his father Azaraiah/Uzziah is stricken with leprosy (15:5). He is given a generally positive assessment by Dtr, which is expanded in 2 Chronicles 27. Dtr's judgment on his son, Ahaz, however, is quite negative for a Judean king, describing him as walking "in the way of the kings of Israel" in his idolatrous practices (16:1-4). Scholars have dated his rule variously: 727–715 BCE; 735–715 BCE; 743–735 BCE. Attempting to coerce Judah into joining their alliance against Tiglath Pileser III's expansionism, Kings Rezin of Aram/Syria and Pekah of Israel attack Judah in what is known as the Syro-Ephraimite War (16:5). In response, Ahaz petitions Tiglath Pileser himself to "rescue" him from his northern neighbors, becoming his vassal and sending him tribute. Tiglath Pileser responds by destroying Syria's capital city Damascus and exiling its upper classes (15:7-9).

Dtr greatly expands on Ahaz's covenantal infidelity by describing his commissioning and instillation of a new altar in the temple that represented his loyalty to Assyria (Sweeney 2007, 384–86). Ahaz will be succeeded by his son Hezekiah (16:10-20).

Having undergone a complex editorial process (Long, 180–83), 2 Kings 17 is a significant one in the DH, because it provides an extended theological rationale for the fall of Israel. It begins by describing its last days under king Hoshea (c. 732–722 BCE), who had rebelled against Tiglath Pileser's successor, Shalmaneser V of Assyria, and was subsequently imprisoned by him. After a three-year siege, Shalmaneser's successor, Sargon, conquers Samaria in 722/721 BCE and exiles its upper classes (17:1-6).

Dtr's theological commentary highlights the covenantal infidelity of Israel, who forsakes the God who brought them from slavery in Egypt to worship other gods (17:7-12). They refuse to listen to the prophets sent by God (17:13-15), and persist in the sin of Jeroboam son of Nebat (17:21-22). God therefore removes them "out of his sight," and Israel is exiled from their own land to Assyria "to this very day" (17:23). A later redactional addition will testify that Judah will suffer the same fate (17:19-20).

The chapter then narrates the consequences of the Assyrian policy of bringing in foreign populations to replace the exiles in Samaria (Oded). Because the Assyrians do not worship YHWH, God sends lions among them (17:24-25). The king of Assyria tries to deal with this problem by commanding one of the exiled priests be brought back to teach the foreigners "the law of the god of the land" (17:25-27). However, this priest originally hales from Bethel, one of the illegitimate sanctuaries established by Jeroboam I, implying that his teachings replicate the "sin of Jeroboam" among the people (17:28). Dtr then details the religious syncretism of the "people of Samaria," who will later be called Samaritans. They are ultimately judged as worshiping YHWH, but also as serving "their carved images" (17:29-41).

▉ THE TEXT IN THE INTERPRETIVE TRADITION

For the rabbis, Ahaz was an extremely wicked man (*Lev. Rab.* 30.3) who, among other things, seized schools and synagogues (11.7), and introduced the worship of Moloch. However, because he was the son (*Gen. Rab.* 63.1) and father (*Eccl. Rab.* 7; 15.1) of devout kings (*Sanh.* 104a), his place was secured in the world to come. In Milton's *Paradise Lost*, Ahaz is a devotee of one of the fallen angels "against the house of God," Rimmon the Syrian deity associated with Damascus (*PL* 1.467–75) (Baker 1992a, 27).

The early church father Ephrem the Syrian had a number of things to say about the final days of Elisha. Regarding his prophecy to Joash, "the Lord's arrow of victory" (13:17) for him "signifies our Lord and Savior hanging from the wood and giving up his spirit." When Elisha dies, the prophet Hosea takes his place as the head of the company of prophets, because the beginning of Hosea's oracles places him during the time of Jeroboam, son of Joash. The resurrection of the man who was tossed into Elisha's grave foretells the future resurrection of all those who have died (Conti, 197–99). Some church fathers used these stories to further their antisemitic views. Origen argues that in light of Jewish purity laws, especially the prohibition of touching dead beings, the miracle of resurrection of the man who touches Elisha's bones reveals "how unsuitable the Jewish interpretation is." John Chrysostom uses the example of Ahaz's sacrificing his son (16:3) and other examples of illegitimate cult to explain the cruelty of the Jews in condemning Christ (Conti, 200, 207).

Josephus's portrayal of the last six kings of Israel expands on their biblical depictions, making them more violent and more reckless in their dealings with Assyria (Begg).

■ The Text in Contemporary Discussion

In these chapters, Dtr provides us with a sustained rationale for why Israel was destroyed and its people exiled. It culminates in 2 Kings 17, which argues that throughout its history the northern kingdom abandoned YHWH to worship other gods. We must keep two things in mind when interpreting these chapters. First, Dtr is assessing the history of these kings *after the fact* from his exilic/postexilic social location. Israel was already destroyed, and Judah is not far behind. His explanation is filtered through experiences of hindsight. Second, the intent of his history is *theological*. There are many other reasons—military, economic, political, social—why Israel was destroyed, the most obvious being Assyria's brutal, overwhelming resolve to gain entry to the Mediterranean Sea. Nevertheless, for Dtr, Israel's destruction is an act of divine judgment because it failed to keep God's covenant.

Dangers in interpretation arise when one assesses history from the perspective of "the rear-view mirror." It is first and foremost *an* interpretation of events, not *the* interpretation of events. Moreover, *theological* rationales of calamitous events pose serious issues, particularly when the judgment is on a group other than one's own. For example, some German clergy asserted that the extermination of the Jews by the Nazis was God's punishment of the Jews (Sweeney 2008, 1–22). The destruction caused by recent natural events like tsunamis and hurricanes has been explained by religious fundamentalists as God's castigation for abortion, homosexuality, and feminism. Theological explanations are difficult to substantiate and often originate from the harmful gender, racial, or other ideologies regarding marginal groups. As such, they should be avoided.

2 Kings 18:1—20:21: The Reign of Hezekiah

■ The Text in Its Ancient Context

Along with David and Josiah, Hezekiah (c. 727/715–698/687 BCE) is one of the most highly acclaimed kings of Judah according to Dtr. Historians have tried to reconcile 2 Kings 18–20 with Assyrian sources about Sennacherib's invasion in 701 BCE, many regarding 2 Kgs. 18:13-16 as the only historically reliable part of the narrative: Sennacherib attacked and captured the fortified cities of Judah; Hezekiah submitted to him; Sennacherib demanded a huge tribute of silver and gold; and Hezekiah gave it to him. The rest of 2 Kings 18–20 has undergone a long traditioning process around this relatively historical piece (Grabbe 2007, 195–200; Grabbe 2003).

The Dtr introduction first describes Hezekiah's cultic reform to centralize worship in Jerusalem, anticipating Josiah's later one (18:1-4). Unlike many of the other Judean kings, Hezekiah removes the high places, pillars, and the sacred pole, a symbol of YHWH's wife Asherah (Dever), and a revered Mosaic relic, the bronze Nehustan (Num. 21:1-9). The recurrence of the word "trust/

rely" defines Hezekiah's reliance on God (18:5, 19-22, 24, 30; 19:10), transforming his story into a theological discourse on faith in YHWH (Brueggemann 2000, 493). This faith and confidence will be tested by the Assyrian envoys. Unlike his father, Ahaz, Hezekiah rebels against Assyria (18:7). However, the juxtaposition of Hezekiah's rule in Judah with the downfall of Hoshea and Israel (18:9-12) implies that Judah will not suffer the same fate, because Hezekiah holds fast to God, who was with him when he rebelled (18:6-7).

Nevertheless, the most historically reliable part of the story seems to challenge Dtr's commendation: Sennacherib's invasion in response to this rebellion, and Hezekiah's handover of tribute for Sennacherib's withdrawal (18:13-16). Instead of withdrawing, Sennacherib sends three officials, the Tartan, the Rabsaris, and the Rabshakeh (chief commander, chief eunuch, and chief cupbearer) to negotiate the surrender of Jerusalem. Details of this Assyrian encounter with Judean officials (Eliakim, Shebnah, and Joah) have parallels in Isaiah 36–37. The Rabshakeh skillfully articulates the shortcomings in Hezekiah's sources of trust. Relying on his ally Egypt is foolhardy, because Egypt is a "broken reed of a staff that will pierce the hand of anyone who leans on it" (18:21). Trusting in God's very self has been abrogated by Hezekiah's destruction of God's high places and altars in his centralization of worship (18:22). Even if Assyria gives Judah two thousand horses, Hezekiah has no riders to put on them, especially if he relies on Egyptian assistance (18:23-24). Finally, God's very self sends Assyria to destroy Judah (18:25). Each of these four arguments has a certain ring of credibility (Nelson, 238).

The Judean officials request the Rabshakeh to speak in the diplomatic language of Aramaic, not Hebrew, so that the populace will not hear his demoralizing words. However, the Rabshakeh arrogantly continues in Hebrew to address those doomed "to eat their own dung and drink their own urine" in a prolonged Assyrian siege (18:26-28). He tells them not to be deceived by Hezekiah into relying on God's deliverance. The gods of Hamath, Arpad, Sephaarvaim, Hena, and Ivvah were unable to save their citizens from Assyrian conquest. YHWH will likewise be unable to deliver Jerusalem (18:29-35). Upon hearing the officials' report on the Rabshakeh's words, Hezekiah sends them to consult the prophet Isaiah, who tells Hezekiah, "Do not be afraid," and that God will put a "spirit" in Sennacherib, so that he will hear a "rumor and return to his own land," where he will be killed (19:1-7).

In the next episode, Sennacherib does hear a report that the Egyptian pharaoh Tirhakah of Cush/Ethiopia has set out against him, but instead of returning to his own land, sends his messengers to intimidate Hezekiah again (19:8-13). Hezekiah then appeals to YHWH in the temple (19:14-19), and Isaiah delivers three oracles to him. The first is directed against Sennacherib, highlighting God's own divine power vis-à-vis the king's human arrogance and future humiliation (19:20-28). The second is a "sign" to Hezekiah that the agricultural fields devastated by Sennacherib's armies will recover in three years, and that a remnant will repopulate the land (19:29-31). The third prophesies that Sennacherib will not enter Jerusalem, because God will defend it for God's own and David's sakes (19:32-34). The chapter concludes with the "angel of the Lord" striking down 185,000 in the Assyrian camp and Sennacherib's returning to Assyria, where he is eventually killed by his sons while he is worshiping in the temple of his god Nisroch (19: 35-37). Hezekiah's trust in YHWH is thus vindicated.

The final two episodes about Hezekiah in 2 Kings 20 seem to describe events before Sennacherib's siege of Jerusalem, because Isaiah prophesies that God will add fifteen years to Hezekiah's life and deliver Jerusalem from the king of Assyria (20:6) and the royal treasury is still full (20:13; cf. 18:15-16). The first episode describes Hezekiah's life-threatening boil (20:7), Isaiah's command that he put his life in order before his death, and Hezekiah's fervent prayer to God to remember his faithfulness and devotion (20:1-3). God responds through Isaiah that God will heal Hezekiah, add years to his life, and deliver Jerusalem from the Assyrians. Isaiah then orders Hezekiah to take a lump of figs and apply it to the boil, to heal it (20:4-7).

The second episode involves envoys of King Merodach-baladan, a Babylonian king who heard Hezekiah was ill. Hezekiah welcomes them and shows them all the wealth in his house, armory, and storehouses (20:12-13). Hezekiah may have entered into an anti-Assyrian alliance with the Babylonian king, which would explain why Sennacherib was not able to capture Jerusalem in a lengthy siege. He would not have been able to divide his forces to deal with conflict on the western side of his empire, and with Merodach-baladan on his eastern flank (Sweeney 2007, 413). However, upon hearing of Hezekiah's overt display of his wealth to these foreigners, Isaiah prophesies that in the future Babylon will come and seize everything in his house, and exile some of his sons, who will become eunuchs—those who cannot bear royal sons—in the palace of the king of Babylon (2:14-18). Although Hezekiah verbally acknowledges the prophecy as good, his inward thought, "Why not, if there be peace and security in my days" (20:19), reveals a negative side to this positively portrayed character: his disregard for disastrous events in Judah and his dynasty after his own peaceful and secure reign.

▌THE TEXT IN THE INTERPRETIVE TRADITION

Rabbinic legends describe Hezekiah as banishing the ignorance of the law that had occurred under his father Ahaz, to the point of ordering that anyone who does not occupy himself with the torah is subject to the death penalty. Needless to say, eventually one could search from Dan to Beer-sheba and not find a single person ignorant of torah. The illness that afflicted Hezekiah was punishment for "peeling off" the gold from the temple to send to Sennacherib (2 Kgs. 18:16). Therefore, the disease that plagued Hezekiah caused his skin to "peel off." Hezekiah is praised for having the traditions of Isaiah, Ecclesiastes, Song of Songs, and Proverbs put in writing.

Rabbinic legends narratively expand on characters that are not developed in 2 Kings. Sennacherib's vast army is described in great detail. He himself was contemptuous when he first saw Jerusalem, wondering why he bothered to gather armies and conquer other lands to gain it. It was smaller and weaker than the other cities he had subdued. Two of the officials sent to meet the Assyrian negotiators, Shebnah and Joah (cf. 2 Kgs. 18:18), were actually opponents of Hezekiah's rebellion. They shot a dart into the Assyrian camp containing a letter, saying: "We and the whole people of Israel wish to conclude peace with thee, but Hezekiah and Isaiah will not permit it." When Shebnah and his supporters left Jerusalem to join the Assyrians, the angel Gabriel manipulated Sennacherib into thinking that Shebnah was fooling him. Sennacherib then ordered Shebnah tied to a horse and dragged to death (for more on Hezekiah, see Ginzberg 1998, 266–77).

Hezekiah is chiefly remembered in Christian tradition for his piety and for the extraordinary answer to his prayer for a stay of death (e.g., Cyril, *Lectures* 2.15; 12.22). In New England Puritanism, he was sometimes described as a type of Christ (e.g., Thomas Frink, *A King Reigning in Righteousness* [1758]) and as a moral example for temporal magistrates (Baker 1992b, 352). The poem "Destruction of Sennacherib," by Lord Byron, in his *Hebrew Melodies* (1815), depicts the Assyrian king's perspective on the siege.

■ THE TEXT IN CONTEMPORARY DISCUSSION

We are presented in 2 Kings 18–20 with an idealized king, a paradigm of piety with an abiding trust in YHWH. God was with Hezekiah wherever he went, prospering in his domestic and foreign policies: his centralization of worship and his rebellion against Assyria. He becomes the total opposite of his father, Ahaz, before him and his son Manasseh after him. Nevertheless, we will soon see that the alternation between good king/bad king is a deliberate Dtr construction. Historical and archaeological reconstructions of the period reveal that Hezekiah's cultic centralization and rebellion against Assyria were foolhardy and had disastrous consequences for the economic and social landscape of Judah. Moreover, we will soon see that the supposedly "evil" king Manasseh actually helped Judah recover from his father's disastrous foreign and domestic policies.

Dtr creates a history "after the fact," from the social location of a community that has experienced the trauma of exile and needs an explanation. The explanation Dtr provides is a theological one: the people were unfaithful to God's covenant. We must keep this in mind as we try to relate Hezekiah's story to our own times. Placing one's trust in God in decisions regarding foreign or domestic policies must work in tandem with dedicated analysis of the broader social and political issues surrounding these policies.

2 Kings 21:1—23:30: The Reigns of Manasseh and Josiah

■ THE TEXT IN ITS ANCIENT CONTEXT

Dtr sets before us two stereotypical models of kingship in these chapters: one utterly "bad" (Manasseh), the other categorically "good" (Josiah). Neither really resembles his historical personage. Dtr describes "evil" Manasseh as reversing all the cult reforms that his father Hezekiah had instigated, comparing him to the absolute worst king of the northern kingdom, Ahab (21:3, 9). His religious abominations even exceeded those of the pagan nations that YHWH drove out of the land (12:9, 11). Because of Manasseh's colossal failures to keep Deuteronomic law (Deut. 12:29-31; 18:9-12; 19:8-10), an unknown prophet declares that YHWH will "wipe Jerusalem as one wipes a dish," casting the remnant off, giving them over to the hands of their enemies (2 Kgs. 21:12-16).

Although blamed for the eventual fall of Judah, Manasseh's lengthy rule (698/687–642 BCE) was historically much more beneficial to the nation than Dtr presents. Following the conventions of ancient Near Eastern historiography, Dtr alternates bad and good kings before and after Manasseh: Ahaz (bad); Hezekiah (good); Manasseh and Amon (bad); Josiah (good) (Evans, 497). Because Josiah is the "golden boy" of the Deuteronomists, Manasseh is set up as his foil. Although he is presented as one of the "good" kings, Hezekiah's rebellion against Assyria was politically and economically disastrous. Sennacherib ravaged the countryside, and Hezekiah lost valuable land in the Shephelah (Finkelstein and Silberman, 251–64). Inheriting a weakened and humiliated nation, Manasseh was left with the task of rebuilding the state after this catastrophe.

Archaeology reveals that Judah experienced a remarkable resurgence under Manasseh's long reign (Grabbe 2007, 201). Collaborating with networks of village clan-based leaders, whose authority was diminished under Hezekiah, Manasseh began to restore those areas of the countryside that were ravaged by Sennacherib. Providing these networks with economic autonomy, his renewal of the rural areas permitted the veneration of the popular agrarian gods, Baal and Asherah, which would later provoke the wrath of the Deuteronomists (Finkelstein and Silberman, 264–67; Halpern 1991, 60–65). Working his position as vassal to his advantage, Manasseh's connections with Assyrian markets enriched his treasuries, trading in luxury goods from Arabia and exporting olives from the Judean highlands for the mass production of oil in the Assyrian-ruled city of Ekron (Finkelstein and Silberman, 267–70; Gitin, 84–87). Despite the biblical condemnation of his regime, Manasseh's rule was a peaceful and prosperous one for Judah. He is succeeded by his son Amon, who is assassinated by court servants, and Amon's son Josiah is placed on the throne by "the people of the land" (21:19-26).

Josiah's birth and rule were already foretold in 1 Kings, when Jeroboam I was offering incense at Bethel, one of his illegitimate sanctuaries. A man of God prophesies against the altar, "A son shall be born to the house of David, Josiah by name; and he shall sacrifice on you the priests of the high places who offer incense on you, and human bones shall be burned on you" (1 Kgs. 13:2). Dtr exalts Josiah among the other Judean kings by describing him as "walking in *all* the way of his father David," and, like Moses and Joshua, "he did not turn aside to the right or to the left" (2 Kgs. 1:2; Deut. 5:32; Josh. 1:7). There was no king before or after him "who turned to the LORD with all his heart, with all his soul, and with all his might, according to the law of Moses" (23:25).

During repairs on the temple, the high priest Hilkiah finds "the book of the law." Hilkiah reports its "discovery" to Josiah, who hears the words of this book as a prophetic judgment from God, "because our ancestors did not obey the words of this book" (22:3-13). Like Moses and Joshua (Exodus 24; Joshua 24), Josiah renews the covenant with the people (23:2-3) and sets about purging the land of idolatrous worship. He begins first with Jerusalem and its environs (23:4-14) and then proceeds to Bethel, the site of the prophecy in 1 Kgs. 13:2, which foretells the destruction of the altar that Jeroboam I erected. Josiah not only tears down the altar but also defiles it by having human bones burned on it, fulfilling the earlier prophecy before moving on to other cultic sites in Samaria (23:15-20). Josiah then centralizes his liturgical reform by instituting the national celebration of Passover held in Jerusalem (22:21-23).

Scholars believed that the "book of the law" was an earlier form of the book of Deuteronomy. However, because of its similarities to early seventh-century Assyrian vassal treaties, they now think that Deuteronomy was composed in the seventh century, just before or during Josiah's reign. Deuteronomy is thus not an ancient scroll that is suddenly "discovered" in the temple but the composition of a Deuteronomistic school (Römer, 45–65). In spite of Josiah's good deeds, he is not able to reverse God's judgment against Judah and Jerusalem because of Manasseh's offenses (23:26-27).

Josiah is killed by Neco, pharaoh of Egypt, at Megiddo, and his son Jehoahaz is anointed king by the people of the land (23:28-30).

■ THE TEXT IN THE INTERPRETIVE TRADITION

Second Chronicles 33:11-13 has Manasseh captured by the Assyrians, who imprison him in Babylon. He repents of his sins, and God returns him to Jerusalem, where he eliminates the foreign gods and restores the worship of YHWH in the land. The remorse of the one who was considered to be the cause of Jerusalem's destruction provided hope and encouragement to the postexilic returnees to Yehud. The apocryphal work Prayer of Manasseh claims to be the one he utters in 2 Chron. 33:13, although this is unlikely. (See "Prayer of Manasseh" in this commentary.)

Manasseh's contrition is expanded by Josephus (*Ant.* 10.40–46), who concludes that Manasseh "underwent such a change of heart in these respects and lived the rest of his life in such a way as to be counted a blessed and enviable man after the time when he began to show piety toward God" (*Ant.* 10.45). Rabbinic legends describe the king of Babylon casting Manasseh into a heated oven, whereupon Manasseh remembers a prayer his father Hezekiah had taught him about calling on YHWH during times of tribulation. However, angels stop his prayer from reaching God, but God, knowing that he would be shutting the doors to anyone who repents if he did not accept Manasseh's penance, receives Manasseh's prayer through a small opening under the throne of his glory. A wind carries Manasseh back to Jerusalem (Ginzberg 1998, 279–80; Hulbert).

According to rabbinic legends, Josiah sought prophetic confirmation after hearing God's judgment against Jerusalem. He consulted Huldah, not Jeremiah, because he believed that a woman would be more compassionate than a man and deliver a more temperate oracle (*b. Meg.* 14b). Knowing that the temple would be destroyed, he hid the ark of the covenant and all its accessories to protect them from enemy desecration (*Yoma* 52b). Although he instituted a purge of foreign worship, Josiah was deceived by the people, who hid their idolatrous ways from his inspectors (*Lam. Rab.* 1.53). Because of this deception and for disobeying the counsel of Jeremiah to allow the Egyptians passage through his land, Josiah was struck by three hundred darts in the clash between him and the Egyptians (Ginzberg 1998, 282–83). Josephus remarks that Jeremiah composed a lament for Josiah's funeral (*Ant.* 10.78).

■ THE TEXT IN CONTEMPORARY DISCUSSION

The biblical portrayals of Manasseh and Josiah are ancient examples of demonization and angelization. Demonization is a rhetorical strategy of depicting rival individuals or groups as embodying all that is considered evil or wicked in a particular context. Angelization is its very opposite, representing an individual or group as all good or virtuous. Neither characterization adequately exemplifies the person or groups in question. Demonization is often used to cast targeted individuals or groups as the other. We have seen that Dtr attributes the destruction of Jerusalem to Manasseh by demonizing his rule, even though he historically helped Judah recover from the disastrous foreign policies of his father Hezekiah, who is angelized by Dtr in spite of them.

We often demonize or angelize individuals in our own time. The Bush Administration demonized Saddam Hussein in order to invade Iraq in the 1990s. The Nazis demonized a whole ethnic group, the Jews, in order to justify the Holocaust. Pro-choice advocates are often contemptuously regarded as "baby-killers." The poor are often vilified as "parasites" and "on the dole." Liberals often label conservatives as "rigid," "ignorant," and "intolerant." Many Roman Catholics "angelized" their parish priests, until the sex scandals that have rocked the church revealed an insidious side to their behavior. Evangelicals have angelized many televangelists until revelations of their financial or sexual corruption have surfaced.

Demonization or angelization of persons or groups close off discussion and further inquiry that would reveal a more unbiased, truthful state of affairs. Our examination of Manasseh and Josiah cautions us to recognize demonization or its opposite when they occur in our own time, and to examine such stereotypical characterizations more fully.

2 Kings 23:31—25:30: The Final Days of Judah and Its Kings

▌ THE TEXT IN ITS ANCIENT CONTEXT

Although in the larger context of Egyptian and Babylonian imperial politics it was probably inevitable that Judah would be conquered and destroyed by the Babylonians, Dtr still judges its demise theologically. The final kings of Judah—Jehoahaz, Jehoiakim, Jehoiachin, and Zedekiah—all "did what was evil in the sight of the LORD as their ancestors had done" (23:32, 37; 24:9, 19). Therefore, God's very self sends their enemies—Chaldeans, Arameans, Moabites, and Ammonites—to attack Judah to fulfill the words of the prophets, because God refuses to forgive Judah for the "sins of Manasseh" (24:2-4). God's wrath is unequivocal for Dtr: "Jerusalem and Judah so angered the LORD that he expelled them from his presence" (24:20).

Jehoahaz (609 BCE) rules Jerusalem three months before he is imprisoned at Riblah by Pharaoh Neco, the same king who had his father Josiah killed (23:29-33). After levying a large tribute tax on Judah, Neco installs Josiah's son and Jehoahaz's half brother Eliakim as a puppet king in Jerusalem, and changes his name to Jehoiakim (608–597 BCE). In 605 BCE, the Babylonian king Nebuchadnezzar defeats the Egyptians at the battle of Carchemish in Syria and Judah becomes a vassal of Babylonia. Jehoiakim submits to Babylonian rule for three years, but he seizes his chance to rebel, probably after Babylon's costly battle with the Egyptians in 601 BCE. Recovering two years later, Nebuchadnezzar strikes back against Judah with the aid of Judah's neighbors Aram, Moab, and Ammon. Jehoiakim conveniently dies during Nebuchadnezzar's siege of Jerusalem in 597 BCE, and his unfortunate eighteen-year-old son Jehoiachin succeeds him (24:8-9).

Jehoiachin surrenders to Nebuchadnezzar, who carries him off to Babylon along with the queen mother, his harem, the officials, the elite of the land, and anyone in positions to instigate a rebellion (24:10-16). Nebuchadnezzar appoints Jehoiachin's uncle Mattaniah as his puppet king and changes his name to Zedekiah. Nebuchadnezzar's conquest, deportation, and installation of "a king of his liking" in 597 BCE are confirmed in the Babylonian Chronicle (*ANET* 563–64).

Twenty-one-year-old Zedekiah becomes Judah's final king (597–586 BCE). His rule is hampered by several factors, the first being the brain drain of Judah's top officials in the 597 deportation, leaving second-tier advisors. Second, he is appointed by the colonizer, while the "legitimate" king, Jehoiachin, is in exile. Third, his administration is plagued by the pro-Egyptian and pro-Babylonian partisan politics at court. These politics are particularly evident in the book of Jeremiah (see Jeremiah 27–28; 37–38). Unfortunately, Zedekiah sides with the pro-Egyptian party and rebels against Nebuchadnezzar, who besieges Jerusalem in 587 and ultimately conquers it in 586 BCE. Zedekiah is captured when he tries to escape, and is brought to Nebuchadnezzar at Riblah. Zedekiah witnesses the death of his sons before he himself is blinded and taken in chains to Babylon (24:20b—25:7). The temple is burned, and all the treasures that were not seized in 597 are taken away. Furthermore, the remaining elites are exiled in a second deportation (25:9-17) (on the two forced migrations, see Ahn). The only ones allowed to remain are "some of the poorest people of the land," who probably constituted the crucial agrarian economic base of Judah (25:12; cf. 24:14).

To establish some stability in the land, the Babylonians appoint a prominent Judean, Gedeliah, as governor at the new capital, Mizpah. However, Ishmael and his men, most likely anti-Babylonian partisans, assassinate Gedeliah and flee to Egypt to escape Babylon's wrath (25:22-26). Their story is recounted in greater detail in Jeremiah 40–43.

The book of 2 Kings ends ambiguously, with the release of King Jehoiachin from prison by King Evil-merodach of Babylon. He is given a privileged seat at the foreign king's table and a pension for as long as he lives (25:27-30). Although the Davidic dynasty has been disgracefully terminated in Judah, the fact that its exiled king is freed from prison and attains some sort of status, albeit in a foreign court, can be interpreted as a sign of hope for a renewed kingship.

▌ THE TEXT IN THE INTERPRETIVE TRADITION

Leviticus Rabbah 19.6 describes the "abominations" of Jehoiakim in 2 Chron. 36:8 variously. He disobeys the prohibitions of Lev. 19:19 and Deut. 9:11 by wearing garments that mix wool and linen together. He is guilty of disguising his circumcision; tattooing the names of idols on his body; having incestuous relations with his mother, daughter-in-law, and father's wife; and executing men to violate their wives and seize their wealth. When Nebuchadnezzar comes up against Jerusalem, he tells the Sanhedrin, who meets him at Daphne of Antioch, that he only wants the insurgent Jehoiakim. If the Sanhedrin deliver him up, Nebuchadnezzar will withdraw. Like the city of Abel Beth-maacah, which saved itself by surrendering Sheba son of Bichri (2 Sam. 20:14-22), the Sanhedrin seize Jehoiakim and slide him down the city walls of Jerusalem into the hands of the Babylonians. Nebuchadnezzar takes him in chains around the cities of Judah, kills him, and puts his carcass on an ass. Another version states that Jehoiakim is cut into olive-sized pieces and thrown to the dogs.

Jehoiachin fares better than his father in *Leviticus Rabbah* 19.6. When Nebuchadnezzar tells the Babylonians that he has installed Jehoiachin as Jehoiakim's replacement, he is told a proverb: "Do not rear a gentle cub of a vicious dog, much less a vicious cub of a vicious dog." Regretting his decision, he then informs the Sanhedrin at Daphne of Antioch that if they deliver Jehoiachin to him, he will withdraw from attacking the temple. When Jehoiachin hears this, he takes the keys of the temple to the roof and bids God to take them, at which point a hand from heaven seizes them. Another version says that the keys remain suspended in midair. Nebuchadnezzar then puts Jehoiachin into solitary confinement. The Sanhedrin begins to worry that the house of David will cease, if Jehoiachin does not beget a son. They devise a plan involving Nebuchadnezzar's wife, Shemirah, to persuade her husband to let Jehoiachin have sexual relations with his wife. When they are about to have sex, the wife notices the onset of her menstrual period. Because Jehoiachin obeys the law and refrains from sex during her impurity, God pardons all his sins.

■ THE TEXT IN CONTEMPORARY DISCUSSION

The book of Kings thus ends the sordid history of Israel's failure to keep God's torah. It is not history as we understand it today, describing "what really happened." Rather, it is a selective history, told from a biased perspective. The Deuteronomistic History records that from the moment the Israelites crossed the Jordan and settled in the land (Joshua and Judges), they were seduced away from their covenanted partner, YHWH, to worship the gods of the land. They even wanted kings "like the other nations," rejecting YHWH as king (1–2 Samuel). First and Second Kings continue the story with wise king Solomon, blinded by his love for foreign women and their gods, the division of the kingdom into Israel and Judah, the "sin of Jeroboam," which ultimately led to Israel's fall, and then to that of Judah, who refused to learn from Israel's mistakes. For Dtr, the end of this glorious nation is the people's continual infidelity to their God and God's covenant.

The conclusion to the book of Kings prompts us to think about the way we also construct history. All histories are written from a selective partisan perspective, even those that claim to be objective. One commonly hears the saying "History is written by the victors," and this is true. The book of Kings compels us to wonder about the voices that are not recorded in its stories: those of the poor, the marginalized, the soldiers who lost their lives or those who were maimed in the continual wars of the kings, the citizens who starved during the horrible sieges, and the peasants whose crops were crushed or seized by invading armies.

What about histories in our own time? Do American history books adequately tell the stories of the indigenous peoples whose lands were appropriated in the name of Manifest Destiny; or the horrors of slavery and the Civil War, the most shameful period of our history? Does this history focus primarily on European immigrants, ignoring those from Asia, Africa, South America, and the Caribbean? What we learn from the book of Kings is that its history is not disinterested, is not nonpartisan. How can we critically examine the histories of peoples, groups, and nations in our own time?

Works Cited

Ahn, John J. 2011. *Exile as Forced Migrations: A Sociological, Literary, and Theological Approach on the Displacement and Resettlement of the Southern Kingdom of Judah.* BZAW 417. Berlin: de Gruyter.

Baker, David W. 1992a. "Ahaz." In *A Dictionary of Biblical Tradition in English Literature*, edited by David L. Jeffrey, 27. Grand Rapids: Eerdmans.

————. 1992b. "Hezekiah." In *A Dictionary of Biblical Tradition in English Literature*, edited by David L. Jeffrey, 352–53. Grand Rapids: Eerdmans.

Bartel, Roland. 1975. "Melville's use of the Bible in *Billy Budd*." In *Biblical Images in Literature*, edited by Roland Bartel, James S. Ackerman, and Thayer S. Warshaw, 30–64. Nashville: Abingdon.

Barzel, Hillel. 1975. "The Biblical Layer in Franz Kafka's Short Story 'A Country Doctor.'" In *Biblical Images in Literature*, edited by Roland Bartel, James S. Ackerman, and Thayer S. Warshaw, 89–102. Nashville: Abingdon.

Baumgarten, Murray. 1992. "Abishag." In *A Dictionary of Biblical Tradition in English Literature*, edited by David L. Jeffrey, 6–8. Grand Rapids: Eerdmans.

Beach, Eleanor F. 2005. *The Jezebel Letters: Religion and Politics in Ninth-Century Israel*. Minneapolis: Fortress Press.

Begg, Christopher T. 1996. "The Last Six Kings of Israel According to Josephus: Ant 9,228–278." *ETL* 72:371–84.

Berlin, Adele. 1982. "Characterization in Biblical Narrative: David's Wives." *JSOT* 23:69–85.

Bird, Phyllis A. 1997. *The Harlot as Heroine: Narrative Art and Social Presupposition in Three Old Testament Texts*. Minneapolis: Fortress Press.

Bowen, Nancy R. 2001. "The Quest for the Historical Gebirâ." *CBQ* 63:597–618.

Branch, Robin G. 2009. *Jeroboam's Wife: The Enduring Contributions of the Old Testament's Least-Known Women*. Peabody, MA: Hendrickson.

Brueggemann, Walter. 2000. *1 and 2 Kings*. Smyth & Helwys Bible Commentary. Macon, GA: Smyth & Helwys.

————. 2001. *Testimony to Otherwise: The Witness of Elijah and Elisha*. St. Louis: Chalice.

Cogan, Mordechai. 1983. "'Ripping Open Pregnant Women' in Light of an Assyrian Analogue." *JAOS* 103:755–57.

Conti, Marco, ed. 2008. *1–2 Kings, 1–2 Chronicles, Ezra, Nehemiah, Esther*. Ancient Christian Commentary on Scripture, Old Testament 5. Downers Grove, IL: InterVarsity Press.

Curzon, David. 1994. *Modern Poems on the Bible: An Anthology*. Philadelphia: Jewish Publication Society.

Dever, William G. 2005. *Did God Have a Wife? Archaeology and Folk Religion in Ancient Israel*. Grand Rapids: Eerdmans.

Dutcher-Walls, Patricia. 1996. *Narrative Art, Political Rhetoric: The Case of Athaliah and Joash*. Sheffield: Sheffield Academic.

————. 2004. *Jezebel: Portraits of a Queen*. Interfaces. Collegeville, MN: Liturgical Press.

Evans, Carl D. 1992. "Manasseh, King of Judah." *ABD* 4:496–99.

Feldman, Louis H. 1994. "Josephus' Portrait of Elisha." *NovT* 36:1–28.

Finkelstein, Israel, and Neil A. Silberman. 2001. *The Bible Unearthed: Archaeology's New Vision of Ancient Israel and the Origin of Its Sacred Texts*. New York: Free Press.

Gaines, Janet H. 1999. *Music in the Old Bones: Jezebel through the Ages*. Carbondale: Southern Illinois University Press.

Garsiel, Moshe. 1993. "The Story of David and Bathsheba: A Different Approach." *CBQ* 55:244–62.

————. 2002. "Revealing and Concealing as a Narrative Strategy in Solomon's Judgment (1 Kings 3:16-28)." *CBQ* 64:229–47.

Ginzberg, Louis. 1956. *Legends of the Bible*. Philadelphia: Jewish Publication Society of America.

————. 1998. *The Legends of the Jews*. Vol. 4, *From Joshua to Esther*. Baltimore: Johns Hopkins University Press.

Gitin, Seymour. 1997. "The Neo-Assyrian Empire and Its Western Periphery: The Levant, with a Focus on Philistine Ekron." In *Assyria 1995: Proceedings of the 10th Anniversary Symposium of the Neo-Assyrian Text Corpus Project, Helsinki, September 7–11, 1995*, edited by S. Parpola and M. R. Whiting, 77–103. Helsinki: The Neo-Assyrian Text Corpus Project.

Grabbe, Lester L., ed. 2003. *"Like a Bird in a Cage": The Invasion of Sennacherib in 701* BCE. JSOTSup 363. London: Sheffield Academic.

———. 2007. *Ancient Israel: What Do We Know and How Do We Know It?* New York: T&T Clark.

Halpern, Baruch. 1991. "Jerusalem and the Lineages in the Seventh Century BCE: Kinship and the Rise of Individual Moral Liability." In *Law and Ideology in Monarchic Israel*, edited by Baruch Halpern and Deborah W. Hobson, 11–107. JSOTSup 124. Sheffield: JSOT Press.

———. 2001. *David's Secret Demons: Messiah, Murderer, Traitor, King*. Grand Rapids: Eerdmans.

Hulbert, W. G. 2008. "Good King and Bad King: Traditions about Manasseh in the Bible and Late Second Temple Judaism." *Stone-Campbell Journal* 11:71–81.

Ipsen, Avaren E. 2008. "Solomon and the Two Prostitutes." In *Marxist Feminist Criticism of the Bible*, edited by Roland Boer and Jorunn Okland, 134–50. Sheffield: Sheffield Phoenix.

Ishida, Tomoo. 1999. "Solomon's Succession to the Throne of David." In *History and Historical Writing in Ancient Israel: Studies in Biblical Historiography*, 102–36. Leiden: Brill.

Jobling, David. 1991. "Forced Labor: Solomon's Golden Age and the Question of Literary Representation." *Semeia* 54:57–76.

Knoppers, Gary N. 1995. "Aaron's Calf and Jeroboam's Calves." In *Fortunate the Eyes That See: Essays in Honor of David Noel Freedman in Celebration of His Seventieth Birthday*, edited by Astrid B. Beck, Andrew H. Bartelt, Paul R. Raabe, and Chris A. Franke, 92–104. Grand Rapids: Eerdmans.

Lang, Bernhard. 1983. *Monotheism and the Prophetic Minority: An Essay in Biblical History and Sociology*. Sheffield: Almond.

Lasine, Stuart. 1989. "The Riddle of Solomon's Judgment and the Riddle of Human Nature in the Hebrew Bible." *JSOT* 45:61–86.

Lassner, Jacob. 1993. *Demonizing the Queen of Sheba: Boundaries of Gender and Culture in Postbiblical Judaism and Medieval Islam*. Chicago: University of Chicago Press.

Long, Burke O. 1991. *2 Kings*. FOTL. Grand Rapids: Eerdmans.

Long, Jesse C., Jr., and Mark Sneed. 2004. "'Yahweh Has Given These Three Kings into the Hand of Moab': A Socio-Literary Reading of 2 Kings 3." In *Inspired Speech: Prophecy in the Ancient Near East. Essays in Honour of Herbert B. Huffmon*, edited by John Kaltner and Louis Stulman, 253–75. London: T&T Clark.

Moore, Megan B., and Brad E. Kelle. 2011. *Biblical History and Israel's Past: The Changing Study of the Bible and History*. Grand Rapids: Eerdmans.

Na'aman, Nadav. 1986. "Historical and Chronological Notes on the Kingdoms of Israel and Judah in the 8th Century BC." *VT* 36:71–92.

Nelson, Richard D. 1987. *First and Second Kings*. IBC. Atlanta: John Knox.

Oded, Bustenay. 1979. *Mass Deportations and Deportees in the Neo-Assyrian Empire*. Wiesbaden: Reichert.

Olyan, Saul. 1984. "*Hašalôm*: Some Literary Considerations of 2 Kings 9." *CBQ* 46:652–68.

Petersen, David L. 1981. *The Roles of Israel's Prophets*. Sheffield: JSOT Press.

Premnath, D. N. 2003. *Eighth Century Prophets: A Social Analysis*. St. Louis: Chalice.

Provan, Iain W. 1995. *1 and 2 Kings*. Peabody, MA: Hendrickson.

Pyper, Hugh S. 1993. "Judging the Wisdom of Solomon: The Two-Way Effect of Intertextuality." *JSOT* 59:37–53.

Rentería, Tamis H. 1992. "The Elijah/Elisha Stories: A Socio-Cultural Analysis of Prophets and People in Ninth-Century B.C.E. Israel." In *Elijah and Elisha in Socioliterary Perspective*, edited by Robert B. Coote, 75–126. Atlanta: Scholars Press.

Römer, Thomas C. 2007. *The So-Called Deuteronomistic History: A Sociological, Historical, and Literary Introduction*. New York: T&T Clark.

Schulte, Hannelis. 1994. "The End of the Omride Dynasty: Social-Ethical Observations on the Subject of Power and Violence." *Semeia* 66:133–48.

Seow, Choon-Leong. 1999. "The First and Second Books of Kings: Introduction, Commentary, and Reflections." In *The New Interpreter's Bible*. Vol. 3, *1 and 2 Kings, 1 and 2 Chronicles, Ezra, Nehemiah, Esther, Tobit, Judith*, edited by Leander E. Keck, 1–295. Nashville: Abingdon.

Smith, Carol. 1998. "'Queenship' in Israel? The Cases of Bathsheba, Jezebel and Athalia." In *King and Messiah in Israel and the Ancient Near East: Proceedings of the Oxford Old Testament Seminar*, edited by John Day, 142–62. Sheffield: Sheffield Academic.

Smith, Mark S. 2002. *The Early History of God: Yahweh and the Other Deities in Ancient Israel*. Grand Rapids: Eerdmans.

Smith, Morton. 1971. *Palestinian Parties and Politics That Shaped the Old Testament*. New York: Columbia University Press.

Snyder, Josey B. 2012. "Jezebel and Her Interpreters." In *Women's Bible Commentary*, edited by Carol A. Newsom, Sharon H. Ringe, and Jacqueline E. Lapsley, 180–83. Louisville: Westminster John Knox.

Solomon, Ann M. V. 1985. "Jehoash's Fable of the Thistle and the Cedar." In *Saga, Legend, Tale, Novella, Fable: Narrative Forms in Old Testament Literature*, edited by George W. Coats, 126–32. JSOTSup 35. Sheffield: JSOT Press.

Solvang, Elna. 2003. *A Woman's Place Is in the House*. JSOTSup 349. New York: Continuum.

Stahlberg, Lesleigh C. 2009. "From Biblical Blanket to Post-Biblical Blank Slate: The Lives and Times of Abishag the Shunamite." In *From the Margins 1: Women of the Hebrew Bible and Their Afterlives*, edited by Peter S. Hawkins and Lesleigh C. Stahlberg, 122–40. Sheffield: Sheffield Phoenix.

Sweeney, Marvin A. 2007. *1 and 2 Kings: A Commentary*. OTL. Louisville: Westminster John Knox.

———. 2008. *Reading the Hebrew Bible after the Shoah: Engaging Holocaust Theology*. Minneapolis: Fortress Press.

Wolde, Ellen van. 1995. "Who Guides Whom? Embeddedness and Perspective in Biblical Hebrew and in 1 Kings 3:16-28." *JBL* 114:623–42.

Yee, Gale A. 1992. "Jezebel." *ABD* 3:848–49.

Younger, K. L., Jr. 1998. "The Deportations of the Israelites." *JBL* 117:201–27.

1, 2 CHRONICLES

Alejandro F. Botta

Introduction

In the same way that Deuteronomy offers a second presentation of the law, the books of Chronicles offer a second recounting of the history of Israel. Christian Bibles include 1 and 2 Chronicles among the "historical books" after 1 and 2 Kings. In the Hebrew Bible and in Jewish tradition, both books of Chronicles constitute a unity, with the name of *dibrê hayyāmîm* ("the events of the days") and are found in the Writings (*ketubim*), the third section of the Hebrew Bible. Chronicles had already achieved authoritative status by the second century BCE, but with the exception of Jerome, the church fathers didn't pay much attention to Chronicles. Neither did it enjoy a prominent place in Jewish tradition. The great Jewish scholar Don Isaac Arbarbanel (1437–1509) stated, "my transgressions do I mention today; I have never read this book in my life and never researched its issues—never before today!" (Kalimi 2009a, 236).

The book itself, like most of the literary works composed before the Hellenistic period, does not include a title or the name of its author. The name given to it by the Jewish sages and church fathers reflects their intention to describe or qualify its content.

Authorship and Relationship with Ezra and Nehemiah

The Talmud attributes part of the authorship of Chronicles and Ezra-Nehemiah to Ezra, and part of it to Nehemiah (*b. Bat.* 15a). Medieval Christian scholars were not so certain. Hugh of St. Cher (c. 1200–1263 CE), a French Dominican, affirmed that the author was unknown, although he trusted the veracity of its content (Saltman, 55).

In the nineteenth century, the great majority of biblical scholars considered the book of Chronicles to form a unity with Ezra and Nehemiah. Nowadays, pioneered by the work of Sarah Japhet

(1968; 1993) and Hugh G. M. Williamson (1977), the consensus has moved into considering the book of Chronicles and Ezra-Nehemiah as two different and independent works. The major arguments behind such a shift are differences in language and style peculiarities (Japhet 1968) and the "substantive differences in theology, purpose, and perspective" (Klein 2006, 10) between Chronicles and Ezra-Nehemiah. Immediate divine retribution, a central theological motif in Chronicles, is not that relevant in Ezra-Nehemiah. The almost complete disregard for the exodus tradition and the Mosaic tradition is not as significant in Chronicles as it is in Ezra-Nehemiah. In Chronicles, there is hope of a future reunification with the northern kingdom (2 Chr. 30:1-31), something absent in Ezra-Nehemiah. The "Levitical sermons," a prominent feature of Chronicles, are completely absent in Ezra-Nehemiah. The most recent major commentaries on Chronicles by Gary Knoppers (2003) and Ralph Klein (2006) have both adopted such a position.

Date

There is a certain agreement among scholars that Chronicles is a postexilic composition. But as Klein states, "the evidence for a more specific date within that period is thin and ambiguous" (2006, 13). The suggested dates by scholars range from 520 BCE to 160 BCE. Chronicles doesn't indicate any Hellenistic influence, so there is some consensus to date the book during the Persian period (539–332 BCE) (Kalimi 2005a, 65).

Literary Characteristics

Chronicles begins with a long genealogical section focused on biblical characters who are significant for the author's theological purposes. Genealogies fulfill various functions in the Bible. Some are meant to show the relationship between Israel and the neighboring nations (Gen. 10:1-32; 19:36-38; 22:20-24; 25:1-6); others are used to bridge the temporal gap between events (Gen. 5:1-32; 11:10-27; Ruth 4:18-22); and others to bring together traditions from different origins (Gen. 5:1; 6:9) (Wilson 1977; Johnson 1988, 77–82). One of the characteristics of ancient historiography was the inclusion of discourses or speeches. As the Greek historian Thucydides (fifth century BCE) stated regarding the uses of speeches in his history, "the speeches are given in the language in which, as it seemed to me, the several speakers would express, on the subject under consideration, the sentiments most befitting the occasion" (*History of the Peloponnesian War* 1.22). Chronicles includes several speeches and prayers: Solomon's prayer at the dedication of the temple (2 Chron. 6:14-42); Jehoshaphat when facing the Ammonites and Moabites (2 Chron. 20:6-12); and a number of speeches labeled by Gerhard von Rad as "Levitical sermons" (2 Chron. 15:2-7; 16:7-9; 19:6-7; 20:15-17, 20; 29:5-11) (von Rad 1966, 269–76). These speeches and sermons are a valuable source of information about Chronicles' theological perspectives.

Chronicles as Legitimate Historiography

With the emergence of history as a scientific discipline under the leadership of figures like Leopold von Ranke (1795–1886), the positive valorization of Chronicles by the church fathers and medieval scholars suffered a strong blow. A more positive attitude toward the Chronicler was developed during the second half of the twentieth century under the influence of scholars like Gerhard von Rad (1901–1971) and Martin Noth (1902–1968). Contemporary scholarship tends to accept Chronicles as a valid historiographical work (Graham, Hoglund, and McKenzie; Kalimi 2005a; 2005b). As Japhet (1993, 32) states, "A consideration of the work's relevant features, such as aim, plan, form, and method, must lead to the conclusion that Chronicles is a history, an idiosyncratic expression of biblical historiography." The Chronicler acts as a historian when he gathers material and sources about the past of his community, decides what is significant for his time, and connects diverse events from his sources to produce a coherent narrative about the past. The difference between a mere past event and a historical event is, after all, how significant that event is for the present community. As Isaac Kalimi (2009b, 192) states, Chronicles "represent the principle of 'each generation with his own historiography and historian.'... Chronicles is the 'right' composition, 'the true one,' for its time, place, and audience."

Sources

Chronicles abounds in citations of works used by the author to compose his narrative. The book of the kings of Israel and Judah is cited several times, although sometimes with a slightly different name (2 Chron. 16:11; see 20:34; 25:26; 27:7; 28:26; 32:32; 33:18; 35:26; 36:8); there is also a mention of the midrash of the books of Kings (2 Chron. 3:22; 24:27). The Chronicler also refers to prophets or prophetic records like the acts of Samuel the seer, the acts of Nathan the prophet, the acts of Gad (1 Chron. 29:29), the prophecy of Ahijah, and the visions of Iddo (2 Chron. 9:29). The Chronicler is also familiar with the genealogical information provided by the books of Genesis, Exodus, Numbers, Joshua, Samuel, and Ruth. There is a citation of what is written "in the law of the Lord" (1 Chron. 16:40), which possibly refers to the Pentateuch; and a reference to a book of laments, unknown to us, that included a "lament of Josiah" (2 Chron. 35:25). The author seems to know the books of Isaiah (2 Chron. 28:16-21), Jeremiah (2 Chron. 36:21), and Zechariah (2 Chron. 36:9). The Chronicler also used information from lists (1 Chron. 6:1-15), and three canonical psalms (Psalms 96; 105; 106) are cited in 1 Chronicles 16. Without being exhaustive, this list of sources shows evidence of a dedicated historian at work.

1 Chronicles 1:1—9:44: Genealogical Registry of Israel

■ THE TEXT IN ITS ANCIENT CONTEXT

The genealogical register of Israel is further divided into subsections, which will be listed below.

Israel's Ancestors (1:1—2:2)

The first chapter of Chronicles is based on genealogical information from the book of Genesis. The author distinguishes an antediluvian generation (1:1-23) and a postdiluvian generation (1:24—2:2), similar to Assyrian and Babylonian cosmogonic genealogies. The Chronicler begins the genealogy with Adam in order to emphatically place the people of Israel in the context of universal history. "Indeed, one can only appreciate the experience of Israel within its land if one has some understanding of lands and peoples relevant to Israel and how they are related to Israel" (Knoppers 2003, 295).

Judah's Lineage (2:3—4:23)

This section consists of three parts: (a) 2:3-55, the genealogies of the tribe of Judah; (b) 3:1-24, the house of David; and (c) 4:1-23, additional genealogies of the house of Judah. The first part (2:3-55) stresses both the divine election of Judah and God's intolerance toward unfaithfulness as exemplified in the case of Er, who "was wicked in the sight of the Lord, and he put him to death" (v. 3), and of Achar, "the troubler of Israel who transgressed in the matter of the devoted thing" (v. 7). The importance of Ram (2:9-17), who is not the firstborn but occupies the first place on the list, is due to his ancestral relationship to David. In 2:13-15, David is listed as the seventh son of Jesse (according to 1 Sam. 16:6-9; 11-13; 17:13-14, Jesse had only four sons). Later tradition adopted the Chronicler's view, as represented in the Dura-Europos fresco (Kalimi 2009a, 123–32). David's sisters are only mentioned here (2:16-17).

The descendants of Caleb are listed in 2:18-24. The first part of the genealogy (2:18-20) deals with Bezalel, a silversmith (see Exod. 31:2; 35:30), who although belonging to a period prior to David, is associated with David and the tabernacle in view of the future construction of the temple by Solomon. The second part (2:21-24) establishes a connection between Judah and a group of descendants of Gilead. It follows the descendants of Jerahmeel (2:25-41), and an additional list of descendants of Caleb (2:42-55).

David's nineteen sons are enumerated (3:1-9), as are the kings of Israel (3:10-16) and the postexilic generation (3:17-24). The extension of David's genealogy to such a late period reflects the importance of David's descendants even during the restoration period (see Haggai 2). The best known of the genealogies contained in 4:1-23 is the one dedicated to Jabez (4:9-10) and his prayer granted by God. The Hebrew version of this prayer presents some difficulties and perhaps would be best translated, "if you blessed me and enlarged my borders, and if your hand might be with me, and that you would extend lands of pasture." This way, the greatest honor Jabez deserves could be attributed to the extension of his territory due to prayer and not to military force. The two genealogical sections of Judah (2:3-55 and 4:1-23) "form an envelope around the genealogy of David and his descendants, who are the centerpiece of the tribe of Judah in chapter 3" (Klein 2006, 142).

Descendants of Simeon (4:24-43)

The tribe of Simeon comes after that of Judah due to geographical proximity. The cities that are listed in 4:28-33 were considered part of Judah from ancient times (see Josh 19:2-8). In times when the people of Israel are dispersed and the prophets are proclaiming the future restoration of Israel (Jer. 16:14-15; 23:7-8; Zeph. 2:7-9), "the author revives the ideal of a larger tribal federation" (Knoppers 2003, 374).

The Tribes of Transjordan: Reuben, Gad, and Manasseh (5:1-26)

This section enumerates the descendants of Reuben (5:1-10), Gad (5:11-22), and the half-tribe of Manasseh (5:23-26). At the beginning of this section, the Chronicler clarifies the reason why Reuben, Jacob's firstborn, does not come first in his genealogy (see Gen. 29:31-32). The author's interest in demonstrating that God often discards the firstborn (see 1 Chron. 2:3; 26:10) seems to emphasize the fact that before God there are no natural rights, only the benefit of divine election. The section dedicated to Gad (5:11-22) points to the theology of the Chronicler when explaining the reason for military success. They cried to God in the battle (see 2 Chron. 14:11-15; 20:5-30; 32:20-21) and God granted their wish (see 1 Chron. 12:19; 15:26; 2 Chron. 25:8; 32:8) because they trusted in him (see 2 Chron. 32:10); therefore, the Hagrites and all those who were with them "were given into their hands" (5:20). The section dedicated to Manasseh (5:23-26) explains the reason for the exile of the northern tribes (see 2 Kgs. 17:7-23). Israel had transgressed against God (see 2 Chron. 36:14), idolatry being one of the main issues; thus God sends a foreign army to punish his people (see 2 Chron. 36:17), and the consequence is the exile (see 2 Chron. 36:18-20).

Descendants of Levi (6:1-81)

The section is divided into two parts: the genealogy of the Aaronide priests and other Levites (6:1-53), and the settlements of the Levites (6:54-81). The lineages of David and Aaron (see 1 Chron. 2:10-17; 3:1-16) are the only cases in which the generations are enumerated from the patriarchal era until the exile. The importance the Chronicler attributes to the Levites is evident in the number of verses dedicated to the tribe of Levi. Together with Judah and Benjamin, they capture the attention of the Chronicler in the genealogy section.

Tribes of the Central Mountainous Region (7:1-40)

Surprisingly, in the genealogies of both Manasseh and Ephraim, there is no mention of any stay in Egypt. Manasseh appears to be associated with Aramean groups in Canaan, from where he takes his wife (7:14-19), leaving aside the tradition of the stay in Egypt and emphasizing the continuity of the occupation of his territory (the northern part of the territory east of river Jordan). Something similar happens with the genealogy of Ephraim (7:20-29), who according to the Genesis narrative is born and dies in Egypt (Gen. 41:50-52; Exodus 16). However, in Chronicles, Ephraim is in no way associated with Egypt. Rather, Ephraim is presented as originally from and settled in Canaan. The narrative of the murder of his sons as the result of a conflict with Gath's men and the foundation of three cities by his daughter Seerah, "who built both Lower and Upper Beth-horon, and Uzzen-sheerah" located in Canaan, does nothing but reinforce the local Canaanite emphasis, which the author of Chronicles places on Ephraim's sons. In a similar vein, Joshua is presented as already established on the land, in contrast to the conqueror role he is given in the book that bears his name. His leadership in the conquest is omitted in Chronicles.

Additional Descendants of Benjamin (8:1-40; 9:1a)

This new chapter, concerning the tribe of Benjamin, is structured in two sections: a list of Benjamite ancestral houses (8:3-32), and a genealogy of the family of Saul (8:33-40). While the previous section dedicated to Benjamin was centered on the military census (7:6-12), the current chapter is centered on geographical distribution.

The Postexilic Community (9:1b-44)

On concluding the descendants of Jacob (1 Chronicles 1–8), the Chronicler adds a final section listing the inhabitants of Jerusalem, paying special attention to the priestly families (9:10-13), the Levitical families (9:14-16), and the gatekeepers (9:17-33).

▌ THE TEXT IN THE INTERPRETIVE TRADITION

The fact that many of the names found in this section are not found in other books of the Hebrew Bible led the Jewish sages to argue that the people listed in the genealogies are actually people mentioned in other parts of the Bible, but under different names. The medieval Jewish scholar David Kimḥi commented that "even though what is written here cannot be found in any of the prophetic books you should not ask how Ezra [the author of Chronicles according to Kimḥi] knew all these things . . . for they are all traditions" (Berger, 69). Theodoret of Cyrus commented that the purpose of the genealogies was to establish that "all human beings are derived from a single man and how our Savior, the Son of God descended from it." Some chapters deserved especial attention by Theodoret, like the genealogy of Judah, because of its connection with the genealogy of Jesus (Conti, 246).

▌ THE TEXT IN CONTEMPORARY DISCUSSION

The genealogical section has a provisionary summary in the opening of chapter 9: "So all Israel was enrolled by genealogies; and these are written in the Book of the Kings of Israel" (9:1). It is likely that its main purpose is to delimit the essential character of exilic Israel; those who cannot prove their genealogically "pure" connection with the ancestors become suspicious. As with many contemporary communities of faith, the exilic community struggled to set standards that would clearly establish who belonged to the community and who did not. In times of crisis, when what is perceived as the core set of beliefs and practices is threatened, those criteria that determine who is and who is not a member of the community tend to become more specific and enforceable. Could this be the intention of the God who claimed through Isaiah of the exile, "I am about to do a new thing; now it springs forth, do you not perceive it?" (Isa. 43:19). Do statements of faith or genealogies serve or hinder the expected inclusive character of the community of the kingdom, here and now?

1 Chronicles 10:1—12:40: Death of Saul and David's Coronation

▌ THE TEXT IN ITS ANCIENT CONTEXT

The death of Saul (10:1-14) is paralleled in 1 Sam. 31:1-13. For the Chronicler, the reign of Saul is more than a prologue to the history of David. Saul's unfaithfulness will be remembered throughout the Chronicler's work (2 Chron. 26:16, 18; 28:19, 22; 29:5-6, 19; 30:7; 33:19; 36:14). It is summarized in 10:13, where Saul dies for disobeying the LORD by not keeping his commands and for seeking guidance from a medium instead of the LORD.

The account of the death of Saul and his sons begins after 9:35-44. The battle takes place on Mount Gilboa, and the results are disastrous. Saul is terrified of what might happen to him if he falls into enemy hands. His apparent self-inflicted death on the battlefield is the only case of suicide in the Bible (see 2 Sam. 1:10, where Saul dies instead at the hand of an Amalekite). The Chronicler replaces "his armor-bearer and all his men" from 1 Sam. 31:6 with "all his house died together," highlighting the end of the dynasty (10:6).

This is the only place in Chronicles where Yahweh directly intervenes to make a dynastic change. The Chronicler clearly points out that the death of Saul is a punishment for his sins. As Klein states, "What happened in the transition from Saul to David . . . was divine retribution at work, and even more, divine providence" (Klein 2006, 291), two essential elements of Chronicles' understanding of history.

King David's coronation is described in 11:1—12:40. Even though the material for this section comes from 2 Samuel 5, the Chronicler presents it with intent to highlight the divine intervention in favor of David. During Saul's reign, David established his power center in Hebron (1 Sam. 30:31), and according to 2 Sam. 2:4, this is exactly the place where he is anointed king over the house of Judah. In Chronicles, all Israel is "together with" David, while in Samuel the tribes only "came" to David. Then David made a covenant with all the elders who had declared their union with the house of David: "we are your bone and flesh." According to the Chronicler's theological perspective, all this happened in accordance with what God had already announced through Samuel (1 Sam. 15:28; 16:1-3).

The new dynasty needs a capital in neutral territory, and Jerusalem is the chosen place (11:4-9). Once again, it is "all Israel" who marches instead of "the king and his men" (2 Sam. 5:6). From this moment and until today, Jerusalem will be the city of David par excellence. The verse "David became greater and greater, for the LORD of hosts [*sabaoth*] was with him," summarizes the essential elements of David's ascent to the throne (1 Chron. 11:9 // 2 Sam. 5:10); "popular and divine election coalesce in establishing David's rule" (Knoppers 2004, 575).

▌THE TEXT IN THE INTERPRETIVE TRADITION

Rabbinic commentaries on the death of Saul focus on the question of whether it is legitimate to take one's life when the alternative is facing unbearable pain or torture. The rabbis portrayed the transition from the house of Saul to the house of David as inevitable, irrespective of Saul's behavior, because the "scepter shall not depart from Judah" (Gen. 49:10). Saul's reign was, therefore, provisional and did not have any future. Gregory of Nazianzus compared the transition from Jebus to Jerusalem with the Christian transition from temple to word (Conti, 248). Augustine read the destiny of David as an example of how futile it is to resist the will of God. Commenting on all the men who come to Hebron, Augustine states: "Obviously it was of their own will that these men made David king; the fact is clear and undeniable. Nevertheless, it was God, who effects in human hearts whatsoever he wills, who wrought this will in them" (*Admonitions and Grace* 14.45, in Conti, 248).

▌THE TEXT IN CONTEMPORARY DISCUSSION

Around the year 1000 BCE, Jerusalem became the capital of the nation of Israel and its religious and political center. Since then, the "City of David," which never ceased to be the religious center of the Jewish people, has witnessed wars; famine; destruction and rebuilding; and foreign occupation by Greeks (Hellenistic), Romans, Byzantine Christians, Muslims, the Ottomans, the British, and Jordanians throughout the centuries. It was not until 1967 that Jerusalem was reunited and reestablished as the capital city of Israel. Today, the ancestral Jewish claim is challenged by Islam, which after its expansion out of the Arabian Peninsula and violent conquest of Jerusalem in 637 CE, occupied the land and built the Al-Aqsa Mosque (completed in 705 CE) on top of the Temple Mount. Alternative narratives are sometimes not equally legitimate and should be examined thoroughly, but is the loss of human life in these successive occupations worth being right?

1 Chronicles 13:1—16:43: Transferring the Ark to Jerusalem

▊ THE TEXT IN ITS ANCIENT CONTEXT

First Chronicles 13:1-4 contains an episode not found in the book of 2 Samuel. It introduces the first failed attempt to transfer the ark of the covenant to Jerusalem, which could in no way be the religious center of Israel if the ark was not there. David's procedure indicates his role as popular leader. It is not by royal decree that the decision is made, but rather after consulting with the commanders and leaders. Such a move needed to have the support of all Israelites, and their priests and Levites (13:1-2). The festive occasion, a narrative climax, precedes the tragedy that follows—from general rejoicing to experiencing the fear of divine mystery. Uzzah, who with all good intentions tries to stop the ark from falling, is killed by God and causes quite a stir (13:10). David retracts his original idea as a response to the uncontrollable divine action, and decides not to take the ark "into his care into the city of David" (13:13). Rather, he takes it to the house of Obed-edom the Gittite. Paradoxically, the ark ends up in the house of a Philistine at the service of the royal household. Contrary to David's fears, "the LORD blessed the household of Obed-edom and all that he had" (13:14).

In 2 Samuel, the first attempt to take the ark to Jerusalem is immediately followed by a second try, this time successful (2 Sam. 6:12-19). In 2 Sam. 6:12, the transfer is triggered by the news that David receives of the Lord's blessing of the house of Obed-edom. In Chronicles, David's religious zeal is presented as the initial cause of this new attempt. According to Knoppers, the Chronicler's accounts of David's attempt to retrieve the ark "ultimately ratify the historical primacy, central status, and continuing privileges of the Jerusalem Temple" (2004, 593).

The Chronicler points out the distinction between the Levites and the "descendants of Aaron," the Aaronide priests (15:4), and then sets out the list of Levites according to their families (Kothar, Merari, Gershom, and so forth): "no one but the Levites were to carry the ark of God" (15:2). In 2 Samuel, the ark is transferred by David, while in Chronicles it is a collective endeavor in which the elders of Israel and the military leaders also take part. Chronicles emphasizes that the Levites are the ones who carry the ark, followed by the main strata of the Israelite society, the military, civilian, and religious groups.

The organization of worship that follows (16:4-42) has no parallel in the Deuteronomistic history and can be attributed to the Chronicler's composition. Once again, David is the one to name ministers, to invoke—literally to "remember"—praise, and to thank the Lord. As a corollary to the above description, the Chronicler includes a song of thanksgiving and praise ordered by David, "by Asaph and his kindred" (16:7-38). The reference to Asaph is important, as the texts that mention him in place of Heman or Ethan are considered very ancient. The psalm of the Chronicler includes parts of Psalm 105 (vv. 1-5); 96 (vv. 1-3); and 106 (vv. 47-48). By including these postexilic psalms, "the Chronicler establishes a continuity between the worship life established by David and that of his own day" (Klein 2006, 370).

■ THE TEXT IN THE INTERPRETIVE TRADITION

The unexpected death of Uzzah while transporting the ark demanded an explanation. David Kimhi suggested that it was David's mistake to try to carry the ark on a wagon (Num. 7:9 states that sacred objects had to be carried on shoulders) and proposes that David reasoned that God's command-ment was only valid for the time of the wilderness (Berger, 126). Salvian the Presbyter stated that Uzzah "was undutiful in his very act because he went beyond his orders," and because "even what seems to be a very little in fault is made great by the injury to God," he deserved his punishment (Franke, 344).

■ THE TEXT IN CONTEMPORARY DISCUSSION

The ark narrative seems to value the sacredness of objects more than human life. Uzzah's good intentions expressed in his attempt to prevent the ark from falling from the wagon do not mitigate God's anger and subsequent reaction. A contemporary commentator justifies God's behavior by stating that "the fate of Uzzah is a fearful warning against over-familiarity with God. His attitude to the thing should have been as reverent as his attitude to the Person" (Wilcock, 67). I disagree. Uzzah's literary killing (of course, gods do not kill people) justifies the death of another innocent victim, adding to the long list of religion-based (literary and real) murders.

1 Chronicles 17:1—21:30: David's Kingdom Is Consolidated

■ THE TEXT IN ITS ANCIENT CONTEXT

Nathan's oracle (17:4-14) is of fundamental importance for the development of the concept of covenant between God and Israel. In both Samuel and Chronicles, Nathan's oracle is preceded by an introduction (1 Chron. 17:1-2; 2 Sam. 7:1-3). The Chronicler omits the second part of 2 Sam. 7:1, "the LORD had given him rest from all his enemies around him," and substitutes the rhetorical question in Samuel—"Are you the one to build me a house to live in?" (2 Sam. 7:5)—with a nega-tion: "You shall not build me a house to live in" (1 Chron. 17:4). This clarifies that God is not against the construction of the temple, but rather against the man who was ready to begin the construction. God offers the reasons by means of the prophet, explaining that since leaving Egypt, God has lived in a tent and tabernacle. Both of these are synonymous and contrast with "house," which indicates a construction with walls. The passage then turns from the negative statement (it won't be David who builds the temple) to the positive one: it will be God who builds the house of David to assure his descendants, and it will be from these descendants that the person who will build the temple will come (17:7-15 // 2 Sam. 7:8-16). God's covenant with David will be perpetuated in Solomon, from whom God will never withdraw his steadfast love (17:13)—the opposite of what happened with Saul, David's predecessor.

David responds to Nathan's oracle with a prayer (17:16-27), which consists of two parts: 17:16-22 and 23-27. The first responds to the content of the first part of Nathan's prophecy: God's benevolence toward David (vv. 7-8). David responds, praising God for his promise to establish David's house, and the enumeration of God's promise to Israel (vv. 9-10a). David also refers to the exodus, conquest, and the covenantal relationship between God and Israel (vv. 20-22). The second part of the prayer (vv. 23-27) claims the fulfilling of God's promise on the establishment and continuity of the Davidic dynasty.

Chapters 18–20 present a summary of David's battles against the Philistines, Moabites, Ammonites, and Arameans based on 2 Samuel 8–21. In what follows, David orders a census and acquires the land to build the temple (21:1—22:1 // 2 Sam. 24:1-4, 8-25). The Chronicler follows the narrative of 2 Samuel in this case as well, noting, however, that it was not God who incited David to "go, count the people of Israel and Judah" (as in 2 Sam 24:1) but "Satan," who perhaps shouldn't be understood as the devil but as "an emissary of the deity carrying out God's punishment of Israel" (Stokes, 106).

▋▌ THE TEXT IN THE INTERPRETIVE TRADITION

Eusebius of Caesarea, commenting on Nathan's prophecy, suggests that Solomon is not the subject of the prophecy, or even the subsequent Davidic kings, who didn't last, but the Messiah ("Christ" in Eusebius's mind), "whose kingdom continues and will continue lasting for endless time" (Conti, 260). After the destruction of the second temple by the Roman army in 70 CE, Jewish interpreters also projected into the messianic era some of the promises to David: "More than God wishes to dwell in a house, He wishes to dwell in Israel's hearts. It is the function of the Messiah to make the hearts of Israel the true House of HaShem" (Eisemann 1987, 248). Regarding the coronation of David (20:2), Kimhi comments on how David could stand a crown that weighed a talent of gold, mentioning previous medieval interpreters that assumed that actually the crown was suspended over his head (the precious stone on top of it was a drawing stone, keeping the crown in the air), but concluding that David wore the crown only for brief periods, therefore being able to withstand its weight.

▋▌ THE TEXT IN CONTEMPORARY DISCUSSION

The project to build a temple, faced by a prophetic reminder of the continuous presence of the God of Israel with his people and with David, makes it clear that God doesn't need a house, and that God is happy with a mobile structure (tent, tabernacle). Communities of faith spend fortunes to improve their "temples." The transformation from "sacred places" to "sacred hearts" (hearts are also mobile!) as proposed above by Moshe Eisemann is a healthy development within religious traditions. Once fiercely attached to certain sacred real estate and ready to wage savage wars to defend or conquer those places, such a movement focuses on the inner presence of God instead of his territorial presence in a place of worship. Paul writes, "Our body is a temple of the Holy Spirit within you" (1 Cor. 6:19). Would it be more in accordance with the divine will to reallocate all the resources spent on "houses of worship," in "sacred places," toward enriching the lives of those sacred vessels that are human beings? It is noticeable that, as described in Revelation (21:22), there is no temple in the new Jerusalem.

1 Chronicles 22:2—27:34: Preparation for Building the Temple

■ THE TEXT IN ITS ANCIENT CONTEXT

This section is structured around David's decisions before his death regarding the building of the temple. Chapter 22 consists of three sections: verses 2-5 describe David's initial preparations; verses 6-16, the charge to Solomon; and verses 17-19, his command to the leaders of Israel. Each of these sections has a rhetorical center—David's thoughts (v. 5); David's words to Solomon (vv. 7b-16); and his words to the leaders (vv. 18-19). Each of the following subsections begins with "David said" or "David commanded," emphasizing David's leadership in the whole project. In this way, Nathan's oracle in 1 Chron. 17:11-14 begins to be fulfilled: "I will raise up your offspring after you, one of your own sons, and I will establish his kingdom. He shall build a house for me, and I will establish his throne forever." In this project, it will not be the Israelites who will be subjected to forced labor (as Solomon would do in 1 Kings 5:27), but rather "aliens residing in the land." The term *gerim* is used in Chronicles when referring to the Canaanites who remained in Israel (2 Chron. 2:16); 8:7-10) as free men with limited legal rights. The description of Solomon as "young and inexperienced" is in harmony with the description of him in 1 Kings 3:7, a young child "who does not know how to go out or come in" (see also 1 Chron. 29:1, where David describes him as "young and inexperienced"). Rehoboam is the other king to whom a similar description applies ("young and irresolute," 2 Chron. 13:7), which suggests that these are not mere descriptive terms but rather pejorative reflections of the immaturity that characterizes both kings.

The changes in the obligations of the Levites after the construction of the temple are explained in 23:26-28. Because they will no longer need to transport the tabernacle, they are assigned additional tasks established in the Pentateuch (23:25-26) as assistants to the Aaronide priests, emphasizing the subordination of the Levites to the priests (23:28-32). Music is central to the worship service and here related to the task of worship prophets. It seems evident that Levites also played this role (see 2 Kings 23:2 // 2 Chron. 34:30).

The army is organized in twelve divisions (27:2-15), each of them of consisting of 24,000 men. All the chiefs are part of the list of the heroes of David (2 Sam. 23:8-11; 1 Chron. 11:10–30). Jashobeam of the tribe of Judah is one of the sons of Judah, and is assigned to lead the first division during the first month (Nisan = March–April). He is also named commander in chief of the army during that period. In a similar fashion, all commanders for the rest of the months are listed.

■ THE TEXT IN THE INTERPRETIVE TRADITION

A midrash reports that God says to David: "'If you were to build it, it would stand eternally, and never be destroyed.' And David said to Him, 'Would this not be all the good?' But God answered him, 'I know that [Israel] will one day sin before Me. I intend to pour My anger upon the [physical] building [rather than on the people themselves, for that reason I do not want a temple which can never be destroyed]" (Yalkut Shimoni to Samuel 145; interpolations by Eisemann 1987, 288).

Some Christian interpreters focused especially on 22:9-10, stating that the reign of Solomon (whose name means "peaceable") was not that long, came to an end, and that the name Solomon was also given to Christ ("he is our peace," Eph. 2:14) (Theodoret of Cyrus, in Conti, 264). Eusebius also argued that Nathan's prophecy (22:10) was really fulfilled by Jesus (*Proof of the Gospel* 6.12, in Conti, 264).

▮ The Text in Contemporary Discussion

The allocation of such a large amount of materials and human effort to the construction of a place of worship makes us wonder: What is the best way to allocate the resources of religious communities? A symbol of power and prestige for the Jerusalem elite, the temple would hardly serve in any way the well-being of the rest of the population, and it reminds us of the failed intention of Gen. 11:4—"let us make a name for ourselves; otherwise we shall be scattered abroad upon the face of the whole earth." David's existential needs (a memorable building, an everlasting lineage) are the literary reflection of our human "unbearable lightness of being."

1 Chronicles 28:1—29:30: Solomon's Investiture

▮ The Text in Its Ancient Context

Although chapters 28–29 relate Solomon's enthronement, the central figure is David. David gathers all Israel's officers (28:1), David says (28:2), David provides (29:1), David says (29:10, 20), David calls to bless the Lord (29:20). This version is different from the story in 1 Kings 1–2, where the people play a mere anecdotic role (see 1 Kings 1:39b-40). In these two chapters, their role is fundamental.

David's speech (28:2-10) focuses on three topics: the construction of the temple, Solomon's divine election, and an exhortation to keep the commandments of God. In the same way that Moses could not enter the promised land and it fell to Joshua to lead in the final possession of this promised land, it will be Solomon and not David who will lead the construction of the temple. The promise of a lasting kingdom for Solomon, which in 1 Chron. 17:4 is unconditional, appears conditioned here depending on his effort to keep God's commandments and ordinances. The conditional character of the divine promise extends to the leaders of all Israel (28:8). From the perspective of the postexilic community, it is clear that the motive by which the Davidic dynasty had been displaced and the people taken into exile was the king and his leaders' lack of observance of the divine commandments. In the same way that the plans of the tabernacle were revealed to Moses and then drawn (Exod. 25:9, 40), so too the plans of the temple were revealed to David and then drawn up (28:2, 12, 18-19). The difference between the times of Moses and the Chronicler is that Moses receives the revelation orally, while the revelation to David is in writing (28:19). For the postexilic community, the inspired word has become the inspired text. David becomes not only the architect of the temple but also the one who dictates the order of service and establishes the hierarchical order of the staff who serve the temple. Even if Solomon is the builder, David is the intellectual author of the whole project.

David's prayer (29:10-19) contains three parts: the doxology (vv. 10b-13), the presentation and dedication of the voluntary offering to God (vv. 14-17), and the supplication (18-19). David asks God that Solomon may faithfully uphold "your commandments, your decrees, and your statutes," a clear reference to the Torah, so the temple may be built.

If it were not for the narrative in 1 Kings 1–2 describing the way Solomon reaches the throne, it would be impossible to understand the bloody family conflicts and palace intrigues that facilitated his ascent to the throne in the narration of the Chronicler (29:20-25). The Chronicler adds the offering of sacrifices by "all the assembly" (29:21) to the narrative of 1 Kings, pointing to the unity of the people in support of the new king ("and all Israel obeyed him," 29:23).

The Chronicler then presents a summary of David's reign (29:26-30), highlighting David's reign over "all Israel" (29:26) without mentioning the fact that while he reigned in Hebron, the territory under his command covered only the tribe of Judah (see 1 Kgs. 2:11). In 29:28, he points out that David achieved everything a king could wish and died "in a good old age, full of days, riches, and honor."

◼ THE TEXT IN THE INTERPRETIVE TRADITION

John of Damascus interpreted God's refusal to allow David to build the temple as a clear indication of the need to separate the political from the religious office. He writes, "Emperors have not preached the word to you, but apostles and prophets, shepherds and teachers" (*On Divine Images, Second Apology* 12, in Conti, 270). Augustine used 1 Chron. 28:9 to argue for the choice of free will, but also maintained that God's grace does not depend on it (*On Grace and Free Will II*, in Conti, 271). Bede interpreted the measures of the temple allegorically. Its height, one 120 cubits, was connected with the pouring of the Spirit onto the same number of men (Conti, 271).

◼ THE TEXT IN CONTEMPORARY DISCUSSION

The conditional aspect of the blessings promised to God's servants is perhaps one of the most important components of the evolving theology of the Hebrew Bible that has been left behind by contemporary communities of faith. Was the church of Germany still in a covenantal relationship with God after supporting Hitler's program? Were the communities of the United States that supported slavery and segregation? Are those who discriminate based on race, gender, or sexual orientation? On the other hand, how can contemporary communities of faith living in a world where gods do not intervene in human affairs interpret the consequences of departing from faithfulness?

2 Chronicles 1:1-17: Wisdom and Wealth of Solomon

◼ THE TEXT IN ITS ANCIENT CONTEXT

See parallels to these verses in 1 Kgs. 3:1-15 and 1 Kgs. 10:26-29. First Chronicles 29:28 shows Solomon already sitting on David's throne, and the opening verse of 2 Chronicles states that he "established himself in his kingdom" (see 1 Kgs. 2:12; 2:46b), an expression that denotes the king's overcoming certain obstacles or conflicts (see 1 Chron. 11:10; 2 Chron. 12:13; 13:21; 17:1; 21:4). Solomon's convocation (1:2-6.) resembles David's in 1 Chron. 28:1. The purpose is to demonstrate that "all Israel" is present in this act of worship.

The Chronicler omits God's appearance to Solomon in a dream and moves directly to God's speech (1:7-13) following its parallel in 1 Kgs. 3:5-14: God's question (2 Chron. 1:7b), Solomon's response (2 Chron. 1:8-10), and God's reaction (2 Chron. 1:11-12). Solomon, previously described as "young and inexperienced" (1 Chron. 29:1), will demonstrate maturity and humility when he asks for wisdom to lead his people. God provides him with "riches, possessions, and honor" (1:12) because of this request, which "demonstrated that Solomon indeed had the wherewithal to build the temple" (Klein 2012, 28).

▮ THE TEXT IN THE INTERPRETIVE TRADITION

Solomon's request for wisdom (1:10) has offered biblical interpreters a rich source for homiletic applications. John Chrysostom commented that the believer should "ask nothing worldly, but all things spiritual, and you will surely receive" (Conti, 274). The nineteenth-century rabbi Malbim (Meïr Leibush ben Yehiel Michel Wisser) clarifies that "wisdom" refers to value (ethical) judgment while "knowledge" refers to information or axiomatic truths (Eisemann 1992, 5). Gregory of Nazianzus praised Solomon as "the wisest of all people, whether before him or in his own time," who also knew "the furthest point of wisdom to be the discovery of how very far off it was from him" (Conti, 274).

▮ THE TEXT IN CONTEMPORARY DISCUSSION

Solomon is certainly a controversial figure. The biblical portrait exalts him as a man of prudence and a great builder, but also as a king who burdened the people with excessive taxation and subjected them to forced labor. "Wisdom and knowledge" are essential components of good leadership, but there is a change in attitude from the very beginning of Solomon's reign. Solomon's sense of entitlement eventually moves away from the best interest of his people. It is too common a development of political leaders.

2 Chronicles 2:1—9:31: Construction, Dedication of the Temple, and Solomon's Achievements

▮ THE TEXT IN ITS ANCIENT CONTEXT

David has already charged Solomon with completing the preparations for the building of the temple (1 Chron. 22:14), which prompts Solomon to force seventy thousand men "to bear the burdens" and "eighty thousand to quarry in the hill country" (2 Chron. 2:2). He also requests the help of Huram ("Hiram" in Kings), king of Tyre, who provides skilled craftsmen, cedar, cypress, and algum timber for the project. The Chronicler emphasizes that the laborers forced to work on the temple are not native Israelites but foreigners (2 Chron. 2:17-18; see 1 Chron. 20:3; 22:2; and 1 Kgs. 5:13-18).

Solomon builds the temple on the site God showed to David (1 Chron. 21:28—22:1); the site is also identified as Mt. Moriah, where Abraham was ordered to sacrifice Isaac (Gen. 22:2), also known as God's mountain (Gen. 22:14).

After its construction, the temple is dedicated to the Lord (5:2—7:22 // 1 Kgs. 8:1—9:8). The assembly gathers in Jerusalem during the seventh month (named Tishri after the exile, but Ethanim in the preexilic period, see 1 Kings 8:2) to bring the ark to the temple. The assembly includes the leaders and "all the Israelites" (5:3). The seventh month is the month of the Feast of the Tabernacles (Sukkot, Lev. 23:34; Deut. 16:13-16; 31:10). In 1 Kings, the priests are in charge of moving the ark, but here the task falls to the Levites, according to what David prescribed (1 Chron. 15:2; see Deut. 10:8; 31:25; Num. 3:31). The sacrifices offered by Solomon and "all the congregation of Israel" resemble the sacrifices offered by David and the people when the ark was moved from Kiriath-jearim to Jerusalem (1 Chron. 13:5).

Solomon's speech (6:3-42) follows the pattern of David's speech in 1 Chron. 28:2-10. After his speech, Solomon turns to the bronze altar, extending his hands in prayer (see Exod. 9:29). Solomon praises God for fulfilling his promise to David, and asks that God keep his promise that the Davidic dynasty be perennial, as long as "your children keep to their way, to walk in my law as you have walked before me" (6:16). The general statement of 1 Kings "to walk before me as you have walked before me" becomes more specific in Chronicles: "to walk in my law as you have walked before me." After the exile, to walk before God becomes to walk in God's law (torah). Second Chronicles 6:18-21 reflects tension between a belief in God's transcendence (see 2 Chron. 2:4-5; Isa. 56:7) and his presence in the temple. Solomon's prayer (6:22-23) suggests that oaths previously made in the tent of meeting or other sacred place (see Lev. 6:3-6; Num. 5:13; Judg. 11:11; Amos 8:14) should now be made in the temple.

The final act of the temple's dedication is the offering of sacrifices. The Chronicler adds two miracles to the story narrated in 1 Kings (7:1-10 // 1 Kgs. 8:54-66). First, fire descends from heaven, consuming the burnt offering (7:1), in the same way that fire from heaven consumed David's offering (1 Chron. 21:26). Second, God's glory fills the temple, preventing the priests from entering the precinct (7:1b-2).

God's answer to Solomon's prayer (7:11-22 // 1 Kgs. 9:1-9) offers a good example of the Chronicler's theology of retribution (7:13-15). The people complete four actions, which lead to God's forgiveness: "if my people who are called by my name humble themselves, pray, seek my face, and turn from their wicked ways, then I will hear from heaven, and will forgive their sin and heal their land" (7:14). The notion of humbling oneself appears previously in 1 Chron. 17:10; 18:1; 20:4, and becomes a key element in the Chronicler's theology from this point forward (see 2 Chron. 16:6-7; 30:11; 32:26; 33:12, 19, 23; 34:7; 36:12). Praying has been connected to the rebuilding of the temple (see 1 Chron. 17:25; 2 Chron. 7:1) and to petitions for salvation (2 Chron. 32:20-24; 33:13). To seek God's face (2 Chron. 11:16; 15:4, 15; 20:4) and "to turn from their wicked ways" also appear as theological concepts in 2 Chron. 15:4; 30:6, 9; and 36:13.

In 8:1-18, the Chronicler contradicts the story in 1 Kgs. 9:11-14. In 1 Kings, Solomon gives away the cities to Hiram of Tyre for 120 talents of gold. The Chronicler considers the promised land sacred, and giving it away is not a proper act for a king like Solomon.

The visit of the queen of Sheba (9:1-28 // 1 Kgs. 10:1-28) follows the parallel story in Kings with little variation. As no other king before or after, he is a source of wisdom beyond the borders of Israel. Verses 13-28 again highlight the wealth of Solomon and his passion for luxury items: he orders "two hundred large shields of beaten gold" and three hundred smaller shields also of beaten gold (9:15-16).

■ THE TEXT IN THE INTERPRETIVE TRADITION

The temple built by Solomon received a number of allegorical interpretations. Origen states, "Let us seek to find in the Church the truth of each statement made about the temple. If all Christ's enemies are made the footstool of His feet, and Death, the last enemy, is destroyed, then there will be the most perfect peace. Christ will be Solomon, which means 'Peaceful,' and the prophecy will find its fulfillment in Him" (*On John* 23). Bede commented on the visit of the queen of Sheba, "The sending of the Ethiopian queen of the treasures of the nations to Jerusalem signifies that the Church would bring gifts of the virtue and of faith to the Lord" (*Commentary on the Acts of the Apostles*, in Conti, 68). The Jewish sages, however, interpreted such visits in more somber ways; Nebuchadnezzar, the Babylonian king that would destroy Solomon's temple, was a descendant of the fruit of her visit (*Alphabet Ben Sira* 21b).

■ THE TEXT IN CONTEMPORARY DISCUSSION

Today, The Temple Mount is an issue of contention. Now, the Al Aqsa mosque (the third most sacred place for Sunni Muslims) stands on top of where the temple stood, and Jews are not allowed to pray in any portion of the 1,555,000-square-foot plaza. According to Arab leaders like Yasser Arafat, there was never a Jewish temple in Jerusalem and there is no connection between the city and the Jewish people. This is a widespread belief in Muslim countries. Israeli security forces are on guard (especially during the anniversary of the destruction of the temple) against a handful of Jewish religious radicals who believe that destroying the Al Aqsa mosque would allow the third temple to be built. Perhaps our species will reach a day when our mother Earth will be considered humanity's one and only sacred place, and every human being her priest and caretaker.

2 Chronicles 10:1—12:16: The Schism of the Kingdom and Reign of Rehoboam

■ THE TEXT IN ITS ANCIENT CONTEXT

After the death of Solomon, the nation of Israel experiences a political schism (10:1—11:4). When the assembly of northern tribes challenges the oppressive taxes that enabled Solomon to pursue his building projects, his son Rehoboam chooses to heed the advice of his young friends and punish the people's disrespect with additional oppressive measures instead of following the advice of Solomon's advisers. As a result, the northern tribes reject Rehoboam as their king and secede. The Chronicler shows that he believes Judah is still part of his ideal "all Israel" by replacing "all the house of Judah and Benjamin" (1 Kgs. 12:23) with "all Israel in Judah and Benjamin" (11:3). As Japhet states, "the people remains one even after the monarchy is split into two, and all its elements and tribes continue to be represented in the kingdom of Judah" (1989, 230).

Afterward, Rehoboam engages in some building projects (11:5—12:16). The list of cities fortified by Rehoboam (11:5-12) does not have a parallel story in Kings. In the northern kingdom of Israel, Jeroboam undertakes religious reforms that revoke the Levites' ability to function as priests. As a result, the priests migrate to the southern kingdom of Judah (11:13-17 // 1 Kgs. 12:31-32; 13:33). For the Chronicler, everything Jeroboam does in matters of religion is reprehensible.

In addition to the reference to David's wives and concubines, 11:18-21 is the only place in Chronicles where the author mentions the names of wives, concubines, and children of a king (Rehoboam in this case). Rehoboam favors Maacah, daughter of Absalom, over the rest of his wives and appoints her son, Abijah, as his successor. Following Solomon's example, Rehoboam appoints his sons in strategic positions to assure his control of the country.

Chronicles adds parenthetical comments to the parallel story in Kings about Pharaoh Shishak's attack on Judah (12:1-12 // 1 Kgs. 14:25-28). The first refers to the consolidation of Rehoboam's dominion and his unfaithfulness to God's law (12:1). The narrative sequence makes clear that Shishak's attack results from Rehoboam's and the people's infidelity. Shishak lists 150 cities captured during his campaign in his inscription at Karnak, most of them situated in northern Israel. This passage is composed with Sennacherib's campaign in mind (2 Kings 18–19). In the cases of both Rehoboam versus Shishak, and Hezekiah versus Sennacherib, the stories highlight the consolidation of power and the subsequent arrogance that brings divine punishment. Also in both cases, the humbling of the leaders and kings prevents the destruction of Jerusalem.

Rehoboam does not receive a favorable judgment: "He did evil, for he did not set his heart to seek the LORD" (12:14). "To set one's heart to seek the LORD" will become an essential component of the Chronicler's definition of faithfulness. Not to do so leads one to sin.

▌THE TEXT IN THE INTERPRETIVE TRADITION

When elaborating on the confrontation between Rehoboam and the people in Shechem, some commentators try to portray it as a misunderstanding; Arbarbanel, for example, states that Rehoboam should have explained to the people how beneficial Solomon's reign had been to them instead of conceding that he oppressed them with a heavy yoke (10:11) (Eisemann 1992, 77). The medieval Jewish scholar David Kimḥi also considered the complaints unjustified considering the peace the land enjoyed during Solomon's reign (Eisemann 1992, 76). Ambrose, however, highlights the fact that justice serves political leaders well while injustice undermines their rule. Augustine condemns Rehoboam for rejecting the counsel of the elders, but emphasizes that this happened to fulfill God's plan (Conti, 78–79).

▌THE TEXT IN CONTEMPORARY DISCUSSION

The oppressive practices of Solomon are evident in this passage, but as the reception history shows, it was hard for some interpreters to accept that the complaint by the people and their request for lower taxes was fair. Communities of faith find it difficult to criticize biblical heroes like Solomon. The question remains, How one can adjudicate a political confrontation like the one depicted here without any additional evidence? It is clear that Rehoboam's reaction was neither wise nor practical, but was the peace and tranquility under Solomon worth the heavy taxes?

2 Chronicles 13:1—16:14: Abijah, Son of Rehoboam, and Asa, Son of Abijah

▮ THE TEXT IN ITS ANCIENT CONTEXT

Rehoboam' son Abijah follows him to the throne of Judah (13:1—14:1 // 1 Kgs. 15:1-2; 6-8). His sermon in 13:4-12 belongs to a significant literary form in Chronicles called "Levitical sermons." The theological message is clear: The northern kingdom has not only rebelled against the Davidic dynasty but also against God himself. In 13:13-21, Chronicles departs from the narrative in Kings to tell the story of the victory of Judah against Israel. Israel has a larger army, but they are no match for God's chosen dynasty. Judah triumphs "because they relied on the LORD, the God of their ancestors" (13:18). Later, Chronicles makes it clear that God himself struck Jeroboam, causing his death.

Asa, son of Abijah, follows his father (14:2—16:14 // 1 Kgs. 15:1-24), and enjoys ten years of peace (14:2-15). He acts as Davidic kings are supposed to act (14:2). Asa "took away the foreign altars and the high places, broke down the pillars, hewed down the sacred poles" (14:3), and also kept the laws and commandments. The blessings are manifested in a period of peace and in the success of his building program. According to the Chronicler, prosperity is a direct consequence of being faithful. God's peace is challenged by a foreign invasion (14:9-15). An Egyptian army led by a Cushite king (perhaps Osorkon I) attacks Judah, and Asa brings his troops to face an enemy much more numerous and powerful. But Judah is not alone. Asa cries to the Lord and the Lord acts by defeating the enemy.

In 15:1-7, the spirit of God commands his prophet Azariah, Son of Oded, to address the king. The speech is another example of the theology of the Chronicler, and it has also been characterized as a Levitical sermon. In the sermon, the Chronicler promises peace, prosperity, and blessings to those who seek the Lord (15:3-6; see Hosea 3:4). Asa reacts immediately to the prophet's demands (15:8-19). He receives the support of all the people of Judah, Benjamin, and the refugees that had fled the northern kingdom of Israel and who had remained faithful to God. The reforms conclude with a covenant renewal, where the people "with all their heart and with all their soul" commit to the Lord. As a consequence, God gives them rest and peace. King Asa even decides to remove his mother, Maacah, as the queen mother because of her devotion to Asherah, although she is not put to death, as the people's oath in 15:13 would have implied. The Chronicler states that Asa was not completely effective in removing all the high places of worship (in clear contradiction with 14:3), but still describes him as a king with a true heart.

Asa cannot counteract Israel's strategic fortification of Ramah, a city in the territory of Benjamin (4.3 miles north of Jerusalem), and has to resort to an alliance with the King of Aram, Ben-hadad, who resides in Damascus, to prevent its completion (16:1-14). The alliance produces the expected results. After Ben-hadad attacks the northern kingdom, Asa is able to take the fortification materials from Ramah to fortify Geba and Mizpah, two other cities in the territory of Benjamin. The story in Kings does not pass judgment on Asa's actions, but the Chronicler is critical of this foreign alliance. The prophet Hanani comes to Asa (16:7-10) and expresses God's condemnation of Asa for his lack of trust in the God of Israel. The theology of the Chronicler demands that kings should put their trust only in God. Asa's reaction is very different from his reaction to the oracle of the prophet Azariah (15:1-7); instead of obeying, he becomes angry. Instead of returning to God, Asa throws Hanani in jail. A king that leaves God cannot act justly with the people or his prophets. When Asa becomes sick, he fails again to look for God's assistance (see Exod. 15:26). Of course, nothing good can come from this act of disloyalty to the Lord. Asa does not recover, and dies.

∎ THE TEXT IN THE INTERPRETIVE TRADITION

The speech of the prophet Azariah was interpreted by some commentators (Kimḥi and the eighteenth-century rabbi Yechiel Hillel Altschuler (Metzudos) as referring to the future, to what will happen if his message is ignored (Eisemann 1992, 106–7). The future without a "true God" symbolizes the years of exile that are coming, where life among idol worshipers equals a life without God. Theodoret of Cyrus reads it as portraying the impiety of the ten tribes who, because of their unfaithfulness, had been deprived of their priests and teachers (Conti, 281).

∎ THE TEXT IN CONTEMPORARY DISCUSSION

Azariah's speech reflects an ancient cosmic vision dominant in the history of the Western world until the beginning of modernity. Today, the idea of gods that mingle in human affairs is not compatible with our understanding of the universe and should be left behind. We have learned that there is no assurance whatsoever that peace, prosperity, and blessings will come to those who seek the Lord. Perhaps the tragic deaths of Jesus, Mahatma Gandhi, Martin Luther King, and millions of observant Jews who perished in the Shoah are a painful reminder of that. We can, however, work with the idea that those who seek the Lord will be able to live a *meaningful* life, a life with purpose and fulfillment.

2 Chronicles 17:1—21:1: Jehoshaphat, Son of Asa

∎ THE TEXT IN ITS ANCIENT CONTEXT

A faithful king, Jehoshaphat (17:1—21:1 // 1 Kgs. 15:24b; 22:1-36, 41-50a), is one of the Chronicler's favorite kings (along with Josiah and Hezekiah). The ongoing hostilities between the northern and southern kingdoms leads Jehoshaphat to fortify cities and to establish garrisons and outposts to prevent Israel from invading Judah. In this unstable situation, Jehoshaphat shows his faithfulness to God by rejecting Baal (17:3) and trusting God. Jehoshaphat's loyalty to God brings him prosperity and security. The mention of "great riches and honor" is similar to the Chronicler's rendering of the reigns of David and Solomon (see 1 Chron. 29:28; 2 Chron. 1:12). His educational efforts offer a concrete example of Jehoshaphat's faithfulness. He sends officials, Levites, and priests to teach

God's law in the cities of Judah. "2 Chronicles 17 is unique in reporting a royal mandate for disseminating torah" (Knoppers 1994, 63–64). This "mission" is, however, peculiar since teaching God's law was a prerogative of the priests (Lev. 10:11; Jer. 18:18; Ezek. 7:26). The exact nature of the "book of the law" that the group carried with them is uncertain. The existence of such a book is assumed in Deuteronomistic texts (Deut. 28:61; Josh. 1:8; 2 Kgs. 14:5). As a result of Jehoshaphat's faithfulness, God imposes fear on the surrounding countries, which not only refrain from attacking Judah but also bring Jehoshaphat tribute, increasing his wealth.

The passage 18:1—19:3 describes an alliance between Judah and the northern kingdom intended to attack the Aramean enclave of Ramoth-Gilead. The Chronicler explains, "Jehoshaphat had great riches and honor" (18:1), and did not need to enter into an alliance with Ahab, king of the unfaithful northern kingdom. However, Ahab "incited" him to do it (NRSV, "induced"), an expression that always has a negative connotation and outcome in the Bible. In the midst of optimistic oracles of victory and triumph, Jehoshaphat wants to hear what Micaiah son of Imlah (a prophet Ahab disliked because he always prophesied disasters) has to say. Micaiah reluctantly declares the word of God: disaster will indeed be the outcome of the battle (18:16). The parallel text in 1 Kgs. 22:32 reports that during the battle, Jehoshaphat, surrounded by the enemy, cries to his soldiers for help; in Chronicles, he asked God for help and is rescued (18:31). Ahab is wounded and does not outlive the day (18:34). Jehoshaphat returns to Jerusalem only to be admonished by the seer Jehu, son of Hanani (19:2).

After that, Jehoshaphat continues his reforms (19:4-11) by traveling around the country to bring the people back to the Lord and by appointing judges that will "judge not on behalf of human beings but on the LORD's behalf" (19:6). Jehoshaphat sets up a final appeals court in Jerusalem presided over by Amariah, the chief priest for religious matters, and by Zebadiah son of Ishmael, for civil matters (19:11).

In 20:1—21:1, the Chronicler reformulates the story in Kings to focus on God's reward for Jehoshaphat's piety. As is usual in Chronicles, the author highlights the religious elements, leaving aside the political or economic aspects of the conflict. The Chronicler reports that Jehoshaphat's reaction to the invasion was pious: "he set himself to seek the LORD, and proclaimed a fast throughout all Judah" (20:3). The Levite, Jahaziel son of Zechariah, proclaims an oracle of salvation: "Do not fear or be dismayed; tomorrow go out against them, and the LORD will be with you" (20:17; see Exod. 14:13-14; 1 Sam. 17:47). In the final section, the Chronicler reports again about the destiny of any alliance with the unfaithful. Jehoshaphat of Judah accepts a partnership with Ahaziah of Israel to build a fleet, and as expected the ships wreck and are not able to reach their destination (20:35-37).

▌ THE TEXT IN THE INTERPRETIVE TRADITION

Jehoshaphat was praised by Augustine, for he "possessed the justice that David first possessed and did not commit the sins that David later committed" (*Against the Pelagians* 2.21, in Conti, 282). Basil the Great exhorts one to take God's forgiving attitude as an example saying, "If you see your neighbor committing sin, take care not to dwell exclusively on his sin, but think of the many things that he has done and continues to do rightly" (*On Humility*, in Conti, 283). The Jewish sages saw

Jehoshaphat's alliance with Ahab negatively, and stated that Moses himself had to intercede centuries earlier for Jehoshaphat's life (*Sifre to Deuteronomy* 33:7). And according to a midrash it was Jehu's admonition that moved him to reform the judiciary.

■ The Text in Contemporary Discussion

The Hebrew Bible contains a strong message against political alliances with the impious, emphasizing trust in God as the only viable source of legitimation, political stability, peace, and prosperity. The risks of such alliances, as reflected in the alliance between Jehoshaphat and Ahab, are great and the danger of compromising the values of God's people is real. Today, globalization makes it difficult not to engage in alliances and partnership with countries where the freedoms that Western democracies consider basic human rights are limited or nonexistent. How can we work for human rights in countries like China and North Korea, where political persecution is the norm; or Muslim countries, where women are second-class citizens, gays and lesbians, are punished by death, and opting out of Islam also carries the death penalty? How are our values being compromised when we engage in alliances and partnership with such countries?

2 Chronicles 21:2—23:21: From Jehoram, Son of Jehoshaphat, to Athaliah, Mother of Ahaziah

■ The Text in Its Ancient Context

Jehoram, son of Jehoshaphat (21:2—22:1 // 1 Kgs. 22:50b; 2 Kgs. 8:17-24), marries a daughter of Ahab and falls to her idolatrous practices. He systematically kills every other possible candidate to the throne. The questionable behavior of the king naturally brings political calamities, and Jehoram is unable to maintain control over his dominion as the Edomites achieve liberation from the Judahite yoke (21:8-11). The Chronicler includes in this section a letter from the prophet Elijah (21:12-15), which is absent from the parallel story in Kings. The letter clearly reflects the Chronicler's theology of immediate retribution. Jehoram's sins are enumerated, and the prophet foretells the consequences of his behavior (21:13-15). This prophecy is fulfilled, and Jehoram dies a painful death (21:16-20).

Azariah, the youngest son of Jehoram, is then made king by the people (22:2-9 // 2 Kgs. 8:25—10:14). All of his older brothers had perished. Several kings appear in the Bible as being put in office by the people (Joash, Uzziah, Josiah, and Jehoahaz; see 2 Kgs. 11:12-20; 14:21; 21:24; 23:30 // 2 Chron. 23:1-3; 26:1; 33:24; 36:1). The Chronicler adds to the story in 2 Kings, suggesting that it was his mother and bad counselors who led him astray (22:3-4). The Chronicler alters Ahaziah's death story to reflect his pernicious alliance with the northern kingdom. His father's piety, however, prevents him from incurring the ultimate dishonor, and his body is properly buried.

Athaliah, mother of Ahaziah, follows him to the throne (22:10—23:21 // 2 Kgs. 11:1-20). In this section, the Chronicler follows the parallel story in Kings with only minimal variations. Details surrounding the foreign character of the troops brought to the house of the Lord (2 Kgs. 11:4) are omitted because they do not suit the theology of the Chronicler. Joash becomes king and Athaliah is sentenced to death by the priest Jehoiada, who leads a religious reform to return to traditional Yahwism.

■ THE TEXT IN THE INTERPRETIVE TRADITION

Augustine used the Philistines and Arab invasion of Judah (21:16-17) as an example of God's stirring up enemies "to lay waste those countries that he judges to be deserving of such punishment" (*On Grace and Free Will*, 21:42; Conti, 284–85). In a similar vein, Rabbi Yechiel Hillel Altschuler Metzudos explains that "God stimulated Philistia's natural greed" (Eisemann 1992, 156). Athaliah's story, however, is what captured most of the attention of the Western world. In 1691, Jean Racine wrote a play about her, and Mendelssohn and Handel used it as the basis for musical compositions.

■ THE TEXT IN CONTEMPORARY DISCUSSION

Religious-based violence was a common phenomenon in the world of the Bible, but today, with some exceptions, violence in the name of religion or religious orthodoxy is something that most religions reject. Centuries ago, however, millions died as a result of religious wars. The Islamic conquest of the Middle East, North Africa, and half of the Iberian Peninsula (seventh to eighth centuries); the Christian Crusades (eleventh to thirteenth centuries) and the Spanish *Reconquista* (eighth to fifteenth centuries); and the European religious wars among Christian factions of sixteenth and seventeenth centuries are just a few clear examples of how religious irrationality can lead people to abhorrent, violent behavior. Violence in the name of religion makes many wonder if religious convictions are the cause for more harm than good.

2 Chronicles 24:1—28:27: From Joash, Son of Ahaziah, to Ahaz, Son of Jotham

■ THE TEXT IN ITS ANCIENT CONTEXT

Joash's reign (24:1-27 // 2 Kgs. 11:21—12:21) is clearly influenced by the life and death of Jehoiada the priest. While Jehoiada is alive, Joash acts faithfully (24:2). After Jehoiada dies, the king abandons the beliefs of his advisor and faces the disastrous consequences of such defiance. During his faithful period, the king restores the temple, but after the death of Jehoiada, the king and the nobles reject the faithful priest's reforms and even kill Jehoiada's son, the prophet Zechariah. His last wish, "May the LORD see and avenge!" (24:22) will be fulfilled. Verses 23-27 provide additional information to the story about Joash in Kings: the army of Aram attacks Judah and Jerusalem "with few men" (24:24), but they achieve a decisive victory because God has abandoned Joash. He is wounded in battle and killed in his bed by his own servants.

The reign of Amaziah (25:1—26:2 // 2 Kgs. 14:1-17) follows a similar pattern to the reign of Joash. There is a period of faithfulness and prosperity during which the king listens to God's prophet and accepts his advice (25:1-13), followed by unfaithfulness and disaster when the king disregards the message of the prophet (25:14-24). His first action is to take revenge for his father's death, killing those responsible but not their children (see Deut. 24:16; Jer. 31:29-30; Ezek. 18:20). The Chronicler expands the only verse in Kings about the campaign against Edom. There is a census before the campaign (see 1 Chron. 21; 2 Chron. 14:8; 2 Chron. 17:14-19), and the king hires mercenaries from the northern kingdom, but a prophet prevents them from participating in the battle. God is not with Israel. Still, if the people of the northern kingdom return to God with all their hearts, God will return to them (see 2 Chron. 15:2). The victory is not the result of human efforts but the direct consequence of relying on God. Paradoxically, it is the booty that Amaziah brings back with him that causes his future downfall. He takes the Edomite gods and worships them. A prophet rebukes the king, but is threatened. Amaziah's destiny is sealed.

The theology of the Chronicler is evident in the differences from the story in Kings, particularly when narrating Amaziah's war against Joash, king of Israel (25:17-28). The announcement of the prophet of God to Amaziah is fulfilled (25:20), and the king faces a terrible defeat, followed by the plundering of the royal residence and the temple.

Two different periods marked by the king's faithfulness (16:3-15) and unfaithfulness to God (26:16-23) also characterize the reign of Uzziah (26:3-23 // 2 Kgs. 14:21—15:4). In his youth, the king follows the good counsel of Zechariah, "who instructed him in the fear of God; and as long as he sought the LORD, God made him prosper" (26:5). But arrogance leads to transgression, and the king encroaches on the privileges of the priests to make the offerings (26:18). The story in Kings does not explain why Uzziah becomes leprous. For the Chronicler, it is clear; God struck him (26:20). Before falling in disgrace, Uzziah leads successful military campaigns. His building projects improve the defense system of the city of Jerusalem and support agriculture, "for he loved the soil" (26:10). His last days are spent in isolation due to his illness, and his son Jotham exercises authority until Uzziah dies. The sequence of faithfulness, prosperity, arrogance, and disgrace is apparent here once more.

Uzziah's leprosy is a living example for Jotham, his son, of the consequences of violating the sanctuary's holiness (27:1-9 // 2 Kgs. 15:33-38). He continues to reinforce the defensive fortifications in Judah. The Chronicler adds to his canonical source in 27:3b-6. Jotham's triumphs in battle and the tribute he receives are the result of his faithfulness because "he ordered his ways before the LORD" (27:6).

The Chronicler portrays Ahaz, son of Jotham, quite negatively (28:1-27 // 2 Kgs. 16:1-12). While in Kings one finds the expression "the LORD his God" (2 Kgs. 16:2), the Chronicler omits "his God," emphasizing the distance between this king and God. The most important event during his life is the Syro-Ephraimite War (see 2 Kgs. 15:27; 16:5; Isa. 7:1-17; Hosea 5:8-15). The result of this war, which exemplifies Ahaz's unfaithfulness, differs considerably in Chronicles from the text in Kings. Jerusalem does not fall in Kings; it does in Chronicles, and booty and captives are taken away from the sacred city. The captives taken by the northern kingdom will return, however, due to the intervention of the prophet Oded. The prophet points out that despite the constant strife between the northern and southern kingdoms, they are still one people.

God shows his displeasure with both Judah and Israel, but denounces the northern kingdom for repeated unfaithfulness (28:13b). The war leaves Judah vulnerable, whereupon the Edomites and the

Philistines take advantage of the situation. Ahaz should ask the Lord for help, but against Isaiah's advice (Isaiah 7), he asks the king of Assyria for help (28:16), and Ahaz is forced to accept Assyrian hegemony. The temple of God is shut down and the Baals are worshiped. It is possible that Ahaz even used the temple to worship pagan deities (see 2 Kings 16), but the Chronicler omits that possibility in order to preserve the sanctity of the temple. According to the Chronicler, Ahaz's burial outside of the royal burial ground, separated from his ancestors, is his punishment (see 2 Kgs. 16:20).

■ THE TEXT IN THE INTERPRETIVE TRADITION

Uzziah's punishment for encroaching on the rights and privileges of the priests was used as a model in the early church to assure the exclusive rights of priests and bishops to perform their duties: "so also do you do nothing without the bishop. . . . So every lay person shall not be unpunished who despises God, and is so mad as to affront his priests and unjustly to snatch that honor to himself" (*Constitutions of the Holy Apostles* 2.27, in Conti, 292). Also Pseudo-Dionysius stated, "Surely, there was nothing unseemly in the fact that Uzziah burned incense in honor of God. . . . And yet the Word of God bars anyone who has taken over a task that is not for him" (*Letter* 8, in Conti, 293). The Jewish sages interpreted Uzziah's transgression as sinful pride and concluded that "one of the causes of leprosy is unjustified pride" (Tanchuma Metzora 3, in Eisemann 1992, 205).

■ THE TEXT IN CONTEMPORARY DISCUSSION

The example of Uzziah is instructive in the sense that he tries to prevent the political powers from encroaching on the religious realm, thereby preventing an unsafe concentration of power. Such radical separation of "church and state" is one of the bases of Western democracies and the natural outcome of the Enlightenment. Within the religious communities themselves, however, the exclusive rights of priests to perform certain functions and rites has developed in a tradition of discrimination against females and sexual minorities, who have been traditionally excluded from clergy positions. Islam and Roman Catholicism are examples of such discriminatory practices.

2 Chronicles 29:1—33:25: Hezekiah, Manasseh, and Amon

■ THE TEXT IN ITS ANCIENT CONTEXT

The restoration of the temple and the renovation of the covenant are the first steps in Hezekiah's religious reform (29:1-36). Hezekiah's speech offers another good example of the Chronicler's theology. The sin of the ancestors brought God's ire on the people, but Hezekiah becomes an agent of divine reconciliation. The sacrifices for the rededication of the temple follow the instructions of Lev. 17:6 and Num. 18:17, including offerings and burnt offerings (see Leviticus 1), and sacrifices of peace (see Lev. 7:11).

From a private family celebration (Exod. 12:1-2), the Passover became a public festival (30:1-27). It also offered the occasion to call the northern kingdom to return to God (30:6). The Passover is celebrated by all the people at the temple. Letters are sent to all Israel emphasizing the religious unity of the people and inviting them to return to the Lord (30:6, 9). The holy city is cleansed from shrines for Baal, and the Levites offer sacrifices for the people. The arrival of ritually impure refugees from the northern kingdom presents a theological challenge that the Chronicler resolves by inserting Hezekiah's prayer, asking God to pardon those people.

Sennacherib reigned in Assyria from 721 to 681 BCE. His campaign in Canaan aimed, among other things, at punishing disloyal vassals. The story in Chronicles of the Assyrian invasion (32:1-33) contains differences from the story in Kings: it adds a description of the defense system prepared by Hezekiah, omits the alliance with Egypt (an act for which previous kings have been punished), and omits the paying of tribute to Assyria. These omissions are meant to uphold the image of Hezekiah as a just king, who dies honored and respected by all the people (32:33).

Manasseh becomes king when he is only twelve years old, and the Chronicler portrays the first part of his fifty-five-year reign (33:1-20) as a systematic program to overturn the religious reforms of his father, Hezekiah. Immediate retribution follows, and Manasseh is taken captive by the Assyrians. When he prays to God (33:12), God hears his prayer and restores him (an event not mentioned in Kings). The Chronicler demonstrates that God hears the prayers of the humble (see 2 Chronicles 6). After Manasseh turns back to God, he begins a building program to repair the walls of Jerusalem (33:14; see 1 Chron. 11:8; 2 Chron. 26:9; 27:3-4), reorganizes the army in Judean cities (see 2 Chron. 11:5-12; 14:6; 17:12-19), and restores the Yahwistic faith. All of these actions are appropriate for a just king. The summary of Manasseh's reign reflects two aspects of his behavior: his apostasy and his repentance. The brief reign of Amnon (33:21-25) closely follows the description in Kings (2 Kgs. 21:21-22), adding that Amnon never repented (33:23). He is portrayed as an evil king whose death at the hands of his servants seems to be the natural consequence of his impiety.

■ THE TEXT IN THE INTERPRETIVE TRADITION

John Chrysostom writes, "For so Manasseh had perpetuated innumerable pollutions, having both stretched out his hands against the saints, and brought abominations into the temple, and filled the city with murders and wrought many other things beyond excuse, yet nevertheless after so long and so great wickedness, he washed away from himself all these things. How and in what manner? By repentance and consideration" (*Homilies in the Gospel of Matthew* 22:6, in Conti, 299).

■ THE TEXT IN CONTEMPORARY DISCUSSION

The Bible postulates that repentance leads to God's forgiveness and restoration. No matter how serious the crimes of the kings of Israel, there is always a chance to return to God and make amends. The rabbis came to terms with the fact that leaders are prone to sin. Sforno commented on the expression "When a leader sins . . ." (Lev. 4:22): "for, after all, it is expected that he will sin." Today we see quite often how political leaders trespass accepted social norms or engage in questionable behavior, and ask for forgiveness from their families and constituents. After a while, they are back running for office. While forgiveness seems to work well within the political realm, there are few attempts to introduce the concept of forgiveness in our legal system, which more often than not fails to reach those in positions of leadership. Should the Chronicler's concept of repentance-for-giveness-restoration have a wider role in the way we deal with social trespasses and crimes?

2 Chronicles 34:1—36:23: Josiah and Last Kings of Judah

▌THE TEXT IN ITS ANCIENT CONTEXT

Josiah (34:1—36:1 // 2 Kgs. 22:1—23:30 // 1 Esd. 1:1-33), along with David, Solomon, Asa, Jehoshaphat, and Hezekiah, belongs to a select group of kings favored by the Chronicler. He becomes king at a very young age, which suggests that the group who brought him to power, the "people of the land," dictated most of his policies. The Chronicler reinforces the positive evaluation of Josiah found in 2 Kgs. 22:1-2 by adding information about his early piety (34:3-7).

In Chronicles, the discovery of the book of the law (34:8-33) is the consequence of a program of religious reform already in place instead of, like in Kings, the result of a fortuitous finding. Josiah's reforms seem to be patterned according to the regulations of Deuteronomy 12 (cf. 2 Chron. 34:24 with Deut. 27:9-26; 28:15-68). The book makes Josiah aware of how unfaithful his father has been. The prophet Huldah confirms his sense that God's punishment is on the horizon (34:24), but the imminence of the punishment does not prevent the renewal of the covenant. The book of the law then becomes the book of the covenant (34:30). The narrative closely follows the story in Kings, but prophets become Levites in Chronicles (34:30; cf. 2 Kgs. 23:2) in harmony with the Chronicler's attribution of prophetic ministry to the Levites (see 1 Chron. 25:1; 2 Chron. 20:14; 29:30).

The Passover celebration is the climax of Josiah's reign. It takes place in Jerusalem, following the precedent established by Hezekiah. The Chronicler considers this celebration a return to the faithful days of Samuel. Paradoxically, the faithful king Josiah dies tragically for not heeding the word of God conveyed to him by Pharaoh. Instead of retreating from battle, Josiah rides to his death.

The death of Josiah leaves the "people of the land" in power again. They skip the firstborn Eliakim and set Jehoahaz on the throne (36:1-4). Pharaoh Neco intervenes, deposing and deporting him to Egypt. Neco declares Eliakim the new king, changing his name to Jehoiakim.

Eliakim/Jehoiakim reigns for eleven years (36:5-8), but the destiny of Judah has already been decided. Their alliance with Egypt makes them an enemy of Babylon, and Egypt is no match for the powerful Babylonians. After they defeated the Egyptian army in 605 BCE, there was no one who could oppose their might. The city of Jerusalem was captured on March of 597 BCE and the elite deported to Babylon. According to Kings, Jehoiakim dies in Jerusalem, but in Chronicles he is taken captive to Babylon.

Jehoiachin, son of Eliakim/Jehoiakim, seems to have been a precocious rebel. The Chronicler reports that at the age of eight he has already begun to do what is bad in the eyes of the Lord (36:9-10). Immediate retribution follows, and within a year he is taken captive to Babylon with the rest of the vessels of the temple.

Jehoiachin's brother Zedekiah was supposed to rule under Babylonian supervision (36:11-13), but the urge to rebel was growing among the elite and the people. After eleven years, Zedekiah rejected Jeremiah's message and rebelled against Nebuchadnezzar. The consequences were tragic; in July 587, after a short-lived rebellion, the Babylonians destroyed the city and the Temple and took thousands as exiles to Babylon.

The last verses in Chronicles (36:14-23 // Ezra 1:1-3) fulfill Jeremiah's words of hope (Jer. 25:11-12; 29:10), as Kalimi states, "showing the fulfillment of God's word in history is one of the Chronicler's literary features" (2005a, 148). The exile comes to an end, and the people return to the land. God has kept his promise.

▌ The Text in the Interpretive Tradition

Kimḥi quotes the sages (*b. Yoma* 52b) who clarified that the scroll was found rolled to the passage of the admonitions (Deut. 28:15), "the Lord will drive you" and so on, as one of the consequences of the passage that begins "But if you will not obey the Lord . . . , then all these curses shall come upon you and overtake you" (Berger, 274). Josiah's reform received high praise, which tended to expand its reach. Some commentators note, "With zeal immense, Josiah, himself a prince, acted in such a way as no one before or after him had ever done!—Idols he dethroned, destroyed unhallowed temples. Burned with fire priests on their altars; all the bones of false prophets were dug up; the altars burned. The carcasses to be consumed did serve for fuel" (Pseudo-Tertullian, *ANF* 4:153–54, in Conti, 301). Josiah's tragic death was explained as a result of his not listening to the words of the Lord (Jerome, *Against the Pelagians* 2.22, in Conti, 302).

▌ The Text in Contemporary Discussion

Religious tolerance is one of the values sorely missing in Scripture. Religion played a different role in ancient societies, where there was no difference between a secular and a religious realm as understood today by most Western societies. On the one hand, it would be extremely difficult for us to grasp what was really at stake behind such religious zeal. On the other hand, it would be a terrible mistake to accept or to justify contemporary expressions of religious intolerance because they are based on ancient texts that religious communities today accept as divinely inspired.

Works Cited

Ben Zvi, Ehud. 2006. *History, Literature and Theology in the Book of Chronicles*. London: Equinox.

Berger, Yitzhak. 2007. *The Commentary of Rabbi David Kimḥi to Chronicles: A Translation with Introduction and Supercommentary*. BJS 345. Providence: Brown University.

Conti, Marco, ed. 2008. *1–2 Kings, 1–2 Chronicles, Ezra, Nehemiah, Esther*. Ancient Christian Commentary on Scripture, Old Testament 5. Downers Grove, IL: InterVarsity Press.

Eisemann, Moshe. 1987. *Divrei Hayamim I*. New York: ArtScroll.

———. 1992. *Divrei Hayamim II*. New York: ArtScroll.

Franke, John R. 2005. *Joshua, Judges, Ruth, 1-2 Samuel*. Ancient Christian Commentary on Scripture, Old Testament 4. Downers Grove, IL: InterVarsity Press.

Graham, M. Patrick, Kenneth G. Hoglund, and Steven L. McKenzie, eds. 1997. *The Chronicler as Historian*. Sheffield: Sheffield University Press.

Japhet, Sara. 1968. "The Supposed Common Authorship of Chronicles, Ezra and Nehemiah." *VT* 18:330–71.

———. 1989. *The Ideology of the Book of Chronicles and Its Place in Biblical Thought*. Frankfurt am Main: Peter Lang.

————. 1993. *1 and 2 Chronicles: A Commentary*. OTL. Louisville: Westminster John Knox.

Johnson, Marshall D. 1988. *The Purpose of Biblical Geneaologies with Special Reference to the Setting of the Geneaologies of Jesus*, 2nd ed. Cambridge: Cambridge University Press.

Kalimi, Isaac. 2005a. *An Ancient Israelite Historian: Studies in the Chronicler, His Time, Place and Writing*. Aasen, Norway: Van Gorcum.

————. 2005b. *The Reshaping of Israelite History in Chronicles*. Winona Lake, IN: Eisenbrauns.

————. 2009a. *The Retelling of Chronicles in Jewish Tradition and Literature: A Historical Journey*. Winona Lake, IN: Eisenbrauns.

————. 2009b. "Placing the Chronicler in His Own Historical Context: A Closer Examination." *JNES* 68:179–92.

Klein, Ralph W. 2006. *1 Chronicles: A Commentary*. Hermeneia. Philadelphia: Fortress Press.

————. 2012. *2 Chronicles: A Commentary*. Hermeneia. Philadelphia: Fortress Press.

Knoppers, Gary N. 1994. "Jehoshaphat's Judiciary and the Scroll of YHWH's Torah." *JBL* 113:59–80.

————. 2003. *1 Chronicles 1–9. A New Translation with Introduction and Commentary*. AB 12. New York: Doubleday.

————. 2004. *1 Chronicles 10–29: A New Translation with Introduction and Commentary*. AB 12. New York: Doubleday.

Rad, Gerhard von. 1966. "The Levitical Sermons in I & II Chronicles." In *The Problem of the Hexateuch and Other Essays*. Edinburgh and London: Oliver & Boyd, 267–80.

Saltman, Avrom. 1978. *Stephen Langton Commentary on the Book of Chronicles*. Ramat Gan, Israel: Bar-Ilan University Press.

Stokes, Ryan E. 2009. "The Devil Made David Do It . . . Or *Did* He? The Nature, Identity, and Literary Origins of the *Satan* in 1 Chronicles 21:1." *JBL* 128:91–106.

Wilcock, Michael. 1987. *The Message of Chronicles*. Downers Grove, IL: InterVarsity Press.

Williamson, H. G. M. 1977. *Israel in the Book of Chronicles*. Cambridge: Cambridge University Press.

Wilson, Robert R. 1977. *Genealogy and History in the Biblical World*. New Haven: Yale University Press.

EZRA-NEHEMIAH

Katherine E. Southwood

Introduction

A key theme in the books of Ezra and Nehemiah is the return from exile and the rebuilding of the temple in Jerusalem. Readers are told within the first few verses of Ezra that the LORD "stirred" the spirit of Cyrus king of Persia to build a temple in Jerusalem and to allow those in exile to return there and build it (cf. Isaiah 44–45). This description of events is often compared to scholarly interpretations of various sources of evidence, each with its own bias, concerning the postexilic context, Persian attitudes to local religions, the movement of populations, and taxation. Cyrus posed a fatal threat to the Neo-Babylonian Empire. He attacked Babylonia in 539 BCE, and after a battle at Orpis the Babylonian ruler Nabonidus was captured. Cyrus entered Babylon, the capital city, in triumph the same year. One of the most prominent sources connecting Cyrus's rise to power and the rebuilding of the Jerusalem temple is the Cyrus Cylinder. Although its propagandistic and stereotypical nature should be noted, the Cyrus Cylinder is a vital piece of evidence that portrays the potential, under Persian imperial leadership, for exiled communities to return to their homelands: "The cities beyond the Tigris, whose dwellings had long lain in ruins. . . . All their people I gathered, and brought them back to their dwelling places." Despite the favorable bias of both presentations of Cyrus, events may have been more connected to the economic organization of the empire into taxable satrapies and provinces, as described by Herodotus, while the portrayal may have been more concerned with gaining the loyalty of subjects and ensuring against rebellions.

Indeed, we have no evidence of any formal Persian policy or recognition of the gods of subject peoples. Nevertheless, there is evidence of the Persians responding to the requests and complaints of the local peoples, including those relating to cultic practice. For example, some of the letters found at Elephantine illustrate Persian authorization for the rebuilding of a Jewish temple that was previously destroyed (TAD A4.9) following a failed request for help from the Jerusalem temple and another, twice drafted, request to the Persians (TAD A4.7; A4.8).

Numerous other inscriptions also illustrate how the Persians reacted to local cultic matters. The Xanthus trilingual inscription, in Aramaic, Greek, and Lycian, which authorizes a cult in Xanthus, shows how the Persian government dealt with the establishment of a local cult. It is striking that nothing within the inscription suggests that the Persians provided any financial support for the cult except to give permission for it to be established. All the expenses, including the donation of land, seem to have been provided by the local community requesting to have the cult established. Likewise, with some similarities to Ezra and Nehemiah, the Udjahorresnet inscription portrays how Udjahorresnet, a high official in contact with the Cambyses, made a petition concerning all the foreigners who dwelled in the temple of Neith in order to have them expelled and to demolish their homes and all their unclean things that were in the temple. Thus, while the Persians continued what was already general policy in the Near Eastern empires—to declare their personal piety in the inscriptions of how they were diligent to obey their god(s) and follow his (their) will, and so on—it is probable that exiled communities such as those described in Ezra would have been expected to support the rebuilding of the temple themselves.

The restoration of the temple provides a physical symbol in the text for the restoration of the postexilic Judean community. As such, striking similarities between the books, and the leaders themselves, occur. Both Ezra and Nehemiah are Jewish officials or leaders (Ezra 7:1-10; Neh. 2:1-2) who become concerned about the state of affairs among the Jews in Jerusalem. Both seek permission from the Persian monarch to carry out their mission (Ezra, implied in 7:6; Neh. 2:1-4); both preside over a number of significant reforms in the Jewish communities in Jerusalem; both write of their experiences in the first person; both are threatened by "foreigners," whether through intermarriage (Ezra 9–10; Neh. 9–10; 13:1-3, 23-31) or harassment (Ezra 4–6; Neh. 4:1-2; 6). Although only a little of the text appears at Qumran, this perceived threat from outsiders may be relevant for discerning the influence of the Ezra material on the sectarian Qumran community, which may have understood itself as the continuation of the postexilic community, as the image of the "holy seed" (Ezra 9:2), developing into a "plant root" in the Damascus Document, a manuscript that forms part of the literature discovered at Qumran dating from about 100 CE, may indicate (CD XVII; Blenkinsopp 2009, 189–227). Likewise, although 1 Maccabees does not refer to Ezra and Nehemiah, the author may nevertheless have been influenced by this construction of Jewish identity (Becking, 143–54).

Opposition to ethnic intermarriage, which emphasizes the perceived threat posed by so-called foreigners, concludes both books. As such, despite the material's age, it is relevant as an illustration of the logic of, and flaws of, ethnic exclusivity nowadays. Rather than interpreting difference as a source of wonder and interest, the narratives represent the failure to tolerate foreign influence. However, what is interesting about this portrayal of ethnic identity is its probable development as a result of return-migration from exile to the homeland (Southwood 2012). As such, the text provides an illustration of the complex impacts migration can have on identity, both for those who migrate and for receiving communities.

The lack of any definite conclusion within both books has activated two responses. Initially, there has been some speculation in later texts regarding the fate of the two leaders. Second Maccabees

1:18-36 depicts Nehemiah as a model legitimating the activities of Judas Maccabeus, but also connecting him to the first temple through the fire on the altar that was never to go out (Lev. 6:12-13). Similarly, despite rabbinic tradition's having Ezra die in Babylon, Josephus eulogizes Ezra, claiming "it was his fate, after being honoured by the people, to die an old man and to be buried with great magnificence in Jerusalem" (*Antiquities* 11.158). The second response to the indefinite, incomplete endings of both books has been the apparent disappearance from written records of the two figures until Ezra's revival in the apocalyptic work *4 Ezra* around the year 100 BCE. Soon afterward, he becomes the second Moses in rabbinic tradition.

Ezra 1–6: The Return from Exile and Rebuilding of the Jerusalem Temple

■ THE TEXT IN ITS ANCIENT CONTEXT

One controversial area within Ezra concerns the various supposedly "authentic" documents that are used to substantiate the temple's legitimacy both in terms of YHWH's support and of Persian imperial endorsement. These documents consist of Cyrus's decrees, which occur in both Hebrew and Aramaic and frame the first section of the book (Ezra 1:2-4; 6:3-12), and of correspondences between the Persian king Darius and officials in Yehud—Rehum the chancellor and Shimshai the secretary, and colleagues, Tattenai, the governor, and Shethar-bozenai (Ezra 4:6-22; 5:6—6:12)—who accuse the Jews of rebellion but eventually establish, having found Cyrus's decree at Ecbathana, the temple's entitlement to be rebuilt (Ezra 6:1-12). Finally, an edict from King Artaxerxes (Ezra 7:11-27), which bestows Ezra with power in Yehud, establishes, at a narrative level, the complete support of the Persian authorities concerning the Jerusalem temple.

The chronology of these letters is confused. Ezra 6:22 refers to the king of Assyria either as a deliberate anachronism or a mistake. Likewise, if taken as a whole, the narrative concerning the rebuilding of the temple jumps from the reign of Darius (522–486 BCE) to his successor Ahasuerus's reign (486–465 BCE; Ezra 4:6), following which point the narrative jumps to correspondence with Artaxerxes I (465–424 BCE; Ezra 4:7-23), before returning to Darius (Ezra 4:24).

Many scholars doubt the supposed authenticity of the Cyrus decree for some of the following reasons. First, like the Cyrus Cylinder, with which the decree is compared and which mentions only "Sumer and Akkad," the Ezra documents suggest direct Persian interest in Yehud. Second, Cyrus is referred to as "king of Persia," an epithet that only occurs in Jewish documents (Ezra 1:1, 8; 4:3, 5; Dan. 10:1). Third, the Cyrus Cylinder is propagandistic and illustrates Persian toleration of local cults, like the Assyrians and Babylonians tolerated such cults. However, the "decrees" within Ezra actually promote the Jerusalem temple. Fourth, there is no reason why Cyrus would have specifically supported a minority ethnic group at such an early point in his reign. Finally, the decrees themselves are full of Jewish theology, relating to the size of the temple, its vessels, and using the designation "the Lord God of Israel," language that recalls how the Israelites left Egypt (Exod. 12:35-36). However, there is no reason for a Persian king to have embraced such language or concepts (Grabbe, 272–75).

Similarly, objections pertain to the documents concerning the reported rebellious nature of the Jews from the officials in Yehud. Despite the careful writing of such documents in the style of and according to standardized literary conventions for letter writing, and in the Aramaic language, the contents of such documents are nevertheless highly suspect. A similar argument may be made concerning the census of returnees in Ezra 2, which may mimic the beginning of the book of Numbers, as the Israelites resumed their journey toward the promised land. Since linking the return from Babylon and the exodus is prominent in Isaiah 40–55, there is reason to suspect the author of Ezra may be using the same underlying concepts, despite the formal presentation of the material.

▌ THE TEXT IN THE INTERPRETIVE TRADITION

The influence of the return narrative in Ezra is significant. Much of the postbiblical Jewish theology and literature concerns a hope for restoration from foreign domination and the gathering of one people around a new and glorified temple. For example, the rise of Jewish nationalism in the Second Temple period is particularly pronounced (Goodblatt). First and Second Maccabees sharply differentiate between Jew and non-Jew/Judaism and Hellenism. Likewise, *1 Esdras* 3–4 (the tale of the bodyguards) illustrates how the builder of the Second Temple came to accomplish this feat and depicts the wisdom of a Jewish youth in contrast to his gentile colleagues within the Mesopotamian court. Similarly, the book of Tobit envisages the return from exile, the rebuilding of the Jerusalem temple, and then in the end time the rebuilding of a glorious Jerusalem. This rebuilt temple later becomes an eschatological expectation in literature such as *1 Enoch* 91, and in the literature from Qumran where the community stands in opposition to the Jerusalem temple, it constitutes an interim temple, and inspires hopes for the establishment of a future temple. Similarly, the author of the *Apocalypse of Abraham* maintains eschatological hopes for a restored temple and sacrificial system for Israel. Later in the book of Revelation, the image of the eschatological temple becomes somewhat dominant.

▌ THE TEXT IN CONTEMPORARY DISCUSSION

The major themes of the narrative within Ezra 1–6 are the importance of exclusivity in rebuilding the temple and community in Jerusalem and the level of opposition the community encounters from "foreigners," or those who are already on the land. Particularly revealing is the narrative within Ezra 4:1-5, when a group of people, deemed by the author "adversaries of Judah and Benjamin," have their offer to assist in the rebuilding of the temple rejected. Following this, the "people of the land" weaken and trouble the rebuilding work and hire councilors to frustrate it (after which point the Aramaic documents accusing the Jews of rebellion appear in the narrative). Labeling such perceived opponents "people of the land" is interesting, especially in light of the fact that in the rest of the Hebrew Bible, as well as in later rabbinic literature, it usually refers to "Israel." Nevertheless, within Ezra, such "nations of the land" are placed in a dichotomous relationship to the "children of Israel" who are confined to the group that came out of exile and who must be purified from the uncleanness of the people of the land: "And the children of Israel, which were come again out of exile, and all such as had separated themselves unto them from the uncleanness of the nations of the land" (Ezra 6:21). Such binary distinctions between return-migrants and those who have remained in their homelands are not uncommon in light of modern discussions of ethnic identity. For example, ethnic Japanese who were born and raised in Brazil have, on return to Japan, experienced alienation and marginalization and as a result no longer understand Japan as their real homeland. They experience the return as a "re-diasporization" (Southwood 2012).

Ezra 7–8: The Figure of Ezra

▮ THE TEXT IN ITS ANCIENT CONTEXT

The character of Ezra only emerges within the narrative at chapter 7, where he is introduced with Aaronic lineage, as a "priest" and "a scribe of the law of the God of heaven" who "had set his heart to study the law of the LORD, and to do it, and to teach the statutes and ordinances in Israel" (Ezra 7:1-5, 10, 12). This illustration of Ezra's legitimacy is further emphasized through a royal edict from Artaxerxes, which establishes Ezra's authority in terms of royal support (Ezra 7:11-26). The blessing at the end of the letter also emphasizes Ezra's divine support and ensures that readers understand that it is YHWH who has stirred the Persian monarch into action: "Blessed be the LORD, the God of our ancestors, who put such a thing as this into the heart of the king . . . and who extended to me steadfast love before the king and his counselors, and before all the king's mighty officers" (Ezra 7:27-28).

Finally, the letter refers to the "good hand of God" upon Ezra, a phrase that, alongside the "eye of God," occurs several times throughout the book to emphasize divine favor (Ezra 8:18 cf. 5:5; 7:6, 9, 28; 8:18, 22, 31).

Several critical issues arise in relation to the letter. Initially, it is specified that Ezra is to "make inquiries" concerning Judah and Jerusalem according to the law he possesses (Ezra 7:14). Precisely what is meant by such a term is unclear, and one cannot straightforwardly assume that it amounts to the same thing as "impose" the law, as the intermarriage episode in Ezra 9–10 may be thought to imply. Nevertheless, one wonders what utility an investigation regarding the law may have had. Elsewhere in Ezra, the verb that is used refers only to searching for records (Ezra 4:15, 19; 5:17; 6:1), and it does not occur in Imperial Aramaic, so there is very little evidence to hand that might help us understand the nature of Ezra's mission. A second problem is how to interpret the term "law." Should we imagine the Aramaic term for law has the same resonances as the Hebrew term *torah*, or might we suggest that what is at stake is the Deuteronomic lawcode? Or should we assume that Persian law is at stake since the letter supposedly arises from Artaxerxes, the Persian monarch? Is the "law" being referred to as some kind of a preliminary version of the Mosaic law, which would later become the Pentateuch? The Aramaic term for "law" that is used here also occurs in Daniel, where it refers to law more generally and includes instructions, edicts, and "the law of the Medes and Persians" (Dan. 2:9, 13; 6:5, 8, 12, 15; 7:25). Again, therefore, the language used is unclear and open to interpretation.

Finally, the letter suggests that all the silver and gold in the satrapy of Babylon is to be given to the temple in Jerusalem, alongside anything freely given and to be used for purchasing animals, grain, and drink. Any other needs are to be paid for from the royal treasury (Ezra 7:19-22). This superabundant generosity sounds more like the "wishful thinking of a Jewish apologist" than reality, and raises the question of why Ezra does not occupy a more official role such as satrap or governor of the territory of Judah, including Jerusalem (Grabbe, 326).

Chapter 8 opens with a list of the heads of the fathers and the genealogy of those who returned from exile in Babylon (8:2-14). The list is organized into families in which a remote ancestor is named and then the immediate head of the family; thus, the list begins with the son and grandson of Aaron (Ithamar and Phinehas). Interestingly, the list contrasts rather sharply with the list provided within Ezra 2 and Nehemiah 7. The list's authenticity is debated; nevertheless, one of its functions appears to be to legitimize the group who returned from exile to Jerusalem through their priestly heritage. There follows a narrative concerning the fast by the Ahava, conducted in order that the group should humble themselves before God and to ask for safe passage, since Ezra claims to have been too ashamed to ask the king for help (Ezra 8:22). This marks a stark contrast to Nehemiah, who travels with letters, army officers, and cavalry from the king (Neh. 2:9).

▮ THE TEXT IN THE INTERPRETIVE TRADITION

The figure of Ezra, who is often portrayed as lawgiver, has influenced later Jewish tradition, appearing as a paradigmatic scholar and as the second Moses. The introduction of the Hebrew square script is attributed to him, as well as the bringing together of the collection of the canonical writings of the Hebrew Bible after the exile. Although modern scholars have argued for separate authorship of Chronicles and of Ezra–Nehemiah, the Babylonian Talmud declares Ezra to be the author of the books of Chronicles and large portions of Ezra (*B. Bat.* 15a; *Sanh.* 93b; Williamson 1977; Japhet). Furthermore, the image of Ezra reading the law with a scroll can be found in the synagogue of Dura-Europos (c. 250 CE).

▮ THE TEXT IN CONTEMPORARY DISCUSSION

One of the many themes running throughout Ezra, but especially dominant within chapters 7–8, is the search for validity and authority. Such concerns are as real today as they were when Ezra was written. For example, many legal systems that are considered authoritative initially require that laws are valid, sometimes with the result that communities sense a moral obligation to obey the law. However, the perspective of the author or editor of the material in Ezra regarding the dominant source of authority is somewhat complex. Rather than acting autonomously, the Persian kings are portrayed as puppets who carry out YHWH's will for the good of the group who are returning from exile, just as YHWH "hardened" Pharaoh's heart in the struggle to leave Egypt (see Knowles). Likewise, what brings the law legitimacy is the idea of divine support and having the correct lineage. In many ways, the need for such recognition suggests some degree of instability and self-doubt. Rather than assuming divine support, evidence of such must be searched for in records and documents and behind the actions of those in power. Rather than assuming legitimacy, genealogies must be consulted or invented to prove the fact. Matters of power and legitimacy certainly do not disappear in later literature. In many ways, Paul's thinking on the matter is similar to that of the author or editor of Ezra, as he claims "every person is subject to higher powers, for there is no power but of God: the powers that exist are ordained of God" (Rom. 13:1). However, such thinking may be at risk of almost divinizing those in power. Ezra's God is a God who also appointed the Babylonians, and as such, the author sees the exile itself as punishment from God rather than the misuse of power from those in authority (Ezra 9:6-15). A stark contrast to this logic is the example of Micaiah ben Imlah, who speaks truth to power (1 Kings 22).

Ezra 9–10: Ethnic Exclusivity

▮ THE TEXT IN ITS ANCIENT CONTEXT

The contentious issue of intermarriage occurs several times throughout Ezra–Nehemiah (Ezra 9–10; Neh. 10:29-32; 13:23-30). Unlike its representation in Nehemiah, which exemplifies the problematic relationship between language and ethnic identity, Ezra 9–10 illustrates the complexity of ethnic intermarriage when placed at the intersection of religious, cultural, and social identities.

The episode is narrated using a variety of different techniques. Initially, a narrative section, which is placed on the lips of the character Ezra, uses reported speech to describe in negative terms the occurrence of intermarriage (Ezra 9:1-5). Within this description is the powerful and loaded self-ascription "the holy seed," who are accused of having "intermingled" with "the people of the lands" (Ezra 9:2). The metaphor emphasizes the community's need to separate from other nations, and to be holy (Deut. 7:3-6), and also underlines the significance of legitimate participation within the community. Only those whose lineage, or "seed," is unsullied may be considered authentic members of Israel (Ezra 2:59-62; Neh. 7:61-64; Ezra 8:1; Neh. 9:2).

There follows an extended penitential prayer on the lips of Ezra that consolidates the ideological connection between "the people of the land" and "abominations" by linking the exile to iniquity and by claiming that intermarriage would be exactly the type of forsaking of commandments that could again risk exile or worse (Ezra 9:14). As such, ethnic intermarriage adds to an already deep-seated source of shame and sinfulness since in response to a "tent peg" of grace—that is, the return from exile to the land—Israel returns to its former behavior. The prayer's portrayal of those who are already living in the land, who had not returned from exile, is particularly derogatory, claiming that the land is unclean as a result of "the filthiness of the people of the lands, with their abominations, which have filled it from one end to another with their uncleanness" (Ezra 9:11). As such, powerful, negative language linked to purity is utilized in order to emphasize the absolute, primordial, ethnic differences between those who returned from exile, who understand themselves as "Israel," and those who remained in the land.

Ezra 10 then reverts to third-person narration, reporting how the community then takes action against those who have intermarried by making a covenant to "cast out" the wives and children of those who have intermarried (Ezra 10:3). It is unclear exactly what is meant by "cast out"; the language is atypical and is unparalleled in the case of formal divorce procedures. Indeed, other pertinent instances of the term may indicate the literal sense in which "cast out" is intended; in cases where a newly married woman's lack of virginity is exposed, she is "cast out" to be stoned to death, as is a woman who has been raped (Deut. 22:21-24). Likewise, when Tamar's irregular sexual exploits are revealed, Judah commands: "cast her out and let her be burned" (Gen. 38:24). Nevertheless, action is taken to ensure that those who have intermarried have two choices; either they must "separate themselves" from the foreign women of the land (Ezra 10:11, 16; cf. Neh. 9:2) or "be separated" from the congregation (Ezra 10:8). Again, loaded terminology, this time relating to ritualized separation for the maintenance of holiness (Ezek. 44:23; cf. Num. 8:14; Deut. 10:8; 29:20), is applied in this instance polemically in order to further polarize and exacerbate ethnic differences between those who returned to the land from exile and the so-called people of the land. Finally, a list is provided naming all those who had intermarried and pledged to cast out their wives (Ezra 10:18-43).

■ THE TEXT IN THE INTERPRETIVE TRADITION

A variety of explanations exist in response to this challenging narrative. Despite the constantly loaded, ritualized terminology that dichotomizes the people of the land from those who self-ascribe the title "holy seed" and "Israel," some nevertheless maintain that the author's, or editor's, motivations were purely religious. For example, Charles Fensham claims that the "influence of a foreign mother, with her connection to another religion, on her children would ruin the pure religion of the Lord and would create a syncretistic religion" (124). However, a number of scholars now contextualize the issue with reference to the resounding influence throughout the narrative of the exile and the move back from exile. For example, Peter Bedford recognizes that "the text confirms the Babylonian exile to be the defining experience for Judeans . . . one cannot claim to be a Judean apart from it" (152). As such, the main threat to the community is of "going native" lest by assimilating with "the peoples of the lands" the community end up cutting itself off from its roots (Bedford, 154). Similarly, the centrality of ethnicity to the intermarriage episode should be emphasized since such a pronounced ethnic identity emerged as a result of the rediasporization experienced by the exiled community on return to their homeland, which, rather than being the same place that had lived on in the hopes of the exiles, had instead changed dramatically.

The issue of intermarriage arises in numerous contexts after Ezra–Nehemiah. Most prominently, the Qumran material attests strong concerns about intermarriage with gentiles. For example, 4QMMT reports a community who claims to have "separated" themselves "from the multitude of the peoples," and like Ezra, the material uses Deuteronomy 7 to warn against the perils of intermarriage. Similarly, William Loader points out that the *Apocryphon of Jeremiah, 4QTestament of Qahat*, and *4QVisions of Amran*, texts found at Qumran, also display hostile attitudes toward gentile intermarriage, designating the offspring of such relationships as "half-breeds" (cf. Lev. 19:19; Deut. 22:9; Loader 2009).

■ THE TEXT IN CONTEMPORARY DISCUSSION

In the modern state of Israel, within ultra-orthodox Jewish movements, some rabbis exercise their religious authority to classify certain marriages as illegitimate on the basis of one partner's supposed lack of Jewishness (Eskenazi and Judd). As such, the effects of immigration continue to give rise to tensions between settlers from different ethnic backgrounds or of divergent religious persuasions such as Ashkenazi and Sephardic Jews, Muslims and Christians, or modern orthodox and reform movements (Eskenazi and Judd, 227).

Modern research arising from social anthropologists concerning ethnicity and intermarriage often explains the phenomena in instrumental terms. Unlike Ezra's representation of Israel and the people of the land as inherently, or primordially, different, modern social scientists would focus more on the economic, social, and political circumstances that give rise to ethnic consciousness. As such, ethnicity itself is to be understood merely as an ideological construct devised by humans to gain power where threats to identity are perceived. Similarly, endogamous, or in-group, marriage may be seen as a measure intended to prevent the diffusion of power to those who are not affiliated to the dominant group. In other words, a tool through which difference is symbolized and accentuated.

To cite a classic example, during the 1950s, urban migrants on the Copperbelt used individualized terms to refer, physically and socially, to more proximate groups, but they resorted to general "tribal" labels when referencing migrants from elsewhere, thereby accentuating differences between distant and familiar groups and emphasizing this difference. As such, a case can easily be made for Ezra 9–10 being as much about power relations as it is about identity.

Nehemiah 1:1—2:8: News of Jerusalem and Permission to Rebuild from Artaxerxes

▋ THE TEXT IN ITS ANCIENT CONTEXT

Nehemiah 1–7 and 10–13, sometimes referred to as the Nehemiah memoirs, recount the missions of the book's namesake, the first beginning around 445 BCE and ending in 433, and the second occurring several years later. Many scholars take the view that chapters 8–9 have been misplaced as a result of some error in transmission, since these chapters include the character of Ezra, who is not mentioned in the rest of the book of Nehemiah, and since this would make for a smoother transition between Ezra 8 and 9 (where the present narrative suddenly jumps from Ezra's preparations to depart for Jerusalem to the intermarriage affair).

Nehemiah 1:11b—2:8 can be described as a court narrative wherein a Jew who has won the respect of a monarch displays wisdom and has a request granted. Numerous examples of narratives of this type, which were a standard element of Hebrew Diaspora legend, can be found, such as the tales of Daniel (Daniel 1–6), Joseph (Genesis 41), Esther (Esther 7–8), Judith (Judith 12), and Ahiqar (see Tob. 1:22). In many of these narratives, as in Nehemiah, the Jew is described as a cupbearer. Nehemiah is cupbearer to Artaxerxes (Neh. 1:11), Joseph to Pharaoh (Gen. 40:1; 41:9), Ahiqar to Esarhaddon and Sennacherib (Tob. 1:22). Many scholars speculate that cupbearer meant one who tasted wine for poison since Xenophon's *Cyropaedia* (1.3.9) suggests that it is a well-known fact that the king's cupbearers, when they proffer the cup, draw off some of it with the ladle, pour it into their left hand, and swallow it down—so that, if they should put poison in, they may not profit by it. There is also speculation about whether cupbearers were eunuchs. The narrative of Ahiqar, found at Elephantine among the Aramaic documents, designates the main protagonist as a eunuch. Likewise, the Septuagint has a variant that makes an interesting misspelling (*oinochoos*, "cupbearer" of Alexandrinus, to *eunouchos*, "eunuch," found in Vaticanus Sinaiticus, and Venetus manuscripts). However, the narrative itself does not appear to be concerned about Nehemiah's role in the Persian court apart from how such a role functions in relation to the condition of Jerusalem. Instead, it is Nehemiah's influence over Artaxerxes, and his request to rebuild Jerusalem, that is at stake.

Why would the Persians have permitted the refortification of Jerusalem? One reason may be the numerous revolts that occurred against Persian domination, especially in Egypt. Although there is no evidence of any imperial strategy concerning Jerusalem, Kenneth Hoglund defends this perspective. Despite some difficulties with this argument, Hoglund's treatment of the Greek sources is commendable. As Jacob Wright comments, "Hoglund has emphasized to biblical research that Ctesias's account of the Megabyzos-rebellion is most probably completely unreliable. Thus, it seems quite plausible that the imperial administration would have desired to tighten its control over the Levant after the intervention of the Delian League and the continued Greek naval operations in the eastern Mediterranean in the decade of the 440's" (81). Unlike the reasons for, or even the questionable historical plausibility of, the Persian monarch's motivations, Nehemiah's motivations are made clear from the outset. The first chapter of Nehemiah is dominated by a penitential prayer (see Boda), detailing Nehemiah's grief-stricken response to the news regarding Jerusalem's present condition. Nehemiah's confession of personal and national sin responds to the echo of Deuteronomistic theology, which views Hebrew misfortunes as punishment for covenantal disobedience (Deut. 28:15-68). Nehemiah also prays that God remember his promises of restoration to the faithful (Deut. 30:1-5). This has many similarities with Ezra's penitential prayer, which also uses Deuteronomistic theology to interpret the cause of the exile as disobedience, and involves mourning and fasting (Ezra 9:5-15).

▌ THE TEXT IN THE INTERPRETIVE TRADITION

The difficulties in transmission are not aided by looking to different versions of the text. In addition to the canonical book, the Greek and Latin texts have different enumeration. The Septuagint version, dated to around the second or first century BCE, contains a compilation of 2 Chronicles 35–36; Ezra 1–10; and Neh. 7:73—8:13. This is known as Esdras α, although in the Latin version it is called 3 Ezra and in some modern translations, such as NRSV, it is known as 1 Esdras. Despite the assumed error in transmission, there are striking similarities between the characters of Ezra and Nehemiah themselves, as well as between the narratives within the books. In both cases, the characters serve Persia in Yehud, initiate their missions with prayer, and deal with an intermarriage crisis. Furthermore, in narratives, they recount opposition from those within Yehud and describe rebuilding work. Both characters are given first-person narration that offers the reader their interpretation of events and that often slides into individual prayer.

Klaas Smelik compares the function of Nehemiah's role as cupbearer at this point to that of seventeenth- and eighteenth-century court Jews who played a significant role in the administration of the various courts in the German Empire. Such court Jews in return for their services attained special privileges, such as personal fortunes as well as political and social influence (see Smelik). Interestingly, 3 Ezra contains a unique account of a competition between three pages at the Persian court, one of whom is identified with the Judean Zerubbabel (3 Ezra 3:1—5:6), an account whose nearest parallel in the history of literature is the Daniel narratives (Daniel 1–6). It is possible, however, that this literary topos penetrated the imagination of Hebrew writers through the Greek fascination with the Persian court, as writers such as Xenophon and Ctesias illustrate. Given this court setting, it is ironic that the narrative designates Artaxerxes as "this man," a phrase that can sometimes be interpreted as disrespectful in tone (Neh. 1:11).

▮ THE TEXT IN CONTEMPORARY DISCUSSION

As Tamara Cohn Eskenazi observes, the cupbearer narrative is dominated by repeated instances of the Hebrew terms *ra* and *tov* ("evil" and "good"), which use the full semantic range of said terms instead of inserting synonyms (Eskenazi 1988). Interestingly, Joseph Fleischman argues that the term *ra* is chosen thoughtfully by Nehemiah in light of Zoroastrian overtones. As such, Nehemiah's dialogue with Artaxerxes shows incredible political, religious, and social astuteness. Given the challenges of interreligious dialogue today, this strategy may be of interest to contemporary readers. Rather than emphasizing the differences between Yahwism and Zoroastrianism, the character Nehemiah draws attention to the similarities in a carefully thought-through manner, thereby creating a common language through which both parties could successfully interact. Although Nehemiah's use of such a tactic may be interpreted as manipulative, the tactic itself is nevertheless effective.

Nehemiah 2:9—7:3: Opposition to Rebuilding

▮ THE TEXT IN ITS ANCIENT CONTEXT

This section of Nehemiah forms part of the so-called Nehemiah memorandum. This possibly independent block that is cast as autobiography orbits around themes such as social, cultic, and economic life in Yehud. Moreover, it contains a repeated refrain-like, stylized vocative, remembrance formula, "Remember [me] . . . Oh my God" (Neh. 5:19; 6:14; 13:14, 22, 29, 31). As such, the sense of the narrative appears as an account of personal actions given before God.

The narrative describes how Nehemiah, having received a commission to serve Persia in Yehud, discovers the city's walls need attention. Following a secretive inspection of the walls by night, Nehemiah's rebuilding project encounters persistent opposition from the start. We are presented throughout the narrative with the move and countermove of Sanballat and Tobiah, and Nehemiah respectively (Neh. 2:11-20; 3:33—4:17; 6:1-19). Each episode depicts total resistance to any interference from outsiders, a theme comparable to that of the rebuilding of the temple in Ezra 4–7; just as foreigners on the land and officials stirred up trouble and made accusations against those who were rebuilding the temple in Ezra, a similar treatment of those who are rebuilding the wall is depicted in Nehemiah.

The opposition facing Nehemiah and his rebuilding project can be divided into two camps. Nehemiah's potential rivals: local individuals with power who apparently worked together to mutual advantage with Sanballat, Tobiah, and Geshem the Arabian, and Nehemiah's fellow Yehudites on the land. However, Lester Grabbe argues that the personality of Nehemiah may also account for some of the opposition, stating that "time and again his actions are confrontational or, at best, insensitive. He evidently had the knack of antagonizing those around him" (Grabbe, 298).

Nehemiah's opponents use a number of other antagonistic tactics to obstruct the restoration of Jerusalem's walls, including anger, ridicule, and sarcasm in Nehemiah 4, when Sanballat mocks the Jews, asking, "What are these feeble Jews doing?" (v. 2). Although there are some problems with the Hebrew at this point, the general force of the derision against Nehemiah is humiliation; even a fox could cause the wall to topple down. The next tactic listed is to "conspire together" and hinder the work (Neh. 4:8). Following this, the fear of attacks against the wall mounts, causing Nehemiah to arm those who work with weapons to the extent that the building goes on with a tool in one hand and a weapon in the other (Neh. 4:13, 17-18). Following this, another tactic employed against Nehemiah is coercion and pressurization. A meeting is called between Sanballat, Geshem, and Nehemiah, which Nehemiah fails to attend. Following this, several invitations to meet are sent to and refused by Nehemiah (Neh. 6:1-4). Finally, the accusation of rebellion is leveled against the building project and against Nehemiah.

Accusations concerning rebellion are a recurring form of opposition. Such opposition is marked in both the Ezra and the Nehemiah narratives at numerous occurrences, in Hebrew and in Aramaic of the term "rebel," *mrd* (Ezra 4:12, 15, 19; Neh. 2:19; 6:6), a serious accusation in light of the political context (see above). This accusation comes to a head in Neh. 6:4-7, where Sanballat writes a letter stating that Nehemiah proposes to "become their king," and accuses Nehemiah of having "appointed prophets to preach about you saying 'There is a king in Judah'" (Neh. 6:7). The accusation is clearly designed, as with some of the Aramaic letters in Ezra, to insinuate sedition on the part of the Jews against the Persian authorities. The completion of the building work is mentioned in Neh. 6:15, but again, this is in the context of opposition to Nehemiah with letters going to and from Tobiah designed, according to Nehemiah, "to make me fearful" (Neh. 6:19). Finally, at the beginning of Nehemiah 7, as soon as the gates are set on their hinges Nehemiah establishes a guard routine.

▌ THE TEXT IN THE INTERPRETIVE TRADITION

Although the realities of Persian taxation lie behind the narrative (see the introduction), the narrative itself appears to be written to preserve the identity and survival of the "Israelite" community (as defined by Nehemiah). This is evidenced in the interpretative tradition, where it is Nehemiah, rather than Ezra, who appears in the praise of the fathers in Jesus ben Sirach (27) as the biblical prototype, and as the initiator of the postexilic refortification of Jerusalem (Neh. 49:13; cf. 2 Macc. 2:13). Why is Nehemiah so prominent in later literature? One reason is that Nehemiah's account of events is very compelling. However, despite this later admiration for the figure Nehemiah, the extent of reliability within the memoirs is questionable. Although the opposition, specifically the political opposition, against Nehemiah is plausible in the context of Achaemenid domination, it is interesting to note that much of the language looks suspiciously like hyperbole. Grabbe argues that "one has the impression that a set of murdering bandits is about to fall upon the poor builders of the wall, that they were opposed by a set of vicious and wily foes who are described in particularly demonic terms" (Grabbe, 299).

Furthermore, the language used draws on the examples of other biblical narratives. "Do not be afraid" is Israel's great battle cry (Deuteronomy 20), the declaration of war through the blowing of the shofar. The phrase "Our God will fight for us" (Neh. 4:20; cf. Judg. 3:27; 6:34; 7:18; 1 Sam. 13:3) presents a picture of Nehemiah as an archetypal leader of Israel. Such stereotypical, resonant language is also evident in Nehemiah's report of the financial crisis (Nehemiah 5). The "great cry" of the people (Neh. 5:1) is mentioned using the same term as the cry against Pharaoh, and the psalmist's cry for God's deliverance from injustice (Exod.14:10; 22:23; Ps. 107:6, 19-20).

■ THE TEXT IN CONTEMPORARY DISCUSSION

It is interesting to note the underlying ethnic division between the characters. Sanballat is given the appellation "Horonite" (cf. Josh. 16:3, 5; Blenkinsopp 1988, 216). The name Sanballat itself appears to be Babylonian (Williamson 1985, 182). Likewise, although Tobiah is a Hebrew name, the appellation he is given is "the Ammonite." Geshem is called an "Arab" (Neh. 2:19). Although the term *goy* may have different connotations in Nehemiah from its modern usage, it is interesting to note that "enemies" are often mentioned alongside a derogative, exclusionary application of this term (Ezra 6:21; Neh. 5:8, 9, 17; 6:6, 16; 13:26). Such ethnic separation and opposition is a general theme in the books and is seen particularly through attitudes toward intermarriage. Many modern ethnic movements rely on this kind of tactic; ethnic unification is achieved by creating a common enemy (Southwood 2011; 2012). For example, political leaders often utilize ethnic division in order to serve their own agenda of seeking to consolidate an electorate by calling for unification against a real or imagined common enemy. Similarly, colonization during the ongoing conflicts in the Greater Horn of Africa led diverse populations to be united into single parties and movements against the colonial administrators who were perceived as a common enemy.

Nehemiah 7:4—9:37: Ezra's Reading of the Law and the Nation's History

■ THE TEXT IN ITS ANCIENT CONTEXT

In Nehemiah 7, we find a list, repeated from Ezra 2, of those who returned and repopulated Jerusalem. The repetition may function as a device for continuity within the books, linking the end of the reconstruction effort with its beginning. The second appearance of this Golah list is introduced by the idea that Nehemiah wanted everyone to be registered according to their lineage. According to Kenton Sparks, these lists determine group membership using participation in the experience of exile as a determining factor. Effectively to be perceived as a "true" Israelite, one must "demonstrate an ethnic origin within the people of Israel and only when this pedigree could be established with written documentation" (Sparks, 314–15).

There follows an account of Ezra's reading of the law that disrupts Nehemiah's memoirs. This disruption, coupled with the introduction of Ezra in Neh. 8:1 and absence of Nehemiah, leads many scholars to conclude that this chapter initially belonged between chapters 8 and 9 of Ezra. Further-more, the date given is the seventh month, before the intermarriage episode in Ezra 9–10, which occurs on the ninth month (Neh. 8:2; Ezra 10:9). Grabbe argues that two separate traditions are combined in Nehemiah 8: a tradition that strongly associates the reading and promulgation of the Torah of Moses with Ezra, and a separate tradition that associates the reading and promulgation of the same law with Nehemiah the Levite, and the people as a whole, without any mention of Ezra (Grabbe, 336). Whatever the original chronological setting of the events, it is interesting to note that they occur on the date later celebrated as the Jewish New Year.

The narrative details how Ezra reads from the book of Moses (Neh. 8:1–3), the Levites explain the law (Neh. 8:7-8), and the people are told to rejoice rather than mourn, because the day is holy (Neh. 8:9-12). Instructions to dwell in booths are found, and booths are prepared, something that had not occurred since the days of Joshua son of Nun (Neh. 8:17), and the celebration of reading the law lasts eight days (Neh. 8:18). A variety of significant details may be observed within the narrative.

Initially, Ezra reads facing the square; thus within a small space a concentration of the popu-lation occurs. As such, Ezra's law is conceived of within the narrative as being in the form of a document, not just a set of teachings. Furthermore, the law is portrayed as accessible to all. Ezra symbolically conveys the accessibility of the law to nonpriests by choosing thirteen lay leaders to stand with him while he reads. Furthermore, we are informed that they read "distinctly, and gave the sense, and caused them to understand the reading" (Neh. 8:8). The general implication of the threefold description of the Levites' work is that the law is for the entire Israelite community, rather than being unapproachable, in the ark within the holy of holies.

▮ THE TEXT IN THE INTERPRETIVE TRADITION

The importance of public reading is highlighted by several scholars as an instrument for dissemina-tion of ideologies. For example, David Goodblatt assigns the public reading of Scripture, found in numerous texts, an important role in the rise of ancient Jewish nationalism. Just as Moses and Josiah read the law, so too does Ezra and many after him (Deut. 31:9-13; 2 Kgs. 23:1-3). Goodblatt cites numerous early accounts of such public reading of Scripture. For example, in the fourth century BCE, Hecataeus of Abdera writes that the high priest "announces what is ordained, and the Jews . . . fall to the ground and do reverence to the high priest when he expounds the commandments to them. At the end of their laws there is even appended the statements: 'These are the words that Moses heard from God and declares unto the Jews'" (Goodblatt, 36). Similarly, the letter of Aristeas reports that the completion of the finished translation of the Torah into Greek was read out to the assembled Jewish community. Also, 1 Macc. 3:46-60, which describes the assembly of the forces of Judas the Maccabee at Mizpah, may refer to a public reading from the Torah (1 Macc. 3:48). By the time of Philo and Josephus in the first century CE, we have clear statements asserting regular public reading of Scripture on the Sabbath (Goodblatt, 24–48). It is also interesting to note that although the origins of the synagogue service are disputed, the practice of public reading from Scripture may be connected to the emergence of the synagogue institution (see Runesson). The reference to Joshua son of Nun may also lend further nationalist overtones to the celebrations.

■ THE TEXT IN CONTEMPORARY DISCUSSION

The ninth chapter of Nehemiah presents, liturgically, national history from creation and election to exodus and the metaphor of entering the land: a metaphor all too pertinent for those who returned from exile. This presentation of a common history may function as a means of underlining, explaining, and consolidating Israelite ethnic identity (Hutchinson and Smith, 6–7). Interestingly, this commemoration of a shared history is an occasion of mourning and separating from foreigners (Neh. 9:2). The prayer acknowledges both God's long-suffering in continuing to fulfill the Abrahamic covenant despite disobedience, and God's justice in using foreign domination as punishment, namely, by Assyria and Babylonia. The sense of a history of shame that emerges from Nehemiah 9 is similar to the sense of guilt within Ezra's prayer (see Ezra 9:6-7). Unlike many modern ethnic histories, which recount past triumphs, it is interesting that in Ezra and Nehemiah national unity is forged on a history of disappointment and disgrace. Nowadays, shame and guilt are often viewed as entirely negative, but the way such emotions are applied within Ezra–Nehemiah also shows that they have the potential to be used creatively and positively.

Nehemiah 10–13: Obligations for the Renewed Community

■ THE TEXT IN ITS ANCIENT CONTEXT

The tenth chapter of Nehemiah is a list of signatories to agreements concerning religious obligations. These obligations include the agreement not to intermarry with people of the land (cf. Exod. 34:16; Deut. 7:1-4), not to conduct business on the Sabbath (cf. Exod. 23:10-11; Lev. 25:2-7), to give up crops and the exaction of debts in the Sabbatical year, and to provide an annual one-third shekel tax for the temple personnel (cf. Num. 18:8-32). Other obligations listed include the wood offering (see Lev 6:5-6) and the firstfruits (see Exod. 23:19; 34:26; Deut. 26:1-11). The ceremony concludes with a commitment by all "to walk in God's torah which was given by Moses the servant of God and to observe and do all the commandments of the LORD" (Neh. 10:29). Interestingly, like the prohibitions against intermarriage in Exodus and Deuteronomy, throughout Ezra and Nehemiah the movement of females is emphasized (see Deut. 7:3; Ezra 9:2; Neh. 10:30; 13:25).

This has led some scholars to the conclusion that the focus on intermarriage within Ezra and Nehemiah concerns female inheritance. For example, Eskenazi states that "the fear of mixed marriages with their concomitant loss of property to the community makes most sense when women can, in fact, inherit" (Eskenazi 1992, 35). There are numerous problems with this argument (Southwood 2012, 79–83). One problem in particular is the reverse of the argument, that if male members of the community married foreign women they could also receive land and dowry, and so increase the community holdings.

As H. G. M. Williamson points out, the similarities between this chapter and Nehemiah 13 are striking (Williamson 1985, 331).

> Mixed marriages 10:31; 13:23-30
> Sabbath observance 10:32; 13:15-22
> The wood offering 10:35; 13:31
> First fruits 10:36-37; 13:31
> Levitical tithes 10:38-39; 13:10-14
> Neglect of the temple 10:40; 13:11

The list of correspondences may indicate that Nehemiah had taken some steps to deal with such problems, following which the community entered into an agreement to prevent their occurrence; thus, rather than indicating two separate incidents, Nehemiah 10 relies on Nehemiah 13. However, Grabbe doubts that Nehemiah ever had the authority to make any major reforms since "he was only the governor of a small province, and he answered to the satrap (a provincial governor) of all the central government." Therefore, it is a reasonable inference that the governor in turn had to deliver a set amount to the satrapal treasury. As such, a "one-off cancellation of some debts might be possible, but it could be disastrous for the local economy if this happened too widely and too frequently" (Grabbe, 306).

Chapters 11 and 12 of Nehemiah are a utopic presentation of Jerusalem as a city built by clergy, populated by those who are blessed, and dedicated with joy. Indeed, unlike the temple's dedication in Ezra, which was accompanied by both shouting and weeping that could be heard from afar (Ezra 3:13), in Nehemiah only the rejoicing can be heard from afar (Neh. 12:43). Oded Lipschits argues that the section of the text is an ideological creation, or a utopian picture in which Jerusalem is envisaged as ruling over all the old area of Judah as a kingdom and also includes all the places in which Jews lived in the Persian period. A list of those who repopulate Jerusalem, which has military overtones, is provided. This names Judahites (11:1-4), Benjamites (11:7-9), priests (11:10-14), Levites (11:15-18), gatekeepers (11:19), and the "remnant of Israel" (11:20-21). The list has important parallels with 1 Chron. 9:1-17, which is alleged to be a list of those who first returned from exile. By implication, those who were originally exiled are the same remnant community who return. However, the broad geographical distribution of postexilic Judahite settlements that the list suggests in 11:27-36 does not so much reflect the historical realities of the day as recall the ideal territorial possessions in the promised land (see Joshua 15). As such, a similar technique of using evocative language to recall stories about Israel's history in order to narrate the return from exile to Jerusalem is used. Just as the events in Ezra 1 are portrayed as a second exodus, the events in Nehemiah 11 portray the Israelites as entering and inheriting the promised land.

Chapter 12 of Nehemiah describes a processional dedication of the wall, starting with another list that records priestly and Levitical families and high priests (vv. 1-26). Subsequently, 12:27—13:3 reports that the people gather to dedicate the wall and even purify the wall itself to make the city holy. Two groups, each composed of priests and Levites, begin the ceremonial procession at the

Valley Gate. One group ascends to the top of the thick wall in a counterclockwise direction, while the second group proceeds the opposite way. The two groups meet at the temple, where they celebrate with singing, sacrifice, and attention to practical matters that David prescribed for the temple service. The list of Levites highlights the singers who are depicted as carrying out their musical service antiphonally (Neh. 12:8-9).

The thirteenth chapter reports events that occur on Nehemiah's second mission to Jerusalem. The narrative describes how while Nehemiah was away the community had violated some of the stipulations made formerly (Nehemiah 10). For example, Tobiah the Ammonite is housed in the temple, portions have not been assigned to the Levites and temple singers, the Sabbath has been violated, and intermarriage has occurred, including intermarriage between priests and gentiles (cf. Lev. 21:14; Ezek. 44:22). Unlike in Ezra 9–10, the intermarriage crisis in Nehemiah focuses on the issue of language, something that is crucial to ethnic identity (Southwood 2011).

▮ THE TEXT IN THE INTERPRETIVE TRADITION

The influence and legacy of Nehemiah's and Ezra's intermarriage reforms are strong. Some Second Temple authors considered intermarriage detrimental to Jews because of gentile immorality (Philo, *Spec. Laws* 3.29; Josephus, *Ant.* 4.8.2; 8.5.191–93). Similarly, Tobit insists that his son should "marry a wife of the seed of your fathers" rather than "take a strange wife, who is not of your father's tribe" (Tob. 4:12). Aramaic Levi also assumes that Israelite seed is holy (see *Testament of Levi* 9:9-10). As Hannah Harrington illustrates, the ongoing influence of Ezra and Nehemiah's marriage reforms is evident in several Dead Sea Scrolls. Harrington notes that like Ezra–Nehemiah, "the Qumran authors who discuss intermarriage do not offer a reasonable acculturation process for the non-Israelite partner. Instead, most adopt a priestly stance to holiness which configures it in cultic terms" (259). As such, intermarriage, even among the laity, compromises the holiness of Israel. This is especially clear within 4QMMT, where we find not only a similar ideology to that of Nehemiah's reforms but also the mirroring of certain key terms such as "the holy seed," "impurity," "intermingle," "sacrilege," and "abomination." Similarly, the author of the *Temple Scroll* quotes almost verbatim from Exod. 34:15-16 and interprets the passage in light of Ezra–Nehemiah's perspective on intermarriage. Likewise, the Damascus Document fails to endorse intermarriage through appealing to cultic language: intermarriage is a desecration of Israel's holiness. Again, in the *Genesis Apocryphon*, the insistence on appropriate genealogy and the concern about defilement mirrors what is found in Nehemiah 13. Finally, in 4QFragments, the concern about unions with foreigners continues. As such, while the intermarriage episodes in Ezra and Nehemiah are not explicitly cited, the language and ideas within the texts is nevertheless dependent on Ezra–Nehemiah (Harrington).

▮ THE TEXT IN CONTEMPORARY DISCUSSION

The building of the wall and the reforms mentioned lead Grabbe to conclude that Nehemiah's goal may have been "to make Judah into an isolated puritanical theocratic state" by "creating his own religious and ideological ghetto" (Grabbe, 309–10). Nehemiah is depicted as a powerful and influential, albeit short-tempered, religious leader. Many religious movements today rely on charismatic leaders. However, such charisma must go hand in hand with ethical, righteous, even inclusive principles if the goal is to establish anything more than the formation of isolated, sect-like groups. The problem lies in deciding and interpreting what constitutes righteous behavior.

Works Cited

Becking, B. 2011. *Ezra, Nehemiah, and the Construction of Early Jewish Identity*. FAT 80. Tübingen: Mohr Siebeck.

Bedford, P. R. 2002. "Diaspora: Homeland Relations in Ezra–Nehemiah." *VT* 52, no. 2:147–65.

Blenkinsopp, J. 1988, *Ezra-Nehemiah: A Commentary*. OTL. London: SCM.

———. 2009. *Judaism, the First Phase: The Place of Ezra and Nehemiah in the Origins of Judaism*. Grand Rapids: Eerdmans.

Boda, M. J. 2008. "Redaction in the Book of Nehemiah: A Fresh Proposal." In *(Dis)Unity of Ezra and Nehemiah*, edited by M. J. Boda and P. Redditt, 25–54. Hebrew Bible Monographs 17. Sheffield: Sheffield Phoenix Press.

Eskenazi, T. C. 1988. *In an Age of Prose: A Literary Approach to Ezra-Nehemiah*. SBLMS. 36. Atlanta: Scholars Press.

———. 1992. "Out from the Shadows: Biblical Women in the Postexilic Era," *JSOT* 54:25–43.

Eskenazi, T. C., and E. P. Judd. 1991. "Marriage to a Stranger in Ezra 9–10." In *Second Temple Studies 2: Temple and Community in the Persian Period*, edited by T. C. Eskenazi and K. H. Richards, 266–85. JSOTSup 175. Sheffield: Sheffield Academic Press.

Fensham, F. C. 1982. *The Books of Ezra and Nehemiah*. NICOT. Grand Rapids: Eerdmans.

Fleischman, J. 2012. "Nehemiah's Request on Behalf of Jerusalem." In *New Perspectives on Ezra-Nehemiah: History and Historiography, Text, Literature, and Interpretation*, edited by I. Kalimi, 241–66. Winona Lake, IN: Eisenbrauns.

Goodblatt, D. 2006. *Elements of Ancient Jewish Nationalism*. Cambridge: Cambridge University Press.

Grabbe, L. L. 2004. *A History of the Jews and Judaism in the Second Temple Period*. Library of Second Temple Studies 47. London: T&T Clark.

Harrington, H. 2011. "Intermarriage in Qumran Texts: The Legacy of Ezra-Nehemiah." In *Mixed Marriages: Intermarriage and Group Identity in the Second Temple Period*, edited by C. Frevel, 251–79. LHB/OTS 547. New York: T&T Clark.

Hoglund, K. 1992. *Achaemenid Imperial Administration in Syria-Palestine and the Missions of Ezra and Nehemiah*. SBLDS 125. Atlanta: Society of Biblical Literature.

Hutchinson, J., and A. D. Smith, eds. 1996. *Ethnicity*. Oxford Readers. Oxford: Oxford University Press.

Japhet, S. 1968. "The Supposed Common Authorship of Chronicles and Ezra–Nehemiah Investigated Anew." *VT* 18:330–71.

Knowles, M. D. 2004. "Pilgrimage Imagery in the Returns in Ezra." *JBL* 123, no. 1:57–74

Lipschits, O. 2002. "Literary and Ideological Aspects of Nehemiah 11." *JBL* 121, no. 3:423–40.

Loader, W. 2009. *The Dead Sea Scrolls on Sexuality: Attitudes Towards Sexuality in Sectarian and Related Literature at Qumran*. Journal for the Study of Judaism Supplement Series 40/2. Grand Rapids: Eerdmans.

B. Porten and A. Yardeni (eds.). 1986. *Textbook of Aramaic Documents from Ancient Egypt* (TAD). Winona Lake, IN: Eisenbrauns.

Runesson, A. 2003. "Persian Imperial Politics, the Beginning of Public Torah Readings, and the Origins of the Synagogue." In *The Ancient Synagogue from Its Origins until 200 C.E.: Papers Presented at an International*

Conference at Lund University, October 14–17, 2001, edited by B. Olsson and M. Zetterholm, 63–89. ConBNT 39. Stockholm: Almqvist and Wiksell.

Smelik, K. A. D. 2012. "Nehemiah as a 'Court Jew.'" in *New Perspectives on Ezra-Nehemiah: History and Historiography, Text, Literature, and Interpretation*, edited by I. Kalimi, 61–72. Winona Lake, IN: Eisenbrauns.

Southwood, K. E. 2011. "'And They Could Not Understand Jewish Speech': Ethnicity, Language, and Nehemiah's Intermarriage Crisis." *JTS* 62, no. 1:1–19.

———. 2012. *Ethnicity and the Mixed Marriage Crisis in Ezra 9–10: An Anthropological Approach.* Oxford Theological Monographs. Oxford: Oxford University Press.

Sparks, K. L. 1998. *Ethnicity and Identity in Ancient Israel: Prolegomena to the Study of Ethnic Sentiments and Their Expression in the Hebrew Bible.* Winona Lake, IN: Eisenbrauns.

Williamson, H. G. M. 1977. *Israel in the Books of Chronicles.* Cambridge: Cambridge University Press.

———. 1985 *Ezra, Nehemiah.* WBC 16. Waco, TX: Word.

Wright, J. L. 2004. *Rebuilding Identity: The Nehemiah-Memoir and Its Earliest Readers.* BZAW 348. Berlin: de Gruyter.

ESTHER

Judy Fentress-Williams

Introduction

The Jewish Diaspora of the fifth or fourth centuries BCE was a community of dual realities, double consciousness, and multiple identities. The theme of multiple identities is present the story of Esther as it employs literary devices of suspense, irony, and plot twists to engage the question of "how" to survive as a Jew in the Persian court. Unlike the court tales in Daniel, where the heroes openly defy the law of the land in their adherence to the Torah, Esther portrays a heroine who works within the system to obtain salvation for her people. Esther manipulates the king like his advisors do, and in so doing saves her people from genocide. The averted genocide gives way to the slaughter of the Jews' enemies and the institution of a new, non-Mosaic, holiday.

Esther is one of the five books of the Hebrew Scriptures that constitute the festival scroll known as the Megilloth. The narrative provides the rationale for the celebration of Purim. Set in Susa, the winter capital of the Persian Empire, the action takes place in the time of the Jewish Diaspora in the Persian Empire, during the fifth or fourth century BCE. The story's heroine is Esther, a Jewish woman who becomes queen of Persia and is thereby able to save her people from genocide.

There are three ancient versions of Esther. There is the canonical, Masoretic (Hebrew) Text that contains no overt reference to the divine. The two Greek translations of a Hebrew text contain additional passages that include prayer and multiple references to God. These additions to Esther afford us a glimpse into the history of translation and development of text (Fox, 269).

The story of Esther opens with a banquet given by the Persian king Ahasuerus (Xerxes) for his officials and ministers that lasted 128 days. This is followed by a seven-day banquet for all the people in the citadel of Susa. The king's banquet is characterized by a lack of restraint, as the king orders the officials to "do as each one desired" (1:8). The queen hosts an additional banquet for the women.

A crisis arises when the drunken king demands the queen's appearance and she refuses. His anger with Queen Vashti is sated when his advisors convince him to depose her. The rash decision leaves the king without a queen. Again, the advisors come to the rescue with a recommendation that will provide a replacement. Young virgins are brought into the palace and undergo a yearlong process of preparation, after which time they "audition" for the role of queen. In the end, Esther, a Jewish girl who is keeping her identity secret, is selected as the new queen.

Almost immediately after becoming queen, Esther is forced into a difficult position because she is a Jew and Haman, the king's top official, has a plan to annihilate her people. Esther is challenged by her cousin Mordecai to champion her people lest she be deceived into thinking her position as queen will protect her. She executes a carefully developed plan of her own as she prepares a banquet for the king and Haman followed by a second banquet where she finally reveals her identity and begs the king's mercy for herself and her people. Esther is successful in gaining the king's favor and exposing Haman. The Jews are allowed to defend themselves against Haman's plot. They kill their enemies, and Haman is impaled on the pole he had built for Mordecai. This victory is followed by the inaugural celebration of the Feast of Purim.

Esther 1:1—2:18: Esther Becomes Queen

▮ The Text in Its Ancient Context

Ahasuerus, or Xerxes, would have reigned from 486 to 465 BCE. The narrative's placement in this historical context does not mean that Esther is a historical account. To the contrary, a number of the details in the narrative do not jibe with the information we have about Persia in the fifth century BCE. For example, neither of the queens' names in the book of Esther, Vashti and Esther, appears in the Persian annals. Furthermore, Mordecai presents the reader with some chronological challenges. If he was with those carried away in the Babylonian captivity, he would have to be well over one hundred years old during the third year of the Persian king's reign. These along with other examples suggest that Esther is something other than a strict historical account. One may safely conclude that the historical elements of the Persian Empire during the fifth century are in service to the narrative.

Esther is often categorized as a novella because it is a continuous narrative. It also has the characteristics of a court tale—a story of Jews in the Diaspora whose survival is linked to their identity. Moreover, the presence of reversals and plot twists introduce the elements of a comedy. In fact, the extravagant details (the feasts of the king) and excessive elements (the number of the Jews' enemies killed) have led some scholars to conclude that Esther is a particular type of comedy, namely carnivalesque. The carnivalesque employs humor and chaos to subvert the dominant culture or power. This term helps us understand the function of the comedic in the face of potential genocide. Esther is a narrative court tale with comedic elements.

▮ The Text in the Interpretive Tradition

The book of Esther follows the structure of a court tale. In these stories, the Jews in the Diaspora must make the decisions that will enable them to survive in the foreign, potentially hostile environment. The court tale depicts the foreign king as powerful, impulsive, and easily influenced by his advisors, who are rivals of the Jewish characters and community. The advisors convince the king to make a decision that goes against Jewish identity, piety, and/or existence. What is perfectly acceptable for the dominant culture could be prohibited in the Jewish community. Even in the Diaspora, the Jews are a people "set apart." They must choose to risk well-being or life itself in order to obey the law and thereby preserve identity. In so doing, they are saved and sometimes the foreign king acknowledges the God of Israel (Dan. 3:28-29, 6:26-27).

As a court tale, the narrative is careful to set up the divide between the power of the ruling nation and the relative helplessness of the Jewish Diaspora. Esther has two names—her Jewish name, Hadassah, which is suppressed in favor of Persian name, Esther. When she is taken along with the other women to become a part of the king's harem, Mordecai instructs her to keep her identity as a Jew a secret. Although the narrative focuses on Esther, the reader should note the king's rash actions of deposing his queen and then finding another result in a number of women who spend the rest of their lives relegated to the harem.

Esther's hidden identity along with her two names highlights the presence of dual consciousness for the Diaspora community. Esther must exist both as a Jew and as a Persian, and as the narrative unfolds, she must make decisions about how and when to claim her respective identities. Her choices have consequences. As was the case in Daniel, the consequences are life and death. Unlike the court tales in Daniel, Esther is not identified as a Jew. The temptation for Esther is to keep her ethnicity hidden and not risk exposure to persecution. She is not asked to take a position of prayer, worship a foreign idol, or violate dietary laws. For all we know, she is not keeping kosher. For Esther, it is not a specific Jewish observance that threatens her people so much as their very identity as Jews.

Both Jewish and Christian audiences are interested in the character of Esther and as a result read this as a narrative of Esther's ascent to the throne instead of the story of Vashti's exile. This reading is encouraged by the fact that there is little character development for any of the characters. No reason is given for Vashti's refusal, and we do not know if Esther is conscripted into the king's service willingly or not. What we do know is that these two women along with the other characters are in service to this plot, which leads the reader through a variety of plot twists on the way to the final goal of the triumph of the Jewish community over those who seek to do them harm. In contrast to Vashti's disfavor, Esther has the favor of those she encounters. In the interpretive tradition, Vashti is demonized to justify her rejection. In a narrative with underdeveloped characters that are either clearly good or evil, Esther is the heroine and Vashti becomes the antitype, the defiant wife who threatens the stability of the kingdom.

■ THE TEXT IN CONTEMPORARY DISCUSSION

Esther did not find its way into the canon with ease. The absence of a direct reference to God meant that it was one of the last books to be granted canonical status, aided by its connection to the festival of Purim (Crawford, 77). It is also distinguished as one of the few canonical books that bear the name of a female who is also the protagonist. As a result, the text is of interest to many who want to explore the role of women in the Bible. Esther takes a position of power in a foreign environment. However, her power is still limited by gender. The queen is not an equal with the king, as Queen Vashti discovers. Both queens must navigate a world where their power is limited. In the opening narrative, Vashti's open defiance of the king is grounds for her removal, even though her refusal may have been out of a sense of virtue or propriety, and Esther's compliance with the wishes of her cousin and the eunuch work in her favor. Contemporary audiences are concerned with mixed messages: Esther complies in contrast to Vashti's refusal, but saves her people when she too defies a royal decree and appears unbidden before the king. Esther's compliance and subsequent boldness may reflect the dual consciousness that is a key to survival in the Diaspora.

Esther 2:19—8:3: Mordecai and Haman

▌ THE TEXT IN ITS ANCIENT CONTEXT

The Diaspora community that originally received the Esther story knew that in order to survive, they needed to occupy the world and worldview of the Persian Empire while living in and preserving an alternative worldview—another, equally real set of rules. Their survival is connected to their ability to move from one to another and to know when they need to exchange one lens or set of rules for another. It should come as no surprise that the book of Esther uses verbal dyads and sets up characters in pairs as foils to one another. Esther is a story with two angles of vision—in other words, the structure of the narrative reflects the worldview of the characters in the narrative (Levenson, 10).

In this second sense unit, the narrative action is played out through a contest between the characters Mordecai the Jew and Haman the Agagite. A postexilic audience would hear in these ethnographic modifiers not only a difference in racial/ethnic background but also a history of antagonism. Haman is an Amalekite, but he is referred to as an Agagite. Agag is the name of the Amalekite king whose life was spared by King Saul in 1 Samuel 15. Saul's decision was made in defiance of God's direct command to destroy all of the Amalekites because of their mistreatment of Israel. Although the prophet Samuel killed Agag, the reference to Haman as an Agagite signals the reader to recall Saul's failure to successfully execute the ban on the nation of Amalek.

The narrative turns on the responses the Jews make to the rules and/or situations presented by the dominant society. The first is Mordecai's response to the edict that everyone must bow to Haman. This legislation comes as a result of Haman's elevation in 3:1. The efficiency of the text in detailing Haman's promotion contrasts the elaborate nature of the banquets described earlier. We are not told how or why he is promoted. What matters in this court tale is that Haman is promoted and that the king orders that everyone bow to him. Mordecai, like the heroes in the court tales of Daniel, must take a stand when confronted with a "law of the land" that is in opposition to Jewish practices. At issue here is, first, the command that a Jew cannot bow to a descendant of Agag (Exod. 17:14-16; Deut. 15:17-19; 1 Samuel 15) and, second, adherence to the law requires knowledge of the law. Mordecai's refusal stems from his Jewish identity that is based on the observance of the law. His behavior enrages Haman and is the impetus for his plot to kill Mordecai and his people. Following the lines of a court tale, Haman convinces the unsuspecting king (with the incentive of a bribe) to issue an edict for the extermination of the Jews on the date chosen by the casting of lots, Purim.

When he hears about the edict, Mordecai responds in a way that again betrays his heritage. He enters into the ritual of mourning by tearing his clothes and putting on sackcloth and ashes. Other Jews also enter into mourning, but it is Mordecai's behavior that gets the attention of Queen Esther. Mordecai wants Esther to plead the case of her people before her husband the king. Esther's response reflects not her intentions but the confines of the Persian kingdom. She tells Mordecai that if she approaches the king without being invited, she will be put to death (4:11). Mordecai's exchange with Esther asserts the reality or worldview of the Jewish community over that of the Persian Empire. In this clash of culture, there is only one right answer, and that is to speak out on behalf of her people.

Mordecai's response makes no direct reference to God, but hints at the divine when he says that if she does not help, "help will rise for the Jews from another quarter" (4:14). Esther responds to Mordecai's challenge by choosing to act: she decides she will risk her life for that of her people. Her preparation involves fasting, the antithesis of the feast. Esther does not have to defy an edict that goes against the Torah or her identity as a Jew; in Esther, there is danger simply in being identified as a Jew. In such a world, the book of Esther raises the question of identifying with the oppressed group when one can blend in to the dominant society, what African Americans refer to as "passing for white." If given the opportunity to move in the world of the dominant culture/society/race as one of them, would one willingly choose to identify with their people and take on suffering if one could avoid it? In the Diaspora, where is the line between assimilating to survive and losing one's primary identity? The fact that this dilemma is posited before the queen is of significance. As queen, Esther is in one of the highest positions in the foreign power. If she cannot ignore her Jewish identity, then no one can. Moreover, Mordecai's challenge reminds Esther and the reader that denying one's identity will not save you, even if you are a favored queen.

Once Esther decides to act, the narrative shifts its attention from a contest between Haman and Mordecai to one between Haman and Esther. Both are close to the king and have the opportunity to exercise influence. Haman tricked the king into signing an edict that calls for the extermination of the Jews. Now Esther must find a way to manipulate the king to achieve her desired end. Unlike the court tales in Daniel, the Jews will not witness a supernatural resolution to their situation. They will fast and pray, but in the Diaspora they must also be cunning. Esther successfully gains an audience with the king, and his words convey his willingness to please her: "what is your request? It shall be given you, even to the half of my kingdom" (5:3). She extends an invitation to one banquet, which is the platform for a second invitation. Esther's request is carefully orchestrated to increase the king's desire to give it to her (he is not a patient man) and to elevate the dramatic tension. What could she want that requires two banquets? Once her request is made, the comedic reversal moves to its climax. The king is enraged near the end of the story just as he was in the beginning. His anger in chapter 1 resulted in Vashti's deposition and Esther's appointment. Similarly, the anger of the king means that Haman will be removed and Mordecai will take his position. The lots that were used to set the date of the Jew's annihilation will serve as the name of the Jewish festival that commemorates Haman's defeat and demise. Esther's plan is successful. Thus, although the absence of God is a theological issue, God's absence may be a literary device intended to re-create in the narrative the feeling of the Diaspora community—one that has come to expect God, but doesn't always readily find an obvious divine manifestation.

▌▌ THE TEXT IN THE INTERPRETIVE TRADITION

Haman and Mordecai are positioned by virtue of their ethnicity, as enemies. Such a contrast, informed by dual realities of an oppressed population, leaves little room for subtleties. In all the ways that Mordecai is faithful, loyal, and good, Haman is duplicitous, self-serving, evil, and proud. The contrast between the two is the foundation of Jewish and Christian interpretive traditions. Haman becomes the epitome of the enemy of the Jews; he is linked to Agag and Esau (Carruthers, 134). In Christian traditions, Haman is seen as the model both for elevation of the undeserving and the enemies of the church. Christians who saw the Roman Church as the enemy equated the pope with Haman's rise to power (Carruthers, 135). In Jewish and Christian traditions, much is made of Haman's pride and his anger, both of which limit him. It is his pride that blinds him to Esther's plan, and his anger separates him from reason.

In Jewish tradition, Mordecai's refusal to bow down to Haman is not tied to the prohibition against bowing down to a descendant of Ahab, but to a more obvious prohibition. *Esther Rabbah* asserts that there was an idol adorning Haman's robe, and it was to the idol that Mordecai refused obeisance (Carruthers, 139). Mordecai is the embodiment of the faithful Jew in the Diaspora. He knows how far to assimilate without forgetting his observance of the law. In the end, he is honored and elevated in the foreign kingdom.

▌▌ THE TEXT IN CONTEMPORARY DISCUSSION

Esther offers contemporary communities the opportunity to face the reality of evil in a world where God does not appear to be present. Although she is the queen, her life is endangered by virtue of being a Jew. Her adopted homeland became hostile in a very short period of time. The post-Shoah world is well aware of how quickly one's home can turn into a battleground and how the lives of a community can be summarily discounted and disregarded. The challenge of the Shoah is that the genocide was allowed to happen. Why was there no Esther or Mordecai? Was God even more absent than in the book of Esther?

Esther 8:4—10:3: The Revenge of the Jews

▌ THE TEXT IN ITS ANCIENT CONTEXT

True to the court-narrative form, the king is unable to reverse the edict calling for the extermination of the Jews, but he does allow the Jewish community to defend itself. Not only is Haman killed on the stake he prepared for Mordecai, but those seeking to do harm to the Jews on that day are killed as well. In Shushan, eight hundred enemies of the Jews are killed. In the surrounding verses, the Jews "fought for their lives" (JPS), killing 75,000 of their enemies. In the end of the story, we see the excess of the Jews "standing their ground" mirroring the extravagance of the two feasts at the story's beginning. On the following day, a celebratory feast is held called Purim, named after the lots that Haman cast in his plot to destroy the Jews.

As a comedic novella, we expect the reversals that come at the end. The death Haman plans for Mordecai becomes his own. Mordecai replaces Haman and inherits his holdings. And perhaps most importantly, Esther "daughter of Abihail, along with the Jew Mordecai, gave full written authority, confirming . . . Purim" (9:29). Just as Haman was responsible for the edicts that went out to announce the massacre of the Jews, Esther, the would-be victim of Haman's wickedness, gives a command that is "fixed" and "recorded." Purim will be remembered by generations to come.

■ THE TEXT IN THE INTERPRETIVE TRADITION

The revenge in the story of Esther makes interpreters uncomfortable. In early Christian traditions, Esther is condemned along with her people for vindictiveness and impiety (Fox, 50). In a number of these early traditions, the condemnation of Esther often became the foundation on which anti-Semitic remarks would be made. In later traditions, there has been a tendency on the part of Christian interpreters to downplay or ignore the magnitude of the revenge in the story. Both of these responses reflect a tendency on the part of the interpretive traditions to fix or explain something that is simply an accurate reflection of the human experience. Perhaps our discomfort in the account of the Jewish people exacting revenge results from the way in which it resonates with that part of us that has suffered.

■ THE TEXT IN CONTEMPORARY DISCUSSION

Esther is not the first court tale that involves revenge. The officials of Babylon who orchestrate the scenario that places Shadrach, Meshach, and Abednego in the fiery furnace are themselves tossed into the furnace with their families. Similarly, after Daniel emerges unscathed from the lion's den, his accusers and their families are thrown in. In Esther, Haman, the enemy, and his family are killed. What is of interest in this narrative is that in spite of Haman's punishment, there are still members of the community who want to kill the Jews. The Jews, acting in self-defense, kill tens of thousands of their enemies. The excessive bloodletting at the end of Esther resonates with the Quentin Tarantino films *Inglourious Basterds* or *Django Unchained*. These films offer a retelling of history that allows the victim to exact revenge on those who inflicted suffering. Esther reminds us that those who have witnessed the horrors of genocide are forever marked by that violence and that in the absence of some sense of adjudication, the imagination craves the opportunity to remember the story in such a way that the victims have the right to gain the upper hand over those such as Haman who embody unexplainable evil in our world.

Works Cited

Carruthers, Jo. 2008. *Esther through the Centuries*. Malden, MA: Blackwell.

Crawford, Sidnie White. 2000. "Esther." In *Women in Scripture*, edited by Carol Meyers, 74–77, 289–292. New York: Houghton Mifflin.

Fox, Michael V. 1991. *Character and Ideology in the Book of Esther*. Eugene, OR: Wipf & Stock.

Levenson, Jon D. 1997. *Esther: A Commentary*. OTL. Louisville: Westminster John Knox.